PASSIONS OF OUR TIME

EUROPEAN PERSPECTIVES

EUROPEAN PERSPECTIVES

A SERIES IN SOCIAL THOUGHT AND CULTURAL CRITICISM

Lawrence D. Kritzman, Editor

European Perspectives presents outstanding books by leading European thinkers. With both classic and contemporary works, the series aims to shape the major intellectual controversies of our day and to facilitate the tasks of historical understanding.

For a complete list of books in the series, see pages 407–9.

PASSIONS OF OUR TIME

JULIA KRISTEVA

EDITED WITH A FOREWORD
BY LAWRENCE D. KRITZMAN

TRANSLATED BY CONSTANCE BORDE
AND SHEILA MALOVANY-CHEVALLIER

Columbia University Press
New York

Columbia University Press gratefully acknowledges the generous support for this book provided by Publisher's Circle members Judith Ginsberg and Paul LeClerc.

Columbia University Press
Publishers Since 1893
New York   Chichester, West Sussex
cup.columbia.edu
Pulsions du temps copyright © 2013 Librairie Arthème Fayard
French edition edited by David Uhrig with Christina Kkona
Copyright © 2018 Columbia University Press
All rights reserved

Library of Congress Cataloging-in-Publication Data
Names: Kristeva, Julia, 1941– author.
Title: Passions of our time / Julia Kristeva; edited and foreword by Lawrence
D. Kritzman; translated by Constance Borde and Sheila Malovany-Chevallier.
Other titles: Original title: Pulsions du temps
Description: New York: Columbia University Press, 2018. | Series: European
perspectives: a series in social thought and cultural criticism | Includes
bibliographical references and index.
Identifiers: LCCN 2018007443 | ISBN 9780231171441 (cloth: alk. paper) |
ISBN 9780231547499 (e-book)
Subjects: LCSH: Time. | Time—Psychological aspects.
Classification: LCC BD638 .K75513 2018 | DDC 194—dc23
LC record available at https://lccn.loc.gov/2018007443

Columbia University Press books are printed on permanent
and durable acid-free paper.

Printed in the United States of America

Cover design: Julia Kushnirsky
Cover image: © Louise Bourgeous, *Seven in a Bed*

CONTENTS

II. PSYCHOANALYSIS

III. WOMEN

IV. HUMANISM

FOREWORD

LAWRENCE D. KRITZMAN

Passions of Our Time represents the work of an exemplary twenty-first century intellectual, Julia Kristeva, a true renaissance woman, a theoretical polymath whose many insights engage in political and social questions. This book takes us on a critical journey examining politics, philosophy, psychoanalysis, gender and sexuality, literary criticism, religion, and cultural critique. Earlier versions of many of the chapters in Passions of Our Time were previously published as articles, lectures, and book chapters. Kristeva's principle concern is time in its broadest sense in the contemporary world. Her attempt is to show how time, in today's world, has become a closed phenomenon and lost some of its kinetic force through digitalized uniformity and hyperconnectivity. Kristeva shows how internal drives, in a Freudian sense, can reactivate the kinetic force of time within us and therefore valorize its singularity in a world that is plural and diverse.

In a first essay, one that functions as a theoretical allegory of her writerly vocation, she demonstrates how her future was overdetermined by an activity she engaged in at a children's festival in Bulgaria—the festival of the Slavic alphabet (the holiday of the Cyrillic letters). This symbolic investment constituted the "letter," her engagement with language as translation, by allowing it to become a sort of fetishistic object in which writing was the medicine that planted the seeds of her intellectual journey and cured her of the ills of living under communism.

As in her previous work, Kristeva engages in psychoanalytic speculation, but she never does so in a dogmatic manner, whereby the analyst would take on the position of an all-knowing subject. Drawing on Freud, Lacan, feminism, and theories of the maternal, Kristeva highlights the importance of psychoanalysis in today's world. As she sees it, psychoanalysis functions as a bridge between humankind and civilization, an activity that enables the unbuttoning of the enigma of human existence. To be sure, her engagement with this heuristic process does not allow the human subject to conform to social norms. Instead it enables the subject to come into contact with the singular freedom that gives birth to creativity and the escapades of the imagination.

Throughout, Kristeva examines the infelicitous consequences of the acceleration of time. What Kristeva perceives as the paradoxical result of this acceleration of time is what she refers to as a "deep nihilistic crisis" in which diversity has given rise to new authoritarian discourses, new anti-Semitisms, and Islamophobia. This crisis was produced by the failure to recognize alterity ("Every I is another") and the refusal to let the other speak. As Kristeva has previously shown in her study of Hannah Arendt, secularization produced the eradication of Jewish difference into the generic "man." In opposition to a cult of identity and the corrosive force of hate produced in a self-contained environment, Kristeva proposes a more felicitous reciprocating questioning that provides a model for living together as a plural phenomenon. The loosening of borders through the activity of globalization has allowed for multicultural cross-fertilization. Yet at the same time it has allowed for the resurgence of abject nationalism because of the infelicitous clichés proliferated by identity politics articulated in a self-contained hermetic world.

At the core of this nihilistic crisis is the failure, metaphorically speaking, of what she terms "the need to believe." This phenomenon does not call for a religious revival capable of producing a dangerous fundamentalism. Kristeva equates "the need to believe" with Freud, who secularized religion and used it as a trope for the ego's drive to create meaning and its desire for knowledge.

The acceleration of time in the digital age has created an identity crisis for both the individual and the nation. The dissolution of a community of differences has had a negative impact on reciprocal trust. To be sure, Kristeva does not espouse the idea that the universe is one, but puts forth the concept of a multiverse open to the fractures of time. This dialogic approach gives new hope to the melancholia produced in the mechanistically closed temporal space of digital technology. The creation of a multiverse allows for the mobilization of creativity as it is libidinally enacted; it therefore allows for the transcendence of dogmatic political ideologies and the authority that technology imposes and regulates. As in the case of the latter, the Internet, that messianic messenger of the contemporary world, forecloses on creativity and imposes the fabricated images of human experience. This foreclosure on creativity functions as a form of political control marked as a new human narrative that undercuts the possibilities of difference. Technological policing closes off the creativity produced in the unexpected fractures of time. The response to new technologies can only be counterbalanced by an enlightened inner life. But this phenomenon, according to Kristeva, can only be realized by giving oneself to another as in the care of the mother for the child and the primary identification of the boy with the father. Accordingly, one is able to live by investing in the other and the subsequent creation of reciprocal links.

What is most moving in Kristeva's book is her attempt to demonstrate how, in multiple domains, globalization can mean more than technological transhumanism. Neither prefabricated ideologies nor unreflected identity politics should undercut the need to believe and the quest for self-knowledge. What is required above all is the commitment to unchain the constraints of uniformity and the desire to think otherwise. We find this practice throughout *Passions of Our Time* in Kristeva's Montaigne-like engagement with self-analysis that is at the core of our being. She enables us to rediscover the paradise lost carried in the potential of language to create through permanent questioning and self-reflection. Doubt is not a handicap but rather a modus operandi that allows us to proceed; hope is produced by a greater level of lucidity that enables one to bypass victimhood and achieve the promise of a singular freedom carrying within it the future of humanity.

As a psychoanalyst, Kristeva shows herself to be an intellectual engaged in the world, a role that positions her in the passions of our time. She calls out to humanity and its mosaic of differences and asks us to seek new freedom and reclaim our sterilized libidinal energy from its enclosure in a self-contained temporality. We are entreated to reconnect with the world and engage in a newfound humanism, such as in her essay on normativity and disability and another on the possibility for Islam and psychoanalysis to meet and enter into a dialogic relationship. The only demand that Kristeva puts on her analysis of figures such as Barthes, Rousseau, Teresa de Avila, and Beauvoir is to uncover their singularities and their rebellious commitment to reflect upon the world.

This intellectually stimulating collection presents Kristeva as a new age humanist; she enables us to come into the presence of a happy warrior who opts for hope instead of despair. She discovers in the human spirit, among its many singularities, a driving force to create and the need to believe. The desire for the infinite as found in religion translates into a desire for knowledge and spiritual understanding.

Out of the malaise to which she bears witness, this happy warrior reinvigorates us with hope and urges us to rediscover the humanity in us. The permanent crisis to which we bear witness allows for endless renewal. Culture must be regarded as a cornucopia and a kaleidoscope in its aspiration to diversity; it is conceived as a kind of being-for-itself in its openness to endless revision. In particular, European culture cannot be defined as a singular entity; it must be conceived as an endless questioning capable of producing new confidences and the discovery of differences. If identity is always already in crisis, it must also be a clarion, a call to constantly reinvent ourselves and rebuild our psychic space. *Passions of Our Time* is an amorous engagement with the world and a hymn to the creative force that gives life meaning and depth.

New York
Winter 2019

ACKNOWLEDGMENTS

We wish to thank the following people for helping us to understand and then translate some of the difficulties.

Dominique Borde
Claire Brisset
Karen Fenn
Russell Grigg
Mireille Perche
Susan Suleiman
Bob Vallier
and Julia Kristeva

I

SINGULAR LIBERTIES

1

MY ALPHABET; OR, HOW I AM A LETTER

AZBOUKA

Today, May 24, is Writing Day in Sofia. It is my first Alphabet Day. I am six maybe seven years old. At any rate, I already know how to read and write, I like that, and I am making fast progress. Bulgarians are the only people in the world to celebrate such a day: in honor of two brothers, Cyril and Methodius, creators of the Slavic alphabet. The country parades along the wide boulevards behind the enormous effigy of these two monks: schoolchildren and teachers of all levels—from kindergarten to science academies—writers, artists, literary types, parents, and more. And on their dickeys, everyone sports a big Cyrillic letter.

Arms laden with roses and peonies, intoxicated by their full-bloom beauty and a fragrance that impairs my vision, blurring my own shape, I too am a letter. One more swirl, a language pirouette, a curlicue of meaning. Nestled in "a rule that can cure anything"—wrote Colette as I would later learn, who cultivated her alphabet in the flesh of the world—even communism. And scattered among all these young bodies dressed in their lightest spring clothes, mingling with those voices offered up to ancient song, to the silkiness of shirts and hair and the ochre breeze in Byzantium or what is left of it, laden by the stubborn perfume of flowers. Imprinted in me, the alphabet overtakes me; alphabet is all around me, yet there is neither all nor alphabet: only a euphoric memory, a call to write, unrelated to any literature. Another kind of life, "cooling and rose," as Marcel Proust would say.[1] I will never forget this first May 24 when I became a letter.

"Alphabet" is *Azbouka* in Bulgarian.

"Why *Azbouka*, Papa? Strange . . . *Az* (meaning "I" in Bulgarian), I get it: it's me. But *bouk*, would it be the book, *le livre*?" After finishing French kindergarten with the Dominicans, and while continuing French at the Alliance Française, I was just beginning English. "Oh no . . . well, yes, in a way . . . it's 'Slavonic,' you know, old Slav. Az Bouki Vedi Glagoli . . . A, a, B, 6, V, в, G, г," he answers me.

A practicing Orthodox, and passionate about letters, my father accompanies me up to my school parade while explaining the etymology of the Bulgarian word for "alphabet": *Azbouka*. We give a *name* to every letter, not simply the phonetic repetition of Greek letters with their meaning going back to their instrumental invention: α, *alpha* (find/invent) for A; β, *beta* (walk) for B; γ, *gamma* (to scythe because it looks like a scythe) for G; nor is it an everyday word for the names of Hebrew letters: א, *aleph* (beef); ב, *bet* (house); ג, *gimel* (camel). "But a life lesson," predicts Papa. "A faith, if you'd rather."

Of course I wouldn't rather. My father knows it, and already suffers from my tomboy and rebellious behavior, where I never miss the chance to mock his teachings and religious beliefs. But today, it is a celebration: I hold my tongue, I listen. Attentively. Because it is my curiosity that feeds my revolt.

"*Az*, A in *azbouka*, designates the first letter, the A, and, as you said, it is clearly 'I' here meaning 'you.' *Bouki*, equal to the letter 6, signifies in old Slavonic 'the letters.' *Vedi*, в or V, our third letter, means 'I know.' *Glagoli*, г for G, is 'the Word'; *Dobro*, Д for D, is, as in modern Bulgarian, 'the good'; *Est*, e for the letter E, is simply the verb 'to be.' . . ."

When my father got it into his head to teach me, his lessons could be interminable. I forgot the rest of the thirty letters of the Cyrillic alphabet as well as their most edifying *names*. Did I ever really know them? But ever since that day, and every *Azbouka* Day that I celebrated from childhood until I left for Paris in 1965, these words came back to me: "*Az bouki vedi glagoli dobro est.*" I would pin the big letter on my white silk blouse and join the parade, repeating this magic formula. I would turn it around, decomposing, recomposing the sounds, the syllables, the words, the verses, the letters, the letter that I was, engraved, joining in songs, roses, perfumed geraniums, flags, slogans, breeze, the May light, all and everything.

"*Az bouki vedi glagoli dobro est*": "I / letters / understand / the word / the good / is"; "I understand the letters, the word, therefore the good exists, it is"; and backwards, the refrain: "The good is I, me I, understanding the letter, the word, and the good." Meaning: "I am the letters, I understand the word, so the good exists." Or else: "Being the letter, I understand the word that is the good." But also, "I am the letter, the word, the good." Or even: "I am Writing." Better still: "I *is* a Writing," because "To write the good is to be," in other words: "The Word writes itself in me only so the good exists." Et cetera. *Az bouki vedi glagoli dobro est.*

The shapes of the letters, the syllables, and the words kept moving, began dancing around, and transporting me into a hallucinating and lucid maelstrom. I turned the curves and the down strokes every which way, the sounds and the lessons of lost Slav reborn in my mouth, under my tongue, in my breast, in my fingers. And out of them, I extracted the ancient melody via present-day Bulgarian, I drew the graphic and wrested meaning from it, I incorporated it, I re-created it. The alphabet came to life in me, for me, I could be all the letters. For this first celebration, I am the letter A, A, *az*, me. The following year I may choose G, г, *glagoli*, word/ verb. Or why not Z, з, *zemilja*, the earth? Or maybe, P, п, *pokoi*, peace. *Azbouka* comes to life again in me as an infinite present, I *is* a letter, I *is* the letters. And here we are, gathered together, four, five, ten, twenty, thirty bodies of girls and boys, women and men, forming a word, a sentence, a verse, an idea, a project: the alphabet has become my organ to take plea-sure (*jouir*) from time out of time.

It seems that nowadays this devotion to writing has become more sub-dued. Perhaps it has even disappeared. No more demonstrations in Sofia; now you *tweet* and *chat*, in Paris, New York, or Shanghai.

Is it still possible to save history? Far be it for me to try, but, just for memory's sake, I will remind you.

Cyril and Methodius, brothers, were born in Thessalonica of an Archon father (a kind of Byzantine dignitary) and a Slavic mother, even possibly Bulgarian. Methodius, the elder, a high-level public servant, left his office and retreated to a monastery on Mount Olympus. His younger brother, Constantine, who was later rebaptized Cyril by the monks, was a fervent man of letters and companion of the young emperor, Michael III. Disci-ple of the philosopher Photios who taught him dialectics, he then became

FIGURE 1.1 Portrait of Cyril and Methodius in the Menologion of Basileiou, eleventh century, Vatican Library.

librarian to the Constantinople patriarch. When Prince Rastislav of Moravia asked Michael III to send him scholars to explain the true Christian faith in their language, the emperor appointed the two brothers to this delicate mission. In fact, it was a question of escaping from Latin! So in 863 Cyril and Methodius departed for Moravia, and there they created the *Azbouka*. Strictly speaking, Cyril was the inventor, the scholar, and the visionary. The role of political promoter and educator fell to Methodius, especially after the death of his younger brother. But their life in Moravia, under a hostile Latin clergy, was nothing but one of privation and suffering. Methodius was even thrown into jail. In the end, the two missionaries finally reached Venice, where they defended the right to write and speak about God outside of the three sacred languages, Hebrew, Latin, and Greek. This could have had a happy ending, as they were ultimately received by the new pope, Adrian II, who endorsed them and recommended that their disciples be ordained priests, but Cyril died in 869 in Rome, barely having pronounced his religious vows.

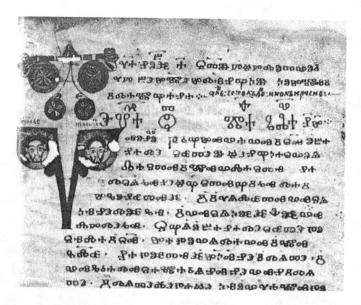

FIGURE 1.2 Codex Assemanius, evangeliary in Glagolitic alphabet, early eleventh century.

The *Azbouka* (feminine in Bulgarian) was nonetheless already completed and being circulated, perhaps even in both of its versions. The older one, *Glagolitza* (from the Slavonic *glagol* in the Christian sense of *Word*), forty-four letters strong, was Cyril's work. It is made up of borrowings and variants of the Greek alphabet as well as Hebrew (proto-Hebraic and Samarian characters), and even Khazar (Central Asian nomadic people) and the Georgian graphic system, *khutsuri* (from the Caucasus); it is composed of two forms, one oval and the other angular. The latter, *Cyrillic*, is a simplified version of Glagolitza, closer to Greek letters. Created by Cyril but undoubtedly completed by his most faithful disciple, Clement of Ohrid, it is this version that is used today.

For me, this long story culminated in the *Prayer for the Alphabet*, *Azboutchna Molitva*, by Constantine de Preslav, another of the two brothers' disciples, whom my father adored. I had a father who prayed for the Alphabet. He asked God to breathe the Word into his heart, the famous *Glagol* from old Slavon, called *Slavo* in modern Bulgarian: "speech and writing reunited" (whereas the word *glagol*, like the word *verb* in romance languages, signifies only the grammatical category designating action, unlike the "substantive" designating the common noun). "Give my heart

FIGURE 1.3 Julia Kristeva, Excellence award at the Cyrillic Alphabet Day, Sofia, May 24, 1951.

a fruitful, potent *slovo* (speech and writing), give me a *slovo* (speech and writing) able to describe your miracles," he murmured to himself, hoping nonetheless to be heard.

I listened to him, acting distracted but ever attentive and, of course, incredulous. He knew this and let it drop. Later on when he visited me in Paris, Papa went to Notre Dame to recite his *Prayer for the Alphabet*. It was composed of thirty-nine verses, each beginning with a letter of the alphabet, in the same order as they appeared in our *Azbouka*. I did not understand all the church Slavonic words that wove this prayer together, but I heard, verse by verse, the melody of the letters of the alphabet strung together, and I restored their *names* just as I had heard them that first day, May 24, when I became a letter of the alphabet: "*Az bouki vedi glagoli dobro est*," "I am the letter that knows the joy of the written word."

THE WRITER AS TRANSLATOR

Out of this blur that was my immersion in the Being, which no word can immediately capture, which the term *joy* trivializes and *ecstasy* embalms, an imperceptible tremor is today seeking the French language, which itself reflects this blur: out of a whole battery of French readings and conversations emerges a luminous fabric chosen by the felt to make meaning exist. Alchemy of naming where I am alone with the French language. And there, in that exile that my imagination attempts to live in French, my suffering comes back. Bulgaria, my suffering.[2]

Thomas Mann's famous text "Germany, My Suffering,"[3] his journal in exile during the Nazi period, was brought to my attention. The writer lived his country's tragedy from inside and out, and while he condemned the shame of Hitlerism, he was nonetheless aware of the insidious complicity that the majority of Germans shared with the one they freely called "brother Hitler." But the violent barbarism of the Third Reich had nothing in common with the collapse of politics and morality in the former Communist empire, a collapse that Western democracies knew all too well. No direct link whatsoever, then, between Thomas Mann's journal and my own inner questioning, too inner, except for my outside-and-inside position and anxiety stemming from the ill effects of this upheaval that hit us with full force and unpredictable consequences.

In the end, and in spite of everything, I cling to French—"other language" for me—because one of the greatest French writers, perhaps the greatest in the twentieth century, was a translator. I am thinking of Proust, of course: "Great books are written in a kind of foreign language."[4] "The only true book does not have to be invented by a great writer because it already exists in each one of us. He only needs to translate it. The duty and the task of a writer are those of a translator."[5]

From the foreigner whom I define as a translator, to the writer translating the universe as his sensitive singularity: are we all foreigners?

I know how demagogic or irritating this pathetic cry of humanistic conscience eager to fight against "exclusion" can sound. We are not all foreigners, and so many writers have been not only fervent ideologists of national identity but nationalists and even fascists as well! But seriously, outside of those extreme cases, to consider one's self as indissolubly tied to the umbilical cord of one's national language and its traditional codes, yes!

Many of us do not even suspect that the expression "unknown to the language"[6] that Mallarmé had hoped to write, and the "translation of the sensible" that Proust envisioned, are, far from being extravagant exceptions, at the heart of the creative act.

I would like to emphasize here the intrinsic and often imperceptible link between the *stranger* and the *writer*, in order to unite them both in a common and unique experience of translation.

I will go even further. If we were not all translators, if we were not constantly exposing the strangeness of our inner life—with its derogations made of their stereotypical codes called national languages—to transpose it into other signs, would we have a psychic life, would we be living beings? "To estrange" one's self from one's self and to continue to be the messenger of this constantly rediscovered strangeness: is this not how we fight our latent psychoses and how we succeed where a psychotic or an autistic fails, that is in naming the sense of time? In my opinion, speaking another language is simply the minimal and first condition of being alive: to reclaim the alphabet, the meaning of the letter, and beyond incredible rebirths, to translate and retranslate them.

2

RELIANCE

What Is Loving for a Mother?

What is loving for a mother?
FLASH, atoms inordinately swollen of a link, a vision, a thrill, of a yet unformed embryo, unnamable.

What is loving for a mother? The same thing as saying, as writing. Laughing. Impossible. A flash on the unnamable, a weaving to tear apart. A body finally ventures out of its shelter, risks it, under a veil of words. WORD, FLESH. From one to the other, eternally, fragmented visions, metaphors of the invisible.

Stretched tympanum tearing sound from deaf silence. Wind in the grass, the seagull's distant cry, echoes of waves, of horns, of voices—or nothing? Or his own cries, my newborn, spasm of the syncopated void. I do not hear anything else, but the tympanum continues to transmit this soundful vertigo.

My body and . . . him/her. No connection. Nothing to do with each other. Right from the first moves, cries, steps, well before his personality became my opponent: the child, he or she, an other. That there is no sexual connection is a meager observation in front of this blinding flash, faced with the abyss between what was mine and what is now irremediably foreign. Try thinking this extraction, this abyss: hallucinating vertigo.

What connection between him and me? None, except this overflowing laughter where some soundful, subtle, fluid identity collapses or emerges, softly buoyed up by the waves.

Tenderness for both man and woman is often described as a desexualization of drive. Wouldn't it also be the case for oviparous animals and mammals when, exhausted by the pleasures and pains of procreation, males and females give themselves over to caring for their newborn? I hold that human mothers—more than female cats and tigers—because they are endowed with language, succeed in sublimating their erotic or destructive drives by this very tenderness. And that they embrace their children (from newborns to grownups who still remain their children), throughout their lives, with this soothed tension, this waning anxiety, smiling and respectful, that makes the newborn the Premier Other.

Maternal reliance as a detotalized universe made up of heterogeneous strategies cannot be fixed in any type of monolithic representation, much less worshipped as a goddess. Surfacing of the visible before and after the separation of forms is the gesture and its trace that might perhaps be the most faithful apparent reality.

The prehistoric artist painted the movement of his drives by imitating his doubles, the bison and horses, running, but did not paint himself: nothing but gestures without "oneself," graffiti, abstract and rough sketches, often completed by "negative or positive hands." Only the female/maternal surfaces in the visible: a giant vulva included in or escaping from living animality gives birth to the visible. But this external inclusion and this internal exclusion do not "represent" maternal eroticism. Like a center of vibratory suspense,[1] maternal eroticism can be perceived in the gesture of this trance, an *archi-writing* links the female sex and the beast.

The Greeks had glimpsed the problem in this representation of the maternal in imagining three Fates, who were none other than weavers cutting and joining Time and Chaos: the Spinner, the Allotter, the Cutter.

As for the Taoist Chinese civilization, it defines the maternal as movement itself, the flow, the "way," also "without name," prior to all entities and linking them all, a "process of emergence within the very body." And calligraphy became an attempt to impose maternal eroticism by infiltrating it into the cultural fabric.

At the heart of our monotheistic tradition, the laugh of Sarah—Isaac's mother—comes closest to maternal eroticism: between destiny (biological) that passes her by (therefore divine), since it is ordered by Yahweh, and

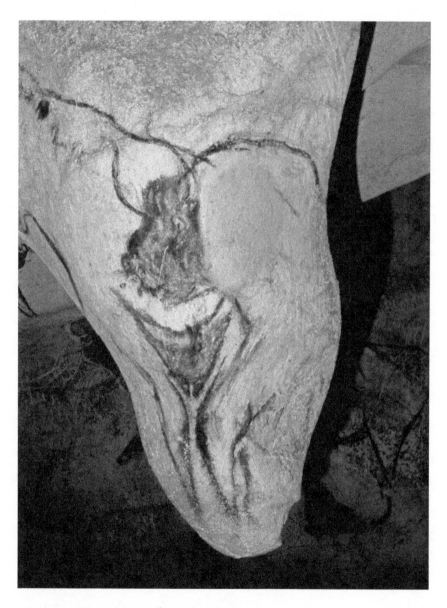

FIGURE 2.1 Venus, painting from Chauvet cave, France.

FIGURE 2.2 The Fates (Moirai) (Clotho, Lachesis, Atropos), Greek goddesses of birth, fate, and life's narrative. Image from the film *Reliance* by G. K. Galabov.

FIGURE 2.3 Xiwangmu, queen mother of the West, Eastern Han dynasty, stamping of a funerary brick, Chengdu Museum, Sichuan, China.

her improbable fertility at ninety years of age, the princess of Abraham just laughs hesitantly with this nameless joy. Incredible and a no less certain reliance on the unthinkable: is it biological or divine?

The Christian and in particular Catholic vision accustomed us to a harmonious nativity, "good news" bathed in tenderness and promise.

FIGURE 2.4 Stamping from unknown provenance, Later Han dynasty (22–220), Paris, Guimet Museum. Laozi superimposed, *Daodejing*, chapter 25: "Something indistinct takes shape even before the Sky and the Earth. Silently, subtly, this thing develops and advances, it circulates undiminished. It can be considered as the mother of the world. As I don't know its name, I call it the Way."

Until this reversal of roles between mother and son, in which Christ himself is transformed into father-mother and holds Mary who has become a babe in arms—"daughter of her son, fixed goal of the Eternal Wisdom," wrote Dante.[2]

Before the Italian painters made off with the *sacra conversazione*[3] of the mother and her male baby to diminish its eroticism, the maternal in Western painting became the male artist's maternal. The draped marbles, the innumerable Nativities, and the Assumptions of the Virgin attest to this.[4]

No one grasped better the catastrophic latency of maternal reliance than German expressionism (does this explain its being considered "degenerate" by the Nazis in 1937?), and in particular, the painter Max Beckmann (1884–1950) in his major works exploring his tragic conception of the world, in *Birth* (1937) and *Death* (1938).

Neither values nor religions, but deeper below them, it is maternal reliance that Beckmann's *Birth* literally tears to pieces. His catastrophe spews a chaos of fragments on the canvas where the spectator can barely make out the remains of the three members of the Holy Family, broken

FIGURE 2.5 Sarah, Abraham, and three angels (Gn 17, 1, 7), prayer for the blessing on the food after the Seder (Birkat Hamazone), Chantilly Haggada (fifteenth century), Chantilly, Condé Museum.

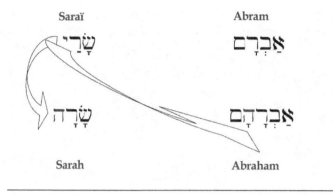

Saraï   Abram

Sarah   Abraham

FIGURE 2.6 Saraï lost the letter *Yod* (the first "masculine" letter of the Hebrew alphabet) and in exchange received an H (symbol of fecundity, letter of the spirit of God; there are two Hs in the tetragrammaton YHVH) to become Sarah. Abram did not lose any letter and received an H to become Abraham.

up objects for improbable subjects in a squalid world. The progenitor of this hideous birth exhibits the horror of her power with a breast more obscene than erotic. Meanwhile, the second panel of the diptych, *Death*, is no longer a Pietà. Forgotten, the placid "Dormition" that had Mary move near her Son-and-Father without experiencing death. Surrounding a doleful, barely visible, mummy in the casket's shadow, angels with trumpets of Jericho sound the new Apocalypse here. Far more than maternal death is the death of reliance itself that Beckmann lays bare.

The unidimensional humanity of last century has been replaced by today's hyperconnected and rushed person who communicates in "tweets" and, whatever the risks of chaos and absence of truth in his virtual world, seems, nevertheless, to reject any supreme authority, whether political or spiritual.

British socialists are seeking a prototype specifically in maternal care to reinvent solidarity and restore the social bond itself. More amusingly, French women writers are remembering they are mothers, and the maternal is making its way into the woman's novel.

If ethics means not avoiding the awkward and inevitable problematic of law but giving it body, language, and jouissance, then this ethic is

FIGURE 2.7 *Madonna and Child*, 1460–1464, Giovanni Bellini (circa 1430–1516), Correr Museum, Venice.

herethical. It demands the participation of women, the mothers in them, and among them, women carrying the desire to reproduce, a stability in movement. Women available so that our speaking species who knows its mortality can bear death. Mothers. Their RELIANCE is this herethical ethic.

FIGURE 2.8 *Birth*, 1937, Max Beckmann, Neue Nationalgalerie, Berlin.

FIGURE 2.9 *Death*, 1938, Max Beckmann, Neue Nationalgalerie, Berlin.

Thus, the private side of moral laws: what makes the bonds, thinking, and thinking of death bearable—the *herethical* is a-death, is love . . . *Eia Mater, fons amoris* (Ah Mother, fount of love). Listen again to the *Stabat Mater* and to music, all music . . . it makes sense . . . until Anton Webern and Max Beckmann shatter reliance, devouring and precluding the need for goddesses. But without forgoing new languages, new reliances.

3

HOW TO SPEAK TO LITERATURE WITH ROLAND BARTHES

I would like to open this conference with a passage from Philip Roth's *Exit Ghost:*[1]

> *To the Editor:*
>
> *There was a time when intelligent people used literature to think. That time is coming to an end. During the decades of the Cold War, in the Soviet Union and its Eastern European satellites, it was the serious writers who were expelled from literature; now, in America, it is literature that has been expelled as a serious influence on how life is perceived. The predominant uses to which literature is not put in the culture pages of the enlightened newspapers and in university English departments are so destructively at odds with the aims of imaginative writing, as well as with the rewards that literature affords an open-minded reader, that it would be better if literature were no longer put to any public use.*
>
> *Your paper's cultural journalism—the more of it there is, the worse it gets. As soon as one enters into the ideological simplifications and biographical reductivism of cultural journalism, the essence of the artifact is lost. Your cultural journalism is tabloid gossip disguised as an interest in "the arts," and everything that it touches is contracted into what it is not. Who is the celebrity, what*

is the price, what is the scandal? What transgression has the writer committed, and not against the exigencies of literary aesthetics but against his or her daughter, son, mother, father, spouse, lover, friend, publisher, or pet? Without the least idea of what is innately transgressive about the literary imagination, cultural journalism is ever mindful of phony ethical issues: "Does the writer have the right to blah-blah-blah?" . . . Everything the writer builds, meticulously, phase by phrase and detail by detail, is a ruse and a lie. The writer is without literary motive. Any interest in depicting reality is nil. The writer's guiding motives are always personal and generally low.

And this knowledge comes as a comfort, for it turns out that not only are these writers not superior to the rest of us, as they pretend to be—they are worse than the rest of us. Those terrible geniuses!

The way in which serious fiction eludes paraphrase and description—hence requiring thought—is a nuisance to your cultural journalist. Only its imagined sources are to be taken seriously, only that faction, the lazy journalist's fiction. . . .

If I had something like Stalin's power, I would not squander it on silencing the imaginative writers. I would silence those who write about the imaginative writers. I'd forbid all public discussion of literature in newspapers, magazines, and scholarly periodicals. I'd forbid all instruction in literature in every grade school, high school, college, and university in the country. I'd outlaw reading groups and Internet book chatter, and police the bookstores to be certain that no clerk ever spoke to a customer about a book and that the customers did not dare to speak to one another. I'd leave the readers alone with the books, to make of them what they would on their own. I'd do this for as many centuries as are required to detoxify the society of your poisonous nonsense.

Amy Belette

I take this "To the Editor," signed by one of the novel's characters, Amy Belette, as far more than an outburst of anger from the author himself. When I suggested a conference on "What is the state of literary criticism today?" to the Centre Roland Barthes, I was close to thinking and sharing what Amy Belette tells us in this "letter to the editor." But this time I was no longer a character of Philip Roth's (as I happened to be once, for example, in his novel *The Stain*). On the contrary, it is in the real world and in my role as reader, literary theoretician, and (sometime) literary critic that I found myself at one with the writer.

In the course of these days, let us not to forget Amy Belette's affects. So that our thinking might at least provide insight into them and become aware of the malaise and, who knows—let's be optimistic—sketch out some necessary mutations.

THREE PATHS TO INTRODUCE THESE ISSUES

1. By its very structure as discourse of or on literature—as metalanguage, for example—whether it is interpretation (hermeneutics) or criticism, all commentary is bound to rigidify the literary experience as an "object." Roland Barthes, on the contrary—whose work is the raison d'être for our Center and the focus of our debates—built on and renewed the wager that writers (from Diderot to Baudelaire or Georges Bataille) have taken up: it is possible to speak *of* literature if and only if we speak *to* literature.

This was my mind-set in 1971 when I attempted to think about Roland Barthes's adventure of taking up in his inimitable style, in a "writing" (as in his meaning), the advances in linguistics, semiology, and more generally social sciences in relation to what he called the "literary competence" of speaking beings. Since no one is a prophet in his own country, you do not know this work, so allow me to review the main and updated ideas of this text called "How Does One Speak to Literature?"[2] and to call my talk today "How Does One Speak to Literature, No. 2?"

2. Because—and this is my second theme—in forty years, the place of language and literature has changed in society, but also in the experience of many of us under the influence of the image and globalization. How does one speak to literature if language itself seems to be receding behind the glow of screens and in their shadows while the Word that used to be "in the beginning" has been reduced to clichés and the novel crumbles in

text messages, in fallouts of autofiction? It is only by surprise that the novel dares a precious look inward, on the memory of a genre and, even more rarely, on the history of thought, to be read later or never.

3. Last, and throughout my reasoning, I will try not to lose sight (of Barthes's body of work, in particular, *The Pleasure of the Text* and *A Lover's Discourse, Fragments*), obviously, of *Criticism and Truth* (1966) to point out the timeliness of this book as much as the yet unthought present that he encourages us to address.

As does Barthes, I will draw attention to two discourses of/on literature:

• The discourse of the "scholar" (interpretive, hermeneutic, analytical) that unfolds the "anthropological" side of meaning—such as Barthes roots it in what Georges Bataille and Philippe Sollers call "experience."[3]
• The discourse of the "critic," who is not the literary columnist (contrary to conventional wisdom that attributes judgment and assessment to the critic) but who is defined as someone who "affirms" his/her "desire."

Two discourses or rather two attitudes that very often crisscross and interweave, at least in Barthes's ideal vision as opposed to that of Picard.[4]

For the *interpretative discourse*, I could refer to Kant's "Third Critique," the Critique of the Power of Judgment, and his Critique of Aesthetic Judgment, founded on taste, the most archaic of the senses that Hannah Arendt revisited in order to envisage another relationship to language and only then another politics.[5]

It can also be connected to Husserl's phenomenology that opens up a material and sensorial sphere, the "prepredicative sphere," in his "porous horizon" of the "predicative thesis," with the challenge to think the sensible.

I prefer to deal with the Freudian unconscious, with the paradoxical regime of drives, affects, and desire as well as their preobjects and presubjects.

All these approaches of literary and more generally aesthetic experience—that jostle the metaphysical categories of sense and the sensible, of the psyche and soma, etc.—have been enhanced by including art and literature as objects of investigation. A really strange "object" when you think of it: because it is not about "commenting" (glossing, paraphrasing) the "substance" and the "form" of the work (descriptions that classic rhetoric and academic discourse excel in targeted by Roland Barthes), but of questioning the *experience* of a Sade, a Balzac, or an Artaud, to show its singularity. And thus how this singular *experience*, this *enunciation* of an utterance, this *writing* (the "concepts" and "notions" keep changing) jostles and innovates the theoretical codes themselves from which the interpreter attempted to approach it.

The "scholar's" interpretive approach enables him to enhance and renew his theoretical framework faced with the discovery of the multiple dormant meanings that Barthes now addresses, not as "object of knowledge" but as "writer's experience"—and I emphasize this—and in which the interpreter himself transfers himself. In the guise of the signification-message-information appears this "whirlwind of hilarity and horror" that Mallarmé spoke of and that has to be investigated by calling on its polysemic economy whose truth contains a general value. "The general discourse of the object is not the meaning but the very plurality of meanings in the work";[6] "science of the conditions of the content, i.e., of the forms; what will interest him will be the variations in engendered meanings, and one might say, engenderable by the works: it will not interpret the symbols but only their polyvalence; in a word, its object will no longer be the full meanings of the work but rather the empty meaning that supports them all."[7] "All the possible meanings will not be organized in an immutable order but as traces of an immense 'operating' arrangement . . . enlarged from the author to the society."[8]

Take Maurice Merleau-Ponty's text *The Visible and the Invisible* as an example of this "scholarly" discourse.[9] What is he looking for in Proust's work, alongside that of Cézanne, understood by the painter as "What I am trying to translate for you is more mysterious and is tangled up in the very roots of the Being, at the impalpable origin of feeling"? Is there a meditative thinking that does not yield to the concepts of its language? Is there a prereflexive state of thought that widens communication with the Being and yet keeps it opaque? Is there an infinite logos that organizes the world where, at the intersection of nature and mind, the germination of meaning and philosophy itself begins? Is it a crossroads or a dehiscence of thought that Proust and Cezanne transferred to Merleau-Ponty?[10]

There is an intertwining of man and the universe, a "hollow," a "fold," a "flesh," as the philosopher would say. Like a barely visible framework, the flesh makes up for what one dares not think. Less than a desire that has an object, more than a *jouissance* that lost it in the fusion with the Being, flesh is this chiasma between sensing and the sensible that exists at the exquisite limits of what is felt. My flesh or that of the world? Both. Imbibed with meaning but stopping at the senseless. Never has consciousness been as ambitious, and for that very reason, as porous as in this hold of what, in becoming me, withdraws from me. In reading Proust, the world touches me and I touch it. You too, Proust and Cézanne, you see me and I see you, copresent and abandoned. Sensible flesh receives sensible time in the communion of the separated. Is it asking too much of a person to live each sensation, why not say it, as a Christian passion? As for Merleau-Ponty, he meditated sensation with Proust, with the effervescence of identities, from outside and inside, from the world and the self, until little Marcel's *In Search of Lost Time* transforms the philosopher, transforms us into flesh; through the imagination fanned out in metaphors and in hyperbolic syntax. As did the writer himself in living his writing. Reading, then, lived as a passionate encounter is an unbearable rite. This is what Merleau-Ponty said in inventing "the flesh" of *In Search of Lost Time*. The concept of "flesh" contaminates us, we are part of it. Through the force of Merleau-Ponty's writing.

In other words, the interpretation the philosopher suggested of the Proustian *Search* introduced in philosophy a new notion of "flesh" inherited from Greek philosophy, Judaism, and Christianity. Proust's text is not for him an "object" to judge, assess, or even less to promote. The Proustian imagination is *experienced* (I maintain the double meaning of the word from *Erlebnis* and *Erfahrung*) as a potentiality within the complex signifying polyphony that the interpreter locates while renewing his theoretical models: rather by re-creating them from this new desire of meaning that the passionate encounter of his reading of the Proustian experience of sensible time, of pure incorporated time, imposes on him.[11]

Let us take it one step further. The fascination of French theory in many universities and cultural institutions throughout the world also comes from this new desire for a new model of meaning that French literary and art theorists have brought to light.

When the poetry of Mallarmé led me to rethink the *Chora* by Plato,[12] this space before the space in *Timaeus*, and to suggest thinking this more-than-meaning of music in letters by the term *semiotic chora*—listening to the drive-bases of phonation as a double for the explicit signification of "A throw of the dice will not abolish Chance" or of "Prose for des Esseintes"—I am not speaking of literature as "object." I am speaking to literature as *subjective experience* since I am joining it in its labyrinth of "mystery in letters" (as Mallarmé liked to say). In truth, this "mystery" that I discern (and analyze) speaks to me: in our transference/counter-transference (between the "A throw of the dice" and "me"), the text gives me the gift of a new interpretative tool that will refine my own perception and enable me to get other texts across differently; I get an analytical tool from it that unfolds the "polyvalence" (Roland Barthes) of this complex symbol which any work is.

Likewise, my reading of Céline[13]—whose anti-Semitism I do not condone nor do I explain or judge—from *Journey to the End of the Night* to *Trifles for a Massacre* alerted me to *abjection* in his novels and pamphlets that underlay the subject/object, child/parent, man/woman links as well as the narrator's link to the other's religion, ethnic group, or race. It called forth and stimulated thinking about psychoanalytic and phenomenological models that I wanted to revisit. I attempt to widen the intelligibility of a subjective experience (that of the author, but also of the reader he appeals to) that takes root in the borderlines of psychic life: fascination and/or repulsion between subject and object, neither one nor the other, ab-jects. I discover *abjection* that subtends the classic aesthetic categories such as "seduction"; from sociology: "racism," and from psychoanalysis: "delirium."

Is this approach of the interpreter "scholar" or the analyst so different from the one Barthes calls "the critic"? Certainly. And yet not absolutely. Writing and its subject, imposed on modern thinking from Maurice Blanchot through Hegel-Mallarmé-Kafka, gave up the speculative labyrinth of absolute mind in Barthes to reach political and mythical discourse, journalism, the *nouveau roman*, and *Tel Quel* with Sade, Fourier, Loyola, and Balzac. And thanks to an alliance between sociology, structuralism, and the literary avant-garde, a new light shone on them. I maintain that for Barthes writing had its apparently irreconcilable origins in, on one hand, the experience of the "fascination" that Blanchot contemplated in writing "given over to the absence of time," "in a loss of the being when the being is missing,"[14] and on the other hand, according to Sartre, in the dialectical conception of writing as objective *praxis*, "more complete, more total than life."[15] But then if the interpreter tries to identify with the writing experience thusly understood, does not the critic do it in his own way? What is that way? Or, on the contrary, do both of them (the interpreter and the critic) remain irremediably strangers to writing? Except if they become writers too . . . by intermittence? Are Blanchot and Sartre scholar interpreters or are they critics? Or maybe writers?[16]

Ambivalence and drama of the critic: was Barthes the first to bring them to light in a culture slipping into the throes of what was not yet called "the media"? On one hand, the critic speaks in his name to another: he introduces desire before expressing any "criticism" whatsoever, be it judgment or evaluation. "Going from reading to criticism means changing desire; it is no longer desiring the work, but its own language."[17] Let us be clear: the critic desires the language of which he is capable. Where the "scholar" interpreter innovates models to think the inexhaustible polysemic experience of works, the critic, said Barthes, is one who asserts the language of his desire: "The critic has to produce a certain "tone," and this tone, all things considered, can only be affirmative."[18] The critic remains glued to his "I," which monopolizes the multiple meanings and which appropriates the polyvalences and signs: "The critic cannot produce the "HE" of the novel but cannot either reject the "I" in pure private life, i.e., give up writing: he is an aphasic of the "I," while the rest of his language remains intact, marked, however, by the infinite detours that the blockage concerning a certain sign imposes on speech (as in the case of the aphasic)."[19] Starting from his opaque "I" toward another's writing, the critic (aphasic of his own narrative experience, unable to tell himself) goes back to his "I" that has remained blocked in a language of affirmation—I mean, that the language of the critic is not a language of experience.

The irony of this going around in circles is not lost on Barthes: the critic has to coagulate an island of affirmative meaning just where writing as experience is constantly and infinitely decomposing and recomposing. Aphasic of the "I" and ironist unable to accept the death wish that triumphs in the act of writing not as a "biography" but as a "thanatography," the critic attests but by his own handicap, however, to this strange singularity of the literary experience. He displays his heterogeneity in the social space of communication but without making it intelligible. With his "decision to say," the critic can only distance himself definitively from the polyphonic logic of writing, from its nocturnal depth edged with senselessness and the sensible.[20]

Here we are at the fault line joining the interpreter and the critic, yet so different from each other: they keep their distance from writing; they are not writers. "A writer is one for whom language poses a problem, who feels its depth, but neither the instrumentality nor the beauty."[21] The writer desubstantializes the meaning of language at the same time as individual identity; his intention takes root outside of language; his secret is intimidating because he is against-communication,[22] that is, plumbs experience.

Rarely and perhaps never has the proximity between interpreter-critic-and-writer, with their similarities-differences and through the mixing of these roles, been so present in consciousness, so minutely analyzed and passionately practiced as in France and in the French language in the latter part of the twentieth century. We should not be inhibited by the apparent technicity of this progress. In clarifying the various modalities of this relation, in calling for each person's constant awareness, it is necessary for Barthes and for us, his friends and accomplices even in our very differences, to show our contemporaries, alienated in their language and without a historical future, that literature is the place where this alienation is specifically and each time thwarted. With a heightened consciousness for some, diffused for others, we must and can resist the ongoing trivialization of minds but also refuse the symmetrical and outdated cult of belles-lettres.

WHAT IS TODAY'S SITUATION?

The third millennium adds new difficulties to this scene. Does that mean that the primacy of the globalized image discredits the central role of language and thus literature, but also interpretive and critical discourse?

Many people think so, and the poverty of literary columns like the opacity of academic discourse, as Amy Belette denounced, would seem to prove it. I have been told that the French cultural message is no longer working, simply because it was based on French language and literature at the expense of cultural industries. How can one not have the ambition to develop these inescapable cultural industries (movies, visual and plastic arts, book, theater, etc.) but also the digital and to reinvent Francophony by the same token! I argue, however, that if we are not able to react to what I would describe as a real and all-encompassing denial of language—and literature—if this "consciousness of the word" that defines the writer, according to Barthes, before any "hierarchy of values" should weaken or even disappear, we would be at a turning point of the human condition that would lead to changes with unpredictable consequences, for better, perhaps, and for worse, as well.

I am not one of those who demonize the reign of images. Nor do I only fixate on language and literature as the major constituents of national identity: even if I am convinced that it is there, not in the cult of language and its literature but in their perpetual transvaluation by writing and interpretive, analytic, and critical discourse that elucidate it, that this mobile identity evolves: not at all a dogma but a constant questioning, a work in progress, an open work that is the identity of a living nation. I will limit myself to emphasizing the fact that—because language constitutes the subject in man and woman (as philosophy and the social sciences have shown for more than a century)—it is the literary imagination that provides the privileged space in which the liberty of the subject is acquired, in, with or without meaning. It is the literary experience—along with its interpretative elucidation that often integrates it in its very utterance—that transforms the man's and the woman's dependence concerning fantasy, that is, the image, but also any univocal idea or signifier. By allowing me to reach the limits of my self as well as the objective possibility of going beyond the sociohistorical, the literary experience is a uniquely complex test of freedom, unique in its complexity, at the very heart of social norms. Proust was saying the same thing when writing, "My imagination, which was my only organ to enjoy beauty,"[23] or "Reality . . . a sort of waste product of experience."[24]

I hear your question. Is it still possible to speak thus to literature as experience when literature itself withdraws, "inrockuptible," in the echolalic poetry of Guyotat; when it focuses—rarely—in a dialogue with philosophy and history according to Sollers; or, more often, when it competes in vulgarity with *Desperate Housewives*?

Protected by the university, but clearly overprotected, only the interpretative "specialized" discourse continues to redeem, cultivate, and awaken this "consciousness of language" that one would wish as or more "sustainable" than the threatened ecosystem. This interpretative discourse should attain the quality of affirmation that Barthes diagnosed in the discourse of criticism: that it decides to be heard, that it chooses to talk in and against the generalized mediatization.

As for criticism itself, it should not orchestrate "celebrity culture." It has to get out of the virtual to which the various screens reduce imaginary constructions and to try to give an anthropological depth to the work of language.

As far as analytical interpretation is concerned, one must reflect upon the place of the image in the complex architecture of meaning, without yielding to the facility of hyperconnectivity that in the fantasy of hyper-communicability promotes the denial of linguistic and literary polysemy and encourages the ideology of decline.

And as far as criticism is concerned, reading has to take precedence over the image, which means changing desire. It has to desire PR less and to desire more the consciousness of language as experience of speech marked out with non-sense, sensations, and infinite recompositions.

Faced with the "crisis of the commentary," Barthes and others in 1966 attempted to join up critics and interpreters with writers. What is threatening in the "symbol that constitutes language"? he asked. And he answered: not the unicity of meaning but the infinite capacity of interpretation and criticism by which the psychic life lives and relives, revolts against dogmas and refounds its links, societies and democracy. The consciousness of language, by awakening the univocal and unidimensional man, would make possible, he hoped, a "social mutation as deep, perhaps, as that which marked the passage of the Middle Ages to the Renaissance."[25]

We are waiting today for an improbable exit from the financial, economic, and social crisis that is far deeper than the malaise prevailing in the pre-1968 civilization. It is no longer a "one-way," hostile to "imagination in power," that threatens us but a real "asymbolia" in which, under the guise of a belief in the image, it is not a "society of the spectacle" that is asserting itself but the space of the "consciousness of speech" as a whole that is closing in. Closing this space means condemning the person and his social links to an in-signifying virtuality, and this new sickness of the soul opens out onto two abysses: disillusioned nihilism, on one hand, and fundamentalist transcendentalism, on the other.

What can the interpretive, analytical, and critical discourse do in this unprecedented situation? We do not know, but we have the possibility of being aware that there is a mutation of the civilization of the word and the book to the benefit of a virtual "culture," a playful metamorphosis of what Freud called a "death wish culture" that corresponds to the "super-ego culture" with its excessive controls and routine breakdowns. Psychoanalysis and criticism are on the front lines of those who can assess the risks and promises of this passage. We must not dodge this seriousness. Think about it and try to talk not *of* but *to* literature.

4

EMILE BENVENISTE, A LINGUIST WHO NEITHER SAYS NOR HIDES, BUT SIGNIFIES

What is a great linguist? Great linguists can be recognized by the fact that as they know and analyze *languages*, they discover properties of *language* through which they interpret and innovate "being in the world" of speaking subjects. I offer this definition in order to see the work of Emile Benveniste (1902–1976) in the context of some of his predecessors who, in spite of appearing meticulous and cold, have nonetheless accompanied and advanced some of the most decisive stages in the human adventure. Think of the sixteenth-century humanists and grammarians such as Scaliger and Ramus, whose analysis of the relationship between language and thought, from Latin to modern languages, laid the ground for the establishment and development of national languages; of Lancelot and Arnauld, whose *General and Rational Grammar* (1660), more than *The Logic of Port-Royal* (1662), by introducing the notion of "sign," by attempting to determine "what is spiritual in language," and by approving the judgment on "grammatical usage," inscribed the Cartesian subject in the syntax of language; of the "historicism" of the nineteenth century and the comparative philology of Franz Bopp and Rasmus Rask, then, last, Humboldt, who, proving after Hegel and Herder the structural link between Sanskrit and Indo-European languages, confirmed the weight of history in the evolutive activity of language.

The tragic conflicts of the twentieth century tend to obscure the fact that it was also a time of exceptional language exploration going right to the heart of the human condition: as a central activity, language conditions, contains, and elucidates all human experiences. Phenomenology, formal logic, analytic philosophy, structuralism, generative grammar, and social sciences questioning the meaning in language of behavior and institutions, not to mention psychoanalysis that added on sex and encroached on biology, developed just as an unprecedented explosion of literary forms, artistic avant-gardes, and stylistic singularities caused an upheaval in the humanities. A lucid adventure that seen in retrospect seemed to herald the breakup of conventional sign systems and the tide of new and virtual hyperconnections that promise as much freedom as chaos.

Emile Benveniste's work is fully a part of this profusion, if we take the trouble to juxtapose the complexity of his thinking with the advances in philosophy and social sciences and with the new forms of art and literature, and it is "in contact with" our century's challenges. It profoundly clarifies the universal properties of language that underlie this creative freedom of the human mind that it never stops probing. The reader attentive to Benveniste's trajectory, one who will not be distracted by a linguistics crammed with technical urgencies in a society losing its meaning and surrounded by "PR," will discover in his *Dernières leçons* that his "general theories" help probe the deep systems that extend even into our digital writing. Are they *chats* lacking "subjectivity" or, on the contrary, ways to "engender" new "signifying processes"?

Emile Benveniste was an austere scholar, a very great specialist of ancient languages, an expert in comparative grammar, and a general linguistics authority. He knew Sanskrit, Hittite, Tocharian, Indian, Iranian, Greek, Latin, all the Indo-European languages, and, when he was over fifty, plunged into the Amerindian languages. But his work, impressively audacious and yet unpretentious and outwardly modest, remains relatively unknown and little read today.

Born in Aleppo, Syria, in 1902 into a multilingual Jewish family,[1] Ezra Benveniste immigrated to France in 1913 where he became a student in the "minor seminary" in the Rabbinical School of France.[2] His exceptional predisposition for languages caught the attention of Sylvain Lévi, who introduced him to the great Antoine Meillet (unless the meeting came from Salomon Reinach).[3] Ezra Benveniste was admitted to the

FIGURE 4.1 Emile Benveniste.

Ecole Practique des Hautes Etudes (EPHE) in 1918 and obtained his degree in literature (*licence en lettres*) the next year and his *agrégation* in grammar in 1922, after which—as a pure product of French Republic secular education—he was naturalized as a citizen in 1924 and chose the first name Emile. During these formative years, he established close links with young philosophers and linguists, more or less rebellious *Normalians*, libertarians, antimilitarists, even Communist sympathizers, and met many surrealists. He left for India in 1924 as a tutor in a family of prosperous industrialists, before fulfilling, willy-nilly, his military obligations in Morocco in 1926. Back in France, he became Antoine Meillet's student, whom he succeeded as department head (comparative grammar chair) at EPHE, where he had a strong influence on his colleagues. He entered the College de France in 1937, again succeeding Meillet as comparative grammar chair. In 1940–1941 he was taken prisoner of war, managed to escape, and took refuge in Switzerland, in Fribourg (where Balthus, Alberto Giacometti, Pierre Emmanuel, and Pierre-Jean Jouve were living), thus escaping Nazi persecutions, although his apartment was looted. His brother Henri was arrested and deported to Auschwitz in 1942 and died there. Along with the greatest names of the Jewish intelligentsia (Benjamin Crémieux, Georges Friedman, Henri Levy-Bruhl, etc.), he signed a joint letter organized by Marc Bloch and sent on March 31, 1942, to the UGIF, calling attention to the Vichy policy of putting Jews into a separate category, a prelude to deportation.[4] After Liberation, Benveniste returned to his teaching at the EPHE and the College de France, forming several generations of students and conducting "in the field" linguistic research in Iran, Afghanistan, and then Alaska. He also participated in numerous international linguistics conferences. He became a member of the Institute (Academy of Writing and Letters) in 1960, director of the Institute of Iranian Studies in 1963, and president of the International Association of Semiotics in 1969. On December 6 of that same year, a stroke put an end to his career, leaving him disabled for the seven years until his death in 1976.

This short biography of an "agnostic Israelite," of a nomadic Frenchman, is above all about a man who made *language* the *path* of a life and through his work transmitted the thought of this experience.

Benveniste left "unfinished work," an expression that might not do justice to the scope of his writing. Unfinished, yes, as his stroke left the man in an intolerable situation: that of a great linguist deprived of the use of speech and paralyzed. But "unfinished" also in an absolutely necessary sense, because such is the *language experience* that he had and theorized in a century where the diversity of schools of thought—which multiplied both the epistemological and aesthetic leads and questions—imposed on this man anchored in his time the *Heraclitian* refusal to "say," to construct a closed, fixed, and definitive "message" in a complete system. In the center of all of this abounding diversity to which he was always tuned in (from comparative philology to Ferdinand de Saussure, from structuralism to Chomskyan syntax, from surrealism to "post–Nouveau Roman"), he practiced what must be called a *Benvenistean* style of thought where the morphosyntactic detail *joined* the constant questioning of fundamental linguistic and/or philosophical[5] categories and which was characterized, other than by the refusal to "say," by shunning the aestheticism that "hides" (although he was sensitive to it for a time, as his literary self-analysis, *Eau virile*,[6] demonstrated), by the will to "signify" (to open to thought, to problematize, to question) and to determine how *to signify* is generated in the formal apparatus of language.

What, then, is "to signify"? The metaphysical question led Benveniste to seek a "material" solution in the very functioning of language: for him, "it signifies" is synonymous with "it speaks" and thus is without recourse to any "external" or "transcendental reality"; it is in the "properties" of language itself that he explores and analyzes the possibilities of making sense, specific to this "signifying organism," the speaking humanity.

The young man born in the heart of the Ottoman Empire, grant student of the Alliance Israelite Universelle, thus did not become a rabbi.[7] At a time in history when the Six-Day War (1967) and the Yom Kippur War (1973) had not yet sparked the desire in many agnostic Jews for a return of God the Father, it was with the motto of Heraclitus, *Oute légei, oute kryptei, alla semainei*[8] (unless it translates the unpronounceable tetragrammaton YHWH: the being identified with what is and will be and with the "signifyingness"), that he summed up his ambition to study the "signifying power" in the very properties of language. A *path* precisely that "neither says nor hides but signifies" and led him from the study of pre-Socratic Greece (explicitly), the Bible, and the Gospels (implicitly) to that of modern knowledge emanating from secularism, and particularly, general linguistics that he attempted to *modulate* in such a way that it might analyze how language is organized to create meaning (*DL*, first lesson).

DOUBLE SIGNIFYINGNESS

Thus Benveniste grasps "meaning" by disregarding its philosophical, moral, or religious "value." It is the search for *meaning in its linguistic specificity* that "orders the discourse on language" of the *Dernières leçons* edited and introduced by Jean-Claude Coquet and Irene Fenoglio.[9] "*We ourselves posit* [our emphasis] that the essential nature of language, which orders all the functions that it can assume, is its *signifying* nature."[10] The "signifying process" that "informs" language thus posited is a property that "transcends" "all particular or general use," or a "characteristic that we place in the forefront: language signifies."

It is December 2, 1968, seven months after the famous May 1968. The naïve reader, then as now, is taken by surprise: is this so original? What good is a language if it does not signify something? Certainly. But do you know what you really mean by "signify"? And what if "to communicate," "to mean," and "to deliver a message" were being confused with "to signify"?

Central to the philosophy of language, but as a bearer of "truth," *meaning* is not really a linguistic issue, reminded Benveniste. *Meaning* is left "outside linguistics" (*PGL* 2:216 [1967]): either "put aside" as suspected of being too subjectivist, elusive, indescribable in its linguistic form; or recognized, but "reduced" (Leonard Bloomfield, Zellig Harris) to structural morphosyntactic, "distributional" invariants," in a "given corpus." According to Benveniste, on the contrary, "to signify" constitutes an "internal principal" of language (*DL*, lesson 3). With this "new idea," he emphasized, "we are thrown before a major problem that embraces linguistics *and beyond.*" If a few precursors (John Locke, Saussure, and Charles Sanders Peirce) proved that we "live in a universe of signs" of which language is the first, followed by signs of writing, recognition, unity, etc. (*DL*, lesson 1), Benveniste intended to show how the *formal apparatus* of language allowed it not only to "name" objects and situations but moreover to "generate" *discourse* with original meanings that are as individual as they are shareable in exchanges with others. Better still, not satisfied with *generating itself,* the language organism also generates other *sign systems* that resemble it or increase its capacities, but it is the only sign system capable of providing an *interpretation.*

Benveniste's works collected in the first volume of *Problems of General Linguistics* (1966), while based on the study of ancient languages and on comparative linguistics, already dealt with these theoretical questions. A *second Benveniste,* clarifying and shifting the principal questions of his *first general linguistics,* appeared in the second volume of *Problems of General Linguistics* (197), published after he suffered his stroke and which gathered the articles written from 1965 to 1972. The careful reading of these two volumes can distinguish two major stages in the *evolution of his thinking,* which the reader should be aware of in order to grasp the whole innovative scope of the *Dernières leçons.*

Starting with the first volume of his masterwork, the theorist proposed a general linguistics that departed from structural linguistics, but also from a generative grammar that dominated the linguistic landscape of the time, and advanced a linguistics of *discourse* based on *allocution* and dialogue, opening the *utterance* toward the process of *enunciation* and toward *subjectivity* and *intersubjectivity*. In the wake of analytic philosophy (performative utterances), but also of Freudian psychoanalysis, Benveniste envisaged *subjectivity in the enunciation* as a far more complex emitter than the Cartesian subject, for he broadened it to the "intentional" (borrowed from existential phenomenology). Furthermore, and without seeming to, he outlined an opening toward the subject of the "unconscious." Not really "structured as a language" but shaped by a (drive-based?) "anarchic force" that language "restrains and sublimates," even though by "tears," it can introduce in it a "new content, one of unconscious motivation, and a specific symbolism," "when the power of the censor is suspended."

A new dimension of general linguistics for Benveniste came out in the second volume. In discussion with Saussure and his conception of signs, the distinctive elements of the linguistic system, Benveniste introduced *two types in the signifyingness* of language: "the" *semiotic* and "the" *semantic*.

The *semiotic* (from *semeion*, or *sign*, characterized by its "arbitrary" link—the result of a social convention—between "signifier" and "signified") is a closed, generic, binary, intralinguistic, systemizing, and institutional meaning, which is defined by a "paradigmatic" and "substitution" relation. The *semantic* is expressed in the sentence that articulates the "signified of the sign," or the "intentional content" (frequent allusion to Husserl's phenomenological "intention," whose thought influenced certain linguists such as Hendrik Josephus Pos). It is defined by a relation of "connection" or "syntagm," where the "sign" (the *semiotic*) becomes "word" by the "activity of the speaker" (*PGL* 2:225). This activates *language* in the situation of *discourse* addressed by the "first person" (I) to the "second person" (you), the third person being situated outside the discourse. "Based on the *semiotic*, language as discourse constructs its own semantics, a signification of intentional content produced by *syntagmation* of words where each word retains only a small part of the value it has as a sign" (*PGL* 2:229).

Formulated in 1966 (*PGL* 2:63, 215) at the Convention of the Society of French Language Philosophy, the SFP, then at the Warsaw symposium, founder of the International Association for Semiotic Studies (AISS) the same year, this *dual* conception of signifyingness opened a whole new field of research. Benveniste focused on surpassing the Saussurian notion of the sign and language as a system and emphasized its importance, both intralinguistic—opening a new dimension of the signifying process, that of discourse (the semantic), separate from that of the sign (the semiotic[11])—and *translinguistic*—elaborating a metasemiotics of texts and works, based on the semantics of the enunciation (*PGL* 2:66). This gave a more precise idea of the immense perspectives that thus opened up: "We are just beginning to think about a property that is not yet definable in an integral way"; this orientation that crosses through linguistics "will impose a reorganization of the apparatus of human sciences" (*PGL* 2:238).

Benveniste's *Dernières leçons* continued this approach by *building on* to a new continent, that of poetic language, seen in his manuscript notes devoted to *Baudelaire* that develop and reorder the lessons' key notions.[12]

Between the second volume of *General Problems of Linguistics* and the manuscripts devoted to poetic language, *Dernières leçons* first attempted to demonstrate that "to signify," which constitutes "the initial, essential and specific property of language," does not lock itself into unit-signs (as Saussure theorized) but "transcends" the communicative and pragmatic functions of language; and, second, to specify the terms and the strategies of this "signifying process" insomuch as it is, strictly speaking, a vital "experience" (as he had said in *PGL* 2:217): "Long before serving to communicate, language served to *live*."

It was fitting that Benveniste introduced this thinking by way of a tribute to Saussure and Charles Sanders Peirce. He recognized the former's "particular importance" and defined his work as a "new moment of analysis," a fundamental step in the history of thought (*DL*, chap. 3, "*Dernières leçons, dernières notes*"), where, for the first time, "the notion of the sign" and of "the science of signs" was formed (*DL*, lesson 3). And in Peirce he referred to the "universal notion" of the sign divided into three "trichotomies" and broken down into multiple "categories," based on "triadic signs," which are also "universal" (*DL*, lesson 2). But this lucid recognition of debt to his predecessors gave him the opening to firmly demonstrate their limits. Thus Ferdinand Saussure "does not focus on the sign"; leaves open a possible "exteriority" of the sign; does not broach the question of relations between the sign systems and the "specificity of language," which "produces" ("engenders") new sign systems, insofar as it is its only "interpretant"; and also "does not deal with language as production" (*DL*, last lesson). As for Peirce, he did not base his theory on language but rather only on the word; his theory excelled in the description of the numerous varieties of signs, but it ignored language, and his logic lacked a systematic organization of the different types of signs (*DL*, lesson 3).[13]

This inventory helped clarify once again the stakes of Benveniste's new general linguistics: "We must pursue this reflection beyond the point indicated by Saussure" (*DL*, lesson 4). And that can be done, particularly by developing a "new relation" that Saussure did not envisage: "the relation of interpretation between systems." Language—unique within the diversity of signifying systems in that it possesses the capacity to self-interpret and interpret others (music, images, kinship)—is, precisely, "the interpretant system": it "provides the basis of relations enabling the interpreted to develop as a system." From this point of view, language hierarchically holds the first place of signifying systems that have *an engendering relationship* with each other (*DL*, lesson 5).

WRITING: CENTER AND RELAY

Language's "double signifyingness" described above is developed through writing that carries out and reveals its capacity for "production" and "engendering." However, while the term "writing" might be at the center of philosophical and literary creation in France,[14] the linguist does not refer to it explicitly but constructs the concept in the framework of his general theory of signifyingness of language.

To distance himself from Saussurean semiology, which, by "associating writing with the alphabet and language with a modern language," postulated that writing was "subordinate to language" (*DL*, lesson 8), Benveniste questioned the act of writing, learning to write, and the types constituted throughout history. He nevertheless took care to emphasize that he was not looking for the "origin of writing" but the various solutions of "graphical representation" of signifyingness (lesson 9).

First, there was the question of the "could not be more intimate" relation elaborated by the civilization of the book between writing, language, speech, and thought, that is, to disassociate these so as to envisage writing "in-and-for-itself" as a specific "semiotic system." Thus, uncoupled from speech, writing appears as a "high degree of abstraction": the writing-speaker extracts himself from the "living" verbal activity (gestural, phono-acoustic, connecting self and other in a dialogue) and "converts" the activity into "images," into "signs drawn by hand." With significant losses, of course, the image stands in for speech as a tool of "exteriorization" and "communication."

Subtle benefits, nonetheless, compensate for these losses, even disregarding the "utilitarian" function of writing (memorizing, transmitting, communicating the message). "The first major abstraction," writing, by making language a "distinct reality," detached from its contextual and circumstantial wealth, allows the speaker-writer to realize that language or thought are made of "words" represented by material signs, in images. Further still, this "iconization of thought" (lesson 8) is the source of a "unique experience" of the "speaker with himself": he "becomes conscious" that it is "not the word spoken or language in action" that writing proceeds from, but from an interior language, "global," "schematic," "ungrammatical," "allusive," "rapid," "incoherent," and "intelligible for the speaker and for him alone," that confronts him with the considerable task of achieving a "conversion operation of his thought" in a form intelligible to others.

Thus understood, the "iconic representation" builds speech and writing *together*: "it goes hand in hand with the development of speech and the acquisition of writing." At this step of his theorizing, and against Saussure, Benveniste noted that, far from being "subordinate," the iconic sign *connects* thought to the graphism and to verbalization: "Iconic representation develops in parallel to linguistic representation," which suggests a "less literal" and "more global" relation between *thought* and *icon* than the relation between *thought* and *speech*.

This hypothesis connecting writing to "interior language," which would be modified later, tied in to Benveniste's earlier questions on the "anarchic force" of the Freudian unconscious (*PGL* 1:78). Might the "interior language" that writing seeks to "represent" be dependent on "weaknesses," "games," and "stray ramblings" whose origin Benveniste, reader of Freud and the surrealists, discovered in the unconscious? *Dernières leçons'* concise notes on writing recall the linguist's former work and complete the phenomenological *intentional content* that he incorporated into the semantics of discourse by a "motivation" of another order. The "interior language" of speaking-writing would not be confined to the propositionality specific to the conscience's transcendental ego and to its "intention" but could implicitly describe a diversity of subjective spaces in its theory of subjectivity: typologies or topologies in the engendering of signifyingness. Baudelaire's "poetic experience," we shall see, confirmed and clarified this advance.

As for the history of writing, it brought a new adjustment to the relation of language to writing and attested to a new stage in Benveniste's theory of signifyingness.

Pictographic writing, a sign of external reality, "recites" a message already constituted by the "language of another" (*DL*, lesson 9): it "does not speak" in the sense that the speaking language is a "creation." As far back as one can go in its prehistory, writing "describes" "events": even though it is "parallel" to language, it is not its "imitation." This statement brings up a question that remains unanswered: does the specificity of the pictogram, which "recites" (reproduces) but does not "create" (does not produce) remain silently latent in all iconization of language? Is this particularity not even more pronounced in certain modern writing (digital, for example)? And, if so, under what conditions? With what consequences for the subject of the enunciation?

Two noteworthy revolutions in the history of writing shed light on the double signifyingness of language. The first resides in the discovery of a *graph* that reproduces the *phonè* in a *limited number of signs*, which means reproducing no longer the content of this message bearer of events but the *linguistic form of this message*. China is in "luck": not only because in the monosyllabic Chinese language (each semiotic unit is a formal unit and not decomposable) one word equals one syllable, but also because of the inventive genius of those who conceived it and who succeeded in attributing a sign (*graphè*, character) to each "signifier" (*phonè*), with "keys" to clarify the homophones (*DL*, lesson 11).

The process of being aware of the flow of speech, of decomposing words, of recognizing that they are polysyllabic, brings about a higher segmentation. For polysyllabic languages, it would be *segmentation in syllables*, with variants: Sumerian and cuneiform writing where "there is clear filiation between the image and the referent"; its adaptation to Akkadian (Semitic); the "rebus" method in Egyptian hieroglyphics (one drawing = one syllable: *chat + pot = chapeau*) (lesson 10).

A "decisive step" in the history of "graphical representations" of language was taken in Semitic *alphabetical* writings. Hebrew is a major example of this, which Benveniste does not develop in particular here, although he recalls its specific organization: the *consonant scheme* carries the meaning (the *semantic*), while the *grammatical function* refers to *vocalization*.

The Greek alphabet, on the other hand, decomposes the syllable itself and gives the same status to consonants as to vowels. This change reveals the role of *voice* in all verbal articulation (*the unit of decomposition* of the word would thus be a vowel or a segment including a vowel [CV or VC]). Moreover, for the linguist as well, the syllable is a *sui generis* unit [lesson 11]) so that "language's natural articulation" can be reproduced and the grammatical relations with which this language specifies the subjective positions in the speech act can be materialized.

Two types of languages emerge from this metasemiotic treatment of their relation to writing: those where the etymological or the semantic predominate (Phoenician and Hebrew), and those where vocalization distinguishes vowels and consonants, and where grammatical variations, which often destroy etymological relations, lead to a refinement of the flexional system (morphologic modifications by affixations expressing grammatical categories).

A "consubstantial" relation between writing and language is thus established, and it can be expressed in these terms: types of writing bring about auto-semiotization, in other words, awareness of the types of language to which they correspond ("Writing has always and everywhere been the instrument for language to semiotize itself" [lesson 12]). *Together,* writing and language constitute *different types of signifying processes.* And since languages understood as enunciation experiences "contain" the referent as well as the subjective experiences of the speakers in their acts and their discursive exchanges (lessons 1–7), these are very different ways of *being in the world* that these types of writing reveal, consolidate, and re-create. Thus a quite clear "dividing line" is drawn: in the East (in Mesopotamia, Egypt, and as far as China) "writing civilizations" predominate, characterized by the primacy of writing, where the scribe (the "wise calligrapher" in China) plays a central role in the organization of the society; while in the West, in the Indo-European world, a devaluing, even a certain contempt of writing (in Homer, *grapho* only means "scribble") prevails (lesson 14).

Barely sketched out, this typology of signifying processes through types of writings is already a mine for research in the semantics and semiology of enunciation. Consideration could thus be given (lesson 14), among other ideas, to determining the semiotic and semantic specificities of biblical texts, and to probing the subjectivity of its speakers as well as its audience. Or questioning the contrast Saint Paul made between "letter" and "spirit": Should it be understood as a dyad joining, on one hand, biblical semiotics (the "letter"), which is always already semantic in Hebrew words (through the polysemic stamp of the graphism memorizing the message or the history of the tradition), and, on the other hand, the discourse of an evangelical subjectivity (the "spirit") that evolves for each expression, appearance, and discursive communication (manifested and clarified by the categories and modalities of Greek grammar)? How can one understand that the "secular civilization" appeared (lesson 14) with "the new notions attached to writing"? Should we conclude from this that the diversity of writings (particularly by means of *translation* from Latin into vernacular languages) and other sign systems that broadened autosemiotization of language in a secularized civilization *increased* its capacity to generate meaning and *predisposed the subjectivities* present in it to create new signifying experiences? Or, on the contrary, that a certain "secularity," successor to Christianity, could benefit the *semantic* of a discourse for communicants to the detriment of the *semiotics* of the interior language?

Without further exploring these barely sketched out programs, and without either going in the direction of linguistic relativism, but in opening perspectives that were complementary to Edward Sapir's, Benveniste remained strictly on the level of general linguistics, which marked a new stage in his thought. He maintained that, in light of the fact that various writings participate in the revelation and development of languages' double signifyingness, writing is not only *parallel* to language (and to types of language) but also *extends* it. Iconization triggers and refines the formalization of language in such a way that writing gradually becomes more literal. "It semiotizes everything": writing is a sign system that "more closely resembles interior language than the discursive chain" (lesson 12).

A new characteristic of "interior language" comes into focus here: even "before" the sacred scribe (who from the start semanticized language by the semantic graphism of Semitic syllabic writings, or by the invention of Chinese characters where each *signified* has its image), it is logically the interior language that "consecrates" by formulating the "myth." And this "interior narrativity," this "train of ideas," such as a writing of "global-ity," tells a "whole story." Is it a kind of "fiction" that Husserl believed con-stituted the "vital element of phenomenology"?[15] Or is it a Benvenistean variant of Freud's "original fantasy" that reveals and frees itself in "free associations"? Or, again, is it about these "narrative envelopes" (much more than "syntactic competences") that cognitivists assume to be the first holophrases of the child who is beginning to talk? Surely, in any case, poetic language—"interior language," created by the choice and combi-nation of words,"[16] and written in condensed metaphorical stories (one thinks of Baudelaire's and Rimbaud's poems: "Mother of memories, mis-tress of mistresses"; "Vast as the dark of night and as the light of day," "*Here is the holy City*, seated in the West!")—is such an example.

Benveniste mentioned this line of research succinctly, always to return to general linguistics and the signifying function that language exercises. "No social behavior," including relations of production and reproduction, exists before language but "consists in its determination." "Encircling" or "containing" the referent, language "operates a reduction on itself" and "semiotizes" itself, writing being the "relay" explicating this faculty. In short, writing definitively makes explicit and reinforces the noninstru-mental and nonutilitarian character of language, which, because of this and more than ever, is neither tool nor communication nor dead letter but "signifying organism" (Aristotle, lesson 12), generating and self-generating.

At this point, Benveniste reversed the initial hypothesis about writing. As "operation" in the "linguistic process," writing is the "founding act" that "transformed the face of civilizations," "the most profound revolu-tion that humanity has known" (lesson 14). This feature of writing in its relation to language also reinforces a final finding: language and writing "signify in exactly the same way." Writing *transfers* the signifying pro-cess of hearing to sight; it is "speech in a secondary form." Speech being the first, "writing is transferred speech." "The hand and speech stand together in the invention of writing," wrote Benveniste. The writing/speech relation is equivalent to speech heard/speech uttered. Writing reclaims speech to transmit, communicate, but also to recognize (i.e., the semiotic) and understand (i.e., the semantic). Writing is fully involved in the *inter-pretence* of language. This relay of fixed speech in a sign system remains a system of speech, provided that the latter is understood as a signifying process able to further generate other sign systems, even including digital blogs and Twitter.

It is certainly not a coincidence if, at the heart of this work in progress on the modalities of the specific signifying process of language, there occurs a reminder of Plato's *Philebus*: within the diversity of sensations and human pleasures, all One is Infinite, and the only way to go against the absence of limits in the state of nature is to have recourse to *numbers*, thanks to which it becomes possible to determine the units in a hierarchical order, to disassociate and to identify. Like "notes" in music, letters in grammar (*grammatikê technê*) are "numbers": in this meaning the activity of the grammarian, who enumerates and organizes the semiotics of language below signification, is "divine" (lesson 13). Recalling the parallel between language analysis and the work of the Egyptian Theuth (Toth in Greek), who was the first to perceive that vowels are "multiple in the infinite," Benveniste borrowed the idea of "number" to articulate that of *limit*, essential in linguistics where it is necessary to "dissociate and identify the units on several levels," to "reach numbers (a limit), and that of the creation of the world by the Word." But he displaced the ontotheology of transcendent meaning and rewove the connotations of this "transcendence" (announced in lesson 1), always inflected in the interior of language, and which continued to be built before the eyes of the reader of his *Leçons*: "The educated man of letters, the *grammatikos*, is the educated man in the structure of language." "The relation of one to many is one that is found in both knowledge (*épistémé*) and the experience of sensations" (lesson 13).

Step by step, Benveniste's theory thus included all referents and, implicitly, the infinity of *res divina*—by definition outside the human world—in and by the signifyingness of language. For this, he drew on Socrates, as seen, to which could be added the fourth book of the Pentateuch, the Book of Numbers, or the Kabbalah, which builds meaning by enumerating. But more than anything else, this dual signifying process of language seems to refer back to the Fourth Gospel, that of John, encompassing the graphical representation (the act of writing and the variants of writings) as well as intersubjectivity and the referent. "In the beginning was the Word." Except that without "beginning," the "divine" is reabsorbed in the engendering of the "folds" (Leibniz) of the signifying process:[17] in the elements and categories of this "given" of language. The linguist does not seek either the conditions of "truth" or the infinite potential and future translinguistic configurations of this given, but he limits himself to "trying to recognize its laws" (*PGL* 2:238).

SIGNIFYING PROCESS AND EXPERIENCE

Taken at its "fundamental" level (unlike "contingent" empirical languages), language become "signifying process" is not a simple complement added to Saussure's sign theory, coextensive with the "social contract." Returning to the idea that linguistic structures and social structures are "anisomorphic," Benveniste aimed to show that the *act of signifying is irreducible to communication and institutions*, and that it only transcends the "given meaning" by the "activity of the speaker set in the center." The notion of "enunciation" understood as "experience" significantly changes the object of the signifying process and/or of language (*PGL* 2:67ff. and 79 sq.).

Far from abandoning the "sign," the *signifying process* includes it in the "discourse" as an intersubjective illocutionary act that conveys "ideas." Signifyingness is a syntagmatic organization comprising various types of syntactic constructions, and as such, it "contains" the "referent" of Saussurian linguistics: on the condition it is enriched by the "unique situation," the "event" of the "enunciation" implying "a certain positioning of the speaker." It is thus the "experience" of the subject of the "enunciation" in the intersubjective situation that interests the linguist, but through the "formal apparatus" of "intentional content," that is, the "instruments of his accomplishment" as well as the "processes by which the linguistic forms of the enunciation are diversified and engendered" (*PGL* 2:81) It is true that "the singular dialectic of subjectivity," "independent of any cultural determination," was already previously announced (*PGL* 2:67–68). But through the intervention of writing, these *Dernières leçons* deepen the "engendering" of the signifying process by moving the subjective experience of an I/you dialogical exchange toward a topology of the subject of the "enunciation," which also breaks with Descartes's *ego cogito* and the Husserlian transcendental *ego*.

The terms for this language dynamic vary: *engendering* but also *functioning; conversion* of the language to writing and of language to discourse;

diversification, language being defined as *production, moving landscape, place of transformations*. But unlike the "transformations" that concern generative grammars and for which syntactic categories are given at the outset, Benveniste's "engendering" of signifyingness was deeply committed to the process of an advent of pre- and translinguistic signification and focused on three types of engendering relations: a relation of *interpretence* (fundamental property, language as "the only system that can interpret everything"); relation of *engendering* (between sign systems: from alphabetic writing to Braille); and relation of *homology* (in reference to Baudelaire's "correspondences"). The last lesson goes back over each of them, recalling the need to review the "formal categories" ("case," "tense," "modes"), and posits that "the whole inflectional system is in question here."

The *subject of the enunciation* himself must feel the effects of this mobility. In this shifting landscape of language and in terms of the writing that helped bring it to light, reflection on the *experience* specific to writing that "poetic language" represents was required. Indeed, Benveniste, in counterpoint to the structuralist reading of Baudelaire's "Cats" by Roman Jakobson and Claude Lévi-Strauss, and echoing the indications of *Dernières leçons,* approached the literary experience in his handwritten notes on *Baudelaire* from the same period (1967–1969).

Closer to "interior language" than to discourse, poetic language requires the analyst "to change instruments," as Rilke wanted (commented on, as we have seen, by the young Benveniste). This "different language" of poetry therefore necessitates a "translinguistics," as the "signifyingness of art" is "nonconventional" and because its "terms," coming from the specific singularities of each subject writer, are "unlimited in number." From the outset, Benveniste established what the singularities of this "translinguistics" were: the poetic message, "completely contrary to the properties of communication,"[18] speaks an *emotion* that language "transmits" but does not "describe."[19] Likewise, the *referent* of poetic language is "inside the expression" while in ordinary language the object is outside language. It *"proceeds from the body of the poet,"* "they are muscular impressions," said Benveniste. Poetic, "sensitive" language "only addresses entities involved in this new community: the poet's soul, God/nature, the absent/the creature of memories and fiction." Why did Benveniste choose Baudelaire to illustrate his point? Because Baudelaire made the "first crack between poetic language and nonpoetic language," while for Mallarmé, this break was already consummated.[20]

Contemporary with *Dernières leçons*, these notes on Baudelaire's poetic experience accorded with the reflections on the "anarchic force" at work in the unconscious that language "curbs and sublimates" (*PGL* 1:78). The expression of an "instant and elusive subjectivity that forms the condition for dialogue," this experience is part of infra- and supralinguistics (*PGL* 1:86), or rather translinguistics (*PGL* 2:66). Translinguistics is devoted to works and is based on the semantics of the enunciation.

These latter reflections, based on listening to ancient Indian poetics from the sacred texts that Sanskritist Benveniste fully mastered, resonated with the late 1960s, where social and generational unrest calling for "imagination in power" sought the secret and innovative rationales of meaning and existence in the experience of (avant-garde or women's) writing.

With hindsight, and in the absence of any explicit reference to psychosexuality, this general linguistics of experience and subjectivity does not recall the Freudian theory of sublimation but rather the unnamed thought process of Martin Heidegger. Indeed, language according to *Being and Time* (1927) is discourse (*Rede*) or speech, with words having no signification outside the *Mitsein* of dialogue. It is up to *Dasein* to *interpret*: it is its localization in existential analytics that is taken into consideration, to the detriment of language as such. Certain resonances emerge between Heidegger's early conception of language and Benveniste's early general linguistics (*PGL* 1) that proposed placing *the formal apparatus* of this language regime—"discourse" and "interpretant"—in society and nature. The Heideggerian approach changed in *On the Way to Language* (1959), where language was considered as "the said," *Sage*, "what is spoken." Dialogue becomes monologue, without being solipsistic, but as it is "interior discourse" and never propositional, without "sound" or "communication," his "interior thought" carries out in *silence* the mental production of a "coming to language." For Benveniste, writing as graphism and as poetic experience—from Baudelaire to Surrealism—seemed to meet Heidegger's definition of "language that speaks only and alone with oneself" and makes sound possible. But he immediately distanced himself from it because to this "letting-go," which is the essence of language and insidiously threatened with becoming "senseless" in late Heidegger, the allusive remarks of *Dernières leçons* and the handwritten notes on Baudelaire juxtapose more than they counter the linguist's vigilance for whom "discourse includes both limit and limitlessness" and "unity and diversity" (lesson 13).

Indeed, Benveniste never failed to emphasize "syntagmation"—probably "reflecting a necessity for our cerebral organization" (*PGL* 2:226)—that confers on the "language instrument" its ability to encode while codifying, limit while limiting, and thus to ensure the semantics of an intelligible and communicative discourse, engaging reality. He added, however, that parallel to language and its relay, writing as graphical representation and poetic experience, although closer to "interior language" than to "discourse," does not eliminate its pragmatic virtues. But writing may be at risk if it moves the limits of language by engendering *singular* signifying systems (the poem) and yet shareable in the "interpretance" of language itself. Neither institutional tyranny nor dreamy hymn, the signifyingness sketched out by this late Benveniste was a space of freedom.

"LINGUISTICS IS UNIVERSALITY"

Everyone communicates today, but rare are those who perceive the force and full scope of language.[21] When Benveniste gave his *Dernières leçons*, the idea that language determines humans differently and more profoundly than social relations do started to become a dangerous thought: a genuine revolt against conventions, the "establishment," the "police state," doctrinaire Marxism and communist regimes. In Warsaw, Italy, Czechoslovakia, in the then Soviet Baltic Republics and elsewhere, *semiology* was synonymous with freethinking. Quite logically, it was in Paris (where French research was most dynamic, whether through the Semiology Section of the Anthropology Laboratory at the Collège de France, the journal *Communications*, or the publications of Benveniste, Roland Barthes, and Algirdas Julien Greimas, among others) where the idea to unite these world movements began. And it was just as logical that, under the inspired authority of Roman Jakobson, Benveniste became the natural president. The International Symposium of Semiotics, organized in 1968, set up the foundations of the International Association for Semiotics Studies, and Benveniste officially became president in 1969.

As a young Bulgarian student with a grant from the French government, I had the privilege—along with linguist Josette Rey-Debove—to be in charge of the scientific secretariat of the "Semiotic Research" publication *Social Science Information* (UNESCO) first, then of the AISS. As I had read with passionate interest volume 1 of *Problems in General Linguistics*, this setting gave me the opportunity to have a unique personal relationship with Benveniste. The meetings were held at his home on rue Monticelli near the Porte d'Orleans. Still today I remember his office as a "sacred" place (as it appeared to the shy girl I was then), where the great scholar with the smile of keen intelligence perfectly captured by the Serge Hambourg photograph[22] seemed to hold the secrets of the immemorial Indo-European and Iranian worlds. It was a rather dark study where books lined the walls and were piled on the floor, and old library collections whose scent, mingling with the vapor of the tea that accompanied the biscuits we never touched, evoked ancient scrolls for me. The administrative details quickly dispatched, the professor inquired about my work.[23] With insatiable curiosity, he was interested in the linguistic and philosophical debates in Eastern Europe (Bakhtin's "dialogism") as well as innovations in literature (then in full swing, with the "Theoretical Group" of Philippe Sollers's journal *Tel Quel*, which met at 44 rue de Rennes).

During these meetings, where Benveniste was as pedagogical and protective as attentive, I remember asking him whether writing was an "infra-" and "supra-" linguistic process (as he had written concerning dreams) or rather *translinguistic*; I suggested that Raymond Roussel's writing could be defined as a "productivity" defying the "product"; and I remember discovering in Jakobson, about whom he spoke to me, the concept of "spotha" (both "sound" and "meaning," and always "activity," according to Indian grammarians).

I recall that the professor advised me to read Madeleine Biardeau's recent book on language in classical Brahmanism;[24] another day, he said he was sorry that Harris and Chomsky had founded a general syntax without taking into account the diversity of languages ("It is regrettable to know only one language," he wrote to a renowned linguist). Most often, he answered my questions with terse, somewhat provocative, remarks: "You understand, I am only interested in little things, the verb 'to be,' for example." And then he would advise me, after his *Problems in General Linguistics*, to look into a publication on this vast subject in a recent issue of the very serious journal *Foundations of Language*.[25] Or, in guise of a response to my questions, he would open the Sanskrit text of the *Rigveda*, to translate appropriate passages for me directly into French. Then, after a few semantic or grammatical remarks, he would return to the contents of the "story" and the "characters" of this great collection of ancient Indian hymns, always in an allusive tone and a bit ironic (referring to Aragon, for example): "Do you, Madam, think that woman is the future of man?"

Another day, when I had just discovered the term *senefiance* in the "journey of the soul to God," dear to the medieval theorists of the *modi significandi*, I asked him what he thought of it. "You read a lot for your age," he replied. "Closer to home, I think that Jean Paulhan's father used this term. Do people still read in Bulgaria? And in Eastern Europe in general? You know that *citati*, the Slavic root for 'to read,' dates back to the meaning of 'to count,' 'to respect' too." I had not thought of that; it was obvious, I didn't know very much.

He never told me that his parents were teachers in Samokov, in Bulgaria. Simply that I reminded him of his mother: a distant resemblance, I suppose.

Husserl's phenomenology greatly interested him, and he seemed surprised that I could have had a few modest notions of his *Ideen*. But we never mentioned Heidegger, whom I had only just discovered.

I had brought Antonin Artaud's *Letters from Rodez*[26] to Warsaw. "Would you lend them to me?" he asked.

Emile Benveniste hid the little book under the photocopied course of the symposium and I saw a shy smile on his lips as he allowed himself to read when the speaker or debate got boring. Encouraged by this show of freedom, I went to speak to our next president during the break, having recently spotted his name alongside those of Artaud, Aragon, Breton, Eluard, Leiris, and a whole galaxy of intellectuals, artists, and writers who had signed the Surrealist Manifesto, "The Revolution First and Always" (1925):

"Sir, what a joy to discover your name among the signatories of a Surrealist Manifesto."

"Unfortunate coincidence, Madam."

The smile was gone, an empty and cold gaze pinned me to the floor, and I collapsed with shame before the group of delegates who surrounded us. Some hours later and without witnesses, the professor whispered in my ear:

"Of course it's me, but you mustn't tell. You see, now I'm at the College of France."

On our return to Paris, he invited me to tea, this time at La Closerie des Lilas.

"This is where we used to meet. A violent time, war. But blood flowed here too, in this same group." Seeing my surprise, he added: "No, the metaphor is not too strong. I soon realized that this was not my place."

Today I am rereading this manifesto.[27] Indeed, Benveniste had fled calls for insubordination, abandoned the bloody Trotskyite-Stalinist revolt (Breton and Aragon), and ignored the harrowing experience of the poetic infinity—which, removed from the social contract, swept away order in language (Mallarmé: "There must be a guarantee: Syntax."[28]) in a vocal explosion (Artaud's glossolalia)—to devote himself to a kind of holy mission for the signifying process in language systems. Academic convention for this firebrand nomad, "poor linguist torn apart in the universe,"[29] was a protection and, necessarily, a restraint. But it did not stop him from reaching out to dissident thinking under communism—which he would not see end, marked by the fall of the Berlin Wall, and which the Warsaw Symposium proved in time to be one of the signs of things to come. No more than it discouraged him from probing the mark of free and creative subjectivity in the duality of signifyingness between the unnamed experience of "interior language" and the semantics of discourse that seeks to communicate and to order.

I remember our last conversation, late November or early December 1969. He had received my book, *Sèméiôtikè: Recherches pour une semanalysis*, which, generous as ever, he had hoped to finish reading and discuss with me in detail before vacation. But soon, suddenly, came the shock: the announcement of the stroke, paralysis, aphasia. The College de France administration and his colleagues took charge of the usual formalities with his sister Carmelia, heroically devoted and sensitive, whom I got to know at the hospital and who accompanied him day after day until the end, in miserable conditions. She talked to me mostly about Father Jean de Menasce, whom I did not know, whose long friendship with Benveniste and own personal experience of a similar stroke from which he luckily recovered inspired confidence in the great linguist's sister.

The situation was deplorable: the patient was hospitalized in a ward where he had to suffer the daily intrusive visits of families, unhealthy overcrowding, and the lack of rehabilitation treatment. Conventional wisdom had it that the aphasic patient no longer understood speech. "But even before the accident, he did not react to family stories we told him either, they bored him," Carmelia Benveniste said. We managed to get the famous aphasia specialist, François Lhermitte, to see him. Lhermitte asked him to draw a house. No reaction. Terrified that the expertise would fall short, I myself tried to get the patient to react. He drew the house. A speech rehabilitation program was then put in place. The result was not deemed convincing. Along with Mohammad Djafar Moïnfar, his faithful disciple, we soon realized that it was impossible to find a better place in a private establishment—distracted as he was, the absent-minded professor had not paid into his health insurance. So we considered launching a fundraising drive with all his friends to regularize the insurance retroactively, but various administrative difficulties made it impossible. Still today, I blame myself for not having been present at his rehabilitation sessions: his affection for me, perhaps, would have made him more cooperative. An illusion, no doubt, but one I always think about. It often seemed to me that his students and foreign friends were the most motivated, the most aware of his distress and the magnitude of his work.

I felt sure that he was still intellectually present. So one day I asked him to dedicate his first book to me, *The Persian Religion According to the Chief Greek Texts* (1929), which I had found in English at an Orientalist antique shop. In a trembling hand, in block capital letters, he wrote his name, E. Benveniste, adding the date, Sept. 23, 1971, which he corrected right away to Sept. 24, 1971: he was present in the act of interlocution and still grasped the notion of time. In 1971 a special issue of the journal *Langages* on "The epistemology of linguistics," of which I was the editor, was dedicated to him: "Hommage à Emile Benveniste"—and he was thrilled. Pierre Nora (director of the Bibliothèque des sciences humaines at Gallimard) and I brought him the edition of the second volume of *Problèmes de linguistique générale*. In 1975 Nicolas Ruwet, Jean-Claude Milner, and I brought out a collection dedicated to him entitled *Langue, discours, société. Pour Emile Benveniste*, published by Le Seuil. He greeted it with pleasure. Of course, the reading was demanding, and he undoubtedly appreciated its existence more than the details. Afterward, unfortunately, the nine hospitals he was subjected to in seven years, my own state (post-doctoral) thesis, then my pregnancy, reduced my visits to him. But he did not forget me, and in November 1975 a letter from Carmelia Benveniste informed me that the professor expressly asked to see me. He was still able to express his wishes and remembered those he wanted to see.

In the course of one of these meetings—at the Creteil Hospital—he asked me to come close to his bed, pulled himself up, extended his index finger as in the photo reproduced in *Dernières leçons*, and, very timidly, with the same adolescent smile, started to "write" on my blouse. Surprised, overwhelmed as much as embarrassed, I did not dare move and could not guess what he wanted to write or draw with this strange gesture. I asked him if he wanted something to drink, read, or hear. He shook his head "No" and again began to draw on my chest these illegible as well as upsetting signs. Finally I gave him a sheet of paper and a pen. And then, with the same writing in block capital letters that he had chosen to dedicate his book to me, he wrote: THEO.

I did not know at that time that Benveniste had arrived in France as a student in rabbinical school. He had never spoken to me about this or the Holocaust. I did not have a global view of his works in general linguistics, and the second volume of his *Problems of General Linguistics* had not yet been assembled, and in any case, I did not have enough knowledge to assimilate it. But I was persuaded that the verbal paralysis had not completely destroyed his intelligence. This "THEO" had a meaning.

Today, reading these last words regarding his published work, I will not attempt to propose an interpretation: "THEO" will forever remain enigmatic. I can only hazard a reading.

The fates of our respective personal histories had put me on his road so that he could send me a message before dying, a message that he insisted on drawing on a body:

Whatever the "the semantic" of our discourse (such as we communicate through dialogues in our temporal existences), *the diversity of our languages and language itself engender this "semiotic ability"* (to which the unpronounceable graphics [YHWH] attest, but that the professor had undertaken to analyze with the tools of Greek onto-theology [THEO] and thanks to its scientific developments) *in the encounter of the "interior languages" of our subjectivities.*

This "original force at work" (*DL*, lesson 7) "transcends" [THEO] all other properties of language, and "it is inconceivable" that "its principle can be found elsewhere than in language." "I," any speaking person, is made up of this duality and remains at this crossroad. "I"—any person— experiences this "SIGNIFYINGNESS" that encircles and interprets history.

I should be grateful to readers of these *Dernières leçons* to add their own path to this crossroad, to this writing.

Articles cited by Emile Benveniste:

Problems in General Linguistics, vol. 1, trans. Mary Elizabeth Meek (University of Miami Press, 1971)

"Categories of Thought and Language," 55–64

"Remarks on the Function of Language in Freudian Theory," 65–78

"Subjectivity in Language," 223–30

"Analytical Philosophy and Language," 231–38

Problems in General Linguistics, vol. 2, trans. Mary Elizabeth Meek (University of Miami Press, 1971)

"Language and Human Experience"

"The Formal Apparatus of Enunciation"

"Language Structure and Society?"

"Form and Meaning in Language"

II

PSYCHOANALYSIS

5

FREUD

The Heart of the Matter

FREUD'S HYPOTHESIS

More than one hundred years ago, a rabbi's grandson, a humanist like Diderot and Goethe, and by profession a neurologist, discovered that there was truth in ancient myths, just as in his patients' fantasies and of course in his own. He transformed the Greeks' *psyché*, the Jews' *nephesh*, and the Christians' *anima* into a copresence of thought and sexuality. You are alive if and only if you have a psychic life: such was Freud's universal message. The human species has never gotten over that, even in this era of automatization and global atomization.

The "Oedipus complex" is the tool for reshuffling metaphysics that imperturbably persists in separating flesh from spirit, desire (for the mother) from taboo (expressed by the father). The Oedipus complex varies according to sex, psychic structures, and civilizations, while maintaining its essential place as organizer of psychic life. Sexuality—about which Freud never conceded—does not biologize man's essence because sexuality is doubly articulated: a biological determination *and* symbolic links that construct the speaking being across generations. Sexuality is not limited to one's erogenous zones or to virtual films that you project in dreams; sexuality is actually a language, advanced Freud in his *Interpretation of Dreams* (1900).[1] But language does not explain it all either. Sexuality is beyond language, beyond ourselves, somewhere in between: it is unconscious drives. And therein lies the pleasure. "As soon as you open your mouth," Mao said, "you're talking propaganda." *As soon as you speak, sex is involved; all you have to do is listen*, Freud maintained.

Transference is the universal consequence of this copresence of sexuality/thought. In the analytic situation, emotional memory is transferred into the present, and from you to me, from me to you: a resuscitation that will enable you to modulate your "psychic apparatus" so that it comes back to life.

The aim of the treatment is not to have you conform to social norms nor to fulfill you with absolute pleasures but to have you discover that you are singular, and only then able to innovate in your thoughts and bonds and to create: this is the third "universal" (along with *drive* and *language*) upon which analysis is based.

Was Freud too subjective in reaching this point? This Viennese man, an adventurer in mind and body, came from afar. Even worse, he was a bad poet, cruel and mocking when he wanted to be, so as to liberate himself from his prejudices and reflect on the burdens of tradition. He wrote to his friend Fliess at the birth of his son, in 1900: "Hail to the valiant son . . . hail to the father, too, who found the key to restraining the power of the female sex. So that he, the son, will carry out the Law."[2] Yet the man of reason continued to watch over the ultra-orthodox patriarch. "He (the father or Freud?) calls on the higher powers: deduction, faith, doubt." And later, this observation: "Woman is totally taboo," which rings like an indictment against all patrilineal and patriarchal civilizations.[3] Discovering that "bisexuality is far more prevalent in the woman than in the man,"[4] and that the intensity of the early daughter/mother relations, rooted in sensorial prelanguage, is "as inaccessible as the Minoan-Mycenaean, second only to that of the Greeks,"[5] he changed his own conception of the Oedipus complex. Klein, Lacan, Winnicott, and Bion, among others, continued to develop the universal vitality of this multifaceted work in progress.

A SOCIAL SCIENCE

Picking a fight with Freud about the "scientificity" of psychoanalysis harkens back to last century's epistemological debates: the involvement of the experimenter's subjectivity in social sciences and its seminal role in analytic effectiveness (transference/countertransference) have been widely acknowledged.

Look rather at the originality of psychoanalysis vis-à-vis religion, and the debate between the philosopher Habermas and the theologian, Cardinal Ratzinger.[6] Since the secularized State lacks a unifying connector[7] as a basis for rational law[8] (according to the German jurist Böckenförde), what is needed is "a trustworthy superior authority" and guarantor of the "normative presuppositions"[9] to manage the frenzied race for liberty: a "conscience become conservative"[10] "would be nourished by faith" (Habermas) or that would be a "correlation between reason and faith" (Ratzinger).[11]

Countering this hypothesis, Nietzsche and Heidegger had already pointed out that the faith/reason, norm/liberty oppositions no longer obtain, if the speaking being I am no longer thinks itself as dependent on a suprasensible (transcendental) world, and even less on a sensible, political, and economic world with the "power of obligation." "I" reveal myself and modify the world by the *link* I weave in language with this strange object of desire at the *crossroads of biology and meaning.* The maximal experience of thought, the summits of art and literature, attest not to a "correlation" but to a reworking of faith/reason.

The theory of the unconscious guides and deepens this reworking in each person's intimate self. Without letting his guard down against the "illusions" that comfort but can inhibit or pervert desires and thought,[12] Freud put what he called "our God Logos" on the couch.[13] He dealt with the "oceanic feeling" that rocks and submerges me in the maternal container.[14] And he emphasized the need to believe (anthropological, prereligious, and prepolitical), with which I vested the "father of individual prehistory,"[15] but then I revolted against the "Oedipus father" to pave the way for the desire to know and for my singular liberty. "Invest," from the Sanskrit *kredh-/straddha,* "credo, believe."[16]

It is not worth denying, ignoring, or decapitating this oceanic feeling and this *need to believe*: it is childish or criminal. But there is also a *desire to know*: question your fantasies to the root of the imaginary, which is the need to believe. It is painful, it is violent: Oedipus is a rebel and so is Orestes. We are all patricides and matricides. This is what Freudian atheism means: "a cruel and drawn-out enterprise,"[17] something not to be left to "public thugs" that Nietzsche feared. Beyond the "broken thread of tradition" (Tocqueville and Arendt)[18] in the multireligious and postreligious planetary era, psychoanalysis encourages the man and the woman not to accept any other "unifying link" but the desire to analyze all identities and all links. And to take pleasure in the work this elucidation procures. Attempts to demolish psychoanalysis do not come from just any imaginary idol but from this transvaluation of the Greek-Jewish-Christian continent of which psychoanalysis reveals the universal anthropological breadth: to rethink over and over.

BENEFITS OF THE TREATMENT

Analysands might say, like Proust: "Those who are ill feel closer to their souls."[19] "The feeling of always being surrounded by one's soul is not like a *stationary prison*; it is more as if one is carried away with it in a *constant movement to go beyond it* . . . which is not an echo from outside but the repercussions of *an internal vibration*."[20] Psychoanalysis responds by offering neither more nor less of the reorganization and permanence of the psychism.

Talking heads claim that because hard sex is now on television and that in political meetings activists bandy about words like "autism" or "being in denial," repression has disappeared, and psychoanalysis, which is omnipresent according to them, serves no purpose anymore. These foes of Freud are ignorant of the fact that far from reducing the psychical life of the organs at work during the sex act, psychoanalysis understands if and how arousal, pain, or pleasure permeate the complex architecture of feelings, words, thoughts, and projects.

They say that hysteria has disappeared. Wrong! The hysterical dissociation between arousal and its psychic and verbal representation—including epileptic-type symptoms—gives way when hysterical hyperexcitability and oedipal traumas find their meaning in "the search for lost time" of free association and the transference dynamic.

Anorexic and bulimic disorders change when one gets to the problem of naming abjection and all extreme feeling in order to untangle the rejection of the feminine and the ascetic meeting with the father's harshness in self-punishment, which lead a person to let him/herself die.

For many analysands, the power of the image worsens the denial of language: they say they are like "perverts" who can "say and do anything" but come to the sessions complaining of being "empty," "lonely," and "unable to love."

At times the perverted scenario itself (film, photo, work of art sometimes done by the analysand) is included in these treatments so that the affects it provokes find the words and bridges are made between the unnamable drives and language that had been until then defensive.[21]

The fact that depression is so common puts us face to face with an osmotic relationship with the maternal container and demands an extremely careful attention to the infraverbal (tone, intensity, rhythm, assonance) to detect the most secret traces of this deadly attachment that the depressed person obstinately cultivates with her/his object of love and other partners.[22]

Contemporary clinical practice in listening has seen innovations to treat people with psychical, mental, sensorial, or motor handicaps by dealing with dependence, shame, guilt, and cohabitation with mortality that goes beyond narcissistic suffering, as well as specific codes of communication that provide spaces of unexpected creativity: a broadening as painful as subtle of human complexity and limits.

In all these new directions, each treatment is unique and as singular as a poetic work. But it is based on theoretical advances leaning on the Freudian foundation and that delve into precocious relations, narcissistic troubles, and their repercussions in borderline cases or psychoses, psychosomatic illnesses but also autism. At the borders of the sensible and sense, psychoanalysis in the past few decades has enriched language theory by identifying its connections with unconscious and preverbal psychical representations. Following Lacan's work on the mirror stage and the signifier, there are multiple examples: Bion's work on the "Alpha and Bêta elements" of the psychism, Piera Aulagnier's on "pictograms," André Green's on affects, and my own contribution on the "semiotic" and "symbolic." Last, the founding principles of Freudian psychoanalysis are able to respond today to psychic distress, this *alter ego* of globalization, visible in all cultures. But these principles get complexified in their relationship with cultures: analytical ethnopsychiatry attests to this.

FIELDS OF PSYCHOANALYSIS

Le temps des cérises and dissident minds are fond of Freud. Why? Because he is a pessimist (the life instinct is inseparable from the death wish); he suggests that the meaning of happiness is freedom: possible, infinitely. Self-knowledge with the other, body and soul, through separation, frustration, castration, sadomasochism, passages of sacrifices, and death: your desires, pleasures, and jouissances are refined and strengthened. Take Simone de Beauvoir, who inspired feminism: "He is one of the men in our century that I most fondly admire," she said in *All Said and Done*.[23] Not only is the heroine of *The Mandarins* a psychoanalyst, but it is in the "Psychoanalytical Point of View" at the beginning of *The Second Sex* that Beauvoir draws the founding idea of her book: sex "is the body lived by the subject. Nature does not define woman: it is she who defines herself by reclaiming nature for herself in her affectivity."[24] Her criticism and simplifications of psychoanalysis that followed, shunting a certain type of feminist away from psychoanalysis, also gave rise to movements favorable to psychoanalytical research and ethics.

Today, some people hope that by applauding surrogate mothers, same-sex marriage, and single-parent families, psychoanalysis will be modernized. This attitude seems as unpsychoanalytical as the contrary, i.e., voting against it. In both cases, one forgets that psychoanalysis is neither sexology, sociology, nor medicine but that it addresses itself to the complex singularity of psychic life. It is not much; it is limited, but it is unique, and it is important to shore it up today. Not to dilute it in "current events" or "fashion" but to change the gaze on these questions themselves. If biotechnology and social consensus can relieve suffering and foster personal creativity, if they take into account exceptional situations, case by case. Prohibiting would be to forget that parentality has changed over the course of history and would encourage transgression elsewhere or secretly. Permitting would be to intensify the tendencies that consider humans as consequences or objects of technical prowess and of the escalation of desires. Let us begin then by analyzing your desire: why do you want to be a parent? What is being a mother for you? Your answer will help you make a decision. It will add to the debate that has to be engaged on this change in civilization at the limits of what is human.

FIREWALLS

For about ten years, Daniel Widlöcher, Pierre Fédida, and I ran a seminar at the Salpêtrière Hospital at the crossroads of the neurosciences, biopharmacology, psychiatry, psychology, psychoanalysis, linguistics, literary theory, philosophy, art history, etc. Serious melancholia, for example, can be treated only by a combined approach: medicine and talking. The complexity and diversity of autisms are being discovered, and while genetic research is being developed without specific chemical treatment, cognitive approaches and ergotherapeutic support are indispensable, as well as psychotherapy. The danger is that the legitimate hope raised by neuroscience could become an ideology that does away with psychic life. *A denial of language is moving in,* and digital hypercommunication, with its "talking points" that dot the minds at the highest political levels, contributes to it. There is a real asymbolia into which rush, on one hand, declinology and, on the other, a sensualist communism, supposed to galvanize people with the promise of hedonism for all. The media indulge in this wave that jeopardizes the civilization of the book and the word far beyond psychoanalysis.

But firewalls kick in too. The psychic anguish that affects all cultures calls on analytic ethnopsychiatry (in response to the distress about immigration in western Europe) and psychoanalysis: after Latin America (Brazil, Argentina, etc.), today eastern Europe, Russia, the Arab world. Is China indifferent? That is to be seen. At Shanghai Polytechnic, an Institute of European and Chinese Cultures and Spirituality, particularly attuned to French psychoanalysis, was created. To my astonishment, the director explained: "So that our engineers don't become kamikazes when they have a personal or social conflict: you open their minds."

Being the guardian and the rebuilder of threatened and often broken psychic space, shrinks only fulfill their duty of memory toward European culture. They are at the heart of today's ills. Here are two examples: motherhood and adolescence.

Between the ecological management of baby diapers and the fear that the emancipated woman might disappear under the nursing housewife mammal and proud to be it, media overenthusiasm has shown that *secularization is the only civilization that lacks a discourse on motherhood.* On the contrary, modern psychoanalysis focuses its research more on the early mother-child relationship. What difference is there between the emotional attachment (linked to pregnancy) and the passion with this first other, at once stranger, myself, and love/hate pole? Dawn of civilization, of maternal madness, of sadomasochism? The mother with or against the lover? How does she transmit language: with the father and with this kind of love—although fed up—that is humor? How does the sublimation of eroticism protect maternal love from pedophilia but also from freezing embryos? And maternal time which is time not only of worry or fear of death but also of continual rebirths, "flowerings" (Colette), the mother rebeginning her time as grandmother, educator, trade unionist, humanitarian worker?[25]

The adolescent[26] is rebellious, a drug addict, anorexic, a vandal, in love: a necessary replay of the oedipal revolt, he pulls himself away from his parents, their shortcomings and absences, and responds to them with an ideal world. There is an ideal partner who will give me absolute, sexual, professional, and social satisfaction, says the adolescent. I believe in it: I'm romantic, rebellious, mystical. Reality never measures up to this ideal nor do ideologies; everything disappoints me. I'm bored. I get violent. *The adolescent is a believer on top of a nihilist.* We are all adolescents when we're in love. Freud had an inkling of it in "Dostoyevsky and Parricide." This attitude runs havoc today in ZEPs[27] and is leading to fundamentalism. Adolescence is an illness of ideality. So-called primitive societies held initiation rites to accompany it. The national education minister himself wants to teach teachers—never enough of them—never safe from depression, to manage violence. Easy to say!

Might psychoanalysis be the only space that can take this need for the ideal and lead it to the desire to know and to re-create bonds? Psychoanalysis . . . as long as it constantly reinvents itself, as Freud himself never stopped doing.

6

THE CONTEMPORARY CONTRIBUTION OF PSYCHOANALYSIS

Alain Braconnier: *Your latest book,* Hatred and Forgiveness,[1] *scans and completes the four main themes that you have developed in depth since the beginning of your psychoanalytic work: the role of language, narrative, and writing; the question of the feminine that Freud and even his women psychoanalyst successors have left uncompleted; the questioning brought up by the religious and the phenomenon of belief, and last, the contemporary contribution of psychoanalysis. Could you establish a personal guideline for our readers to understand the connections that led you to concentrate successively and at the same time on these different research themes?*

Julia Kristeva: Freud's ambition was originally and fundamentally therapeutic: his theoretical genius and his vast Jewish culture that endorsed the ideas of the *Aufklärung* often make us forget that. Confronting our delirium as speaking beings, he discovered that desire was the carrier wave, and that in this amorous intersubjectivity which would become transference, language was the best vehicle and the optimal (the only?) means enabling each of us to infinitely reconstruct our fragile and ever-threatened identities. If I summarize here both the Freudian pessimism and his therapeutic commitment, it is also to outline the scope as well as the limits of his approach, of our approach.

First the scope: psychoanalysis is a clinical practice, a limited field, a "frame" accompanied by theories, but it is also intrinsically dependent on conditions of existence, on analysands and on analysts. This does not mean that only "outside the frame" interests us and is understood in transference and countertransference, but also that the psychic "facts" that concern us are immediately social, historical, and political "data." This also goes for the adjustment of desire/love, need to believe/illusion, and even the boundaries of male/female sexual difference. Psychoanalytic "collected data" are certainly universals, but they are also economies or mobile structures, malleable in human history: Freud never ceased to deal with them in his archeology of civilization. And we must recognize that we are finding it difficult to pursue and update this perspective.

Now the limits: in *Moses and Monotheism*, Freud considered that "the first individual in the history of humanity"[2] was Amenhotep IV, this eighteenth-dynasty pharaoh[3] who imposed monotheism on his people at the very time Moses would have lived. Freud thus admitted that the psychoanalytic subject sprang from the monotheistic subject: moreover, the presages of Freudian discovery are rooted in Sophocles's *Oedipus Rex*, with the father's structuring role implied in the prohibition of incest. A being at the crossroads (remember that Oedipus killed his father at a crossroads in the shape of γ, the Greek gamma, bifurcation between desire and murder), lover of his mother, Jocasta, and murderer of his father, Laius, Oedipus must nevertheless recognize these crimes to free Thebes from the plague. In conducting his investigation, in questioning himself, in thinking, the man of desire and murder "psychologizes," or better, *subjectivizes* the fate inflicted by the gods, and only at this price can he become a divided tragic subject that is, at the same time, subject of desire and subject of knowledge. Indeed, his desire to know the truth by uttering it can only be fulfilled at the cost of renouncing his desire, of guilt, and of punishment: these are all necessary for the acceptance of the truth along with paternal and/or city authority. It is understandable that the Greek myth, as modulated in Sophocles's obviously binding, and even outright legislating, text could seduce Freud, concerned with recognizing jouissance with its delights and its risks, symbolized by both prohibition and knowledge together. Because "*jouissance* is prohibited to him who speaks as such," "it can only be said between the lines for anyone who is subject to the Law, because the Law is founded on this very prohibition," Lacan said later.[4]

The founder of psychoanalysis thus drew his conception of tragic subjectivation, which constitutes the speaking subject as subject of the Law, and at the same time the ethics of psychoanalysis with its active pessimism, upon which the analytic experience is based. It is imperative to remember this, because the "new maladies of the soul" that now reveal the foundations of this subjectivation—which often remain irreducible to it—highlight the difficulties if not the impossibilities of individuation in some regressive states. They evoke human experiences of another kind, which challenge the legitimacy of the analytical frame, putting into question the universality of the Oedipus complex itself. Does not, for example, Aeschylus's *Oresteia* point to a very different "subjectivity," rebellious to paternal law and, in a sort of throwback to mythical matriarchy, requiring the fantasy of matricide as a liberating psychic condition? This is what Melanie Klein suggested. Similarly, can Euripides and his *Bacchae* and as well as the Pentheus/Dionysus duel, which offers at least two directions in the maternal traversal, be dismissed: the *mère-version* of Pentheus and the Dionysian sublimation, including the "double birth" that prefigures the Christic resurrection? The list of Freud's "forgottens" is longer still, and they have given rise to innovations in modern clinical practice, in early mother-child relations as well as in psychosis or autism. And there is great temptation to shake Freudian topographies themselves in favor of a "third way" or, in a less "parricide" style, to get to the oedipal problematic with psychic fragmentation models and borderline cases.

My exploration of the aesthetic experiences of modernity (literature and visual arts) in the area of psychosis, as well as the experience I have had of a totalitarian regime repressing individuals' creative possibilities by threatening them with excessive automatization in a paranoid-schizoid political and cultural context, have convinced me that psychoanalytic listening has to accept new psychic configurations that require new interpretative attitudes to carry out treatment, before and along with the Oedipus complex. The crisis of "monotonotheism," despite outbreaks of "returns to faith" and other spiritual revivals, the mixture of fundamentalism and nihilism generated by globalization, the rise of "new maladies of the soul" (addiction, psychosomatoses, melancholic schizophrenia, vandalism, morbid perversions masking severe depression in the manic exaltation of *jouir* unto death, etc.), all these symptoms that dominate the postmodern era most obviously require that the oedipal subject's antecedents as well as its failures be reconsidered (desire-guilt-working through-sublimation).

I am convinced, however, that the "topographies of splitting" between true and false self that are necessary in psychoanalytic actuality, the nonmentalization or the primitive unconscious outside representation based on originary phantasms, and affective more than cognitive projective identification phenomena do not have a specific autonomy but have to do with symptoms or subjective pathologies that can be understood and treated only in the context of oedipal neurotic integration. It is not to reduce them to this approach but to remember, lucidly, that the analyst must take this approach if she/he does not want to be complicit in what Freud called the "plague": the plague of more or less occult complacency, with regression, fragmentation, and madness.

Thus, attentive to preoedipal bonds in borderline patients or in the treatment of children and adolescents, I have begun to rethink the "object relation." Faced with problems of separation between "subject" and "object," and without postulating a similarity with the paranoid-schizoid split, I argue that the mother and the *infans* constitute themselves in the early existence of the baby as "ab-jects."[5] Neither subjects nor objects but poles of attraction and rejection, they begin the subsequent separation in the oedipal triangle, except that in the modality of subjectivation in question, logically and chronologically prior to the Oedipus complex, the interaction of "abjects" is based on the "direct and immediate" "primal identification" with the father of individual prehistory and is materialized in the preverbal exchanges that I call "semiotic" (the drives via the sensorial pathway, and prelanguage expressed in intensities, rhythms, and intonations). At the dividing line of primal repression, the "abject" and "abjection" enable analysts to refine their listening, by inscribing the negative transference in translinguistic, "semiotic" communication. It also enables analysts to closely follow their analysands, in the position of the ab-ject mother (desired and detested as in a female representation in paintings of Picasso or de Kooning) as well as in that of the "father of individual prehistory,"[6] pole of "primary identification" and not yet of "oedipal taboo." You see that this type of listening, temporary or intermittent in the long process of treatment, works around the Oedipus complex rather than dismisses it and, in my opinion, provides the intrapsychic conditions for a reconstruction of the analysand as subject of desire and thus of creativity, integrating him into transference/countertransference from his preoedipal latencies. For, as of the "archaic" stage of his unmet needs, the analysand is listened to and interpreted in the ambivalence of the early objectal link in the process of constitution and rejection. In my *Powers of Horror,* I proposed a psychoanalytical approach to these early modalities of subjectivation, which have also been "treated" throughout history as defilement purification rituals in various religions (Judaism, Christianity, Hinduism) or whose sublimatory failures have been noted, as in Celine's anti-Semitic ravings, for example.

Alain Braconnier: *How have you succeeded in going beyond those who sometimes pitted Freud's and Lacan's contributions against each other in a caricatural way? Is it your initial training as a linguist?*

Julia Kristeva: My training as a linguist would have been insufficient if I had not added semiology: Saussure, Benveniste, Greimas, Barthes. I was lucky, very young, to participate in this opening of the studies of meaning through the "language" object of linguists toward translinguistic "signifying practices": literature first, but also the image, with painting and film, and also music, gesture, etc. This period and these studies, now too easily forgotten or discredited, and which have also often locked themselves in an archly technical esotericism, appeared to me and still appear to me as the pinnacle of contemporary thought. I considered *meaning* as a dynamic process, a *signifying process* that mobilizes—along with language—other means of signification. Beyond structuralism, I helped bring the subject of the enunciation in history to the fore: my work on Bakhtin, the body and the carnivalesque discourse, was pathbreaking in this respect. But it was also necessary to question linguistics in the light of phenomenology, which is what I tried to do in my thesis on the *Revolution in Poetic Language: Mallarmé and Lautrémont.*[7] Through a detour toward Husserl's transcendental Ego, I wanted to escape Chomsky's Cartesianism, which tended to lock language in grammar and introduce two parameters in studies of meaning that semiology ignores: "matter" (*hylé*) and the "other." I then proceeded to a rehabilitation of drive and desire in the interpretation of poetic enunciation. I understood by "revolution" first the return of repressed instincts, and only then its impact of surprise, even mutation, in the tired code of normative social exchanges. Thus revisited, "language" or rather the "language system" of linguists was no longer my objective: it was to interpret the text, writing, with their subject in crisis and reconstruction in a specific biographical and historical context. Freud and Lacan had no more reason to be in opposition: they participated in this refoundation naturally.

Alain Braconnier: *Considering contemporary work on language and its avatars and your own work in this area, what do you think of Lacan's famous and still partially enigmatic formula: "the unconscious is structured like a language," emphasizing as I think you do "like"?*

Julia Kristeva: My work as a semiologist and literary theorist was prepared and accompanied by a very empirical and concrete "in the field" investigation. Even before starting my own analysis, I devoted myself to the meticulous observation of the two edges of language: language acquisition by children (recordings and analyses of echolalia, then first phonemes, morphemes, syntax, etc. at the nursery at Censier), and speech disorders, even of language ability itself, in psychoses (at La Borde Hospital). In Lacan's formulation, I put the emphasis on "like." Lacan himself spoke of "lalangue," alluding to "lallation," to echolalia, pre- or translanguage. The speaking being is subjected to the influence of the family linguistic code, and every mother tongue imprints itself on the organization of the "own," including one's own body. The unconscious of my Russian or English patients is not the same when they talk to me in English, French, or Russian. Yet Freud's position, for whom the unconscious is constitutive of drives, is so complex that we have to support it with new data and with semiotics and biology: the unconscious is not only language. Affects, drives, sensations-perceptions, these *entities of signifyingness* are irreducible to language, of which they make up the heterogeneous double. On this level, I agreed with André Green's positions, and I developed the language/drive heterogeneity in the *Revolution of Poetic Language*. In my analytic practice, I understand these entities as heterogeneous facets of subjectivation: at certain moments of the treatment, I note them in their own carnal, perceptive specificity—pleasurable, painful, and hallucinatory. I draw the analysand's attention to these bodily "experiences"; I name them in metaphors, figures, and stories, so as to interpret their unconscious impact in transference/countertransference. Necessarily and inevitably, I use language to open the inter- and intrapsychic space to what is not "of language," to the unconscious heterogeneous experience of language. I knew a very erudite person who liked to say that "the unconscious is structured like a language" and admitted in this context to being proud of having done an "analysis based on the superego"! There is no reason to be proud of a language impasse.

Alain Braconnier: *Can you remind us of the distinction you make between the "symbolic" and the "semiotic," from a psychoanalytic point of view?*

Julia Kristeva: As a counterpoint to structuralism, which sees meaning as a structure, and as of the *Revolution of Poetic Language*, I suggested that there was a signifying process in language, a dynamic process of subjectivation/desubjectivation, which is constituted in the interaction of two signifying modalities (or modes). The semiotic is a first encoding of drives under the influence of the mother tongue, in rhythms, melodies, and intensities, then in echolalia of pseudoconsonants and pseudovowels; prior to the mirror stage and translinguistic rather than prelinguistic, the semiotic incorporates (as Racamier would have said) the mother-*infans* coexcitation. The semiotic carries the interactive, affective, and sensory *meaning* without *signification*. This comes about with the constitution of the "predicative thesis" (in Husserl's meaning) and the mastery of syntax, which already carries the "narrative envelopes" and begins tracking the speaking subject in the Oedipus complex.[8] I call this second signifying modality *the symbolic*. The semiotic/symbolic distinction allowed me to analyze the polyphony of poetic language that precisely attaches to the explicit "message" in a text (poetry or prose) a whole undecidable polyphony that we receive as "musicality" of a "style." But this distinction also identifies important strata of subjectivation in what are commonly diagnosed as psychotic speech disorders.

For example, I recently had the opportunity to make a "patient interview" at Sainte-Anne. The patient was schizophrenic, a runaway, capable of self-mutilation, and had made a serious suicide attempt by jumping out of a window. Very quickly, B "introduced himself" by introducing his mother. He spoke as if he was in "place" of his mother, constantly referring to her, telling a dramatic story that I knew was his own but that he appropriated and formulated as his mother's: SHE scarified HER own body, SHE attempted suicide, SHE complained about being "the black sheep" of the family in her childhood, SHE demanded that her son "monitor" her, which B confessed he could not "digest" because invisible forces he could not oppose "directed" him. He also tried to interpret his state of fusion with the "black sheep" emphasizing his father's absence, his sibling conflicts, and his mother's intrusiveness. I heard a cold and set speech, like a reduplication of words from different therapists who had explained his "case" to him since childhood, echoing also the "shrink" readings he had done. B was a philosophy student. I also heard he spoke French as if it were a second language: was he Belgian, Swiss, or was it a kind of flight, an attempt to break the maternal "monitoring" to "throw himself out the window" of the hold of the *abject*? B had spent one year studying in England. At a particularly intense moment of our conversation, he referred to himself by an English nickname. I decided to continue our conversation in English. And it was a renaissance. B brightened, his hitherto impassive face became expressive and smiling, he found the courage to entrust me with his conflicts with his brother and his teachers and his desire to "vent his malaise," and to write a thesis on the "absolute good." Clearly, he regretted the end of the meeting and asked if we could see each other again.

A psychoanalyst who "plays dead" has no place in treating a melancholic schizophrenic. The long and perhaps impossible separation with the maternal *abject* frozen into a psychotizing *alter ego* cannot take place without restoring a "semiotic communion" between the two psyches: that of the patient and that of the analyst. In the meeting with B, it was the only way of "digesting" the "overbearing" mother who parasitized him and with whom he mixed himself up in the guise of a "black sheep"; a bête-noire with whom he could not think together but that he could only stubbornly flee or destroy by destroying himself.

English, the foreign language, was his way of "distancing" himself from the "black sheep" that she was and he was: a playground finally at hand—with me, escaping from the mother tongue—that had become available to his thinking process in our own duo. A translanguage of hope in which he could allow himself to relearn to speak and think with *another mother*, to provoke me, to work out his projects of "absolute good" and even to suggest how difficult the reparative hope was: his smile implied that he might have told me about the "ridiculousness" of this repair, if the interview had been longer. Paradoxically, but in fact necessarily, it was a foreign language that enabled him to remake an *unnamable* and no less transitive, transitional *semiotic link*—by which he felt he existed, able to discuss, contradict, think, and laugh. Was it because "it" had happened but had been foreclosed by the injury of a hyperaggressive oedipal complex brought about by his parents' divorce? Or because "it" had not occurred in the mother tongue of the early mother-son link, and that the foreign language, English, gave him the opportunity of a "graft" of narcissistic reassurance, the only way from which B could meet me without catastrophic anxiety but in reinventing strategies of "imaginary matricide," starting with the most innocuous and perfidious: irony, laughter, seduction. With the foreign language offering B a solid semiotic base, he almost found the narcissistic flexibility of the neurotic.

Alain Braconnier: *In your latest book, you write: "We do not know much about femininity as a product of the feminine imaginary alone," indeed referring to the rarity of women painters. What can you tell us about this feminine imaginary that, perhaps paradoxically, so intrigued Freud?*

Julia Kristeva: I will respond to the part of your question concerning the ever-persistent enigma of the "feminine." I maintain, along with others, and in my own way, that the complexity of the "feminine" cannot be grasped without considering the two oedipal complexes that structure the female subject.[9]

I call "Oedipus Prime" the initial mother-daughter coexcitation, in which the prelinguistic sensorial experience is decisive: effraction and passivation of the hollow body, including the vagina, by the maternal other; aggression and oral, anal, vaginal, and clitoral possession of the other; and last, repression of excitability and compensation by a psychic and sensorial overinvestment of the maternal object, which prematurely creates a psychic introjection, and which will develop in the form of this "mysterious" interiority of the woman, dependent on the object, in "communicating vessels" with it, fascinating and consuming. Although the maternal object at the outset transmits the link to the father, this early dependence on the mother is essential and different in girls compared to boys, because her female genitor erects her less as a phallic prosthesis (which the boy is) than she projects on her own narcissistic fantasies and sadomasochistic and depressive latencies, resonating with the little girl's orificial and sensorial jouissances. In other words, the sensorial reality of the object, the actual presence of the mother (and, later on, of the lover) are required—by the little girl—as compensation for the effraction of the hollow body and the psychic introjection constantly at work. You see, I do not think there is an early, preobjectal, and serene "being," prior to any "drive-based happening" in the early mother-child relationship, with either the girl or the boy. Winnicott's "distilled" and "pure feminine" may be a countertransference fantasy. Moreover, even the philosopher most attentive to the "serenity of the being"—Heidegger—does not think of it as devoid of "negative" but inevitably "embedded" in "nothingness," when he is not insisting on the "malignancy of the being."

As for "Oedipus 2," it exposes the little girl to what I call the complexity of the "phallic meeting": identification with the paternal taboos, integration of the law, social codes, construction of the superego; and simultaneously substitution of the maternal object by the father as erotic object. Phallicization and objectal receptivity (rather than passivity) constitute the woman from here on as a subject of phallic law for certain, but as intrinsically "foreign" to the phallic order of the law, because she is indebted to *Oedipus Prime*, from the "Mino-Mycenaean" continent according to Freud, meaning to the "semiotic" sensorial imprint. This unconscious attraction of the primal maternal controls the "more accentuated psychic bisexuality" in the woman, with its two symptoms: depressive latency, on one hand, and hysterical dissatisfaction, on the other (which Hegel feared, or welcomed, when he saw in the feminine "the eternal irony of the community"). *Femininity* developed as an attempt to close this constitutive dissociation of the *feminine* between *Oedipus Prime* and *Oedipus 2*, with the implicit "I know but still": seduction, masquerade, erection of the body of the *girl* (when it is not the androgen) as phallus that masks castration, cunning, artifice, and even "false selves" that get the hysterical taken for a borderline case. So many traps into which modern clinical practice seems to be falling, forgetting hysteria in favor of "borderline cases." Motherhood can be the opportunity for a real encounter with the *other* that *Oedipus Prime* and *Oedipus 2* prepare and which will be the *child* conferring to the woman the incarnate fantasy (as in Kleinian fantasies) of finally existing. Fleeting certainty, however, as multiple pregnancies are called for to maintain it, when the lack of desire and object does not ravage the matron, who collapses, a tired and depressed housewife. The psychic work of working through and sublimation can be proposed as one possible way out of this complex process that specifies the subject-woman and destines women to be the most numerous, and even the best, analysands and analysts. It is not sure, however, that these particularities of feminine psychosexuality prepare the feminine imaginary to excel in painting. This requires an investment of the gaze more than of the invisible, of the outside more than of the inside, of aggression more than of repair. There would have to be a strong phallic identity, such as that of Artemisia Gentileschi or Georgia O'Keefe, and that the evolution of psychic female bisexuality like Louise Bourgeois's expresses itself in "forms" of modern art so that a specifically *feminine* and necessarily evolutive *imaginary* can be discerned or not.

Alain Braconnier: *You have written three books on feminine genius. What meaning do you give to this notion of genius and especially feminine genius? What determined your choice of Colette, Hannah Arendt, and Melanie Klein?*

Julia Kristeva: I distinguish, on one hand, the "originary meeting of the genii" celebrated by the Greeks and Romans (imagining a *daimon* or a genius, a divine spirit that presides over each person's birth) and then crystallized in the Jewish *chosenness* and the *ecceitas* or Christian singularity, that psychoanalysis finally considers as a specific creativity of each subject; and, on the other hand, its displacement or metonymy secularized in the genius of "great men" that held sway from resurgent Humanism up to Romanticism. The uncertainties of secularization nowadays reopen this recurring problem in a new form. The ruins of the onto-theological continent too quickly declared gone appear less and less as "dead letters" and more and more as laboratories of living cells, whose exploration would clarify current aporias and impasses. Neither sacred destiny nor divinity's romantic return to reality, are we reduced to being only trivialized numbers or digitalized "differents"?

Facing the trivialization of discourse, the collapse of authority, the technical specialization of knowledge that makes it impossible to communicate its excellence, and the surge of greedy needs of satisfaction-seduction-cancellation, the word *genius* remains a hyperbole that awakens our capacity for surprise, that ultimate thought-provoker. So I go back to the word *genius* but try to delete its romantic inflation. And, temporarily putting aside the idea of "great men" that Hegel dwelled on (I will return to it), I take up its archeology and its meaning before its resurgent fetishization. In the three volumes of *Female Genius*—Arendt, Klein, Colette—I understand "genius" as the loving singularity that Christianity discovered and that has since had unforeseeable developments, both in what is called the history of arts and letters and in the Freudian discovery of the unconscious. Still invisible—but nonetheless in effect—the Freudian discovery of the unconscious, reread by Lacan, in my view, makes it possible to rethink the work of the signifying process through love in the singularity of the human adventure. It thus opens a new page in the "philosophy of immanence" (going back, with Y. Yovel, to Spinoza[10]), which suggests another way of looking at the old questions of singularity and genius that are pertinent to our conversation today. Is not the goal of treatment, precisely, to reveal the analysand's specific singularity, thus promoting the creativity that seems to be the best criterion for the end of an analysis?

The three volumes of *Feminine Genius* are inscribed as part of the foregoing and are to be read also as a response to massifying feminism. What is it? Eliminating the question of *being* to replace it by the security of belonging ("being *part of*"), women have been "massified" as the bourgeoisie, the proletariat, the Third World, etc. were once massified. Against this massive myth of "all women" gathered in the "community of women," I looked into their *singularity* (*l'ecceitas* according to Duns Scotus), and I analyzed it concretely in Arendt, Klein, and Colette.[11] I seized the provocative term "genius" to demonstrate that I am a "Scotus" "feminist." In the life and work of these three women, I first identify some specific traits of female psychosexuality in general. Not nearly as narcissistic as it is said, and even far less narcissistic than a man, a woman from the start constructs herself in relation to others: to live is to live of and for the other, including and especially when it is impossible and traumatizing. Rarely locked into the obsessional palaces of pure thought, thinking for a woman is inseparable from carnal sensoriality. The metaphysical body/soul dichotomy is unbearable for these three women geniuses: they dispense thought as physical bliss, and *eros* is for them inseparable from *agapè*. Their time is haunted by the worry of finitude, without it being a race to death, and yet it subsides in the miracle of birth, of flowering. "To be reborn . . . never beyond my powers":[12] this exorbitant exclamation by Colette evokes not only women's capacity for adaptation but also the psychosomatic flexibility of the mature woman after having passed through the pitfalls of phallic claims and envy. It is especially the *specific* realization of these common features in Arendt, Klein, and Colette that interested me to invite my women readers not to be "like" but to seek to be incomparable. Incommensurable genius can exist only when taking the risks that each one is capable of taking, by putting into question his or her thinking, language, time, and whatever identity (sexual, national, ethnic, professional, religious, philosophical) is harbored there.

Alain Braconnier: *About religion now, you seem to follow a path similar to the one Freud generally took, starting with the question of drive and individual neurosis and then leading him, through his research, to the malaises in civilization. Would you agree with my reading of your chapter on this subject in your latest book?*

Julia Kristeva: Absolutely. And I recently picked up on this problematic at a symposium with psychoanalysts from Columbia University and the IPA (International Psychoanalytical Association) on "The Dead Father."[13] The creation of a Standing Interdisciplinary Forum: Psychoanalysis, Belief and Religious Conflicts was then envisaged in Jerusalem by the Psychoanalytical Society of Israel and the Department of Psychoanalysis at Hebrew University in Jerusalem, with psychoanalysts, historians of religion, philosophers, writers, artists, biologists, and physicists, and perhaps one day, theologians, around the questioning that psychoanalysis has brought to the fore. Certain believers, and not the least of them, have begun to think that hermeneutics and psychoanalysis can elucidate the subject of "God" and would be of interest. Along with Freud, we dare say that "god" is analyzable. It is beginning to take hold.

Alain Braconnier: *Who are the great figures in psychoanalysis who have influenced you the most?*

Julia Kristeva: After Freud, Melanie Klein, Winnicott, and Lacan, of course. And I learned a great deal from my supervision with André Green.

Alain Braconnier: *Psychoanalysis has been strongly criticized recently. What would you say to its critics to defend it? What do you think is the future of psychoanalysis?*

Julia Kristeva: Discussions begun with neurobiologists, such as those we had started to conduct in the seminar at the Salpêtrière Hospital with Daniel Widlöcher and Pierre Fédida and in the Centre du Vivant at the University of Paris-7, Denis Diderot. Active and public interpretations on "social issues": parentality, assisted human reproduction, motherhood and the modern woman, and religions. And, in particular, not to get bogged down in discussions with malicious and revisionist detractors but to highlight our advances.

Alain Braconnier: *Are you interested in pursuing here the current discussions on the respective place of psychoanalysis and what is called psychoanalytic psychotherapy?*

Julia Kristeva: Article 52 of the law on the use of the professional title of psychotherapist requires theoretical and practical training in clinical psychopathology. I approved, and I argued before the decision-making bodies, the Paris Psychoanalytical Society proposal to amend the legislation, particularly in the formulation of the specific content of university master's degrees. This formulation must necessarily distinguish psychoanalysis as an approach distinct from systemic, cognitive-behavioral and integrative psychotherapies. It corresponds to the need to uphold the place of psychoanalysis in the university, taking into account the different psychotherapies that respond to the social demand, and the need to reserve rigorous psychoanalytic clinical training for the psychoanalytic societies.

Alain Braconnier: *Your book* Black Sun, *which you published in 1987, provided essential insights into depression. Has your view on this topic evolved?*

Julia Kristeva: I have not changed my theoretical position on the problem, and I have nothing to add, neither to my clinical observations nor to my analysis of the depression/sublimation relation. However, I will probably develop the depressive background of certain perversions, notably in life-threatening acting out that threaten unconscious, rejected or repressed masculine or feminine homosexuality.

Alain Braconnier: *At the request of the president of the Republic, you have written a report on disability and issued a letter to citizens with disabilities.*[14] *Could you tell us what brought about this commitment and what conclusions you draw from this report?*

Julia Kristeva: The word of a psychoanalyst, wife, and mother proved necessary when the "republican worksite" concerning the exclusion of disabled people had to address the need to "change public opinion's view" of considering these men and women not as "deprived objects" but as subjects capable of creativity, whatever their limitations, and therefore as *political subjects* in their own right. After this first phase of my involvement as president of the National Disability Council, I gave up the actual presidency, but I still try to develop a less political and more analytical discourse on the creativity, specifically, of the vulnerable subject, at the intersection of biology and sense, especially in the field of psychoses and sensorimotor disorders. Besides, this approach to disability goes back to many aspects of my early theoretical and semiotic work. It will take everyone—parents, government, and public opinion—considerable time and effort before we can draw conclusions about a subject as complex as that of "disabilities," a subject that, beyond the narcissistic and castrating ordeal, puts us squarely in front of our anxieties in facing death and the limits of the species.[15]

7

A FATHER IS BEING BEATEN TO DEATH

... who have been called Christians for two
thousand years, are just a psychological
self-misunderstanding. Examined more
closely and in spite of all "belief," they
*have been governed only by instincts,—*and
what instincts they are!

—FRIEDRICH NIETZSCHE, *THE ANTECHRIST* (TRANS. JUDITH NORMAN)

The "dead father" is a clinical experience I have often encountered with my analysands in a number of variations that resonate with my countertransference. My own personal experience of this was especially strong when I lost my father in dramatic circumstances in September 1989, in my native country of Bulgaria, two months before the fall of the Berlin Wall. He was murdered in a supposedly socialist hospital where experiments were performed on elderly patients; family members were not allowed to visit for "fear of germs." Then, the bodies of practicing Christians were cremated to prevent religious gatherings. While I was mourning, I could only talk about this by writing a novel.

It was the "metaphysical mystery" genre that I found myself writing for the first time, a genre in which I continue to work at the moment, which necessarily combines philosophical, political, poetic, and psychoanalytical approaches. This first detective novel is entitled *The Old Man and the Wolves*.[1] To be brief, my father's death drove me to see society as described by Freud: "based on complicity in the common crime."[2] The other consequence of this event was the loss of inhibition that underlies my thinking today: it goes through the desacralization of the lover couple and the unveiling of its sadomasochistic repression in the links between the characters, Alba and Sebastian, who accompanied the novel's "dead father."

I will not linger on this subject today, which has already been largely transposed in a mythical form in my "whodunit." I mention this story, however, only because the grief and melancholy I felt after my father's death, as well as their working through–sublimation, underlie the analyses that I intend to speak about today, and in which you will clearly hear personal auto-analytical and countertransferential connotations. In particular, I will examine the fantasy of the "father being beaten to death" while maintaining that this fantasy lies at the foundation of the Christian faith. At the same time, I will take a brief moment to examine Freud's other fantasy familiar to you all, "A Child Is Being Beaten to Death."

A Coptic manuscript, translated from Greek in the third and fourth centuries and unearthed in the 1970s, was published by *National Geographic* in April 2006.[3] It brings to light the fact that Judas did not "betray" Jesus but rather "fulfilled" his design to be put to death. The image of Judas as the unworthy disciple, which has fed two thousand years of Christian anti-Semitism, is thus broken. The analyst, as far as he or she is concerned, has no need of this kind of "proof" in order to understand that the putting to death of the Christic body is not an unfortunate accident (such a betrayal, such an internal conflict in Judaism, etc.) and is still less a Gnostic resurgence of the Platonician soul (which rids itself of the body in order to attain the idea of the Good and the Beautiful). On the contrary, the "father being beaten to death" appears to the analyst as a logical necessity in the Christian construction of the subject of desire, which removes the guilt of *incestual love* of the father and for the father, by its displacement onto *suffering-passion* as the only possible path for *sublimation*. This logical necessity begins by transferring the prohibition or abandonment of incest in the form of a punishment of and by the father, lived as a form of passionate suffering, before finally allowing the love of and for the father in "reconciliation" by "infinite intellectual love" (Spinoza), by sublimation.

Should I mention that I am an atheist and yet convinced that psychoanalysis has the formidable privilege of lending its listening to the religious sphere whose "clashes" are worsening, when they do not condition, the malaise of men and women at this beginning of the third millennium? This assessment applies to all psychoanalysts, whatever our "school" or whether we are believers or nonbelievers imbued with the consequences of our cultural and religious environment. There will be obstacles and progress that engage the future of psychoanalysis as an outcome of this listening. We are very much behind in the treatment of these new variants of the "crisis of civilization," and I can only hope that meetings such as this one will help us make progress on this difficult path.

I will argue that the "father complex" is universal but is nevertheless modulated very differently through the history of the various civilizations and religions; and today, when confronted with the new methods of procreation, we need to take into consideration these different varieties of this complex that concern real fathers in their relationship to the structural figure of the "dead father," or rather in the plural, the "dead fathers." As children of the Enlightenment and as disciples of Freud, we have hastened to declare the death of God and have remained blind to the complexity and paradoxes in the history of religion, especially as they pertain to the role of the father, both living and dead. My intention here is a reading of Freud's *Totem and Taboo* inflected by my interpretation of "A Child Is Being Beaten,"[4] in which I examine the guilt that underlies the murder of the father as the symmetric other side of the desire for him and of its elucidation.

FREUD: "A CHILD IS BEING BEATEN"

While he postulates the existence of *originary fantasies* in our unconscious, which stem from either the observation of certain events or a "prehistoric truth" going back to "the *originary* times of the human family," Freud mentions only three: the primal scene, castration, and seduction. The "a child is being beaten" fantasy, introduced in 1919, seems to occupy a particular, pivotal place among these fantasies that structure the psychoanalytical interpretation of desire and the variety of individual sexual scenarios in which the singular eroticism of speaking subjects unfolds. Halfway between "originary" and "individual," the mythical and the poetic, might "a child is being beaten" be the origin of individuation, the decisive time when the subject constitutes himself in his *sexual choice* and in a *speaking identity* in the ternary structure of oedipal kinship? In fantasizing myself as "a beaten child," I, male or female, excluded from the primal scene, look for my place between father and mother in order both to mark out my difference and to find my place among the ties that are inseparably those of love and speech, both passionate and signifying.

I schematically sum up this text, underlining that Freud distinguished between the "a child is being beaten" fantasy for the little girl and for the little boy.

The little girl (and the woman) protects herself from her incestuous love for her father (first stage of the fantasy: "He loves me"), and from her defensive masochism (second stage of the fantasy: "No, he doesn't love me, he beats me"), by projecting them, preferably inversely on another person of the same sex as the coveted paternal object (third stage: "He's beating a boy"). Two questions arise here: How does this delegation of female desire to another object of the same or rather the other sex, the male sex, happen, and that shelters her as a subject of desire? How does this reversed delegation of desire come about, which, strictly speaking, is not repression but rather what I would call an introjection of affection for the father and of the father: an introjection of the *père-version*?

As I have commented elsewhere,[5] the little girl experiencing her first oedipal stage with her *mother* constructs an early alterity, experienced as a sensible and preverbal presence, which is simultaneously a pole of attraction and adversity with which she will continue to compare herself, measure herself by, and separate herself from. You or me? Such is the question she asks herself right from the start, unable to position herself as Narcissus sure of his Ego and imbued with his image. The little girl puts herself outside the bounds of arousal, which nevertheless agitates her, and protects herself from her passion, which is first incestual, then masochistic, by concentrating on others: "He doesn't love you because he hits you."

Who is this "you," this beaten second person who protects my guilty desire of loving and being loved?

Freud interprets: repression, which follows desire, turns love of the father and for the father into the punishment of another person who is jealously hated. The prototype of this other beaten person can only be the *mother*, the little girl's humiliated rival, even in the best of patriarchal families.

And yet the ambivalent love of the little girl for her mother continues to protect the envied matron and looks for other targets to keep the loved/hated maternal object sheltered. Thus other children usually replace this beaten rival in the little girl's fantasy. But why this displacement and this masquerade?

The founder of psychoanalysis does not stop at evoking daily observations of siblings or of children at school who are frequently subjected to paternal punishment. He suggests that the guilt internal to the voyeur's own repressed desire creates the necessity for punishment, with or without observation of punishment scenes. And revives the inquiry: where would this guilt-laden repression of the love of and for the father that reaches its acme in the fantasy of punishment or even thrashing come from?

There is one single answer: this repression would be but a repetition of the repression of incest constitutive of the history of humanity and dictated by it. Foundation of the culture that specifies our species, *the repression of incest*, which is thus an *originary repression*, necessarily and universally engenders guilt and its corollary, masochism. This prehistoric guilt can (in certain circumstances) lead to strong individual drives, powerful incestual overtones in the family, and intense regression to prior stages of psychic development –before genitality: to oral-anal arousal (spanking), to onanistic satisfaction, or to variants of punishments-thrashings that take the entire body for an erogenous zone.

I suggest adding to the Freudian vision of this originary, primal, or endogenous masochism commanded by the originary repression of incest the fact that this very repression, pushing away incestuous desire, leads to a final displacement of arousal, this time not to another "object" ("a boy") but to the *medium of expression and communication itself*: repression of incest leads to an investment of language and thought. On this particular point, I would like to situate the "primal identification" with the father of individual prehistory that I developed in *Tales of Love*[6] that conditions the preverbal sublimation (*semiotic*) of drives in real linguistic signs (in *symbolic*).[7]

I say, therefore, that parallel to the fantasy that "another is being beaten" who comes to protect me from the prohibited genital satisfaction and/or the incestuous desire to be loved and to love (Daddy, but Mommy as well: Freud concentrates less on the latter, as love of and for the mother seems more natural, less prohibited), I, the little girl, shift the intensity of my desire to speaking and thought, to representation and psychic creativity, relying on the fantasy that "a boy/child is being beaten."

This shift of my libido onto language and intelligence is not a simple defense against guilty genital desires. It especially creates a new object of desire, which becomes a new source of satisfaction, complementary to the pleasure of the erogenous zones: it is simply the capacity to infinitely represent and name—up to giving words and sense or non-sense to genital and masochistic arousal itself. All this in the hope not only of finding partial substitutes to prohibited incest, which would be my own activities or symbolic works, but of deserving this prohibited, guilt-ridden love, turned into masochism: of deserving it by this extravagant capacity of sublimation that all humans possess but which I, little girl, work harder than anyone else to excel in.

In addition to masochistic perversity ("I take pleasure in the fantasy of being beaten") and its sadistic reversal ("I take pleasure in seeing a boy beaten") is the sublimatory jouissance of my own capacities to say and to think for and with the loved/loving one. You see it in the beginning: sublimation accompanies the *père-verse* defense, and the *père-version* is sublimation's double. Let's keep in mind this sublimatory movement: we will come across it again, reinforced to the extreme, in the nuclear fantasy that I see as essential to the Christian narrative: "A father is being beaten to death."

Thus we are led to this: the terminal fantasy "One beats a child" erases the representation of the masochistic scene from the girl's consciousness ("He beats *me*") and replaces it by a double movement. On one hand, the sadistic version of the fantasy: "He beats *him*"; and on the other, its accompaniment by an imaginary and cognitive hyperactivity, as well as by a critical moral consciousness identified with the parental superego in which the feminine superego takes root, and even by an observant vigilance that can go as far as a delirium of self-observation. It is clear, then, that the conflicts between this symbolic construction and excitability can engender the symptoms of these conflictual, split personalities called hysterics, very frequent in women but that do not spare men who have similar backgrounds. In favorable familial and historical contexts, these conflicts can also be powerful stimuli for the development of women's symbolic creativity, on a backdrop of tamed masochism, thus merely tempered.

But this strong identification, at once defensive and creative, of the girl with the paternal superego mixed with the phallic function occurs to the detriment of her female identifications. It causes the repression of the mother reduced to a castrated, sick femininity, gives rise to virile mimetism, and propels the female subject into a glorification of spirituality, all of which work to reunite the little girl and the woman she will become with the symbolic father.

Admirable twistings and interminable polyphonies of the hysteric adventure! How many have given up and asked: "What do women want?"

Nor does the little boy escape this sadomasochistic economy. With the difference that his thrashing fantasy is experienced as passive from the outset: "I am loved by the father" (implying: like a passive woman). To protect himself from this feminine position and the homosexuality it involves, the boy superimposes another fantasy on the defensive fantasy: ("I'm being beaten by the father"), one that represses the father by inverting the sexual attributes of the punishment's author: "It's not he who beats me, it's *she*, a woman, it's the mother." This is the third stage of the masculine, masochistic fantasy.

Male masochism, which culminates in the flagellation scenario of a woman wielding a whip, protects the male subject from this ultimate danger of the father's sadistic desire, against which the son must defend himself at all cost; for it is this very desire that persists, both as an unconscious homosexual attraction and as the ultimate danger. And although this masochistic fantasy of being beaten by a woman does in no way keep the man from occupying a feminine position given the nature of his passive role in this scenario, it offers him a double benefit. Not only does the sadomasochistic scene not take place between men, since I come with a woman, in a duo of women. But I give myself the passive feminine position, even if I avoid the choice of homosexual object. An apparent heterosexuality is maintained. Moreover, the child beaten by his mother who I now am is not even just a passive woman: because this man suffering with the mother, that is, joins up with the suffering that I had suspected in my own father, this humiliated man who was always overshadowed by the power of maternal hysteria. Beaten, I join my belittled father once again; we are at last united by these nuptials under the whip. After all is said and done, my man-beaten-by-a-woman masochism is the only compromise able to make me a man, somewhat diminished, but who finally exists, as I myself exist, through the experience of suffering, of his, my father's, suffering. I am the man of my mother, of course, the man I have always desired with a fearful desire and whose sadism I no longer have reason to fear.

On the woman's side, on the man's side: the throes and delights of sexuation, suffering and dying each in their own way?

INCEST TABOO: SUFFERING AND NUPTIALS, A SUBLIMATION

Had you recognized me you would
have known the Father.

—JOHN 14:7–12

If the murder of the father is a foundational *act* at the origin of human civilization, Freud also offers the hypothesis that with Christianity, the religion of the Son, this murder is finally *admitted*, in order to be transcended. I take these considerations into account, while nevertheless distancing myself so that my attention is focused exclusively on *psychic reality*, which generates fantasies in those who believe in such events, whether or not they actually occurred.

Another point: although the Person of Christ is that of the Son, Saint Paul declared that it is God the Father himself who suffers the Passion and dies. It really seems difficult to dissociate the Son's suffering to the death from that of the Father who, in the mystery of the Trinity, is consubstantial with him. What would happen if Jesus were not only a child or a beaten brother but above all a father—and a father being beaten to death?

A similar situation for the little girl means that the one she loves (object of maternal desire and phallic function which supports her access to representation, language, and thought) shares the victim-state of the boy in the girl's sadistic fantasy as analyzed by Freud, where it is not she but a boy who is being beaten. But here a beaten father becomes by the same token a kind of brother. By combining father and son, this scenario has the double advantage of appeasing the incestual guilt that weighs on the desire for the Other (sovereign Father) and of encouraging virile identification with this tortured man, but only under the cover of a masochism that such a movement valorizes, even encourages: "This beaten father and/or brother is my double, my fellow man, my *alter ego*, myself, endowed with a male organ."[8]

The path is thus open in the unconscious so that the father agent of law and prohibition can now merge with the subject of the guilty amorous passion that "I" am as a girl loved by this same father, superman who is humanized as soon as he becomes my brother; even more, who is feminized by the suffering undergone, and becomes in fact my ideal double. A complicit "us" gets worked out by and in the father's passion. From there on we share love, guilt, and punishment.

For my unconscious this father is from now on not only the agent of prohibition and punishment but clearly the object of the prohibition, suffering from this prohibition and punishment like my brother, my fellow, like me. I thus pledge to him an idealization in which the ego ideal and the superego are mixed and which is added on to my perception as excluded minor from the primal scene, to the point of absorbing this exclusion. I thus return to the first phase of my oedipal fantasy: "I love him and he loves me." Thus, because of our osmosis in the paternal passion, this love expresses itself differently: "We are both in love, and guilty, we deserve to be beaten to death together, death will bring us together again."

For the unconscious, these father/daughter reunions *suspend the incest taboo* in and by the suffering of the two lovers-and-punished protagonists in such a way that this suffering will necessarily be a *marriage*. The suffering sexualized under the "whip of faith" in the father being beaten to death, "this love without pity" (to paraphrase Baudelaire), is the paradise of masochism and of its only way out: sublimation. Why is this so?

By placing the fantasy of the father being beaten to death at the summit of the evangelical narrative, calling for believers' identification,

Christianity does not just stop at reinforcing the prohibitions but paradoxically displaces them and opens the way to their working through or their sublimation.

First, the neurotic person continues to be both curbed and stimulated by the fears of judgment, condemnation, and expiation of all kinds that mutilate and rekindle his desires. However, being beaten as this son-father, the subject can overcome his suffering from guilt over his unconscious desires and invest in what must be called sovereign, divine suffering. This is no longer the suffering of guilt, of transgression, but a suffering as the sole way leading to the union with this ideal subject, the Father being beaten to death. A new kind of suffering: Christic or Christian, which is not the flip side of the law but a suspension of law and guilt to the benefit of a *jouissance in idealized suffering*. A jouissance of the appeal, of longing, of the essential failure of assuaging the desire for the father: suffering-jouissance in the ambivalence of the *père-version*.

The father being beaten to death does not make suffering banal, nor does it authorize incest. By the glory and grace of our suffering-together, of our com-passion, it consecrates and justifies them.

Nonetheless, the adoration of the beaten father brings about another, far more fundamental consequence: with and beyond the surreptitiously accepted incestual link with the father, it is the *symbolic activity* itself that I am encouraged to sexualize through paternal passion. How so?

Since it is by representation, thought, and language that I connect with the Other, it is indeed this activity of *representation* of my desires, albeit frustrated, that promotes the Father-Passion that took the place of the Father of the Law. The resexualization of the ideal Father as Man of Passion brings about an unprecedented resexualization of the representation itself, of the fantasizing and language activity. First, while favoring compassion, the Passion of the Father of pain invites me to act out my own sadomasochistic drives, not only in everyday reality but also beyond: in sacrificial devotion, mortification, and penance. In addition, my sadomasochistic drives are diverted beyond the reality of suffering unto death in the *kingdom of representation* where language can appropriate it: more than in fantasy communion, I become his chosen one, the chosen one of the Other, by the thought and speech that I create around the subject of the father being beaten to death.

The activity of representing-speaking-thinking, attributed to the father in patrilineal societies and which connects me to him, now becomes the privileged realm of sadomasochistic pleasure, the "kingdom," indeed, where suffering burgeons, justifies itself and abates. Along with Freud, *sublimation*[9] is this displacement of pleasure starting with the body and sexual organs in representation. *Perversion and sublimation are the flip and the right sides of this loosening,* if not of this fabulous suspension of the incest taboo induced by the beaten father. No religion, not even that of the Greek gods, has promoted the sublimatory experience so effectively. By the intervention of this fantasy of the beaten father, Christianity has maintained, on one hand, the inaccessible ideal (Jesus is a God, thus a forbidden Father who forbids me to touch Him and to approach him); on the other hand, and without eluding the paradox, he resexualizes also the son-Father ideal that connects me, under the cover of guilt, to His Passion, first through the Eucharist and then by the intense activity of so-called aesthetic representation. Of course, it is only too clear how Christianity was able to construct itself at certain moments of its history as a consecration of vengeance, calling for the crusades, initiating the Inquisition, and inciting pogroms. Let us here try to retain the intrapsychic truth aspect that I would summarize this way: the myth of the being beaten-to-death father states that the incest taboo is more than merely privation of pleasure, since it suggests that arousal skips a beat, and while staying inside me, passes through my sensorial or genital organs to translate into representance and psychic acts: ideality, symbolism, thought. Great artists like Mozart or Picasso experienced the intensity of such a dialectic in the sustained fever of creation. With the Baroque rupture in particular and what came afterward, Catholicism brilliantly promoted it by maintaining and transgressing sexual or carnal taboos and by giving form to this fortunate guilt.

A TRAVERSAL OF THE DEATH DRIVE?

You might be wondering: theater of sadomasochism, does not Jesus as the beaten father free the death drive at the very moment when he claims to "reconcile" it, to distill it further?

Differing in this from other religions that exacerbate the same funda-mentalist offshoots, the Christic knot, in particular in the Roman tradi-tion between desire, suffering, and sublimation, has also encouraged working through, even the analysis of these deadly extravagances by the mediation of theology, writing, and art. "Liberated," the death drive thus found itself on the road to its own deliverance, and to its semiotic and symbolic unloading.

Yet it is another moment, essential to the "a father is being beaten to death" fantasy, that, strictly speaking, not only liberates the death drive as a sadomasochistic aggressiveness but, still further, combats this drive in the profound and radical Freudian sense, as an *unbinding*[10]of the drive-based links and of the living being itself. This is what the Gospel implies when God the Father in person espouses nothingness.

In the Passion, when the reins of Eros and Thanatos are released, the identity of the body and even the spirit gets undone, passing from suffer-ing into nothingness. But a supreme difficulty awaits us here: Christ is not only a Son abandoned by his Father ("My God, why have you abandoned me?") nor a beaten father, but really and truly *the* Father ("Had you rec-ognized me you would have known the Father") [John 14:7–12], who died, as Paul wrote ("Christ is dead") [Romans 14:9], before rising from the dead. Let us stop at this death that Catholic theologians approach pru-dently but to which Protestants and Orthodox Christians seem to give more importance.[11]

In Greek, this "descent of the Father himself to the deepest recesses of the earth" is referred to as *kenosis*, which means "nonbeing," "nothing-ness," "inanity," "invalidity"; but also "senseless," "deceptive" (cf. the adjective *kenos* for "empty," "useless," "vain"; and the verb *kenoun* for "to purge," "to cut," "to annihilate"). Beyond the beaten father's sadomasoch-ism, we are confronted with the suspension of the paternal function itself, that is, the canceling out of the capacity of representing-symbolizing that this function upholds in psychoanalytical theory. For the theologian, it is no more and no less than a matter of the death of God. In philosophical terms and in reference to the death drive as a "carrier wave" of all drives, we can say: only "Thanatos is," as Gilles Deleuze wrote, meaning: only nothingness is.[12]

In the Christic Passion, it is God himself who "suffers." Such a scan-dal, which theology is hesitant to confront, prefigures modern times up against the proclamation of "the death of God." "God is dead, God himself is dead" is a prodigious, tremendous representation "that presents to representation the deepest abyss of schism."[13]

Barely evoked, however, Christianity refuted the death of the father and/or of the symbolic function in the miracle of the Resurrection! What therapeutic power in this linkage of recognized-desired death and its denial! What a prodigious restoration of the ability to think and desire is offered by this harsh exploration of suffering to the point of losing one's sanity and even dying! It is because the Father and the Spirit themselves are mortal, canceled out through the intervention of the Man of pain who thinks even in his suffering to death that they can be reborn. Thought can begin again: can this be an ultimate variant of the freedom that Christian suffering announces? Nietzsche did not fail to notice that this yielding to *kenosis* endowed human and divine death on the cross with "this freedom, this sovereign detachment" that places suffering "above any resentment."[14]

With *kenosis*, we are confronted with the *sacred*, understood as a traversal by the thought of the unthinkable, of nothingness, of uselessness, of the vain, and of the senseless. Mysticism already ventured into these areas through the voice of Meister Ekhart: "I ask God to leave me free of God."[15] But perhaps Saint John of the Cross best expressed this presence of the impossible in the tension of desire and thought, this nothingness that punctuates the "vain pursuit"[16] specific to the need to believe. Anthropology, ethnology, sociology: the humanities try to approach this "return of the sacred," without seeking to bring back new variations of the paternal function nor without exploring the possibility of maintaining the work of meaning in the modern subject threatened by fragmentation, criminality, and delirium. Is this not, on the other hand, the task of psychoanalytic interpretation? From *Black Sun* and up to *Hatred and Forgiveness*,[17] I have been suggesting that *interpretation* is forgiveness: neither the religious nor the sacred, but the possibility of giving a sense to non-sense, of deciphering desire and/or hatred through the elucidation of transference in countertransference and vice versa.

To put it another way, Christianity both admitted and denied the putting to death of the Father.

Christianity promoted, or tried to promote, a direct relation with the Father comparable to Freud's "primal identification." This is the experience of faith. We know its wonderful legacy in works of the imagination. I claim that the survival of faith does not only concern the religious domain but also answers to the social need to believe: thus this lack of pragmatism, this fervor that surges in riots and revolutions, so frequent in post-Catholic societies like France, which can be interpreted as so many sadomasochistic appeals to the loving Father.[18]

"I" renounces incest in order to rediscover the desiring and desirable father as a symbolic father and to join him by an appropriation of the symbolic capacity itself. This new beginning ("In the beginning there was the Word" [John 1:1]) is suffering: the child who speaks must renounce his desires and repair his guilt, the child who speaks is a "beaten child" (psychoanalytic models, like Freud's "separation-frustration" and Klein's "depressive position" attest to this).

And yet, by relieving this infantile, incestual, and speaking humanity—and speaking humanity is a suffering humanity—by the suffering of the Father who is reincarnated as his Son to be beaten to death, Jesus shakes up the capital constituents of the human condition that *Homo religious* bequeathed us. Psychoanalysis is the heir of this psychosexual construction and undertakes its deconstruction. How? Incest, with both parents, and more specifically with the Father, is not only an unconscious desire, it becomes a preconscious desire. The splice between the two scenarios, the "beaten-to-death" and the "resurrection," can also act as an impasse and an inhibition; but in the context of an optimal oedipal complex, it could also stimulate the sublimatory performance of the subject.[19]

For the girl: "Transforming oneself, rebuilding, rebirth have never exceeded my powers," we can say with Colette.[20] Psychoanalytic inquiry as well as detective novels, which enable us to discover the origin of desire-to-the-death, could provide a gateway to this rebirth.

For the boy: the identification with the beaten-to-death Father and his resurrection represents the anxiety-producing threat of passivation and feminization while it could at the same time calm it. Thus the optimal working through of homosexuality opens up the possibility of thought that is not mere calculation but a resource for the imagination.

In this context, ancient heroism, and in another way, monotheistic man's phallic all-powerfulness, appear to be untenable. "Superman does not exist," says the beaten Father-Son, because all sovereignty is symbolic and depends on the sadomasochism of elucidated desires. The libertines of the Enlightenment and up to Sadian hyperbole never stopped developing this baroque breakthrough. Following the Counter-Reformation, this gave rise to a new renaissance in Europe and continued with the rise of the bourgeoisie and the ambiguities of its moral code, reconciling the law with transgressions.

As for repression, there is no way out of the *père-version* other than to reverse it in *sublimation*. Since the subject can only be *père-verse* (*père-version* is in the process of being depenalized and depathologized in modern secular society), he can only become a glorious body if he maintains himself in the ideal (ideal Father), while resexualizing it and working through the sadomasochistic desire. And it is art, thought as art or art as thought, in all its variants and modulations to come that will form its element and environment.

As for the death of the Father that crowns this sadomasochistic course, it de-eroticizes the incestual passion, leaving the possibility of another psychic experience gaping: the experience of the abolition of the symbolic and/or paternal power (*kenosis*). This nihilistic possibility brings with it all the risks of psychic, social, and even biological disorganization the global era already entails. But it is also laden with all the libertarian unknowns generated by the traversal of the religious: contingent on reinventing new variants of this "loving intelligence" with which Spinoza identified God, and to which the love of transference is currently our modest and arduous counterweight. Through interpretation and working through that are woven in transference-countertransference, with and beyond sublimation, the Father dies and is reborn in an infinity of moving figures in me, if and only if I am a subject in analysis.

In conclusion, following these psychoanalytic and cultural considerations, I would like to summarize, in a more general way, my reading of *Totem and Taboo*, with regard to "A Child Is Being Beaten." Freud noted that the prohibition of incest, on which human culture is founded, begins with the discovery by brothers that the father is an animal to be killed. Of Totem and Taboo, only the Taboo has been preserved, to be transformed into rules for the exchange of women, into laws, names, language, and meaning.

After the Holocaust, the Freudian approach was the only one that emphasized the sadomasochistic desire for the law of the father that feeds the moral order, as well as the dark Eros that subtends *père-version* and the sublimation of *Homo religiosus* as a double of *Homo sapiens.*

The beginning of the third millennium, with the collapse of paternal and political authority and the massive return of the need to believe, enables us to perceive something else: the Freudian "dead father," a condition of existence for the human condition, died on the cross two thousand years ago. The founder of psychoanalysis, who was a man of the Enlightenment, began by putting love on the couch. He went back in time to the love of the father and the mother, taking the gamble (which is not a matter of faith but rather of play between needing to believe and desiring to know) that "I" can free myself from my genitors, and even from myself and my loves, provided I am in analysis, perpetual dissolution, in transference-countertransference. This supposes that there is not only one dead Father, but figures of paternity and of numerous loves in which I take pleasure, and which I kill and resurrect when I speak, love, and think. Before you, psychoanalysts, I argue that the need to believe is an ensemble of *impassable père-versions* of the speaking being, and that the *mère-versions* themselves—successively discouraged and encouraged by feminism, contraception, and various forms of medically assisted procreation—are no exception to the rule. And finally, that the "clash of religions" could be clarified, if not elucidated, by our psychoanalytic listening.

INFINITE ARE THE METAMORPHOSES OF THE DEAD FATHER . . .

It was thought that "Big Mother" had replaced the oedipal Father. But the truth is that the Freudian analyst, whether a man or a woman, works with a new version of the "paternal function," which is neither totemic animal, nor Laius/Oedipus, nor Abraham-Isaac, nor Jesus and his abandoning and resurrecting father. In the love-hate relationship of transference, the father is not only loved and hated, put to death and resurrected, as the scriptures would have it. He is literally atomized on our couches and nevertheless incorporated by the analysand. This continuous dissolution-recomposition for which the analyst stands as the guarantor enables the analysis of drug addiction, somatization, criminality, and other borderline cases. The subject of these "new maladies of the soul"[21] emerges with a paradoxical identity, which suggests the Brownian motion of Jackson Pollock's drip paintings called "One."

Where has One gone? Am I still One when I analyze and when I am an analyst? Definitely, yes, but my identity remains undecidable, deprived of an immobile center and freed from deadly repetition. A little like serial music or an improvised dance with an underlying order nonetheless, as in l'Ouvert. Free associations, as Freud wanted, alluding to a long history.

I read in this the troubling, fascinating secret of European culture. This Old World humanity has been shaped by its diversities that Christianity has been generating over the past twenty centuries and with which secularization, along with the social sciences, continues to cope. Psychoanalysis seems to be the surreptitiously best equipped to advance an interpretation of this secret, this hold, like those of other religions. We can thus offer an enlightened space where elucidation takes the place of these deadly confrontations and where regression competes with the explosion of the death drive, which threaten globalized humanity today.

8

MATERNAL EROTICISM

SEARCHING FOR RELIANCE

Living and thinking the maternal as an *eroticism*: would that be just as scandalous as speaking of *infantile sexuality*? One might think so, as so many social crises pander to the maternal presumed to satisfy all needs, while some hasty interpretations wrongly suggest that today's psychoanalysis assigns sexuality exclusively to the woman lover, granting to the maternal only the untenable destiny of the object relation.

The principal reason for this difficulty in properly recognizing the maternal we are dealing with here is first in the very conception of *eroticism* that took root with the invention of the unconscious before acquiring its definitive form with the couple Eros/Thanatos, binding/unbinding, which Freud, as early as 1911, formulated as a "psychic revolution of materiality" in *Formulations on the Two Principles of Mental Functioning*.[1] In line with J-M. Hirt, I see in this Freudian discovery a gradual differentiation of materiality and psychization,[2] contemporaneous with work on narcissism and psychosis;[3] it would find in Lou Andreas-Salomé a modulation of passion.

What did Lou really say? Several of her provocative works anticipated the Eros of the second topography. It should be recalled that without forsaking anything of his earlier theory of sexuality, Freud defined Eros as follows: "by bringing about a more and more far-reaching combination of the particles into which living substance is dispersed, *eros* aims at *complicating* life and at the same time, of course, at *preserving* it,"[4] thus paving the way for ontogenesis and phylogenesis. Sexuality in this meaning of eroticism, for Lou, who developed and amplified the master's words, is "what ruptures the limits of our ego,"[5] "reestablishes . . . contact with the original, fleshly being,"[6] and reconnects "materiality" rather than "distinguishing us from it." And she invited Rilke, Freud, and all her readers to "reach out, groping into space . . . and into our very bodies, with confidence, like *one hand stretched out toward the other* . . . with all the 'inwardness of a creature' for whom this relation is no longer obfuscated."[7] This was before attributing to the *maternal* precisely this capacity to *establish* and *overcome* the "pathological split" in order "to actualize the connection" between internal and external reality, matter and symbol, masculine and feminine, and "to restore the loss from which the process of individuation suffers."

Maurice Merleau-Ponty would use the same metaphor of "two hands touching,"[8] one belonging to the *ego* and the other to *objectal reality* in his *Phenomenology of Perception*, to illustrate a subjective experience where the interior/exterior, matter/spirit gap is reworked by this "reciprocal insertion and this interlacing of one with the other," which the philosopher ultimately called "flesh," "the transition from the mute world to the speaking world."[9]

A century after 1911, which I have taken as emblematic of the encounter between Freud and Andreas-Salomé, and I am including Merleau-Ponty, the development of psychoanalysis enables us to have a real debate about my "theoretical fable" (this three-way meeting) without the risk of betraying psychoanalysis with either a spiritualist detour or a reduction of the libido to genetics. On the contrary, this is an attempt to give back to *maternal eroticism* its biopsychic complexity, for the well-being of the child no less than for the emancipation of the woman—in and by the maternal as well.

Biology itself is today confronted with maternal eroticism (and thus with psychoanalysis) when it tries to explain certain hormonal upheavals in the pregnant woman, even beginning with her desire to conceive. Might there be a "permeability" between biology and psychism? While medical literature points out the high rates of mortality and fetal risk in diabetic women, isolated clinical experiments report that some diabetics, on an individual basis and with certain types of diabetes, actually improve their glycemic control during pregnancy or when planning a pregnancy. Here, then, is a new direction for psychoanalytic research: what is the correlation between the intensity of phantasmatic and hallucinatory functions *and* certain biological changes in the pregnant woman?

Based on conversations with my colleagues and my own clinical and personal experience, I will try to sketch out some elements of this maternal eroticism that I will call *reliance*.[10] I hypothesize that *reliance* is a specific economy of the drives such that, *countercathected* by psychic representation and thus *fixed* by *inscriptions*, the energy of this *originary split* both maintains and spans primary and secondary repressions. Without necessarily displacing them as in a psychotic-type regression, maternal eroticism renders the fixation of the life drive as well as the death drive both problematic and available and puts them in the service of the living as an "open structure," linked to others and to the environment. Analyzing maternal eroticism in this way thus leads me then to posit at the outset the extreme fragility of this economy and investigate its translatability.

I will deal with the reasoning that points out the reliance on *the mother's side* where psychoanalytic advances seem more tentative, compared to the exploration of transitionality on *the child's side* where the future subject's autonomy is worked out.

LIFE'S "STATE OF EMERGENCY," THE LIBIDO, PRIMARY REPRESSION, AND THE SUBLIMINAL CYCLE

1. By *reliance* I mean *experience* in the double meaning it has in German. Experience (in the sense of *Erlebnis*) brings to life a new preobject: an emergence, a flash, a fulguration. Progressively, in its second phase, experience becomes understanding, patient knowledge (*Erfahrung*). Whether she is prepared or not by a desire for motherhood, every expectant mother is immediately overtaken by biopsychic events like pregnancy, labor, and breast-feeding, so that maternal reliance is not only irreducible to an irrevocably social "symbolic function" like the "paternal function," but it is also a *passion*. Modern biology uses the term *passion* to designate the transformation of *emotions* (attachment or aggression) into *love* and its corollary: *hatred*. Narcissism and/or object relation,

tenderness and depersonalization, even psychic catastrophe, "suffered" and "endured" but not "passive," passion is in the end integrated into the logics of the unconscious—so as to better pierce it.[11] Like the "dark energy" in modern astrophysical theories of the cosmos that break up the Universe into the *Multiverse*, maternal reliance *naturally contains the void, as well as the collapse of passion*. The "I" created in maternal passion from then on becomes the "multiverse."

Yet this *passion* is also a *vocation*. Never deprived of signifyingness for the mother as a speaking being, this passion is inscribed in the cultural heritage and in the imaginary and symbolic capacities of each singular mother, capacities that *give meaning and signification* to the drives and to the pregnancy that transform them.

Passion-vocation. This biosychical zone that surrounds maternal reliance defies rationality and haunts philosophy and literature. Plato alluded to it in *Timaeus* and apologized for using "bastard reasoning." Space before space, *chora*, he said, is both nurturer-and-devourer, prior to the One, to the Father, to the word, and even to the syllable: a modality of *sense* before *signification*, and what I call "semiotic."[12] Colette's intuition takes hold of these *metaphors* that, through writing laden with sensations and affects, become *metamorphoses*: the writer "procreates" the flora and fauna of the countryside, her mother Sido, and even the flesh of the world through writing. Nevertheless, this belonging of the speaking subject to materiality that she calls *flowering*[13] is not Lou Andreas-Salomé's fulgurant ecstasy in sexual orgasm. The self-exile suggested in *Reliance* is an enduring ex-stasis. It punctuates time for death in a temporality of new beginnings: jubilatory affirmations and anxious annihilations that literally put me outside myself and, without annihilating me, multiply me. In the face of this multiverse of maternal eroticism as reliance, facing its risks, its endurances, and its creativities, psychoanalysis seems to hesitate. We relate them to concepts that demarcate a *universal subjectivity* (originally masculine), like narcissism, phallic assumption, masochism, borderline states, psychosis, etc. That is how we consolidate *Homo sapiens* and its internal double, *Homo religiosus*. Do we dare propose new objects of analysis, when the practice confronts us with the unknowns and difficulties of reliance?

2. Before it becomes a "container" from which the creation of *psychic links* are detached,[14] maternal eroticism (passion/vocation) with its

biopsychical horizon is a *state*: a "state of emergency of life," the *Not des Lebens* that Heidegger and Lacan deal with.[15] It is an always already psychosomatic quality of energy in the speaking being, given and received so as to be up to what is "necessary for the conservation of life." This state called "*Das Ding*," the Thing, would be "foreign," sometimes hostile (in the sense of an absolute exteriority to the subject), outside of the signified; it is a "gap" between me and the world, subject and object, a between two. Neither "I" nor "you" but "behind us" and "beyond the object," moving from one "in the direction of," it is an "emotional relation" that the subject experiences as a "primary affect, prior to any repression."

Does this experience, accessible through hallucinations and phantasms, place the subject who undergoes it at the dawn of *originary* repression?[16] The analysis of the early mother-child bonds sometimes leads the analysand to it, who becomes *psyche-soma*[17] in his dependence on the Thing from which he will separate himself: melancholic jouissance at the edge of the road of repression. But what happens if "I" experiences the Thing-itself, this strangeness, the "primal fixated affect" in "originary repression," and "in the direction of" the other, "secondary," repression, that establishes the signifying chain of language? What if "I" clears out, "takes off" into the Thing: what to make of this woman/mother-subject which *looms* at the frontier of originary repression and *seals* her destiny?

More than a frontier, it is really a "primal split" that Freud imagines with this enigmatic "originary repression" that could also be developed as an *anchoring of perception in the symbolic world*. I hypothesize that maternal eroticism inhabits this split. Or, rather, it is a victory over the persisting split that confers this aspect of "natural folly" as well as "natural maturity." How is this possible?

It is possible as a result of the "paternal metaphor" (Lacan's hypothesis) or the "psychic revolution" of materiality (according to Freud, more biological and social). The crystallized unconscious at the threshold of originary repression, Freud says, is not yet verbal but is composed of elements borrowed from the *imaginary*. Let us say it conveys some *imagos*, some unconscious *fantasies*, some *complexes* able to be translated into the mother tongue, or, on the contrary, that resist any translation.

Maternal eroticism surfaces in this strangeness, this regression, this "state of emergency of life." The various logics of maternal reliance that build up over the course of a mother's life attest to that eroticism; they reactivate its dynamics and transmit its traces. And what if it was also *this* that the pathetic "desire for motherhood" seeks—and that the refusal of motherhood refuses—beyond settling scores with the mother's mother, the denial of castration and the harnessing of the paternal penis or even the phallus on this side of the mirror stage? The "horizon" of the Thing in the subject/object gap evokes what Sophocles, in *Antigone*, called Até: the paradoxical frontier, before laws were enacted, a fascinating and yet atrocious place.[18] It is "atrocious" for the emerging consciousness in the "psychic revolution of materiality" that the ego hides from us and defends for us. Até: Hegel and Lacan, make this the beginning of ethics.[19]

In addition, the female *lover's libido* never stops orienting this life urgency—its discharges, negativities, investments, and sublimatory cycles—toward the *drive-based satisfaction*. This libido does not disappear in the mother. If the lover's libido were lacking, *maternal eroticism* would be merely defensive or operative, and it would bring about deficiencies in the child's sexualization, such as its ability to think. Conversely, when the lover's libido diverts (from *seducere*: seduced) its unsatisfied drives onto the child, it is the *mère-version* (using Ilse Barande's expression[20]) that structures the infantile psychic life. But while the lover's libido is dominated by the satisfaction of drives, maternal eroticism deploys (or "tends toward") its libidinal drives as tenderness: beyond abjection and separation, tenderness is the basic affect of reliance.

3. *Discharge* is the second component I have chosen to bring up in what I see as the multiverse of maternal eroticism. It is by *discharge* (*Ausstossung* and *Verwerfung*, rejection and negativity) that the Thing is released from its Thingness and releases another living subject to the world. Freud locates discharges in the development of psychic representation, in the child's thought and language acquisition. But it is maternal eroticism that carries them from the beginning, from the violence of labor in which the mother risks her own psychic and physical integrity, no less than that of the child.

4. This always biopsychic and drive-based violence perpetuates itself in the destiny of the death drive that I call *ab-jection*: the inevitable process of fascination-repulsion, where there is not yet either a subject or an object, or even "objeux" (Francis Ponge anticipating Winnicott), but only "abjects."[21] The child "loses" me ("kills" me) in order to leave me: Orestes before Oedipus. From my side, in order to separate myself from the child

and rebecoming "I," I leave him by "abjecting" him, and at the same time, I abject the Thing in which we were fused, the biopsychical *continuum* I had also become. For psychization to be finalized, and for biopsychical negativity to ensure the creation of links, maternal eroticism lets go of the death drive in the vital process, while connecting itself to it: the maternal transforms the *abjects*, rejected by the death drive, into the not-yet mother-*infans* space, into objects of care, survival, and life.

Always inside and outside, self and other, neither self nor other, an in-between: maternal eroticism separates and connects: hiatus and junction.[22] Thus there is "normal maternal madness,"[23] but also the maternal influence that obstructs the psychic and sexual life of its progenitor and often explodes in hatred: there are multiple symptoms that manifest the paroxysmal disasters of this *ab-jection*, which is a "normal" psychosexual component of maternal eroticism.

5. Is it because of this weight of abjection in maternal eroticism that its structuring role in the constitution of the ego-ideal is not sufficiently considered? The Father of primary identification (*Einfülung*)[24] is an ideal imago of the sexual partner recognized and recomposed by the maternal eroticism that had *invested* him as the loved/loving father of their child. The "I" of the future subject emerges only by the investment (cathexis)/recognition that this "Father of individual prehistory" signifies to me, provided I am connected by the maternal investment in him.

Investment: *Besetzung* (German), *cathexis* (English), from the Sanskrit root *kred-*, *srad-*: credo, credit. Cathexis of the paternity of the loving father, maternal eroticism here *elects* the father of *election*. Because she repeats or repairs the election that her own father has (or has not) signified to her, the maternal Thing adds a new capacity to its aptitude for abjection: that of electing the Third for her/their child. It is a vocation in response to the Other (to the father).

6. Overwhelmed, often desubjectivated by the "state of emergency of life," by the work of abjection and by the exile in election, reliance is clearly the work of the negative. But it couples it with a *fabulous investment in the state of emergency of life* with that negativity, linked to cathexis in physical and psychical *survival*, in the *care* of the living and the *concern* for transmission. Simply put, the negative is at work if—and only if—its *unbinding* is immediately recathected and *reconnected*. That is, maternal eroticism adds this refusal to collapse that cannot be reduced

to a dubious resistance to its secret and natural familiarity with *apoptose* (cellular death that sculpts the living body) while being aware of the masochism it often turns into. *Stabat Mater*: *she holds*. Let us be careful not to see this way of being/tenacity as merely a neurotic or even paranoid defense. Just as the "capacity to be alone" is not only a melancholic indulgence in solitude but also an aptitude to sublimate loss, a wound, or even narcissistic deficiency, so also the capacity of maternal eroticism to accompany the living through the threat of mortality and even death seems to me an integral part of it. She holds: *Stabat Mater*. A phantasm, but it is erected on a psychic and somatic reality as fragile as it is indelible: maternal *reliance*.

7. Two factors within maternal intersubjectivity promote the metabolism of *destructive passion* into *reliant dispassionateness*: what I call the woman's "oedipal biface"[25] and the maternal relation to language. I will not go into the self-analytic or defensive potentialities of these repetitions and displacements of *primary Oedipus* (primary homosexuality with the mother) and *secondary Oedipus* (access to thirdness by the father) that maternal eroticism inscribes in and works through the couple with the loving father, as well as in the primary maternal preoccupation. Let us just say a few words on the subject of the maternal relation to language.

The *child's language acquisition* is a language relearning process by the mother. By speaking the echolalia and her child's language (and thus rediscovering the instinctual foundations of phonation, as Sabina Spielrein has demonstrated), each mother in her own way carries out the Proustian search for "lost time" and step by step resolves the "incongruence" separating affect from cognition—about which the hysteric endlessly complains.

8. A whole *sublimatory cycle* is built on these two pillars, the oedipal biface and language acquisition, where the mother positions herself by differentiating herself from the newborn. I would like to compare it to the sublimatory cycle that Freud observed in emitting and receiving *witticisms*: the emission of "verbal or preverbal enigmatic signifiers": the drive-based withdrawal of the mother, who does not invest in her own message but remains attentive to the child's reaction only; the "incentives" to experimentation, to "traps," to "the right to error." Finally, the mother in return acquires an even greater jouissance from the response of the child whom she idealizes and encourages, through this circulation that is not without a certain perversity.[26]

9. On the other hand, the failure of *dispassionateness* replaces reliance with its opposite: *possession*. Neonaticide and infanticide do not *give* death: they are the work of *possession*. The female genitor, incapable of giving and who commits these acts, has scotomized reliance. She has taken hold of life and made it a nonobject, outside of time and place in her totalitarian narcissism with its ultimate stage of "dead matter," "dead nature," and antimatter; dead body or frozen, without bonds, out of time and out of bounds. More commonly, when the woman's libido makes the child the ultimate goal of her drives, maternal reliance ends up in enthrallment. Would the mother's death, then, be the only event capable of freeing the son from his incestuous fixation? Unless, because of an ultimate debt to maternal possession, does he feel the "right" to die in the guise of recovered freedom?[27] On the other hand, "the good enough mother" tries to inscribe mortality itself, her own and that of her children, in reliance. This results in a dramatic reliance, that of birth/rebirth/rebeginning, which Colette describes this way: "That [in flowering] is where the essential drama resides, and not in death, which is just a banal defeat."[28]

Allow me to rehabilitate this word, *reliance*, in the back and forth between Old French, French, and English. Reliance: *to link, to gather, to join, to put together*; but also *to adhere to, to belong to, to depend on*; and therefore *to trust in, to confide in, to ease ones thoughts and feelings, to assemble*, and *to be yourself*. After highlighting separation and the transitional object with Winnicott, I am convinced of the need to focus today on this maternal side that *maintains* the cathexis and the countercathexis of the libido and Thanatos itself in more and more extensive psychosomatic links, to be re-created. I call a *reliance* this specific eroticism that *maintains the urgency of life and up to the limits of life.*

AN UNREPRESENTABLE JOUISSANCE
WHERE THE VISIBLE SURFACES

"How can we represent reliance?" means: how can it be given a place in the social contract?

Is this a psychoanalytic question? Not really? And yet, yes. The eroticism in question of which social consensus denies the sexual component to retain only an idealized or pathological "love" has such a vulnerable tenacity that only maximum tact could avoid the two recuperations that disfigure it throughout human history and that psychoanalysis perhaps alone tries to escape: *heroization/sacralization*, on one hand (thirty-thousand-year-old ancient mother-goddesses to whom the religiosity of *homo sapiens* pays its debt and settles its score with maternal eroticism by "statufying" it); and on the other hand, *mère-version* (in orgiastic Taoist rites faintly evoked in Georges Bataille's *My Mother*, leaving the mother with only one way out, that is, to kill herself).[29]

Is man capable of desacralizing maternal eroticism? Women themselves indulge in it, with obvious libidinal benefits. Freud's heroism delves into it, nonetheless, in writing that the only way to "free" oneself from the "respect" of woman is to "come to terms with the representation of incest.[30] I would add that, in order to detach oneself from the power of the phantasm, even the phantasm of a maternal sovereignty, it is necessary to go backward, with incest, to the *mirror stage* itself.[31] Some people, like Lewis Carroll, have nevertheless risked it. But to get to the other side of the mirror, he transforms himself into a little girl, Alice: an anagram of Lewis—his maternal side? While Céline, brave explorer of a generalized abjection, immolates himself in political compromise and the Godless Apocalypse.[32]

Today two competing versions of the maternal take issue with the deep logic of maternal eroticism and impose it, without sacralizing it: the gesture that traces the movement of the flesh toward the image, before and beyond sound (Venus, fig. 2.1); the emergence of Chinese writing in the "mother of the world" (fig. 2.3); and Sarah's laughter (figs. 2.5, 2.6). This laughter alters her, shows her to be double: incredulous and/or confident. It keeps her available in the crack between believing and not believing. But Sarah, smiling at her Isaac (who laughs), dies by taking on herself the death of the son, he himself saved, because of the same *Akeda*. It is therefore by the anguish of what is closest, at the deepest level of self, that the maternal, according to Sarah, seals the covenant.

Civilization's unease today lies in the hands of these two forms of maternal eroticism: the Chinese mother's calligraphic ease, in the globalized context, and the wisdom of Sarah, willing to die for laughing at fertility and immortality. Like a line from Antigone, Sarah anticipates Mary in the Pietà and the round of smiles joining da Vinci's Virgin and Child with Saint Anne.

DETOTALIZED UNIVERSE

Have Mary's blessedness, the promise of the nativity, and the maternal jouissance held in man's maternal side that pervade Western Christendom's aesthetic sublime (fig. 2.7) definitively vanished, as the paintings of Max Beckmann (1884–1950), *Birth* (1937; fig. 2.8) and *Death* (1938; fig. 2.9), attest to?[33] In 1937 Freud had already published *Beyond the Pleasure Principle* (1920), and Otto Rank, *The Trauma of Birth* (1924); Melanie Klein had discovered the "depressive position" in 1934 and the "paranoid-schizoid" in 1936; Winnicott had begun his second analysis with Joan Riviere (1936) and had only published his first book, *Clinical Notes on Disorder in Childhood* (1931). In 1935 Bion had undertaken the analysis of Samuel Beckett that lasted only two years: while listening to Jung lecture at the Tavistock Clinic, Beckett realized he had "never been properly born," broke with Bion, who pressured him to take some distance from his mother, and decided that his "duty was to his mother" and to literature, waiting for Godot in the trash-can of old age.

Today this deconstruction takes other paths (Kleinian sociologists of the Labor Party, novel-writing mothers). After making sexuality our *logos* and our God, and the paternal *phallus* into the guarantor of identity, psychoanalysis today encourages us to revitalize our ambitions for freedom in more mobile, more archaic regions, yet no less rich-with-potential regions, where the One (identity) does not achieve being or is not content with being simply One.

It was thought that women wanted to be free by keeping themselves from being mothers. We now see that women want to be free to decide to be, or not to be, mothers. Many who want to be mothers turn to medically assisted pregnancies, willingly and without reservation: is this because the presubjective side of feminine eroticism familiarizes them with this *dispossession of self* that science requires at the most private level? Although we have heard them, we have yet to find the right balance between being attentive to the individual demand, scientific prowess, and a given ethical moment of social tolerance.

By analyzing the history of established religions, Freud identified *religiosity,* or *the need to believe,* as a universal element of psychic experience that he endlessly deconstructed through the *desire to know*—even including the "infidels" that Jean-Michel Hirt analyzes in his trilogy.[34] The *reliance* specific to maternal eroticism reveals a logically and chronologically prior biopsychical economy, and just as universal. Reliance is a separate dimension of *religere*, even opposed to its laws and powers.

HERETHIC

It is not because secularization is the only civilization lacking a discourse on the maternal that religions and religiosity contain the truth or the trace of reliance. They are rather *symptoms of its repression* that psychoanalysis flushes out in our metaphysical heritage. It is up to us to create new metapsychological concepts so as to develop—by listening to the sexuality of the woman lover—*the elucidation and support of maternal eroticism* in all its specificity. Without that, the emancipation of the woman-subject is fated to be no more than an ethics-less ideology. While love (for Spinoza) is the intimate side of ethics, maternal eroticism is not an ethics but seems to us to be like a *herethic* of love.[35] Thus, far from being censored, the urgency of *eros* countercathected (fixated, psychized) in this new other ("my other"), the child frees the death drive (unbinding) itself and gains its libidinal satisfaction only by relinking this drive-based disunification with the pleasure of vital care and the sublimatory cycle.

"The free woman is just being born," wrote Simone de Beauvoir in *The Second Sex*.[36] No woman will be free as long as we lack an ethics of the maternal. This ethics is just being born; it will be a herethics of reliance.

9

SPEAKING IN PSYCHOANALYSIS

From Symbols to Flesh and Back Again

W hat speech in psychoanalysis?" I am intentionally reformulating the task of the two rapporteurs of the Congress,[1] "The Talking Cure."[2] Because it is this question they are answering when, far from settling for this metapsychological discourse that is unfortunately increasingly becoming the secret code of psychoanalysis, they put the theorization of "speech in analysis" within the vast field of "studies of the mind." They do that while also calling for a *new return* to Freud that enables us to better differentiate speech in psychoanalysis from the "cognitive unconscious" or "philosophical deconstruction." They are helping to make this traditional meeting a veritable epistemological event that could take place only in the context of French and francophone psychoanalysis. Let me explain.

WHAT IS MEANT BY "FLESH"?

When the disciplines of phenomenology, and then semiology, lent an ear to the Freudian discovery of the unconscious—but also to the "gay science" of language brought by the modern "great writers"—a revolution was, and still is, underway concerning the understanding of what "speech" means. It is a question of crossing the surface of the "language" object, made of signs (words) and predicative syntheses (logic, grammar), to aim for what Husserl called the *hylé*, the material left outside of the "putting into parentheses" in the act of signifying. Merleau-Ponty accomplished this upheaval in researching a "prereflexive" state of thought that increases communication with the world (with the Being), where nature and the mind intersect: a "passage from the silent world to the speaking world" that the philosopher described this way: "The seen world is not 'in' my body and my body is not in the visible world . . ., flesh applied to flesh, the world does not surround it nor is it surrounded by it . . .; there is a reciprocal insertion and intertwining of them with each other."[3] "Flesh" was thus defined as a "chiasma"[4] between the ego and the world, leading him to his *Phenomenology of Perception*.[5] But perception/sensation[6] could be introduced into the linguistic sciences only when they were beginning to develop around the "subject of the enunciation" and, a fortiori, around the subject of the enunciation worked on by the unconscious.

Thus, when Emile Benveniste, the first linguist who wrote "Remarks on the Function of Language in Freudian Theory,"[7] turned his interest to "opposite meanings of primitive words," it was in no way to validate Carl Abel's etymological speculations—where Freud had sought a justification to his theory that there is no negation in the unconscious. Benveniste's article calls attention to the fact that the same word does not signify two opposite "meanings" but rather two "perceptions" by the same speaking subject when he moves in space.[8] This analysis suggests that there are vestiges of primitive languages found in today's communication codes that, like those of dreams and the unconscious (that of the Id and not unconscious representations), carry sensorial quasi-signs. That meant that the sensation-perception of a pre- or translinguistic "acting" of the speaking subject in the world was included in the object "language."

Antoine Culioli's linguistic theory deepened this perspective in taking up the ancient notion of the Greek Stoics, the *lekton*—forgotten by the "sign," according to Saussure—that is, the *signifiable*. Indeed, the linguistic sign[9] does not refer to an opaque referent-object but through it to an open ensemble made up of sensations-affects-drives that reveal the conscious/unconscious negotiation necessary in the subject's "act of signifying." This approach brings to mind the Freudian model of the sign: representations of words vs. representations of things,[10] provided one adds that in psychoanalysis the unconscious "thing" is never "in itself" but rather a thing of desire, thus of "enaction" (of acting):[11] the "representation of thing" is contextualized and acted and, consequently, gives itself right away in what Daniel Stern calls a "prenarrative envelope."[12] The linguist thus discovers that language itself can function as a predicative articulation of quasi-signs and micro narratives that are not just metaphors but unleash a "more-than-metaphoric" sensorial experience: I would say a metamorphic experience. The "signifiable" will be a mix of sensations, affects, and cultural memory: for example, *au ras des pâquerettes, qui dort dine,* or *avoir les yeux plus gros que le ventre.*[13] This creates the charm and magic of this identity link of the mother or national tongue, but also its power of subjugation, the double of fascination and horror.[14]

The signifiable pushed to hallucinatory metamorphosis (of which the speaking subject bears the onto- and phylogenetic mnemonic traces) becomes—by the intervention of language—a coded and transmissible metaphoricity in the language system itself. But metaphoricity finds its maximal expansion in what our culture considers a "literary style." Here the "simultaneity of the sensorial and verbal mnemonic traces" belonging to quasi-signs (sense-and-sensation) acts in a surprising way, defying the clichés of the national code. That is the economy of the passage in "Mr. Seguin's Goat," which interested René Diatkine and Laurent Danon-Boileau: "Suddenly the wind freshened, the mountain turned violet. It was night."[15] Here where the speaking subject does not exist—for Blanchette is frozen with fear—the *sensations* of the outside world into which she projects herself impose on the reader the *affects* of worry, danger, and fear. The metaphor metamorphosizes the reader by situating him in the chiasma between the outside world and the inner feeling: in the "flesh of the world."

Our rapporteur is correct to pay particular attention: it is not only a question of an arrangement of words but of a condensation of the mnemonic traces that must be brief,[16] even if these "holes" in the signifying chain can be strung together infinitely, as in Proust's sentences and little margin notes.

Baudelaire, who had an affection for coenesthesis,[17] brilliantly commented on the tipping over of the *sign* into the *sensation* and, through it, into *desubjectivation* under the influence of hashish, wine, or simply, if I can say such a thing, the sublimatory act called "inspiration." For example, "Your eye fixes itself upon a tree . . . that which in the brain of a poet [insinuating: a bad one] would only be a very natural comparison becomes in yours a reality. At first you lend to the tree your passions, your desire, or your melancholy; its creakings and oscillations become yours, and soon you are the tree."[18] I myself do not write metaphors, I transmit metaphors to you, Baudelaire says in essence. Daniel Widlöcher takes up the term: "The psychoanalytic past is not registered in time but in a forever-there, an infinite universe of metamorphoses."[19]

I agree with him. When an autistic child melts in front of a puddle of water, he *does not make a metaphor*: he *acts a metamorphosis* in the sensorial chiasma between a non-me and the nonworld. He is in a failure of signs, for lack of a "symbolic thirdness." He is in the presubjective flesh that Merleau-Ponty called the "flesh of the world."

On the other hand, when the analyst "verbalizes" this emersion in the flesh of the world by a metaphor (in thinking and saying that "the puddle" makes the autistic person feel his unnamable anxiety), the autistic person may be able, perhaps, little by little, by dint of transference of his infantile sexuality on his therapist, and if his "type of autism" allows him to understand the interpretation, to advance, himself, toward an experience of quasi-signs.

As for the writer whose "force of language" we admire, he "succeeds where the autistic person fails."[20] He has experienced "metamorphoses" in an autistic way[21]—I am thinking of the Proust narrator enveloped in lilac perfume in a urinal, or in the "pink and quivering matter"[22] of a stained glass window. The writer nonetheless succeeds in formulating these sensorial intensities in the form of metaphors that he calls "transubstantiations"[23] (a "holy" word borrowed from the Catholic Mass). They come about through the narrative structure that either hosts or can be torn by the insights into the "unconscious thing" in which—as in the free association of the analytic treatment—compacted sensations of drive-based acting transit via the narrative envelope. The "madeleine" episode—in the first drafts, the delicious "madeleine" was no more than a dry "toast"—is overdetermined by a crisscrossing of several narrative strands:[24] a scene in which the narrator's mother was reading a novel by George Sand, where the incestuous mother's name is Madeleine, including the secretly coded ritual for homosexuals of the time, who, to profane the Catholic communion, ate toast dipped in urine that they called "tea" in the urinal slang of the time.

Also think of Colette: "one" does not remember the plots of her tales, mundane stories of jealousy and adultery, but one does recall the wow effect (to speak like Danon-Boileau), the sensorial impact of her metaphors-metamorphoses that move us from the strata of the linguistic sign in the sensation of the object mentioned, in the pleasure felt from the contact of its fragrance or color, and that become as many "clues" of the affect of solitude and despair: "Black rose, a compote of fragrances."[25] "From now on I am that solitary and upright woman, a woman like a sad rose which carries itself the more proudly for having been stripped of its leaves."[26] You can hear it: the emphasis on alliterations fosters the rupture of the abstract contract between the "signifier" and the "signified" and loosens the afflux of the affective and sensorial memory.[27]

But it is Artaud who, starting from psychosis, focuses on the fact that the fine film of sensations themselves adjoins an otherwise more rebellious, drive-based turbulence: "Feelings are nothing / nor are ideas / everything is in motility / of which like for the rest, humanity only took a specter."[28]

Freudian conceptualizations on the paths of the mnemonic trace in the *Magic Notebook* (1925), Derrida's works on writing, "trace" or "impression" prior to vocal language,[29] those of André Green on the heterogeneity of the drive-supported signifier,[30] and others whom I cannot take up here come to mind to help us interpret these literary or clinical advances in the *sensorial substratum of language* as relays between *signs* and *drives*. I would add my own research on the translinguistic "semiotic" (as opposed to the "symbolic," which occurs with the acquisition of signs and syntax): the "semiotic" mode of language condenses and moves the drive paths that metamorphose the subjective affects into stories on desubjectivized, even prepsychic, sensorial experiences.[31]

How do these meetings between analysts' clinical experience and certain modern approaches of language fit into Freud's language models? Or, rather, how do Freud's language models modify them?

FREUD'S THREE LANGUAGE MODELS

I use the word "models" because at least three can be identified:[32]

- The asymptote model
- The optimistic model
- The signifyingness model, which buttresses language and shows itself to be accessible through it in transference.

A *first model*, which had its origins in *On Aphasia* (1881) and *The Origins of Psychoanalysis* (1885), points up the inadequacy and the imbalance between the sexual and the verbal. Sexuality cannot say itself—entirely. And this *asymptote* induces, if not an absence of translation, then at least a deficient translation between unconscious representations of objects (which will become *thing-representations*) and those of words (*word-representations*). This deficiency generates symptoms that need an intermediary, another language, "speaking in psychoanalysis," if they are to be lifted. I would like to stress the heterogeneity[33] inherent in this "first language model" that Freud developed later with the theorization of the *drive* and of its *figurability*.

The psychoanalytic model that I call *optimistic* came on the scene with the institution of the armchair/couch treatment and its fundamental rule of "free association," clearly formulated in *The Interpretation of Dreams* (1900). It is close to the structural conception of language and was the model that Lacan drew on, except that the structural approach to language in psychoanalysis would, curiously enough, keep silent about this Freudian innovation that took over. And yet the invitation to the patient to provide a *narrative* profoundly modified the classical conception of language: it is this representation of *acting* and/or its unconscious substratum, *fantasy*, and not *signs* and *syntax*, that allows for this modification. What is happening? Because "from the outset" it carries fantasies ("prenarrative envelopes"); language possesses a signifiable that language sciences overlook: *desire* and *drives*. Freud said that language was "preconscious,"[34] which implies—already in *The Interpretation of Dreams*—that it is a language of "contact," as Dominique Clerc's report makes clear.

A turning point in Freud's thought occurred between 1912 and 1914 that profoundly modified his conception of language and, faced with resistance to analysis, launched a "third model": with *Totem and Taboo* (1912), "On Narcissism: An Introduction" (1914), "Mourning and Melancholia" (1917), by introducing the death wish, "Beyond the Pleasure Principle" (1920), and finally, *Moses and Monotheism* (1939).

Two aspects of this third model are of interest for "speaking in psychoanalysis": first, the *fluidity* of the topographical concepts that promotes both resistance and catastrophe as well as psychic reorganizations; second, as if to optimize this fluidity, Freud's concern to focus listening and interpretation on the analysis of the *paternal function*, its unbearable fragility, in particular. This was forgetting, or underestimating, the mad endurance of the maternal vocation, but that will be a subject for another conference.

The Ego, wrote Freud in *The Ego and the Id*, consists of *verbal traces* and *perceptions:* "perceptions may be said to have the same significance for the Ego as instincts have for the Id."[35] This copresence of perception and verbalization exists henceforth as a "region" or a "district" bordering the Id (deep unconscious) and the Superego (consciential), and consequently, as the *object* par excellence of the treatment. As the aim of interpretation is to bring the *Ego* into being where the *Id* was, it is clear that speech in the treatment is supposed *to transform into perception/verbalization* the inexpressible mnemonic traces of the more or less traumatic "thing alone," but it can be modulated in the oedipian transference helped by the treatment. Freudian theory and practice also mean that in substance the analytic interpretation will always be in view of the Oedipus complex, not to be confused with a formulation reducible to the Oedipus complex. From the flesh to signs, or vice versa, and because he deepened his analysis of the paternal function, Freud constantly set limits but also openings-passages-porosities in the signifying process.

Freud never stopped thinking up to the last words of his final apophtegme (1938) that "speaking in psychoanalysis" was indefinitely capable of reaching the drives via the sensations concerning mysticism: "Mysticism is the obscure self perceptions of the realm outside the Ego, of the Id."[36] This testament needs to be set alongside his *New Introductory Lectures* (1932–33): "Perception may be able to grasp (*erfassen*) happenings in the depths of the Ego and in the Id."[37] Let us be clear that what distinguishes psychoanalytic treatment from the mystic hole is that, for mystics, the *Ego* has disappeared in favor of the *Id* that perceives itself. Mystical raptus is limited to the glimpse (vision) which makes an *instantaneous* breach ("*psychoanalysis of the instant,*" wrote D. Widlöcher) in verbalization; it leaves the thing perceived, and the underlying drive, to act in silence, before Eros makes noise again, leading the mystic to invent a language, a writing. On the contrary, analysis is a *processual event,* temporal and interactive, continually constructing/deconstructing the oedipal link.

Question: what is the *specifically psychoanalytic framework* that distinguishes "speaking in psychoanalysis" from the esthetic or mystical raptus?

The analytic treatment, in substance, reveals to its analysand that there is meaning (of the symbolic), and it is the Oedipus complex that constitutes its inter- and intrapsychic support. But meaning (the symbolic), and the Oedipus complex with it, is neither a transcendental imperative nor an absolute norm. We can deconstruct and renew them, by analyzing the law and love in transference-countertransference. Without any roadmap other than the ability, acquired in this experience, to open language to its heterogeneous doubles (semiotics), sensation and drive, and to flesh. The Oedipus complex thus understood through the behavioral scheme, like a never accomplished becoming of the speaking identity bordered by catastrophes, collapses, and rebirths, proves to be a formidable extension of the field of speech: a *signifying process* to endlessly reconstruct. And it is this *tragic* (one cannot insist enough) *oedipian destiny of Homo sapiens* that structures the *ethics of psychoanalysis* that Freud outlined toward the end of his life (*Analysis Terminable and Interminable*, 1937), at the same time that he laid the foundation for *analytical listening and interpretation*. He helped us as well to distinguish mysticism from psychoanalysis. For it is in deconstructing the Oedipus complex in the transference-countertransference that the analyst makes language not a system of defense (as the obsessive demands, as social conventions advocate), nor only—rarely—a metaphoric grace (as the poet and mystic desire), but a psychosexual reconstruction experience that is the basis for psychic curiosity and the desire to know. The two rapporteurs show in fact how the risks of oedipal transference are the "royal path" that continues to make language the privileged grounds and principle tool of psychoanalysis, including in the care of autism. If one opens listening and interpretation to the heterogeneity of signifyingness, speaking in psychoanalysis has possibilities of success too often and too quickly denied to it.

Thus, faced with the patient Ada's discourse saturated with sensations that are inextricably bound up with their "violence and poetry," faced with the nostalgic defense that bars her access to the self-analytic process and imposes a seduction on the analysis that "castrates listening" by its sensorial grasp, the analyst interprets by outlining a *link*: "Well, there is the dream . . . the scene with Pietro . . . the scene in the cafe . . . your mother's words." But Ada retorts: "The link? Oh, you've stumped me there, an exam." This vignette that Laurent Danon-Boileau presents shows that this analysand's speech, compacted with sensations and designed to attract the analyst, is searching for her father who died when she was ten years old. And when, going beyond the end of the session, she opened up a new associative path in mentioning her grandmother: "She loved me. I don't remember," echoing this missing "link" to this father who died too early, I can hear her analyst thinking: "The link is that someone is no longer there, someone died too early for you to be able to remember that he could love you."

I emphasize the necessity of including the oedipian link at this moment in the transference because the reminder of "infantile sexuality" in Laurent Danon-Boileau's vignette enables it. And because the "third Freudian model of language"—*signifyingness*—has helped us to see that Ada's father's death has left her wide open to the introjection of the primary identification [*Einfühlung*] with the loving father of her preoedipal period. This "direct and immediate identification" with the ideal Father, Freud wrote, marked the birth of the Ego Ideal. But the patient is not able to "decompact" the language-sensation that she throws out to her therapist as a desperate call from the other until the analyst's interpretation, speaking in the name of the loving father prematurely passed away, opens the way to speech able to construct the necessary psychic transition between the flesh (maternal, too maternal, grandmotherly?) that imprisons this young woman and her scientific excellence that destines her to solitude.

On the other hand, when Dominique Clerc's "Don't touch" patient complains about not feeling anything about her because of the "age difference," and the analyst tactfully interprets: "It's true, I could be your mother," the subtext is, "I could be your mother, whereas you need your father so that I won't touch you too much." This oedipal implicitness remains insinuated, and only the analyst's tact can determine when and how the fear of incestuous desire and the appeal to the thirdness of the father and/or the analyst can be said.

INTERPRETATIVE SPEECH AS A QUESTION[38]

Gradually, as Freud theorized the death drive and as narcissism turned out to be powerless to stop it, the *object relation* appeared as the buttress able to modulate the *unbinding*, in the way André Green uses the term.[39]

Modern psychoanalysis refers to it often, without emphasizing enough, it seems to me, that this movement of Freudian thought is accompanied by *the emergence of signifyingness*: identification, working-through, idealization, superegoization, sublimation—so many psychosexual and intralinguistic logics that I see as in-depth studies of the discovery of the Oedipus complex and the Freudian *paternal function* that regulates the speaking animal's destructiveness.

Lacan's "signifier" (not to be confused with the strict meaning of "signifier" in linguistics), refers to this layering of *signifyingness* (my terminology), which includes the transformation of thinking acts (such as, among others, Brion's system), the *regulation* model of processes (metapsychology),[40] but both integrated *from a genetic point of view*, which makes the organization of the psychic apparatus and its structures depend on Oedipus complex accidents. Indeed, a vigorous reworking took place in late Freud between the "genetic point of view" of the stages (oral, anal, phallic, and genital), the phases of the Oedipus complex and its differences in men and women, as well as the object relation that depends on or challenges it. Thus, refined by Lacan, *the exploration of the paternal function* combines the topical, dynamic, and economic models with ontogenesis and phylogenesis. And it is indeed this *signifyingness of the free association discourse, anchored in the destiny of thirdness*, that associates, or even subordinates, the *transformation* model of thoughts (Brion) as well as the *regulation* modal (metapsychology).

Neither only genetic nor only historical, I choose to call "signifyingness" this translinguistic thought process that the third model of speech has bequeathed us and that Freud encourages us as analysts to hear.

For whatever its stages or strata, free association carries within it the *signs* of the language. The evolution of family structures that a more and more regulated filiation accompanies inevitably links the most intimate (the ineffable) to historical upheavals: signifyingness thus puts *history* in what "speaking in psychoanalysis" means.

Freud, an irreligious man of the Enlightenment, considering that the paternal function concerned the introduction of signifyingness and its accidents, nevertheless put forward the idea of "a superior essence of humans": *das höhere Wesen in Menschen*.[41] Far from betraying some sort of idealistic regression, this postulate, on the contrary, clarified the logics of an immanentization of transcendence that the father of psychoanalysis saw appearing by and in the "talking cure" he launched. This capacity of language that the Freudian revolution uncovered comes in two moments: *primary identification* and the *castration complex.*

The *Einfühlung* of primary identification is not based on loving/hating/knowing (Bion) but of course on this "need to believe," this "believing expectation" (*Gläubige Enwartung*), that follows fearful anxiety,[42] emphasized by Dominique Clerc. A totally different "objectality" then takes shape: the father is no longer invested as an "object" of desire, even desire unto death, but as the psychic *investment* of my *investment*, provided that this father is a loved/loving father.

From this point of view, it must not be forgotten that *negativity* (*Negativität*), whose figures Freud dealt with in the oral and anal spheres,[43] adds *the phallic test* to structure the signifying chain. Its binary structure (marked/unmarked phonemes), like a psychosomatic computer, transfers the psychic representations of swallowing and excretion, of approbation and rejection into verbal traces.

This means that language acquisition is after all a negotiation of the *ordeal of castration*, in which the subject takes over oral appropriation and anal expulsion to construct a signifying chain which will be its ultimate diversion—and its distraction—against and with the death drive.

I want to link a psychic activity that Freud did not give sufficient attention to but which is for me foundational for the analytic situation to the phallic phase and to the symbolization of the drives that it completes: *it concerns the allocutory act, par excellence, of questioning,* which challenges the identity and authority of the other (of the real and of the object).[44] The jubilation of the child who asks questions is still inhabited by the metamorphic (hallucinatory) certitude that all *identity* is a constructible/deconstructible representance. This is before the Ego is subjected to the consciential and communicational Super-Ego dictatorship, this "pure culture of the death drive,"[45] which generates unidimensional, security or virtual systems and orders.

But it happens that some people can no longer not be able to stand symbolic castration, which, from diversion to diversion, pulls us out of *flesh* to put us in *code* and perpetuates deep traumas that become unbearable out of hypocrisy. These people become "analysands": they ask the analyst to open the Pandora's box of signifyingness.

Transference as a process of signifyingness gives rise to questioning that is neither consciential nor philosophical, as it presupposes no response. "Speaking in psychoanalysis" is precisely interrogating this horizontal questioning, because on the vertical of language and conscience, it undoes what language has constructed and, with it, the tyranny of identification and its substitutions of the paternal function. Does the whole meaning of the treatment not emerge when the self, who no longer corresponds to "anyone" and escapes the "real," frees himself from the signs in which he was trapped and so can touch the sensitive flesh? "I" remove myself and "Id" speaks. Thus, as I speak, I confront silence: the silence of the analyst, the silence of anxiety. But as long as transference lasts, it is still and always about a silence awaiting meaning: one of a possible new beginning.

In the treatment, the analysand touches this link, which is none other than *the link of investment in the symbolization process as process: as signifyingness.* For the *object*, whatever it be (sexual, professional, symbolic, etc.), and even if it is provisionally optimal, exists in the long term only if the speaking-analysand subject is able to indefinitely construct-deconstruct the *meaning* and the *Thing* (the sexual affect, refractory to repression).[46]

Thus Freud imagined "talking," a new experience of language that does not reveal one truth but detects one of its potentialities: this is one of the formidable privileges of psychoanalysis. Touching on morality and religion, but also on the "spiritual sciences," "speaking in psychoanalysis" has provided a new relationship with the process of signification that constitutes the human. But this *transfer of the word in relation to himself,* this essential yet imperceptible revolution, specific to the analytic practice, worries the world. We must be ever more conscious and mindful of its formidable singularity, and even more, let us be proud of it. Psychoanalysis is alone today in being able to "save" a culture that it has shown to be a death-drive culture by enabling us to distance ourselves from it: it staves it off, wards it off, diverts it. An infinite process, the analytic treatment is thus the only experience that, while taking hold of language, gives access to the inexpressible: back and forth and vice versa.

10

AFFECT, THAT "INTENSE DEPTH OF WORDS"

I bring you three pieces of good news:

• Affect is at the heart of the discovery of the unconscious, if one considers that the major impact of Freudian psychoanalysis lies in the refoundation of metaphysical categories (body/soul; matter/spirit; inside/outside; interior/exterior, etc.). Why affect? Because affect is both an energizing process specific to the drive-based impulse (to its quantitative force) and already a qualitative expression (subjective tonality). Example? Horror, pity, modesty, disgust, shame, anger, anxiety, phobia, fear, hate, violence, the feeling of dying, mourning, pain, and more. But also joy, jubilation, tenderness, tranquility, pleasure, exaltation, etc. The German terms *Affektbetrag* (Freud) or *Affektwert* (Breuer) define in technical terms what Baltasar Gracián called "the intense depth of words."[1] I am purposely using this expression for the title of my talk. Is it not an "interior castle" (*morada*) that Teresa of Avila described as "see[ing] nothing with the eyes of the body or with the eyes of the soul" but both at once?[2] Or rather a psychosomatic space of an even greater depth and height? "The soul has no need of reflection—because Our Lord gives it the fruit of the apple tree, all picked, all prepared, all *incorporated*, to which the Spouse compares it" (my emphasis).[3]

- Bernard de Clairvaux, the great interpreter of the Song of Songs, developed the most complete theory of affect as tributary of the senses as much as of the will: because the speaking being, as a spiritual being, is moved by one and the same logic. This ambivalence of affect, according to Saint Bernard, that plunges the human in the animal so as to better ennoble it does not necessarily make it a precursor of the psychoanalytic affect. But it brings it so close to contemporary psychoanalysis that it leads me to my second piece of good news: far from being cut off from modernity, Catholic tradition, and in particular the mystical one, encourages us to reread and reinterpret it. Not only to restore it to European cultural memory—which seems to be turning away from it—but to stimulate the modern analytical experience itself, more and more attentive to the frontiers between biology and sense.

- The convergence of these two discoveries (the affect of Freud and of Bernard) suggests that a new humanism is in the making in the very heart of secularization that is not merely the disastrous reduction of men and women of globalization to virtual systems of consumers or kamikazes in religious conflicts. In probing the microcosm of the intimate, psychoanalysis does more than proclaim "God is unconscious."[4] As psychoanalysis has a grip on affects and is attentive to the techniques that take over the body and procreation at the same time as the economy, it is for me like a meticulous worker that Incarnation would need, if Incarnation could find a place in the twenty-first century! And for that very reason, psychoanalysis seems to me to have to be considered one of the main levers for a refoundation of humanism.

AFFECT WITH FREUD AND LITERATURE

Affect theory for Freud (and even more so with his followers) varies in its manifestations but remains necessarily linked to drive: affect is an offshoot of drive. Drive (*Triebe*) as a borderline concept (some people call it a "myth," or even the unthinkable itself) consisting of excitation (hormonal or electrical energy) and representation (representation of thing/representation of word, leading to language), affect is part of the psychical representation of drive. Because of this and very specifically, affect itself is already dual. How?

Affect applies to the energizing part of the representation of the drive, which is the rudimentary state of psychic representation and which joins—or not—this other part that Freud called "ideational representative." This is exclusively psychic. Affect is thus the place of copresence between a moving quantity of drive and its first psychic tonality: the crossroads where the energizing quantum becomes a subjective quality. Moreover, in an article written in French,[5] Freud translated *Affektbetrag* as "affective value," with "value" being understood as expressing a "quantitative and qualitative" notion:[6] "Each event, each psychic drive comes with a certain quantity of affect (*Affektbetrag*) that the Ego gets rid of, either by a motor reaction or by psychic activity."

Three kinds of transformations occur in the destiny of affects, essentially transformable through their border position between psyche and soma: (1) conversion (conversion hysteria); (2) displacement (obsession); and (3) transformation (anxiety neurosis).

As for the origins of affects, early in Freud's work, in *Studies on Hysteria*, he showed the relationship of "emotional movements" to "well-motivated acts" in the past but which have since weakened, leaving only the impact of sensations and/or highly charged affective memories. A remarkable fact from Freud's pen is that language (which links these memories to the event that provoked them) is not a simple intellectual operation but an "act and discharge through words." Does that mean that the "origin" of language itself is affective, or at least parallel to that of affect? Would that make affect a kind of "language," a "prelanguage"? And make language itself a "second-order" affect? "The human being finds an equivalent of the act in language, an equivalent thanks to which the affect can be abreacted in the same way."[7]

Retaining this common, drive-based source of language and affect as the abreaction of a traumatic act, I will come back to it in my theory of language that I consider not as a "structure" but as a *signifying process*. For now, affect, both drive-based impulse and representative of the drive, is already a psychicization but an incomplete one, or a mobile "psychic trace" (rather than a "sign"), barely more than the neuronal energy flow. Another essential characteristic: moving quantity and subjective quality, so the affect discharges itself . . . toward the body, toward the interior. It leaves the body and returns to it: the zero degree of call/response, looping autoerotic reflexivity, self-perception. Even before representing an exteriority (the object, the other, the world), and while assuming an outside, affect sweeps over the interior: it marks a psychic depth different from the acts and words oriented toward the exterior.

Two consequences follow from these Freudian advances that I am summarizing:

On one hand, the Unconscious (and even more clearly the Id) in which these traces of affective charges are engrammed is a heterogeneous structure that includes not only representatives of a linguistic type ("The unconscious is structured like a language")[8] but also the facilitations of affects that can—or not—link themselves to words and grammar, while continuing to constitute an elementary psychicization. While accompanying the perception of an exterior object, the affect is not aimed at the object, since it is concerned with psychicizing the somatic excitation itself on the side of the subject grasping itself as such, distinct from the grasping of an object. Affect tracks the somatic path of the drive as an underlying condition and, in this sense, one that is prior to my being in the world with others. Since every drive has a source (organic) and a goal (the object, the outside), the speaking body could not place itself in an exterior world without it becoming "the second world exterior to the Ego":[9] without being itself equipped with a certain degree of representation (or of "sense," different from "signification"). And it is precisely the affect, experienced as motion and/or as psychic impact in the act of emerging from the energizing motion, that is my interior correlative to the exterior where the object of the incitation, of the lack, and of the appeal is situated.

In other words, as far as the analysis delves into the emergence of the speaking being, there is always a certain "sense" already present. The affect is the internal correlate of the positioning of the Ego in the outside world. Husserl called this positioning a predicative thesis, and it posits the Ego as a transcendental Ego. Affect precedes and exceeds the predicative thesis.

I am highlighting here the differences between phenomenology and psychoanalysis. The experience of affect in psychoanalysis, and even more in modern psychoanalysis faced with borderline states and psychoses, takes us to the conditions for the emergence of the Ego confronted with the other, in the advent prior to the "thesis" of the subject aiming for an object: by exploring the occurrence of drive-based sense underlying the signification of the subject of desire and of knowledge. The transcendental Ego of the predicative synthesis cannot grasp its antepredicative sphere, since "the inherently possible individual consciousness" and the "experienced driveness," while supposed to be antepredicative, are immediately caught by the intentionality of the transcendental Ego (in which any driveness "resembles" intentionality). Freud himself doubted the existence of unconscious affects. On the contrary, it is the unconscious destiny of the affects internal to the drive-based impulse itself that the treatment of psychoses and borderline states observes and that it interprets "on the path from its origin to its goal [where] drive really becomes psychic."[10]

I could have broached here the role of fantasy, especially that of originary fantasy (Oedipus, castration), which acts as mediator in the structuring of the subject. Attracted by the affects (of lack, distress, anxiety) and then inducing scenarios-representations with which the psychic interiority structures itself, fantasy is always already doubly determined: by the (somatic) facilitations of affects and by the imaginary representations of object desire.

I would prefer to limit myself to a few succinct comments on my attempt to go beyond the structuralist, but also generativist, model of sense and signification to take account of this dual affective content of language in poetic experience.[11] To introduce the drive-based and thus affective dimension of language in the language model, I suggested not reducing it to a system but understanding it as a subjective dynamic of construction/deconstruction of the subjectivity that I call a signifying process (echoing the *senefiance* of the *modi significandi* established by logicians of the Middle Ages).

Two logical modalities are involved in this signifying process: translinguistic affective marks that organize the *semiotic chora* (might it not be Teresa of Avila's *morada*, her "interior castle"?);[12] and the symbolic register that comes to the fore with the acquisition of language made of words-signs and their syntax. I borrowed the term *chora* from Plato's *Timaeus*: "bastard reasoning," he said, indicating a "space before the space," nourishing and maternal, mobile, unstable, anterior to language and even to the word, to the syllable, to the father and to the One.[13] Only a metaphoric, pictorial rhetoric (the *chora* rather than a concept) enabled Plato to suggest this bodily motion that already made sense but did not posit any signification that referred to an exterior object, since we are in a precocious and fragile state of psychic representation.

Concretely, what belongs to the *semiotic chora* are children's echolalia before the appearance of words and grammar; but also, in adult language, all these modifications of the conventional code that make of ordinary and used language a style, "a total, new word, stranger to the language" (Mallarmé),[14] and that breathes into the discourse "mystery" or "music in the letters": alliterations, intonations, silences, syntactic distortions (for vocal gestures); but also the condensations, displacements, ellipses, etc. that form the rhetorical figures and inscribe a reflux of sometimes namable, sometimes diffused or even eclipsed, affects, in a series of connotations. The nonverbal arts (music, painting, dance) belong to the *semiotic chora*. They elude linguistic signification but have a grip on our affects: interiority that is unnamable but yet present that, thanks to these techniques, talents, and geniuses, obtains the exteriority of this object of desire, of this medium, even this communion of the work of art.

Two extreme and opposite experiences put you in contact with the risks and delights of this affectivity that makes sense in and beyond the consciousness that speaks, thinks, and judges.

Analytic treatment reveals states of regression where, below the threshold of consciousness and farther than the unconscious itself, the analysand loses his/her identity to become what Winnicott called a "psyche-soma."[15] In psychoanalysis, this regression refers to archaic states of osmosis between the infant, or even the fetus and the embryo, and its mother and maintains a fleeting link to self and the other by the infralinguistic sensibility alone whose excessive acuity matches the loss of the abilities of judging abstraction. Another "thought" results from this, an *a-thought*, a deep plunge to the depths in which the terms of "sensorial representation," of "psyche-soma," are more appropriate than "mind." As if the reasoning "mind" handed over the reins of the being in the world to an imaginary elaboration whose seat would be the whole body touching-feeling the outside and the inside, its own physiological functions as well as the exterior world, without the protection of "intellectual work," without the help of the judging consciousness. Winnicott questioned that the "mind" was located in the brain, since the regressive states of his patients attested to the fact that, according to him, all the senses and organs were involved in autoperception as well as in the perception of the world: that the psyche is body (soma) and the body psyche.

It is, however, possible—mystical states, esthetic "inspiration," and, Freud hoped, moments of grace that psychoanalysis can attest to—that the Ego does not settle for regressing to these states of psyche-soma but manages to translate them into a renewed code of expression, widening its own frontiers and those of our means of communication. Without lowering our guard against the madness of telepathy or occultism, the *Introductory Lectures on Psycho-Analysis* stated that mysticism and psychoanalysis dealt with the "same point": the "perception by the deep Ego of the Id"; and that they aim at the same goal: to widen the scope of the Ego (and of language) by reaching the Id's drives so as to "translate" them and to render them conscious, free of superego censorship and thus shareable.[16]

Thus in the two "experiences" of mysticism and psychoanalysis, a topical reshuffling of subjectivity occurs: the psychic instances—the Id / the Ego / the Superego—change places, and their functions are transformed. But these reshufflings are radically different.

The mystical path thrusts the Ego into the Id by a kind of sensorial autoeroticism ("obscure autoperception") that imparts an omnipotence to the Id (the Id places itself "beyond" the Ego) and imposes a failure on the knowing Ego, tempted by the obscure reign of the Id, which is where this fluctuation so particular to the mystical state, between revelation and absence, jouissance and depression, comes from. All and Nothing. The mystic gets pleasure from the visual or auditory representation of the Thing or Object of desire, and this unsayable jouissance can become a perverse or psychotic impasse. The final 1938 apothegm said: "Mysticism: obscure autoperception of the reign of the Id, beyond the Ego."[17]

The psychoanalytic treatment is directed at the same pleasurable (*jouissive*) meeting of the Ego and the Id, but it enables them to move around thanks to the transference-countertransference relationship: back and forth from the Id to the Ego. Yet few analytical treatments lead to these states of grace by encouraging transmission of shareable consciousness. The pleasurable autoperceptions of the Id saturated with affective flux alternate with melancholic states but also manic exaltations pushing the person who is experiencing them to commit aggressive, warlike, and authoritarian acts. The artist of genius, who is nevertheless aware of criminal excess, crystallizes the good fortune of the delights and risks of these borderline states.

Such is Proust's imaginary experience, for example, in the time found of sensible memory: "My imagination, my only organ through which I could take pleasure in beauty." Meanwhile, his personage, Baron de Char-lus, is being whipped to death in a brothel for men; Marquis de Sade's work illustrates the omnipresence, in fantasy, of what is now called sado-masochism, and which, accompanying more or less secretly the immer-sion of sense in affects, would thus underlie the imaginary literary and, more generally, esthetic creation.

The bankruptcy of moral codes and family models, the regression and rigidifying of religious institutions, the decline of writing as an act of sub-limation to the benefit of hyperconnectivity and the toxic hold of images, in addition to the uncertainties of globalization make for a context that, more than in the past, exposes men and women of the third millennium to the benefits and risks of regression, that is, to the limits of originary repression where sense is absorbed by affects. What spaces can modern society offer to welcome these regressions and lead them toward the con-quest of the truth of self, toward the flowering of beauty? This is the diz-zying question that is posed today.

Spiritual orations are no longer "top quality," and Ignatius of Loyola's *loquella* is an untransmissible regression, whereas the "imposition of the senses" in the *Exercises*, which awaken the sensations to be able to declare them in conformity to the Passion, remain rituals reserved for forming an elite group.[18] When these depths of the intimate are unattended to, and out-of-control affects fracture social links instead of amplifying them, every-one thinks him/herself an artist or writer; everyone can become criminal. Psychoanalytic experience tries to accompany this errancy; to interpret its construction-deconstruction and to make it a rebirth with the means and in the context of modernity. An exorbitant ambition that you can hear. Why you, here? Because of Bernard de Clairvaux and Teresa of Avila.

EGO AFFECTUS EST. SAINT BERNARD: AFFECT, DESIRE, LOVE

Bernard of Clairvaux imposed an idea of man as loving subject in twelfth-century Europe.

Beyond the affirmation of the *ego cogito* that Descartes bequeathed to us directly from Saint Thomas, another idea (and another experience) of man can be seen at the very heart of this first resurgent or precolonial expansion that the Crusades were for the West. Saints and troubadours seemed to be proclaiming *Ego affectus est*. They infuse their love with will, illuminate it with reason, color it with wisdom to raise it to the dignity of a divine essence. And man, uncertain, passionate, sick, or happy, identifies with this affect. Because God is love.[19]

AFFECT: SHAME AND GLORY

Love, for Bernard[20] is only one of the four affects (with fear, sadness, and joy), and the notion of affect, central in his work and of a sometimes ambiguous complexity, allows us to approach the density, if not the conflicts, that his experience and thought on love lead him, but also his modernity. Tradition distinguishes *affectus animae*, *affectus mentis*, and *affectus cordis*. Eager to tame this diversity since the speaking being, being spiritual, can only hope to conform to divine law, Bernard constantly pointed out the difficulties of his task: not only because the flesh is resistant to will but also because divine law itself, being love, is no exception to this tension.

Affect, notion bordering that of *desire*, designates man's link to exteriority: God's and the world's. What differentiates the two notions (for Aristotle and for psychoanalysis) is that *desire intensifies lack*, whereas *affect*, without neglecting it, *accentuates the opening to the other* and promotes reciprocal attraction.

Bernard used the term *affectiones* often with the meaning of affect, at the same time attributing a more specific signification to it: he designated the various affect-composed feelings that the soul experiences for God (for example, *timor, spes, obedientia, honor, amor*). He distinguished three types of affections, thus hypothesizing that affections infiltrate the highest abstractions: one affection that comes from flesh, another that governs reason, a third that establishes wisdom. "The first is where the Apostle says that it is not and cannot be subjected to the Law of God," wrote Bernard in the same *Sermon* (50:4), and one can find that he often emphasized a first degree of affect or of love irreducible to divine law.

However, and although the basically passive affect can develop into passion whose primary characteristic is against the Law, it unburdens itself of it to become love, while maintaining the ambiguities as well as the tensions of passion. Among other definitions, the following one is indicative of this complexity, which for some authors is just a contradiction: "The affections, simply said, are found in us by the fact of nature; it seems as if they come out of our own substance; what completes them comes from grace; it is clear that grace does not control anything but what creation has given us, so that virtues are no more than controlled affections" (*On Grace and Free Choice*). Bernard does recognize that the four affects can produce irregular, impure, and ignominious effects, to be understood as pathetic or drive-based. "There is no human soul without these four affections (love, joy, fear, sadness); but for some they are for shame and others for glory. If they are purified and well ordered, they are the glory of the soul crowned by the virtues; be they out of order, they are confusion, abjection, and ignominy" (*Sermons on the Song of Songs* 50:2). However, other definitions suggest that spirituality is inherent to the affect (*Sermon* 42:7).

REGION OF DISSIMILARITY. THE BODY-COW

Without applying the Trinity dialectic to human affects as did his friend Guillaume de Saint-Thierry; nor without removing flesh from a spirituality that would thus become too ethereal; but also without forgetting the presence of the spirit in this flesh that forms a fundamental region of dissimilarity between man and God. Basing himself on the notion of *regio dissimilitudinis*, which he borrowed from Saint Augustine, Bernard put forward a conception of affect as inhabited by the divine but of a "dissimilar" logic: affect, which is not without sense, does not share the ordained sense of the divine.

Unlike the dualism of Baius or Luther, this dissimilarity is endowed with dignity inasmuch as the same movement that designates the animal (the "cow") in the human civilizes it by domesticating it. What led Bernard toward this dissimilarity (which is not a duality) of human experience and whose ultimate expression is love was perhaps the heterogeneous and secretly conflictual characteristic of Christianity incarnate. Regardless, the loving thought of he who was both a valiant warrior and a very sick man, suffering from ulcers and tormented with vomiting, confirms the reality of a body that he compared to a "cow": "There are two places for the reasonable soul, the inferior one that it governs and the superior one where it rests. The inferior one that it controls is the body, and the superior one where it rests is God. . . . Our body is situated between the spirit that it must serve and the desires of the flesh or the powers of the shadows that fight against the soul, as would be a cow between the peasant and the thief" (*Sermons on Different Topics* 84).

This dissimilarity governed, strictly speaking, Bernard's thought. The more the mystical goes beyond the body-cow, the more he assigns its place as animal residue, the more the "cow" takes importance in affect and in love however managed, dictated, and implanted in us by the grace of the Other.

DESIRE: VIOLENT AND PURE

For Bernard, it must be remembered, the notion of *desire* that completes that of *affect* is attached to this dramatic conception of *love*. If Augustine is to be believed, desire is *rerum absentium, conscupiscentia* (carnal *concupiscence* is *desire* for things forbidden). While affect covers proprioceptive emotions, desire designates attraction toward an object. On a different level, desire for God, according to Bernard, is anchored in the first human desire, which is simply a "voracity." Far from lacking desire, God the Father is the one to desire us first. Does Bernard refer us to the image of a voracious God? "The wedding feast is ready. . . . God the Father is waiting for us, *he desires us* not only because of his infinite love—as the only son who is in God's breast tells us: My Father *loves you*, but for himself, as the Prophet says: It is not for you that I will do it, but for me" (V. nat., 2, 7).

It is understood that desire follows a mirror movement, in which my desire will be satisfied by Him, because His desire was satisfied at the moment He created me in His image. For several Church Fathers, and in particular for Saint Thomas, this specular quality of Christian love, based on a loved ideality to love, becomes accessible to the individual through reference to the immediate objects supposed to satisfy his desires. The sublimation of narcissism inherent in this specular love goes back to a kind of "primary narcissism," that only the position of an Other presupposed before us and himself warned of this aspiration to auto-satisfaction and total satisfaction—including affective—can help us go beyond.

COMPLETENESS AND DEPRIVATION

Only the desire for this Other, the desire for an absent one—voracious, absolute, impossible desire—desire punctuated by affect, can let itself be directed by will and wisdom so as to purge itself, recover its plenitude in the fusion with the supreme Loved one, God: "Your actions, your zeal, your desire are like lilies from their candor and perfume" (*Sermons on the Song of Songs* 71:1).

Nevertheless, Bernard did not forget that the path toward this completeness in beatitude includes the deployment of the whole range of the affective experience, including deprivation as the a priori condition of the identification with the ideal Object. And he always emphasized the dissimilarity, the heterogeneity (of the lover and the friend, of the wife and the husband, of man and his God) triggering a surge of affects: love is also fainting, crying, whining, tormenting oneself to try to be with the other. Suffering would thus condition jouissance, and jouissance would stimulate a new suffering quest.

Is this a masochistic dialectic of jouissance expressed as the injunction of an ideal as loving as it is fundamentally harsh? This symbiotic identification with the ideal, *ad unum*, overtaken then by beatitude and unremittingly diagnosed by Bernard, is part nevertheless of an exceptional movement of balance and limitation of desire.

Carnal love placed at the origins (originary in fact if not in law), as a double for the sublime love due to God; completeness but also deprivation that regulate sublime love itself; his holy violence with heresy and liberty alongside each other and including the rapture with which desire is accompanied with indomitable yet sublimated affects ("From there, this satisfaction without disgust, this always-awakened but never anxious curiosity, this eternal, inexplicable desire whereas nothing is lacking") (*On Loving God* 2:33), their intertwining for the Bernardine conception of love makes a complex construction that defies "pure love" as well as the Pelagian thesis of a "happy nature."

Here is one of the many expressions of these ambivalences: "We also love our spirit carnally when we break it in prayer, with tears, sighs, and moans. We love our flesh with a spiritual love when, after submitting it to the spirit, we practice it spiritually for the good and watch over its conservation keenly" (*Sermons on Different Topics* 101).

The maintained heterogeneity of these edges, at the same time as their indisputable subordination to the essential priority of divine Ideality, makes Cistercian mysticism, more than any other doctrine, the appropriate and powerful way to define man's being as loving experience. Neither sin nor wisdom, neither nature nor knowledge. But love. No philosophy will match this psychological success that has provided satisfaction to drive-based narcissism, while at the same time raising it beyond its own region, thus granting it a radiance aiming for Alterity.

MORALITY AND FELICITY

In the Bernardine construction of the affects-desires-loves that are both separate from one another and copresent, there is only the essential that is lacking for the moderns: the moral felicity of the link with the other—my fellow creature, my brother. It is the Unique Other raised as an authority of the supreme Good, it is God who guides, orients, and moralizes the wanderings of human loves by subordinating them to his magnificence at the risk of obscuring them. But not to the extent of preventing the analysis of human loves with an implacable yet fortunate lucidity: as did Bernard de Clairvaux, this suffering, subtle, and finally happy psychologist, thanks to his faith in Him.

When faith starts to disappear or at least to withdraw "in parentheses," the sense of moral duty it leaves us (in the manner of Kant) does not seem to suffice to give us this loving happiness by which the human fact, it would seem, defines itself. Thus either disillusioned humanity will be reduced to a mass of consumers disappointed by sexual and other technical means of creation and procreation, or loving experiences in which interior and exterior come together and tear each other apart get built and get destroyed, will continue to complicate their games, as did the most baroque of the saints, Teresa of Avila, allowing herself to play chess with her God, all affects infused in his infinite purity. As for psychoanalysis, more sober and even more insolent, it pursues the experience: moral duty passes through transference and countertransference to flush out flashes, not of divine love, but of sense and signification. To specify the ways of their dissimilarities in the affects of flesh that no longer or does not speak, to find desire and try love's chance. The logical dissimilarity of affects interests us; we are going to clarify it, says the analyst. Because not only am I if and only if I am affected, desiring, and in love, but I am if and only if I desire to clarify affect, desire, and love, confirms the analysand.

But since no one has spoken better of the immanent impact of the exterior loved one in the interiority of the loving body than Teresa, I can only open this colloquium on the presumed "exteriority" of God with an evocation of Teresa's affective experience.

INFINITESIMAL TERESA

Body and soul, Teresa was torn apart and put back together in and by a violent desire to feel and to think—simultaneously—the Other.[21] A desire based on the proximity of touching and touched bodies, of affected bodies: a desire accepted in its affective violence and perpetually lightened in elucidations.

The touch of the other always already present to one's fellow man, the touch raised as a principle of the Other, consecrates the stranger (and any alterity) as an element of affects from then on intimate and indelible for Teresa, and thus of physical and psychic vitality. Water (with its four variants) will be the "fiction" (her term) of the affect. Water for Teresa can feel and understand how touch, this primary sense (for Aristotle) (I feel water through the skin and the mucuses), becomes the original feeling of the contact between inside and outside, flesh and spirit, me and the other. I see in it more than a metaphor, a metamorphosis (à la Baudelaire: the poet is not like water; he becomes water) that designates the fluid dynamic of the *affective sense* that no signifying process, no signification can capture definitively (and that Plato had already dealt with in the "bastard" concept of *chora*). Water, like affect, simultaneously evoked for Teresa the ultimate instrument of the survival of animals, the permanence of bestiality in the human *zôê*, the supreme humanity of tact, the keen attention given to the tolerable, psychic flexibility.

Teresa thus confers an ontological status on the always already touching/affected and desiring body, all the while attributing a polyphony, a polysemy, and a ductility through ambivalence of bestiality/tact that the many mansions of this new soul attest to. Consequently, these psychic and bodily interior castles are not fragments of a submerged continent nor ruins expecting to be abandoned to infinity but, on the contrary, points of impact of infinite desire, sites contacted by and in its infinite movement.

Following the fluidity of the waters in the first books of her *Life* is the permeability of the seven mansions of the *Castle* that in no way resemble a fortified castle but rather the grace of a transparence infiltrated by the infinite play of sense with the senses. The extraordinary novelty of Teresa resides in this incorporation of the infinite that, inversely, restores the body to the infinity of links that she built by her writings and in their foundations

Such is the Teresa revolution that Leibniz (1646–1716) understood, discovering in her ecstasy a premonition of the infinite monad. Indeed, the polyvalent soul-body ensemble that was built and written with and thanks to Teresa was possible only if it did not settle for being the sign of the Being-Other that would be affixed to him, placed from the exterior (as in Mme Guyon's sublimity with Fénelon). This is possible if this body-soul ensemble is experienced as a point that infinity does not just bathe but a point in which the infinity of the Being-Other *insists* as such. If the speaking subject, body and soul, is an infinity-point; and, on the other hand, if the infinite of the Being-Other "presents" itself in the point that I am. Even more, Teresa the biblical, perhaps without really wanting to know, and without ever recognizing her Marrano genealogy, specified: "He" / the Other is "engraved" in me. I translate: I am affected by it.

The "mystical marriage" and other exorbitant formulations such as "I am transformed in God" as well as numerous and just as extravagant metaphors-metamorphoses begin to herald this modulation of the subject that consists in and with the Infinite—and that, very often but not always, Teresa herself rejected as pure "madness." I am not a "sign" that "suggests" an exterior Being (Creator or Savior, loving or judging). I participate in it, I am part of it, I seek myself in Him, I am him even though I am not equivalent to him. I am a site of unlimited signifyingness.

In this continuous transition dynamic that is mine, Teresa seemed to say, knowledge is no longer a totalization but a procedure of removal,[22] of exhaustion by which the infinite—never absolutely exterior—gets closer to an always fleeting end. Here, Teresa stops languishing, and the suffering "dissimilarity" becomes baroque profusion. Why, she suggested, do you say "lack," "suffering," "persecution"? I escaped your world of "Egos," orphans of the All, since I am the very impact of the Infinite, infinitely. My All that is Nothing has nothing to do with the full All. Infinity inhabits in my own point, in this nothing.

This is the real Teresa as subject (her soul, as she said) if one thinks that this "subject" is infinity "put into points." A subject that would not be either exterior or interior of the Being-Other but a deictic/anaphoric subject. Its function is comparable to that of an adverb or a demonstrative pronoun: *ecce* (here is); *haec* (this). Its purpose is to designate infinite plurality, to inscribe it body-and-soul right here. *Here is infinity.*

It was this contact of the subject with infinity, in the region of dissimilarity itself, that would be source of jouissance for her: libidinal energy, watched over writing and historical action, which were her veritable, her noninfantile, serenity.

Baroque art, especially Italian (Bernini with Teresa!), showed the experience and demonstration of this touching, of this logic of the copresence of flesh/spirit and man/god, that contains in it the seed of Incarnation (see fig. 13.1).

IN CONCLUSION

Teresa's self-analysis, extraordinary for the depth of what she "felt and expressed," enabled me to dream of a humanism that would move away from that of the French Enlightenment because it would follow the discovery of a loving unconsciousness formed by affective and/or loving, transgenerational, and historical links, underlying the speaking being.

Indeed, Freud was not far from thinking, without ever formulating it, what Teresa exalted by all her written experience. Is it not love saturated with affects that Freud put on the couch? Moreover, it is love that is transferred in the listening we do to the speech, drives, and affects of our patients. Freud's philosophy refers to the Enlightenment; his unconsciousness is certainly kabbalistically and talmudically Jewish, but the transference on which he founded psychoanalysis is baroque. Baroque—inconstant, mobile, playful, to be reinvented in movement—is this loving principle that Freud pointed out in the discourse of his analysands, that he emphasized by examining the history of myths, religions, arts, and letters, and that Teresa crisscrossed with her joyful faith, without forgetting the demons of excitation unto death.

We are here at the heart of the baroque revolution that was able to refound Christian faith and transmit a new loving body to the men and women of the Enlightenment. The troubadours and Bernard. Teresa the baroque and the Enlightenment. Why are Catholics not prouder of the baroque revolution that made an infinite-point, an impact of infinity of each body, sound, or color?

Before the five hundredth anniversary of Teresa in 2015, it is time to think with her that a refoundation of humanism is possible starting with the European tradition: to take up in all its diversity, in the light of contemporary experiences.

11

THE LACAN EVENT

Q: *You arrived in France in 1966. What did Lacan mean for you at that time?*

A: An event that, like psychoanalysis, is fascinating and unsettling. I was preparing a thesis on the *nouveau roman* and met Philippe Sollers, who brought me to Lacan's seminars. Lévi-Strauss had "structured" the myths and the exchange of women in so-called primitive societies. Benveniste compared structural and generative linguistics to the Freudian unconscious and the Indo-European pantheon; Goldmann went back from Marx to Hegel; the subtlety of Barthes, attentive to *Tel Quel*, irritated the Sorbonne immensely; Derrida, also attentive to these language experiences, rewrote the phenomenology of Husserl and Heidegger in the form of a grammatology. But the real event was Lacan. He did not teach the classics, did not recite packaged ideas; he lent his presence and his word to the dreams and anxieties of his public to transform them into thought. And this thought was being constructed out loud before us in the flesh of a French language as demanding as dreamlike. I must admit that the theatrical ritual, part surrealist, part Catholic, of this grand bourgeois made my head spin. But as curiosity is my only vice, I tried to understand. So I dug in my heels and, with Sollers as my guiding light, I took his seminar at the Ecole Normale, and then at the law school.

Q: *So you then took up psychoanalysis?*

A: Not right away. I began first by reading Freud, and then Lacan's teaching entitled "Return to Freud." My education in Bulgaria had oriented me toward German philosophy, but my knowledge of Freudism was limited to the Bulgarian translation of *The Interpretation of Dreams* that my father made sure I read, while hiding it in the "depths" of the family library as psychoanalysis was considered to be a bourgeois science in Eastern Europe.

Q: *Lacan became a friend of the couple you formed with Philippe Sollers. How did he act with you, young intellectual that you were?*

A: "Friend" is a little strong, and as for "couple," psychoanalysis recommends a perpetual refoundation. Each of us interacted with Lacan through friendships based on true intellectual seduction. My own began during an interview I was to do for a semiology journal: since his theory of the unconscious "structured like a language" seemed to contradict the Freudian unconscious understood as a reservoir of drives, the semiological research based on Pierce and Saussure necessarily had to grasp this renewal. We had dinner together at La Caleche, his regular restaurant, and a very strong bond founded on mutual respect developed between us. Coming out of the restaurant, Lacan asked me my father's first name. I told him his name was Stoyan (Bulgarian version of Stephan), a "signifier" whose etymology my father playfully traced to the Latin root *stostare*: "he holds." Lacan stopped and looked at the moon for some long minutes and then finally said to me: "I see that it holds true." I will always remember his expression, keen, enveloping, and very respectful. In the end, I never did the interview, but the exchanges went on.

Q: *And yet, you did not want him to be your analyst?*

A: We knew each other too well for him to be my analyst. Back from our trip to China—a trip he canceled at the last minute for personal reasons—I went to see him nonetheless, asking him to advise someone from his school for me. And the name he suggested was an intimate friend—of his intimate woman friend at the time.

Q: *Why?*

A: I asked this myself. Maybe because he wanted me to be in his clan, his erotic circle, as if adherence to his thought passed through a kind of incest, or maybe he considered that it had no importance at all and that, after all, an analysis should take the passion out of all that to get to the truth. . . . What is a psychoanalyst? Someone who is in touch with his unconscious and permanently maintains a certain connection with culture. But a great psychoanalyst? He is free with his unconscious and possesses both ancient and modern culture so well that his practice and his theory are able to think the present. Nonetheless, I turned down the game Lacan proposed to me and I joined another group: the Psychoanalytic Society of Paris.

Q: *And he did not hold it against you?*

A: How would that be possible? You know, when you go as I did from totalitarianism to Saint-Germain-des-Prés, you are always in a mind-set of death and resurrection: "Keep walking or you're dead." I had found my solution for walking: to try to transform curiosity into creativity. Question the situations and ideas that seemed interesting to me and give my own version of them. I was all the freer insofar as I belonged to no community, neither the *Normaliens*, the *agrégés*, nor militants of any kind. It seemed to me that Lacan respected this state of freedom. And in a certain way, he even encouraged me to persevere in my independence.

When my first book, *Polylogue*, appeared in 1977, he was intrigued by my choice of cover: a throng of flying angels by Giotto. I told him that it represented the plural logic of the imaginary: the supposed "individual" bursting out in the variants of his sublimations, not really asexual experiences, but singular and singularly crisscrossed sexualities. "I see," he said to me smiling, "the contrary of members of a school, they're not really singular, alas, but *you* don't need all that." He dissolved "all that," his school, during that period. He feared that his thought would end up being transformed into a Band-Aid.

Q: *But did he influence you in your analytical practice?*

A: I practice long sessions, in the best of cases, three times a week, with Freudian-type interpretations. Is it not the Freudian attention to language that the founder of psychoanalysis applied from his first dream analyses that Lacan took up and amplified in the context of structural linguistics? Lacan put great value on this power of language to lock—and also unlock—inhibition, symptom, and anxiety by claiming that it was a simple "return to Freud." Rhetorical modesty or protective deviation? I especially saw in it the extreme attention given to the mother tongue, French in this case, that Lacan placed at the heart of psychoanalytical listening.

He asserted, in essence, that the mother tongue is the supreme way to understand the singularity of each analysand. And to make each treatment a "Poïesis" experience that brings out the incommensurability of each speaking being. It seems to me that here is where the secret of the strange seduction of Lacanian theory resides, totally impenetrable for his various detractors. Countercurrent to trends in globalized psychoanalysis, which reduces the unconscious to abstract, even "cognitive," patterns, Lacan comes across as quintessentially "Frenchy," baroque, or literary.

Q: *In L'Etourdit, Lacan affirmed that the psychoanalyst is a linguist . . .*

A: Yes, but he also loved "mathemes" that track the intra- and interpsychic devices that are transversal to language. And he readily modified his structuralist-inspired positions to suggest replacing "linguisterie" with the term *lalangue*: babies' "lallation," infantile prelanguage, echolalia, and also "music in letters" like Mallarmé. These approaches are limited when psychoanalytic interpretation is confined to word games and pure formalistic deconstructions of sounds, vowels, and syllables, ignoring affects and drives. Some of his followers have fallen prey to these simplifications. On the contrary, the specific originality of psychoanalysis resides precisely in the "heterogeneous" conception of signifying activity in human beings: at the same time energy and sense, drive and signifier.

Q: *So in the end you have gone further than Lacan in analyzing language?*

A: Research in psychoanalysis exists, despite its detractors, including in the copresence of sexuality and thought in language. After Melanie Klein, Winnicott and Bion in England, Piera Aulagnier's work in France, and especially André Green's work on the heterogeneity of the signifiying process oriented my own work as semiotician and psychoanalyst attentive to Lacan. I am particularly interested in this dimension of meaning, what I call "semiotic" and which is in the nature of prelanguage, melodies and intonations, and where the affects and sensations proper to early mother/child drive-based relations are imprinted. The analyst hears it in both depressed people's speech as well as in people who, in our world of images, reduce their verbal expression to "tweets" and SMSs, while the truth of their unconsciousness is hidden as if encrypted in this more archaic register.

Q: *What is left of Lacan today from a theoretical point of view?*

A: Three openings that we have not yet fully developed.

He reopened the bridges between psychoanalysis and the vast continent of thought: philosophy but also theology, of course social sciences, and the other sciences too. Without this breath of life in which psychoanalysis originates—let us not forget that with Freud, psychoanalysis was born of the Enlightenment and its encyclopedism—psychoanalysis would find itself reduced to a psychologizing governance.

By encouraging analysts to hear the inscription of traumas, joys, and pain in the furrows of infantile speech, he reinjected an unexpected vigor into cultural diversity that is much needed today: the truth about our trivialized and globalized bodies passes through the native language; it is there that the singular trace of every speaking subject is inscribed. And so it is through multilingualism that it can develop unexpected creativities.

Without having systematized his thought on the feminine or on religions, Lacan's contributions to "feminine jouissance" or the "other jouissance," adding to his insistence on the "paternal function" and the "Name-of-the-Father," form the precious bases for thinking about the history of religions, but also religiosity (before and beyond religions, monotheistic or not) and including the "need-to-believe" as a universal component of speaking beings. I dialogue with these positions in my book *Teresa, My Love: An Imagined Life of the Saint of Avila*, dedicated to Teresa of Avila, that Spanish Carmelite whom I discovered during Lacan's seminar entitled *Encore*.

His findings revitalize psychoanalysis in its historic and political scope that seems to me to be an essential stake in the Freudian discovery but which current psychoanalysis tends to ignore or obscure when it becomes too esoteric or, on the contrary, popularized.

Q: *Philosopher Slavoj Zizek presented Lacan through the lens of Hollywood cinema: would he have appreciated that?*

A: Like all "isms," Lacanism gets all tied up in its own schools and disciples. But by sowing in the wind as he did, the Lacan event also opens up to being read in the original, and it is important that research in psychoanalysis, as well as analysands, wherever they come from, develop the polyphony of his teaching. With the risk that this piles up in the "Big Mall" of psycho-spiritualistic merchandise where everything is equal to everything else and nothing is worth anything. Yet rigor exists: it consists in holding to the fundamentals of Freudian theory in which sexuality—whether it be a tragedy or a divine comedy—is accessible to language while respecting the play of transferences and counter transferences. One criterion only: analysis. That is what protects us from the somnambulistic digressions of new gurus who attract the media.

III

WOMEN

12

ANTIGONE, LIMIT AND HORIZON

Who are you, Antigone (by Sophocles, 440 BC)? A child (*pais*), a girl (*korê*), an offspring (*gennêma*) of Oedipus, a fiancée (*nymphê*), a virgin (*parthenos*), called by this name only as a corpse desired by Haemon, your cousin, the son of your enemy Creon? Creon even suspects you of being a man: "then she's the man here, not me" (550 *anêr*),[1] exclaims your maternal uncle, this tyrant whose reason you oppose by defying his edict: the prohibition of burying your brother Polyneices, which makes you an outlaw, a criminal. A rebel, for sure; you are certainly not a warrior: no connection with Joan of Arc or even with a dutiful heroine like Corneille's. You are a fierce resistant to tyranny into which the reason of state inevitably tips, and maybe even political thought, in general, when they neglect this "absolute individuality" in which you stand and claim for your brother. That is your sacredness arrayed with the indestructible desire to the death whose "divine use" is not lost on you.

Might you be an irreducible loner? Fearless? Cold, rigid, and frigid if your enemy Creon—he once again—who, clearly, hates you (but he will end up yielding and will collapse in a kind of pitiful chiasmus, inverted double of your annihilation: let's wait for the end of the show). "You understand [he threatens Haemon who wants to marry you, what a weird idea, you, the virgin fiancée of death!] how such embraces can turn freezing cold when an evil woman shares your life at home," a girl who "disgusts," only good enough to "marry someone else in Hades" (v. 743).

Unless you are, on the other hand, a charitable person who comes to the aid (*ophelein*) of the dead themselves (vv. 559–60)? Not to all, of course. You have your favorite, one of your brothers, it is understandable as descendants of the incestuous Oedipus and Jocasta: it will be Polyneices,— how surprising!—*Poluneikes*, the one who "is full of dissensions," as his name indicates, who takes pleasure in attacking his own city-state, his father/motherland, and, frankly, an anarchist who wants to destroy his own. OK, that does not stop you from being charitable, in your own way, an Ophelia, if one understands the Greek word *ophelein* in the Shakespearean sense. And crazily turned, like her, toward death, twenty centuries before Hamlet fell for it.

Black Eros caught in flashes, *imeros enargés*, "radiant desire" that enchants the Chorus's elders seduced by "the bride's desire seen glittering in her eyes" (v. 905)? Hanging out nevertheless with a psychorigid who protects herself from her incestuous links the Labdacides family likes so much? "This girl is passionate—her father was the same" (v. 535). "The strongest iron tempered in the fire to make it really hard—that's the kind you see most often shatter" (v. 539). More than anyone else, rightly so? A "poor girl, [who] disobeyed the royal laws" (v. 430), a "little guilty Antigone"? Worse, you are supposed to be resistant to all civilization, raw—*omos*—that is, wild, inhuman? And so cruel to Ismene, to begin with, your cautious sister, "the one who knows," since that is how your father named her; intending her for wisdom; enough blindness in the family.

No? Maybe not, after all. You think only of Polyneices, but since you are splittorn (I would say "cleft") between the City and Hades, Creon's world and that of death, political logic and that of your blood if and only if it is blood of an insurgent, of rebels, of transgressors (the most active political logic is obviously murder), and so if it is Polyneices's blood that triggered a civil war—well! In one of these oxymorons you and Sophocles are so good at, you define yourself as a "saintly criminal" sister, desiring simply to rest near your brother, "dear to who is dear to me," purity of post mortem weddings. To Creon who takes your mortuary pity for a kind of hatred and a lack of friends, you retort with another definition of yourself that will surprise those who do not understand you: "But my nature is to love. I cannot hate (*symphilein*)" (v. 598). And countless romantics will mourn, for centuries and centuries, this "love," your mystical antimarriage: poets, feminists, and melancholy souls!

Beginning with the guard in your play who catches you on your second criminal act, washing and covering Polyneices's body with dust to protect it from the sun, birds, and dogs. The brave servant cannot prevent himself from sympathizing, perhaps even from rejoicing, in spite of Creon's edict: "That made me happy—though it was painful, too" (v. 493). His feelings are in reality yours at the moment of the funereal love act, and the Chorus itself clearly shares them because it is Dionysos's mouthpiece: so that this first *kommos* of the tragedy that bears your name involves the whole audience in your emotion in which pain and exaltation ally with and cancel each other out. As for Creon, he will not have the right to empathy in the *kommos* dedicated to him at the end of the play. You are the winner, Antigone, and we are still wondering what that really means.

Ungraspable, indefinable, lacking any fixed identity in your very authenticity, you slip away from yourself, Antigone. I understand that you would prefer the obscurity of the underworld; you are not of this world. Yet there is nothing indecisive in this evasion: your word is law (*nomos*)! In your insolent autonomy as Oedipus the transgressor's daughter, you know in advance that you are excluding yourself from political justice, and even from human norms. But your knowledge (that attests nevertheless that you "are in it," in this social world, at least partially) does not bother you very much. On the contrary, you persist in your obstinate, invincible and sublime certainty. "She was not afraid at all. . . . She just kept standing there, denying nothing" (v. 491). "I admit I did it. I won't deny that" (v. 500). And to Creon who cannot get over that you dare defy the law even though you know it, that you go to your death fully aware: "Were you aware there was a proclamation forbidding what you did?" You reply: "I'd heard of it. / How could I not? It was public knowledge" (v. 507).

No madwoman, this Antigone. Or else a madness that reveals a superior and clear logic, an intrinsic logic that will turn out to be contagious, maybe eternal, universal?

Is Antigone the way she is because she is the fruit of incest? That she is suffering the consequences? That she carries them to their climax and their tragic end before the customs of the city-state begin reframing these confused clannish passions and before Plato's *Laws* establish in all lucidity a family and political order that already prefigures ours? A vestige of the past, good only for shrinks' archives?

Or is Antigone Antigone because she is a woman? Her stony solitude, her cadaveric desire, her endurance in the "no" thrown to common sense: do they show specifically feminine characteristics that would act like a permanent corrosion of social links? Far more dangerous than the "eternal irony of the community"[2] that Hegel diagnosed?

But then, this "no" that she pitted against Creon's laws (his totalitarian abuses or his political common sense? Enormous subject that democrats specialized in human rights have not yet sorted out): is it a dynamic, prospective, Faustian, or dialectical "no?" Or rather, in seeking this limit where the human being outdoes itself and that the sacred is attracted to, does Antigone's defiance condemn him to prove the existence of the uncompromising death wish that Freud bequeathed to us without any other details or precautions?

The death drive is not this virile aggressiveness present in both sexes that eroticizes fights to the death in the guise of desires and that scrutinizes the erotic torture described by the Marquis de Sade, for example, as the ultimate cunning of the supreme Being, especially when it collides with its victims' indifferent harshness. No, Antigone demonstrates a placid energy that cuts links, a *de-liaison*, precisely, that cancels out identities and differences, to set up the subject, beyond loss, depression, and suffering, in the pathos of defusing. There is no difference here between suicidal laissez-faire and endurance; indifference can shine in care and abjection of life can perpetuate itself in raging disobedience that renews social links. White psychosis? Or triumph of sublimation at the edge of originary regression, at the frontiers of the living, that the speaking individual perceives as a foray out of self, borderline states of an unsharable identity? Mature, sovereign.

The world of the Labdacides is dominated by the obsessive quest of the *auto* and the *homo*[3] because it is woven of links and of incestuous and incestual intersections. But it does not seem to know the other, except as stranger, murderer, or troublemaker of civil wars. The self-birthing union between mother-wife and son-husband, autoengendering, autoaffection, automutilation: it belongs to, it happens in, it depends on the *same* family, the *same* womb, the *same* hand. The "sameness" loops around with the same blood and is reflected only in reciprocity, in mirroring, by reversible kinship among offspring of the same womb and who share a mobile, problematic, and virtual improbable identity (*autos*). Capable, however, of delving into the uncovering of one's own self, of the permanence of self, as Antigone does by pushing self-knowledge (*auto-gnotos*) up to this metallic certainty of self that Creon envies/criticizes in her. The sovereignty thus won by exclusion (*anti*) is quick to be abolished just as quickly in the annulation of self, but only by a tragic act, as Antigone does not hesitate to do by letting herself die to herself, in a manner of speaking. As if she assassinated—like always and in herself—the parent/the relatives she fatally identifies with, whom it would be impossible for her to join for good except in the wedding tomb (Authentês, the murderer would have been first the one who committed the act—murder being the act par excellence—of a parent, the double of oneself, recalls Nicole Loraux with Louis Gernet).[4] But finally whom of her own does she join, with and through Polyneices and his identarian overlappings?

In this labyrinth of identification/disidentification, losses and reunions of the same in the closing of the "sameness," *homo* emphasizes similarity more than identity itself (*auto*) and plows the furrow of reversible kinship. On this side, Antigone is homologous with her brother Polyneices, and he is homologous with his father Oedipus (both of whom are the sons of Jocasta); but also with the *man* in his *virility*, since in seeing herself in the mirror that Polyneices holds out to her, she captures the male characteristic that her uncle Creon criticizes her for, a brother also, but from Antigone's mother, Jocasta's brother.

Here we are: Jocasta! The one and only, the only one unnamed, an unpronounceable center around which the infernal chase of *auto* and *homo* revolves. Focal point of the tragic imagery of the play, never designated explicitly but always allusively evoked: "from the same mother and father, too." This means that Jocasta, the mother, is the *only* one who persists in her own identity because she is everyone's mother, including Oedipus; Oedipus's father is himself also the child of this mother, but he is not the "only" one since he is not Jocasta's father.

Curiously, Antigone does not want to recall that this universal Mother is still the lover of the son/father, her Only Rival, while being the Only Mother. Antigone censors Jocasta's desire/pleasure so as to think of Jocasta the genitor alone: of the fertile blood of the womb, of the one and same maternal blood that lends itself as reality and metaphor engendering (literally and figuratively) the fluid identities of the blood relatives. Loving and/or murderous identities because, like blood, they are destined for procreation and carnage, and never one without the other. Mixed up and confused identities of brothers of "the same blood" (*homai-mos*), incestual siblings who can only manifest their autonomy in similarity by deploying themselves in bloody wars with each other. Unless there is an end to fecundity? And therefore to its double, that is, war?

Heroine of self-analysis, you will discover, Antigone, the secrets of the tragedy. But without saying it, merely by obstinately holding yourself in *de-liaison*. Strangled by the closing of the incestual family, the "sames" in their *auto* and *homo* intertwining are condemned to generation and killing: the engendering family is a killing one. Worse, suicidal, because killing one body of the same blood in the consanguineous labyrinth of ambivalences, ricochets, and reflections means—for this family here— "suiciding" one's "sameness," *committing suicide*: the deaths of/in the family are the family's suicides. The internal, interfamily, and intrafamily wars go on and on and especially in the form of continuous political conflicts: your brothers Polyneices and Eteocle fighting each other in a civil war; Haemon their cousin paying this inexorable spiral of deathly generations, of matrical blood with his life. Still today, wars among national and religious "communities" are involved in the same tragic, suicide-threatened logic, hidden in their supposedly symbolic "sameness."

This implicit assessment that threads its way through *Antigone*'s tragic story had inevitably to lead someone, necessarily a woman, a descendant of Jocasta, to cut the thread in the inextricable line of the *auto* and the *homo*. This will be the solution of Anti-gone (anti-engendering), faced with the death that continues—the Chorus is there to remind you—as the one and only situation against which the human species, even though full of clever tricks, reveals its fatal powerlessness. When you are against the *gonê*, when you repudiate the family line, you find a "thing"/charm/remedy: you tame death. No blasphemy against motherhood, nor matricide either, that is good for Orestes. You settle for repudiating (*anti*—against) motherhood and "in its place" (other meaning of *anti*), for imposing a certain reflexive resemblance with it, according to the same logic of *auto* and *homo* that motherhood comes from. But in another world that is no longer "of this world" living by dint of the womb.

You can see, fixed in your subterranean universe on the banks of the Acheron, you continue to perpetuate the desire for motherhood. Do you not know that you hinted at it, this maternal vocation? Yes, you did. Recall the funereal care bestowed on your brother/father/son, washed / in his dead flesh: does that not betray a maternal solicitude? And more: "I'd never have swaddled with dust and purified/protected done it for children of my own, not as their mother . . ." (v. 1015): Did these words escape you? The moans you uttered in front of the bodily remains of your Polyneices: are they not "just like a bird who's seen an empty nest, its fledglings gone" (v. 479)? And finally, your death, Antigone, "hanging by the neck, held up in a noose—fine woven linen" (v. 1359), a copy of Jocasta's hanging?

Except that Antigone does not hang herself on stage; only a messenger attests to a "she," third-person impersonal, a nonperson: making commentators lose the thread. Who hanged her? She herself? By her own hands? Or not? I prefer to think that the messenger's vision was only a rhetorical figure of Sophocles to say that "she," Antigone, in her opaque and absolute coldness was always a silent, constricted vengeance, against the prohibitionless mother, the Only Mother, the All Mother. A mother to kill and whom, in the toxic flux of the "samenesses," you cadaverize instead of her.

It was thus necessary for the desire to meet her own in death, announced at the very beginning, to be already inscribed in the heroine's first name: *against* the Mother and/or *in her very place*. To try to be free, or at least autonomous, you dedicate yourself, Antigone, to embodying the death of the desire for life, the double of Eros. Even though this logic leads you to be one of these suicides of the incestual family discussed above, this death of the desire for life is neither a black sun of melancholy nor a theology of nothingness. Nothing to do with gloomy Nerval's complaint; nor with the apology of nonbeing dear to the cut-off tongue of an Angela of Foligno (that your lapidary style nevertheless irresistibly recalls); nor with the happiness of a Zen monk whose meticulous garden you will never know.

Antigone triumphs over Jocasta by taking her son from her in whom she does not find the blind sage in Colonus, but the discordant Oedipus finally appeased as a dead baby. On this condition only, the shadow of the melancholic object has no need of falling on her but is crystalized in the *endurance of the death wish.* I repeat: the death wish in the full meaning Freud gave it in the second topography, not to be confused with the erot-icization of aggressiveness and sufferance now called sadomasochism. Nothing to do with it. For Antigone, Thanatos cut the necessarily erotic links with the living as we have seen. Only attempting to exceed the limit (*Até*) of the human, Jocasta and Oedipus's daughter is as if sucked in by and *in the limit itself:* "atrocious,"[5] indeed, in the "in-between" of the death wish.

Short of narcissism, farther than autoeroticism, in radical *de-liaison.* Instead of neurotic depression, around the masochistic *père-version* whose tortured object finds jouissance to the death—to the point of becoming insensitive to the pact even between the master and slave. Anti-gone got herself out of neurotic humanity. Divine Antigone? The Chorus suggests this hypothesis in an antistrophe that the offended reclusive one violently rejects.

Because she knows that her sovereignty is simply human, but fully human, exceptionally human. In the place of the mother, Antigone gives birth to an imaginary universe: she repairs the loss of her own by re-creating the virtual world of a life that is possible on the edge, in the *Até* itself. Those who go beyond this threshold sink into delirium, lose their human forms, and pass away. As for Antigone, she triumphs in her cadav-eric construction because it provides her with the benefit of consummat-ing the love for her brother in tender loving care, in maternal gestures. She has to accept dying for herself and for her body (and Creon will be the unwitting accomplice of this Antigonian desire that precedes his edict) to accomplish the maternal vocation of tenderness and care but not the ges-tation of a child: the sublimation inherent to the maternal vocation. This is the reward for her sacrifice. Antigone does not know it because the tragic world has not invented the child-subject (the Bible and the Gospels will do it later). She struggles in the inextricable interweaving of Eros with Thanatos and fights back, petrified in the timeless love of a dead brother and a sister ready to die to save their autonomy and their validation.

In this place if you do not go mad, if you do not lose the limits of lan-guage in mental confusion, it is the pathos of solitude that petrifies the living man or woman. He/she is elsewhere, within or beyond, inaccessi-ble Self, indestructible diamond. But its mortified narcissism, sure of itself and triumphant, can also become available, which confers on it this enigmatic radiance perceived by the Chorus. A meditative and glacial availability, that of a saint, sometimes that of a superefficient nurse, Ophelia, reborn from the waters and care giving. No suffering, pity, compassion. She does not feel anything: "If I shall die before my time, I count that a profit (*kerdos*). . . . to face such a fate as this is pain that does not count. . . . But if I dared to leave the dead man, my mother's son, dead and unburied, that would have been real pain" (vv. 521–29). The death of self, as the apotheosis of the *auto*, finally delivered of the weight of living reproductive links and held tightly in the ivy of the knowledge of its limits, of the Limit: Could this be the ultimate "profit"?

Profit from manic-depressive psychosis, I would have said, if one had to settle for the shrink diagnosis that, however insufficient, is still real. It does not explain, however, how Antigone's pathos not only does not become pathological but, reverberated on Creon, makes him wear the suit of the complaining neurotic: "I am no more a live man than one dead" (v. 1469). Meanwhile, Antigone now invisible, hanged offstage, does not stop growing in the minds of spectators and readers present and in the future, as the only heroine of the eponymous play.

Antigone's magisterial solitude is at its height when her autoanalysis of the coexistence with the death wish claims to be rebellious not only to the political spirit (of Creon) but also to that of the gods themselves. Lacan was right: it is not that Antigone does not recognize Creon's right to recognize himself in Zeus; it is *she herself* who breaks away from herself and from Zeus: "Zeus did not announce those laws to me" (v. 508), and from the *dikè* of the gods. Her *de-liaison* does not have to do with their prescribed "laws" but "laws not written by the gods": *a sort of trace without representation that a human being cannot transgress.* Less or more than the *dikè* of the gods, it is a question only of a *horizon* (*oros*), from the verb separate, delimit, determine, linked to limit) that Antigone allows herself to aim for to the point of appropriating it for herself in the radiance of her sovereign identity.[6] A region that absorbs her because she is thinkable only as transversal to language, rules and laws, even though delimited/ fixed by them: horizon of the sense of time, of affect, of the drive at the crossroads of biology and sense.

Certain to aspire to the limit of the living and to be aspired by it, but always inhabited by desire—also oedipian—to know the truth that her parents left to her by their *crime* or fault and its very revelation, Antigone is sure of her experience. Does it let her know the power of "programmed death" that is at work in life as soon as there is life, according to biologists today? Let us thus read her debate with Creon on the *dikè*: alone in the apperception of this carrier wave of the life instinct that is the death wish, Antigone holds herself in this blinding, illegible double of the laws that would be the gods' *unwritten laws*: there where there is neither prescribed nor prohibited but where it is felt, it is experienced, where it is lived and dies. At the limit of madness, the horizon of a psychic sovereignty can open.

The Chorus, although Dionysian, seems stupefied by so much pretention. And it recalls that the human beings trapped by death take refuge in "baffling sicknesses [where they] discovered [their] own remedies" (vv. 413–14). I suggest here a new interpretation of the Greek text that differs from the usual translations and extends Lacan's reading: indeed, Sophocles speaks of an escape into sickness (νόσων δ'ἀμηχάνων φυγὰς ξυμπέφ ρασται) and not an escape from the sickness in such a way that this "sickness" would finally be *impossible* (μηχάνων). This is an early psychoanalytic reading of sickness that eluded many (pre-Lacan) translators who always understood incorrectly that human beings can only "escape *in the face of* sickness." In fact, what strikes the chorus in its Dionysian understanding of the heroine is that unlike ordinary humans, Antigone *does not escape into sickness.* And even more, what "common sense" considers as sickness is for her more than a defense: it is a pseudo-sickness, "one holy thing" (ἀμηχάνων), adds Lacan,[7] as the symptom of an unconscious revolt or an insupportable desire by which Oedipus's daughter escapes from human and divine laws. She is not sick at all; her diamond-brilliant pathos has nothing pathological about it! The confusion of the guard himself, beyond the fear of being massacred because of being the messenger of bad news, is perhaps also due to this enigma of the not-at-all-mad girl, in her troubling and yet so familiar strangeness. How could this be possible?

Suppose first that Antigone's truth shouted from deep inside her nuptial tomb is only a historically dated truth: that of the *tragic advent of the individual* in the suffocating net of the incestual family that has not yet found its rules for combatting the prohibition of incest. The history of Indo-European vocabulary shows that the identity of the very Self, foundation of the free Individual, could only be formed *outside* of bonds of kinship, only in alliances external to blood links. Thus the Sanskrit root *swe*, "self," *soi* (in French), *svoy* (in Russian), etc., is found in Greek in "ally" (*étēs*) and in "ethic" (*éthos*).[8] Slow and uncertain emergence of free subjectivity, thanks to alliances. Whatever might have been the political society's laws that had to frame and replace incestual uses in family clans, they did not have the power to decide among the tragic intertwinings through which *identity* sought to construct itself alone. Was not this, finally, the tragic? And its delicious seduction.

The power of God creator of monotheism would replace sacrifice and self-sacrifice by *separating prohibitions* (food, sexual, moral), thus guaranteeing the emergence of the subject in man. The text of the Jewish Bible and its people's rigor in their rituals will seal this historical mutation by the "chosenness" that defines the self only facing the Other, this One to posit and to hear in all the others; and simultaneously by the necessity of generation—to multiply infinitely—so as to guarantee the perpetuation of alterity. Adonai and Yahve cut short the confusion of the sames in the blood *sameness* of the more or less matriarchal family of paganism by prohibiting the spilling of necessarily impure blood ("Thou shalt not kill!"): that of killings as well as of menstruation; while inciting—via the mothers—the perpetuation of the posterity of the sons of their fathers: nominal identities in the succession of the chosen.[9]

And it is with Christ not only that the father's murder (oedipian) will be admitted, as Freud discovered through Moses, but that Antigone's exploration of the death wish will be revisited—it too recognized and metamorphosed—what Freud omitted to recall.

Placed as the focal point of the imaginary, the death wish / the desire for death of the subject Son/Father beaten to death[10] cannot be reduced to the killing of a victim by a rival religion's court. An experience of mortality gets recognized as not being the end of life *but a permanent coexistence of death in the temporality of the living.* As a result, and beyond the sadomasochistic experience of death and suffering, and even female passivation in which the passion on the Cross excels, is added the annihilation (*kénose*) of the Son/Father dying in hell, evoking Antigone's tombal adventure, walled in because of her desire to join Polyneices, her brother/father, beyond the *Atè*.

As for Antigone-mother in the place of the genitor, Mary the Virgin carries out the eternal return spectacularly and culminates in the Pietà that attaches her to Jesus, like a young woman descendant of a Sulamite who had dreamed of Antigone.

Except that—and the difference is radical—the fable of reunions in death is traversed by that of the resurrection in which the incestuous love for and of the Son/Father is allowed, finally, rehabilitated at the price of sublimation. Antigone the sublime was not unaware of the absolute work of the drive that changes aim (it will be the love unto death in place of erotic links), but she had no inkling that it was possible to say/paint/make music instead of letting herself die in a tomb-like dungeon. The transcendence of the tragic dimension will follow the chalice drunk to the dregs the day of Christ's Passion, nevertheless included in the body of the Son/Father who becomes corpse the more to be exalted in a glorious body living to the right hand of his Father.

Christ and Mary, differently and together, recognize Antigone's sovereign lucidity, but they pull it out of tragedy to found, in place and against the reproductive world, the myth of possible love: beyond, infinitely. And they invite all women, the natural mothers of the species, not really to stop the flow of pregnancies but to join with them (Christ, Mary) at these possible intersections of Greek and Jewish memories.

This adventure has all too often crossed out the female body. But it has nonetheless encouraged the spiritual or sublimatory development of women who have accompanied the history of Christianity (from female monachism, through women storytellers, letter writers, writers, witches, warriors, and other revolutionaries, up to feminists and presidents of all types). Teresa of Avila's[11] ecstasy and her jubilatory writings are inseparable from death to self, in the poignant tests of closure and in the identification as passionate as forsaken with the Son/Father beaten to death. Thus confessed, the incestual fantasy surpasses and relieves itself finally in this new Judeo-Christian promise that the Greek world did not know: love of the Other who elects and forgives. From then on, the death wish not only is tragic but also introduces the tragic as the other face of love.

Shall I suggest still another hypothesis? Far from being a vestige of the past, Antigone's universality resonates in the psychic life of women today. Beyond the so-called classic family that generally observes the incest taboo, that secularization detaches from Jewish and Christian dogmas, and that does not stop recomposing under the pressure of procreative techniques, of the emancipation of the "second sex," and of the mixing of the various religious and cultural traditions,[12] the anthropologically universal dimension of female solitude, confronted to the drive of *de-liaison*, is clear in clinical observation as well as in social behavior. Solitude and *de-liaison* that do not necessarily reject motherhood but insist on and accompany it. Female depression and maternal criminal behavior attest to this. One must nevertheless be aware of the new solidity of those women who have the possibility and ability to produce knowledge, an art or a way of life/survival: a remarkable consequence of female emancipation still in progress.

Indeed, Oedipus prime,[13] which attaches the little girl to her mother in early mother-baby links, marks the woman's psychosexuality with an endogenous primary homosexuality; it is "unwritten" because it is pre-linguistic, sensorial, and virtually unsharable. Oedipus II transfers her to the father, installs the woman subject in the world of language, the ideal, and the social superego but without eliminating her prior dependence. Formed in this two-sided Oedipus, the inconsolable sorrow of Oedipus prime and the improbable accomplishment of Oedipus II make a woman an eternal stranger in the political community, an inexorable refugee of the initial osmosis with her genitor.

Homosexuality will provide the occasion to relive the delights and discords of the lost continent. Motherhood will be an opportunity to go out of Oneself in order to love, at last—like oneself—someone other: the child of, a third, the father. Miracle also of the maternal vocation, but how threatened by maternal madness, this recurrent pathos of the autoerotic and narcissistic "sameness," in the permanence of Oedipus. Miracle also of symbolic motherhood that gives up the bodily reproductive cycle and constructs itself, like Antigone, at the limit of the human and of language. But who, unlike Antigone, seeks its meaning to understand the death drive in the dispassionating of sublimation.

There is an Antigone in every mother who succeeds in freeing her children from herself. I risk my life like Antigone in each work that surpasses me. Because with or without the experience of motherhood, but especially concerning current attempts to construct a modern discourse on maternal passion in the present, it is perhaps becoming possible for women to approach the limits of the living to which the ambiguities of their oedipal experiences confront them. Limits of their own sexual identities (the endogenous psychic bisexuality of women); of their children's lives:

always fragile and objects of solicitude; of the life of the planet threatened with new cataclysms; of new reproductive techniques that play with life and death without sufficient precautions.

Apocalyptic current events including acts of maternal infanticide do not cancel out the increasing number of women who face the borderline states of human experience with Antigone's indestructible serenity. And that reveal themselves as a horizon, for better and for worse, from which laws themselves, since they are necessary in a social order, are apt to be transformed, but first in the depth of psychisms, before perhaps being consecrated by political justice.

This can occur only if language, thought, and interpretation of our solitary solidity in coexistence with the death wish are developed. If not, it is the barbarism of frozen embryos, children raped or sold for organ trade, sterilized or flouted pregnancies, repressed or repudiated women.

Antigone "in the place" of the mother? At the heart of Winnicott's joyful mother lies an Antigone. She cut the ties; she traversed her *auto* and *homo*; she is dispassionate: a certain annulation. What is a good mother? She knows that the "other" emerges at the point where her own identity-ambition disappears and the horizon of possible alterities opens, veritable singularities. Against the pathos of the mother and in her place: maternal love, borderline state, and inaccessible horizon.

Antigone, you have experienced the conditions of accession by taking risks. Vestal virgin of the death wish that adjoins crime but that is purified in the identitary emancipation inherent in a work of art and in this work of art that is the insupportable dispassionating of maternal care. Thus your experience is ungraspable and yet concise, in defiance of common sense but of an absolute rigor and mysterious clarity. A necessity of silences and precision of voice, it marks the death of self, punctuates the flowering of the other in the child, leaves pending and frees up interpretations: open, personal, and traced because foreseen but imprescriptible. Like these unwritten nonlaws of the gods. A musical élan. Sublime.

13

THE PASSION ACCORDING TO
TERESA OF AVILA

T he extravagant experience—called mystical—that Teresa of Avila lived and wrote about coincided with the beginning of the decline of the Spanish conquistadors' power as well as the Golden Age. The theories of Erasmus and Luther shook the traditional faith, and, while new Christians such as the *alumbrados* accepted women and Jews, the Inquisition put books in the Castilian language on the Index and more and more people on trial to attest to the *limpieza de sangre*. Daughter of a *cristiana vieja* and of a *converso*, Teresa de Cepeda y Ahumada (1515–1582) witnessed in her childhood the trial in which her father's family had to prove that they were really Christian and not Jewish. Much later, the Inquisition examined the "case" of Teresa herself, a cloistered nun practicing the mental orison of amorous fusion with God that led her into a state of ecstasy. Later on, the Counter-Reformation discovered the extraordinary complexity of her experience as well as its usefulness for a Church seeking to marry asceticism (required by the Protestants) and the intensity of the supernatural (propitious to popular faith). Teresa de Cepeda y Ahumada was beatified in 1614 (thirty-two years after her death), canonized in 1622 ("saint" forty years after her death), and in the 1970 prolongation of Vatican II became the first woman doctor of the Church along with Catherine of Sienna.[1]

In my brief presentation of some aspects of her mystical experience, I will begin with two general ideas, philosophical and political, hoping they will coincide with the approach of this conference.

Catholic mysticism at its two apogees—in the twelfth century with Rhineland mysticism, then following the Council of Trent and the Counter-Reformation with, in particular, the Spaniards Teresa of Avila and her friend John of the Cross—was situated in an internal exclusion within Catholicism: a margin that reveals its heart. From this paradoxical position, the mystic carries a deep anthropological knowledge that psychoanalytical interpretation would transform into analytical and semiotic truth (I mean in relation to sexual and linguistic economy). I consider three elements among others of this knowledge-ignorance that Teresa's experience brought to a never-before-attained paroxysm and clarity.

The Christian faith professes an unshakable confidence in the existence of an ideal Father and in the absolute love of this loving Father at the source of the speaking subject, which is none other than the very subject of the loving word. Father of Agapê or Amor, then, and not Eros. The syllogism of the believer, "I love because I am loved, thus I am," could summarize Teresa's experience of her visions and ecstasies. Far from rejecting the existence of this "loving father," Freud alludes to it in *The Ego and the Id* when he discovers the "primary identification" with the "father of individual prehistory" (not to be confused with the father of collective prehistory of the "primal horde"). Endowed with the qualities of the "two parents," identification with him is direct and immediate (*direkte und unmittelbare*). For the psychoanalyst, this is just a variant of the "oedipal father." On the other hand, unfamiliar with Oedipus, the Christian faith retains only de-eroticized Love of and for the Father as the foundation of the possibility of the Word, which exists only if it is the word of love. One could go back in time—and Teresa as well as other mystics did not fail to do so—to the Song of Songs as a source of this copresence word/love.

Nonetheless, such an extreme idealization can be affirmed only in a pure state—with an injunction of repression—in the Church's exoteric message. The mystic, on the contrary, in her position of internal exclusion never ceases to resexualize it. Freud highlighted this logic of alternations in the drive-based economy where the processes and excitations become eroticized when they exceed certain quantitative limits. Yes, mystics, and especially Teresa, not only relate to this turnaround but for some, and our saint more than others, even name it. From then on, the alternation idealization-desexualization-resexualization, and vice versa, metamorphoses love for the ideal Father into rampant drive-based violence,[2] into a *passion for the Father that turns out to be a sadomasochistic père-version.*

There are thus long fasts and grueling penances, going as far as self-flagellation with nettle branches on open wounds, these mortifications bringing about convulsions and leading even to epileptic comas in cases of neuronal or hormonal fragility. I mention here only a few of the extravagances that mark the aftermath of "exiles of the self" in Him (to use Teresa's expression), her transferences in the Other. The believer, and in a paroxysmal way, the orant, identify more with the "beaten Father" venerated in the Christic Passion than with the "beaten child." This is a gratifying manner if ever there was one to support suffering humanity, as well as the passive femininity of both sexes, up to sadomasochistic violence. Dostoevsky's observation ("It is too idealistic . . . and thus cruel")[3] can be read as a summary of the mystical *père-version* and that of Teresa.

Militant dolorism finds relief in the oral satisfaction of the *Eucharist,* which reconciles the believer with the beaten Father;[4] and going further, she adjoins the attributes of the nourishing mother to the body of this Man of Sorrows that "I" become myself in swallowing the Other. In the Middle Ages, many melancholics and anorexics thronged to churches with the sole motive of nourishing themselves with a thin slice of the bleeding and tortured body of the Man-God, and this food was sufficient to enable them to survive long years of exaltation in spite of the hunger that they experienced by oral and symbolic assuagement alone. Having oralized idealization-resexualization, Christianity also made the word itself an ultimate object of desire and love: "Not that which goes into the mouth defiles a man; but that which comes out of the mouth, this defiles a man" (Mathew 15:11; Mark 7:15).[5] Not only is Teresa conscious of this essential orality of her love for the Spouse endowed with maternal attributes, but she claims it forcefully, disarmingly making the leap from this mammalian God to the pleasure of saying, from the pleasure of suckling to verbal sublimation. And from suckling pleasure to that of saying, what is the difference? Is it not the same jouissance? "The soul said . . . that she savored the milk flowing from God's breast," writes the saint in her *Thoughts on the Love of God* (5:5).[6]

At the same time, she comments unremittingly on the renowned verse of the Song of Songs: "Let him kiss me with the kisses of his mouth," before adding: "This word can be understood in many ways; but the soul cares not for that. *What it wants is to pronounce it* (*El alma no quiere ninguno, sino decir estas palabras*) (1:10). Is Teresa on the verge of becoming a psychoanalyst by observing the "word" that evokes pleasure? In any case, she is taking that path.[7] Consequently and in her fantasizing, genitality is done away with, replaced on the pleasure of being reborn by orality. A "holy anorexia" is the result.[8] This rebirth is doubly assured: by the oral-stage identification with the beaten Father and by the reconquest of Time in the form of the eternity of the word which becomes the *princeps* object of desire (object "a"), a narration open to the infinite quest of necessarily subjective sense.

These three aspects of Christian faith can be summarized in this way: (a) an ideal Father exists; Faith is love for and of this father; (b) this idealization resexualizes itself: the Father is a beaten father and my pleasure with him comes from his castration and his killing; (c) but I also associate myself with Him through the two virtues of orality, the Eucharist and the word, creators of a veritable parthenogenesis of a self-engendering of the Ego that opens up to me Time and sublimation that will be valorized by the mystic. They form a subtle system of formidable efficiency, sometimes provoking and then simultaneously accompanying through numerous modulations the accidents that the drive-based disintrication, or the dissociation of the erotic drive and the death drive: somatization, perversion, sublimation.

The libidinal system thus constituted reduces the feminine and the maternal in the permanent reconquest of a *demanding singularity* of the subject of sublimation. Duns Scot's focus on the *ecceitas* formulated this fulfillment of the Christian faith in "truth," understood as incommensurably singular. The privileged experiences of such an accomplishment were for Teresa writing (as elucidation of experience) and foundation (as a political act that invents not only institutional space but also communal temporality).

The future saint undertook the reform of the Carmelites into Discalced Carmelites sometime after having begun her *Book of Life* in 1560[9] and continued writing while founding seventeen monasteries during this twenty-year interval. In doing so, she showed herself to be both "the most virile of monks"—"I am not a woman, I have a hard heart," she wrote—and a staunch defender of female specificity. She maintained, for example, that women are more fit to carry out the spiritual experience of the liturgy than men and pressured the Church hierarchy and the royalty to promote female monasticism. This would not be the modern issue of "sexual difference" but the economy of sublimation, intrinsic to the Catholic faith that Teresa practiced with her particular genius in her visions and writing.

Teresa lost her mother whom she was very close to at the age of thirteen. The only girl among seven boys (before another girl and boy came along and increased the number of siblings), Teresa was very attached to her brother Rodrigo, her paternal uncle Pedro, and her cousin, son of her second paternal uncle, Francisco: this comfortable family of incestuous inclinations was in decline. On November 2, 1536, at the age of twenty-one, Teresa decided to become Carmelite in the Incarnation Convent. She was torn body and soul between *guilt-ridden desires* that she evokes in her *Life* (specifying that her confessors kept her from expressing them) and her adoration of Mary (Virgin Mother) and Joseph (symbolic father) in a kind of *idealizing exaltation.* In her beguilingly sincere biography, the young woman made no secret of the symptoms of her agony: convulsions, fainting spells, and comas lasting sometimes for four days. The French epileptologist, Pierre Vercelletto, like his Spanish colleague E. Garcia-Albea, diagnosed this as a "temporal epilepsy."

Teresa also spoke of the "visions" that accompanied her fits—what neurologists call "auras," and that I interpret as "embodied fantasies." She felt with her whole body the comforting *embracing* presence of the Spouse. This loving father is none other than the reverse side of the ideal one who molested her for her "temptations," her "lack of honor" and her "dissimulations" that gnawed at her very core. Teresa succeeded where the president [Daniel P.] Schreber failed. Freud analyzed these divine torments: because God loves her, He no longer judges her.

The gradation of recounted and shared "visions" relieved the malaise and acquired the therapeutic value of a life-saving alchemy. First in the appearance of a "severe face" that disapproved of her too-casual "visitors"; then in the form of an expanding "toad"—could this be the visitor's sexual organs? And lastly, the vision with the features of the Man of Sorrows, the one Teresa passed in the convent courtyard, this Christ on the cross, martyr with whom she identified.

Rapture reunited her with "Christ as man (*Cristo como hombre*)," she took nourishment from it, lost herself in it: "Certain that the Lord was within me (*dentro de mi*)." "It was impossible for me to doubt that He was within me, or that I was totally engulfed in Him (*yo todo engolfada en el*)" (*Life* 10:1). The exultation of the senses swings inescapably into nothingness: the soul becomes unfit for "work," only "abandon" subsists, a delectable passivation in bliss: "One does not feel anything, there is no sense of anything but pleasure, without any knowledge of what is pleasurable"

(18:1); "deprived even of feeling" (18:4); "a kind of delirium" (18:13). Positive or negative, jouissance or pain, contraries in the extreme, always linked, succeed each other. The crushed body escapes and collapses, and the psychism is in turn canceled, "out of itself," until the soul takes over and initiates the narration of this state of "loss."

Before her Dominican and Jesuit fathers authorized her to put pen to paper, Teresa confided the heights of these cenesthesic "visions" to her worried and/or charmed confessors. Reproduced in marble by Bernini in 1647, and mentioned by Lacan in *Encore*,[10] here is the baroque hymn of this *Transfixion*:

> Oh, how often, when I am in this state, do I remember that verse of David: *Quemadmodum desiderat cervus ad fontes aquarum* . . .
>
> When these impulses are not very strong, things appear to calm down a little, or at least the soul seeks some respite, for it does not know what to do. . . . But there are other times when the impulses are so strong that it can do absolutely nothing. The entire body contracts; neither foot nor arm can be moved. If one is standing at the time, one falls into a sitting position as though transported and cannot even take a breath. . . .
>
> Our Lord was pleased that I should sometimes see a vision of this kind. Beside me, on the left hand, appeared an angel in bodily form. . . . He was not tall but short, and very beautiful; and his face was so aflame that he appeared to be one of the highest rank of angels, who seem to be all on fire. They must be of the kind called cherubim. . . . In his hands I saw a great golden spear, and at the iron tip there appeared to be a point of fire. This he plunged into my heart several times so that it penetrated to my entrails. When he pulled it out, I felt that he took them with it, and left me utterly consumed by the great love of God. The pain was so severe that it made me utter several groans. The sweetness caused by this intense pain is so strong that one cannot possibly wish it to cease, nor is one's soul then content with anything but God. This is not a physical, but a spiritual pain; though the body has some share in it—even a considerable share. . . . But when this pain of which I am now speaking begins, the Lord seems to transport the soul and throw it into ecstasy. So there is no opportunity for it to feel its pain or suffering, for the enjoyment comes immediately (*porque viene luego el gozar*). (*Life* 29:11–14)

FIGURE 13.1. *Ecstasy of Saint Teresa*, 1647–1652, Bernini (1598–1680), Cornaro Chapel, Santa Maria della Vittoria Church, Rome.

The mystic's "torment" is "bliss," and this fusion of autoerotic pleasure and pain is felt as a "spiritual jouissance," she said, while being well aware of the "corporal form." Christ's humanity is a recurrent subject during this era of Erasmus and "the illuminated," converted Jews and those women known as *Alumbrados*. Teresa's ecstasies immediately mix images with physical sensations, spirit and flesh, or else the contrary: "The body has some share in it—even a considerable share." The experience is thus immediately dual: Teresa is both "object" of her transports and "subject" as well; her "graces" and "raptures" betray an incredibly extravagant lucidity. Lost and found again, inside and outside, and vice versa, Teresa, like her element water, ripples and flows: "I . . . am so fond of this element that I have observed it more attentively than other things" (*The Interior Castle* 4D, 2, 2)—her way of thinking is so well reflected in this water.[11]

But the saint's raptures do not pierce their mystery as much as her recounting of it. Does she in fact go beyond the narrative? The power of this famous text lies in its ability to transcribe the shock and drive-based discharge using Catholic codes and their constraints, assuring Teresa her survival and posterity. The Carmelite Teresa knew it: "This imagining (*hacer est ficción*) is necessary that we may truly understand that within us lies something incomparably more precious" (*The Way of Perfection* 28:10).

From the Teresian "fiction," I first of all note this state that religion calls *ecstatic* and in which I find what Winnicott defined as a "psyche-soma." I will then move on to the *metaphor* of water—more than an image, I think it is a *metamorphosis*. Lastly, I will analyze Teresa's identification with the divine and the paradox of a God who exists only in the depths of the writer's soul.

Teresa introduced her "research" through a *suspension* of "powers" (theologians' term to designate understanding, memory, and will), enabling her to attain what must be called a state of regression where the thinking individual loses his identarian contours and, below the level of consciousness, becomes a "psyche-soma."[12] It refers to the archaic states of osmosis *in utero* and with the maternal container, an underwater dive without the help of the judging consciousness, given over to the feeling-touching body and its imaginary elaborations.

How to express this self-perception of psyche-soma that occurs in the passionate state—that of Teresa, wife of Jesus, or of an intense counter transference in borderline cases?

The Teresian style is intrinsically anchored in images destined to transmit these visions that do not have to do, or do not only have to do, with sight but inhabit the whole body-and-mind, the psyche-soma. Such "visions" can first of all and essentially only be given to touch, taste, hearing, before passing to sight. Let us say that a *sensible imaginary*"—rather than an "imaging," "imagination," or "images" in the scopic meaning of these terms—summons *words* in Teresa's writings so they become the *equivalent of her feeling*, and to put into play the feelings of her addressees: the *La Madre* confessors who demanded and encouraged her texts, her sisters who glorified her, and ourselves, the present and future readers in Time.[13]

Metaphor words, comparison words, or metamorphosed words? How did Teresa appropriate the Castilian language to make it say that the loving bond of a cloistered woman to the object of desire, to the other being—in and/or outside of oneself—is then a *sensible bond*? How to describe in a communicable way this alterity that made her experience separation in love, but which could also fulfill her by love? And which is neither abstract law nor a spiritual vocation, nor a metaphysical concern, but inevitably reciprocal and nonsymmetrical calls-and-answers between two bodies living in a desiring contact? A bond between two communicable desires?

Intimate fulgurance, resurgence of the evangelical theme of baptism? Or faithfulness to the spiritual alphabet of *l'alumbrado* Francisco de Osuna who guided Teresa's mental orations and whose *Third Spiritual Alphabet* abounds in images of water and oil to evoke the state of abandon (*dexamiento*) favored by the illuminated, a state this author freely associates with what the infant feels at its mother's breast?[14] Undoubtedly all the above, not excluding the more or less unconscious regression of the lover of her ideal Lord in the embryonic state touched-bathed-nourished by amniotic liquid.

And so Teresa sought refuge in her condition as woman and used her inaptitude for "spiritual language" as a pretext of to be pardoned for her "re-creation," which was her recourse to "comparison"! Thus justified, she distinguished four steps of oration that she described as "four waters" (*Life* 11:7) that watered the garden of the praying subject: wells, the noria and buckets, the river, and rain. Reading her texts I realize that for the cloistered religious woman, water figures as the bond between the soul and the divine, a loving bond that puts the dry earth of the Teresian garden in contact with Jesus. Springing from outside or from within, active and passive, neither one nor the other, and without being confused with the gardener's toil, water transcends the earth that I am and changes it into garden. I, earth, become garden only by the contact with this restorative liquid medium. Being earth, I am not water; but water is not God either, since He is the Creator. Water is henceforth *fiction*, the sensible representation of our encounter; it designates space and body-to-body time, copresence and the copenetration that makes being: *living being*. For the fiction of water connects me to God but does not identify me with Him; it maintains the tension between us and, while filling me with the divine, spares me the madness of merging with Him. Water is my living protection, my vital element. As the image of the mutual contact of God of the creature, it dethrones God from His suprasensible status and brings him down, if not to the role of gardener, at least to that of a cosmic element that I taste and that nourishes me, that touches me and that I touch.[15]

Husserl thought "'fiction' was the vital element of phenomenology like of all the eidetic sciences."[16] This value of fiction as the "vital element" to know "eternal truths" has perhaps never been as justified as in Teresa's use of water for writing-describing her states of oration, an oh so "telling" example of a quest for sublimation by a word that aspires to resexualize by blending in with the loving regression-exaltation experience.

In other words, not only does the word "water" stand for the encounter of the earth person with her heaven, but in the state of oration, Teresa immersed herself before the barrier of word-signs in the psyche-soma. She escaped the "powers" evoked above through her fiction (better and other than by epilepsy). From then on, what remains of the "words" is no longer a "signifier-signified" separated from "referents-things," as is customary in the understanding that obtains with "words-signs" of an exterior reality. On the contrary, the oration that mixes the self and the Other also mixes the word and the thing: the speaking subject comes close to—when it does not fall prey to—the catastrophe of mutism: the self "loses itself," "liquefies itself," "hallucinates." Midway between these two extremes, a fine membrane rather than a barrier separates the word from the thing: they contaminate each other and disassociate from each other alternately, the self loses itself and finds itself, devastated and jubilant, between two waters.[17] On one side collapse, on the other, rapture: the fluidity of the aquatic touch accurately translates this alternation.

Teresa plunges into her mother tongue as if into a bath that is consubstantial with the engendering experience of a new self, coiled against the Other, a self loving the Other that this self diminishes and that the Other absorbs. Water is vital as the absolute and inevitable fiction of the loving touch, by which I am touched by the touch of another who touches me and whom in turn I touch. Water becomes fiction of the decanting between the other being and the unnamable intimacy, between Heaven and the vagina, the exterior milieu and the interior organ. Neither comparison nor metaphor, but the two together, without failing to play them against each other like symmetrical contraries, even canceling the water by fire, and reciprocally, in superimposed contradictory images to lose the logical thread of these multiple inversions and cancelations to create a perceptible fluidity of sense itself. And to contaminate us by the psychic, physical, cosmic, and stylistic dynamic of her own metamorphoses. . . . Not to be *like* the other, but *to be* the other. "Water is not like divine love, water is divine love and vice versa. And I am of it, we are of it: I, you, God himself," such is the sense of the Cartesian image of water that takes us away from the stylistic to put us before the touch of psyche-soma that Teresa tried to transmit.

From our skeptical third-millennium perspective, Teresa wrote a decomposition of her intellectual-physical-psychic identity in and by the loving transference with the Being-All-Other: God, the paternal figure of our infantile dreams, elusive spouse of the Song of Songs. By this deathly and pleasurable metamorphosis that cures the melancholy of her inconsolable pain of separation and abandonment, she appropriates the Other-Being in an infracognitive and psychosomatic contact that brings her to a delicious and perilous regression edged with masochistic pleasure. It is not rhetoric that helps us read her, but Aristotle's dazzling revelation in *On the Soul* and *Metaphysics* that attributes the touch, the most fundamental and universal property of all the senses. If, in fact, every living body is a tactile body, the sense of touch that characterizes the living is like that with which I enter into contact and that enters into contact with me. At first sight, and through the fiction of water, Teresa, who saw herself bathed by the Other, masked the mediation and fantasized herself immersed in her Spouse as he was immersed in her. But at the same time, in diffracting the water between God, the gardener, and the four ways of making it come, she implicitly criticized this immediacy, distanced herself, and tried to deploy her simultaneously painful and jubilant autoeroticism in an accumulation of physical, psychic, and logical acts. So many tales and stories of water!

It is not water but the fiction of water that diffuses the fantasy of an absolute touch in a series of auxiliary parables (noria, wells, rain, gardener, etc.); she coupled it with its contrary (fire), charged it with contradictory states before seeking other images, then she lost interest in the images, words, and writing; turned away from exchange and love. Would water, then, be as much the fiction of the divine sensorial impact on Teresa as an unconscious, implicit, and ironic criticism of the impact of the divine itself?[18] Going as far as the dissolution of the ideal Father, of the Other in the praying person, in Teresa the writer?

If water is emblematic of the relation between Teresa and the Ideal, we realize that her interior chateau is not a fortress but a warren of "dwelling places," *moradas* with permeable walls. A sort of Teresian "metapsychology" that "travels" her through the stages of the psyche to her truth. This is to say how immanent transcendence proves to here: the Lord is not beyond, but in Teresa!

Supreme audacity of the Incarnation dogma, or irony that borders on atheism? In a page not included in *The Way of Perfection*, Teresa advised her sisters to play chess in the convent, even if it was not allowed by the rules, in order to "checkmate the Lord."[19] An impertinence that resonates with the famous words of Maître Eckhart: "I pray God that he may make me free of God."

Or else it can be interpreted in the manner of Leibniz, confiding in a letter to Morell on December 10, 1696: "And as for Saint Teresa, you are correct to esteem her works; I found in them this beautiful idea that the soul must conceive of things as if God and itself were alone in the world. In philosophy this even influenced considerable thought, and I have found it useful in one of my hypotheses."[20] Was Teresa an inspiration for Leibnizian monads, always and already containing the infinite? Was Teresa a precursor of infinitesimal calculus?

This sublimatory passion is sublime in risks, sublime in jouissance and in lucidity. I call it, of course, masochism. We in our modern lives claim to be free of it. Is it so sure? And at what price?[21]

14

BEAUVOIR DREAMS

J uxtaposing Beauvoir and psychoanalysis brings to mind the famous movie director John Huston, who liked to point out the coincidence of the invention of psychoanalysis and of cinema. See no mischief in my substituting feminism for cinema. It is just an invitation to think, beyond any historical coincidence of feminism, cinema, and the invention of psychoanalysis, of a back-and-forth, or even of a reciprocal challenge. The provocative connection to John Huston is striking because it points to an unthought idea: do not subordinate one side of the equation for the other; recognize the similarities so as to better appreciate the incommensurable. For example, while psychoanalysis and the cinema share the freeing of inhibitions of desire and fantasy, on the contrary, psychoanalysis obviously attempts to *elucidate* while the cinema aims to *seduce*. And this is to grasp the respective differences, autonomy, and limits of the two arts as well as their reciprocal questionings. So what of the crossfires between feminism and psychoanalysis? The same applies when Beauvoir and psychoanalysis are put side by side. Let me explain.

Simone de Beauvoir "adored" Freud more than she read him ("He is one of the men of this century for whom [I] had the most respect and affection," she said in *All Said and Done*),[1] which took courage in a period when the discovery of the unconscious was still relatively unknown in

France (but the philosophy professor was already speaking about it to her students, and the Education Ministry did not really approve). In spite of the criticism she leveled at psychoanalysis starting with *The Second Sex*, I argue that Beauvoir drew from psychoanalysis this foundational idea of the book, and that was like a slap in the face of the establishment. It is still upsetting today. This is how she expressed it: "Sex," she said in essence, in defining the "psychoanalytical point of view," is "the body lived by the subject. . . . Nature does not define woman: it is she who defines herself by reclaiming nature for herself in her affectivity."[2]

In taking up and thus affirming what remains essential in the Freudian discovery is the refoundation of the metaphysical dualism body/soul, flesh/spirit, nature/culture by the promotion of "sex" to the rank of a "psychosexuality," Simone de Beauvoir showed herself to be more complicit with Freud than many phenomenologists who, with Heidegger, accused the Viennese doctor of "biologizing the essence of man." Nevertheless, and in spite of this deep and as if immediate embrace, Simone de Beauvoir maintained a constant ambivalence concerning Freud and Freudism. She went as far as including psychoanalysis among "the religions";[3] she accused Freud of knowing "women only as clinical cases";[4] of reducing the Freudian oedipal theory to a competition between genital organs (vagina and clitoris versus penis deified as phallus of the other); of forgetting the symbolic sense of the paternal function—so fundamental, particularly in later Freud.[5] All these simplifications were bound to spur the rush of a certain feminism, especially in the United States, against psychoanalysis. But on the other hand, they also sparked movements that then tried to learn what was going on in psychoanalysis and that led to the birth of the Psychoanalysis and Politics movement in France.

In fact, more than a feminist outraged by woman's originary castration (a vast continent that has not stopped uniting and dividing Freudian and post-Freudian psychoanalysts and theorists), it was the phenomenological philosopher Beauvoir who rose up against what she thought was an "absence of the original intentionality of existence" in Freud, or his "systematic refusal of the idea of *choice*."[6] She countered him with Alfred Adler's positions. The complex architecture of psychic life, according to Freud's two topographies (the unconscious vs. the id; drive-affect-desire vs. narcissism-identification-ideal-of the-ego, superego, etc.), did not seem to be taken into account by the theorist. It would be doing her a disservice, and not fair for her work, to drag her into a debate on the fundamentals of the discovery of the unconscious.

For Beauvoir, the "fundamentals" lay in her commitment to elucidate and promote women's existential freedom at the heart of a given historical context. To do this, she reworked the phenomenological-existentialist discourse itself, borrowing various liberating discourses in which psychoanalysis was given a very choice place in this recomposition—but a choice that Beauvoir assimilated into her own personality and integrated into her own cause.

I will not voice any objections that are obviously easy to make after the fact, today, when psychoanalytic research (far from limiting itself to Freud, but in developing his discovery with and after Klein, Lacan, Winnicott, and a few others) continues to explicate and develop Freudian paths in areas of sense, desire, sexual difference, and ethical issues.

ALL SAID AND DONE, DREAMS

I will take another track by rereading first this surprising gift Simone de Beauvoir gave us as a digression in *All Said and Done*: twenty pages of dreams! "I want to speak of an area I have never broached: my dreams. It is one of my most delightful diversions."[7]

With her usual intellectual honesty, the author admitted that sleep gave her "euphoric states" similar to certain drugs: states she "does not experience when awake because they imply total abandon." She "keeps them at bay"—ah: Beauvoir's distance, even in her dreams! "Often I think I'm playing out a psychodrama rather than really living." Always in control, the inevitable ascendancy over drives, mastery of self, even in sleep. "Keep at bay," "abandon" itself, is that dreaming? Right from the start, this lucidity of analytical inspiration: "I will not try to give this a Freudian interpretation: dreams can deliver their deepest meanings to the analyst only if taken within an analysis as a whole."

Nor will I give a strictly Freudian interpretation to Simone de Beauvoir's dreams. I will choose a few of her summaries and juxtapose them with my reading of the philosopher's other writings as well as with some "free associations" that these notes waken or reawaken in me.

It begins thus: "Very often, I walk from one point to another." This sentence with all emotion whited out triggers an avalanche of trips, foot or bike races, trains and train stations, cars and planes, even helicopters, no: it is Sartre who becomes the helicopter in person, and this is not funny. Lost baggage that is rarely found, unlikely maps, confused itineraries, flights and falls, in Europe, Asia, America, in France, of course, and often in Paris; corridors-cafés-restaurants, known or weird and sometimes political or familiar characters, expulsions-separations-rarely reunions. This gets sometimes mixed up with deportation, if not exile; there is no lack of assassinations, as dreams should have, nor some admissions of suffering—but in a minor key. And suddenly, the shadow of the woman destroyed standing alongside the liberated woman lover, the woman traveler, the woman walker. Walking or not walking? "Very often, I walk from one point to another. . . . We were going by road and path, and suddenly a house blocked our way. That happens very often: I go into the house, I vainly look for the way out, I'm not supposed to be there, I panic and sometimes someone is chasing me."

Reading the accumulation of these long walks, I hear a continual motor excitation, a constant beating without discharge but that crashes out of fear. Sleep does not erase it, as it meticulously works at translating it into spaces, with great care, without rest: "no way out," "I don't know where the brake is," explains the dreamer. "I suddenly realize I don't know where the brake is, I can't find it, I wonder how I'm going to stop: in general, I end up gently hitting a wall; I come out of it without a scratch, but I was afraid." This *pertuum mobile* that Beauvoir was (if one believes her autobiographical writings and her friends' accounts) has trouble settling: trouble finding her home port, her markers, and even more, her house whose image in her last dreams is her mother's fifth-floor apartment on rue de Rennes.

Paired with her motor excitation: clothes problems. Beauvoir accumulates dreams of unrecognizable clothes, unhappy fittings or feverish disguises, useless piles of accessories: to fight against the cold "over there," cold "down there"? All this ritual is meticulously subjected to the critical examination of the dreamer, and—like a strange skin or an unfaithful mirror—it expresses a shaky, disconcerting self-image, sealed by the words "hole," "emptiness," and "fear": "I'll mention one [of her many clothing dreams] that is rather exceptional for its reflective and critical side. I was getting ready to go to my class in Rouen, and suddenly I had a memory block. . . . I saw in the mirror that I was wearing a yellow blouse and a plaid skirt: I didn't recognize them. I was afraid. . . . Many people surrounded me and I still felt this emptiness in my head: impossible to remember what clothes I had in my wardrobe. I said to the doctor: 'I don't understand anything. *Unless I'm sleeping*.'[8] . . . I stuff clothes into a big blue trunk; it's too small because it's very cold 'there,' and I have to take a lot of things with me."

TWO EVENTS PUNCTUATE THE LABYRINTHS OF BREATHLESS EXCITATIONS

Falling: let-down of excitation without discharge, bitter dissatisfaction *in fine*, unshed tears. And flights, swirling euphoria, usually, here and there tinged with a hint of worry and anxiety, except when they become a "played out" psychodrama, emphasized the dreamer who judges herself while dreaming.

Frequently, the writer dreams of her mother: "woman" without a face, an attractive yet inaccessible girl, to love or to kill; this maternal presence that has to be called dreamlike wends its way into the imaginary name of a city, "Mersépolis" (instead of Persepolis that had been talked about a lot that day, said the dreamer).

The emblematic dream about the mother at the lake surprisingly led the dreamer to Nelson Algren. The same cold water separates her from mommy—first love and hate object—to the favorite lover: metaphor-metamorphosis of frustration, insurmountable wound, frigidifying remoteness. "Another night, I caught a glimpse of my mother—a young and beautiful, silhouette, faceless—who was at the edge of a stretch of luminous water that I had to cross to meet up with her. I thought of the little lake in front of Algren's garden: but there was no boat to cross it. It was also a fjord that was really hard to get around: you had to jump into the water where you could drown. But I had to warn my mother of a great danger threatening her." Remember this lake: memory of an inaccessible mother, psychically absent, impossible to conquer, threatened-threatening? Or is it a defensive reconstruction against her attraction: against the desire for her and against her desire for the dreamer?

TWO OTHER DREAMS COMPLETE THIS MOTHERHOOD, ELUSIVE AND TO ELUDE

First, the dream of the "stupid woman"—but might she not be an alter ego of the dreamer, since the dreamer and her heroine are the same age? "I was walking with a stupid girl: I was the same age as she was . . . she answered that what was important for a 'woman' was to have a day care center nearby. She irritated me because in speaking of herself she kept saying 'woman.' We went into her house that was a real palace." We met a man "dressed in a long white coat that he had been wearing the day before last during the demonstration for abortion rights. I was happy to see him. On a table there was a dish of raw eggs out of their shell. Someone took a fork and stuck it into the whites. I shouted: 'Don't do that!' They were embryos and if you touched them they would become handicapped children. This dream was obviously influenced by conversations that I had had about our demonstration." Of course. This "stupid woman" dream that ended in a dream of eggs that the dreamer was going to beat with a fork also expresses the anxiety of infanticide: through one of her characters is the fear of the deficient child, the disgust of eggs, ovaries, female fecundity, and its dangerousness.

Another latent thought attests to the depth of the self-analysis Simone de Beauvoir sought to pursue. Killing the mother in the egg is a dream that belongs to the same constellation as that of the sister burned and/or unfit for marriage. Dreams of matricide, of the fight to death with the other woman—"two people—one was my sister even though she didn't look like her and was a very young girl. Her nose and her right arm were burnt tree branches. She didn't seem to mind that, but I said to myself: 'She'll never get married. These burns are too ugly.'" The mother of the dreamer herself dies, mixed up with her daughter, "stretched out on a sheet, as if I had been in a bed, I felt I was going to fall; . . . At that moment, a woman dressed in white—maybe a wedding dress—fell twistingly and crashed to the ground. I said to myself: 'It's my mother.' . . . 'My mother has just killed herself,' without feeling anything, as if I were playing a role." Is it the coldness of the mother of the lake that impregnates the girl herself to the extent of giving her a "false personality," a "false self"? Or is the girl who "steals" the place of her mother in the bed of the bride and ends up "falling" . . . crashing without pleasure, because of unknown guilt? The dreamer refuses this primal incestual passion by playing all the roles, being omnipresent. To protect herself from choosing: from loving or hating, desiring or taking vengeance?

Enter cruelty, a well-tempered cruelty that Beauvoir does not dwell on. But she repairs it, including in her dreams, by adopting Sylvie, dreaming of her as a kind of sister—"someone who was both Sylvie and my sister," "I was with my sister Sylvie," "a charming young woman in furs." Sylvie: reassuring and loving companion in the labyrinth of stations, trips and other lost and found baggage, in counterpoint to a Sartre, essential and no less unassailable.

Did the father really disappear from the nights of the second sex? Beauvoir makes it clear that her father did not appear in her dreams: "I said in *A Very Easy Death* that my mother appeared often in my dreams while my father was absent from them; in the past, she was a dear presence but I was often afraid of falling back into her power. Now I see her in our old apartment on rue de Rennes. I feel uncomfortable about it and in addition we don't seem able to meet up: either I don't manage to get to the house or she is not there. When she does appear she is in general far off and young."

Yet the father is not so absent as all that in these dreams that emphasize the maternal absence. But when the dreamer remembers, it is a paternal figure that she assassinates.

Beauvoir does not kill her own father explicitly: he is merely someone who comes to mind after mentioning walks with Sartre, after finding herself with him in a kind of desert and without baggage, without her pretty embroidered blue skirt bought in Greece, after having lost her key. Will Sylvie's arrival in the dream erase this bitter sequence? Not really. The answer is in the dreamlike logic that follows with another dream: the murderous dream itself. She who dared in *The Second Sex* to question the father's authority brought a boy's oedipal complex on stage in a bloody scenario: "a big bad man attacked our friends and I plunged a knife down his throat; I fainted while thinking: 'I killed! It's impossible.' Recovering, I anxiously wondered if I would be congratulated or put on trial: I was rather disappointed because nothing happened at all."

And it is the same "murder of the father" theme but better concealed, twisted in the meanders of a cemetery full of men in stone (diminished replicas of the statue of the Commander?), who reappeared in the dream about Solzhenitsyn, a perfect figure if ever there was one of the patriarch, beside the dreamer's mother: "I was told: it's Solzhenitsyn. . . . He asked . . . : 'Whose fault is it that my father is dead?' . . . At that moment I left: my mother was waiting for me for dinner in our old apartment on the fifth floor, rue de Rennes (it comes back rather often in my dreams.) I found myself in a village. . . . I went into the cemetery. And there I had an astonishing vision: it was like those dreams in movies that seemed so false to me. On the ground were many coffins covered in black material; men in black clothes and top hats lined up on each side while others paraded in the background: under the top hats some had skull heads. . . . They weren't men's but heads of stone sculptures." Is modeling the dead father into a statue a "rationalization," as Beauvoir's commentary suggests? Or also a defense against the aggressiveness concerning the father, replaced by a work of art, the sculpture idealizing and neutralizing the acting out of the knife? Other dreams, explicitly dreams of suffering, associate the "man of stone" with Sartre, also with a heart of "stone": "Silent sufferings were unbearable for me, and I have already said that I was no longer able to die in my sleep. Sartre during the night had always been for me either the companion he is in my life or a man with a heart of stone that my criticisms or prayers, my tears or my faintings left indifferent."

Yet there is a selfless, soothing motherhood that repairs the inaccessible mother-at-the-lake and the burned-arms sister, the (aforementioned) dreams of the dreamer with Sylvie, her adopted daughter. Sylvie, who merges into an enhanced sister, a complicit double, a soothing companion, a counterweight to an uncertain Sartre. This Sartre who is sometimes a carrier (like a helicopter), sometimes elusive because he prefers to eat but does not if the dreamer wants to also: does he not share the same bread? Does he not have the same taste or not the same appetite as those of the dreamer? "I'm going to eat as well," she says after getting lost and at last finding Sartre sitting in front of a dish with "appetizing hors d'oeuvres and a chestnut cake." "I've had enough, I'm full," cuts in Sartre "humorously." Other trips, interrupted by a tired Sartre, would continue with Sylvie.

I will stop here with the possible free associations that Beauvoir's dreams, generously offered to her readers, could awaken in the "public's" unconscious. Is giving one's intimacy to the public an act of seduction? Of power? Or is it a call out of love, or out of fragility? Does it record the intimate in the very heart of the political pact: to avoid the "Beauvoir" cult or to better solidify it? I would like to think that Beauvoir offers her dreams to us to avoid worship, to weaken it.

Might it be because she continued to analyze herself until the end of her life and in the limelight of what was becoming a society of the spectacle that Beauvoir's thought has taken an indelible place in women's and the world's history? Her recorded dreams reveal only "the most pleasant" ones to tell and do not in any way exhaust the breadth of her work. At the heart of "all said and done," they attest to the fact that Beauvoir's genius lies in her ability to reveal the most intimate possible, making it compatible with the difficulties of a period, transforming them into political crises. My angst is yours; it is up to you to "transcend" it on the world stage: this is what this dreamlike "diversion" seems to be saying in substance.

From then on, psychoanalysis, which cannot be reduced to the *microscope* of the interpretation of dreams and the intimate, could try to prolong the dialogue by broaching her work with this *telescope* that could be a social-historical interpretation attentive to the analytic experience.

I tried elsewhere to examine through a telescope the three areas in which Beauvoir innovated by recording her unconscious (and whose dreams reveal a few bumps) in the social-historical existence of twentieth-century women: the universal and the female; the destroyed-reconstructed couple; the novel as a refoundation of the intimate in politics. These subjects are always present; they reveal and keep alive Beauvoir's presence in us and around us, more than ever, sixty years after *The Second Sex*. I would like to refer you to it.[9] You will find a path leading to the writing of this free woman. Before her work became a political project and while becoming one, Beauvoir liberated her interior experience, including her dreams and desires, by writing it: "Writing remained my life's great affair."

IV

HUMANISM

❖

15

A FELICITY NAMED ROUSSEAU

We do not live, we wait to live.

—BLAISE PASCAL

The purpose of human life is human felicity . . . but who among us knows how to attain it?

— JEAN-JACQUES ROUSSEAU

WHOSE FAULT IS IT?

Who are you, Jean-Jacques Rousseau? A fixed star in the constellation of the Enlightenment, "Voltaire-Diderot-Rousseau"? The founder of the political philosophy of globalized modern times, with "people's sovereignty" and "general interest" in addition? The theologian of the republican religion "Liberté-Egalité-Fraternité"? Or rather, if Voltaire is to be believed, a "madman," an "apprentice clockmaker," a "maniac" who "crossed the limits of ordinary madness"? "The first modern man, an idealist and a rogue," a "runt planted firmly on the threshold of modern times" who wanted a "return to nature," according to Nietzsche? A "desolate vagabond" who "adopted the walk of life," as Hölderlin said? A "deserter from the *Social Contract*," to use Sollers's words?

After your two speeches in Dijon, the polemical "Letter to d'Alembert," *La Nouvelle Héloïse*, and *Emile*, finally came the beacon book: *Of the Social Contract* (1762). The prerevolutionary ideology is taking shape as you write! Debates, criticism, enthusiasm, and conflicts of all types are only just beginning; even the Encyclopedists are tearing each other apart. But a new period is emerging and you are its prophet, in the eye of the storm.

The work is banned in France, the Netherlands, Geneva, and Berne. Yet you were aware of some of the objections to your two speeches: your *Social Contract* does not stigmatize the social link itself but suggests refounding the pact by adjusting progress to natural values. Your "state of nature" is not the savage state but a philosophical hypothesis based on a relentless and preventive criticism of social abuses. Can a new political convention guarantee justice? Can citizens be just? You suggest basing the social contract on a one and only "sovereignty": exit that of the prince, long live that of the people! Without any particular vested interest—privileges, "partial associations," egoism, or sectarian communities—arriving and distorting the "general interest." "Each of us puts his person and all his power in common under the supreme direction of the general will; and in a body we receive each member as an indivisible part of the whole."

The effort you ask of the legislators of this ideal state seems insurmountable, and so you inform the reader: "Gods would be needed to give men laws!" And only the advent of a new humanity will be able to create your paradise on earth: to "inform the general will" men have to change, and "they have to be made indivisible parts of the whole." Has this outsized ambition for such a vision really been heard, for better or for worse?

Might you be a republican saint? Undoubtedly a reader of Saint Augustine: "*Socialis est vita sanctorum*," wrote the bishop of Hippo. But you are not yet at the *Confessions* chapter. Right from the outset, though, your political faith is steeped in asceticism, and this virtuous inspiration, sometimes considered puritanical, troubles your aspiration for social happiness. Perusing *Julie, or the New Heloise*, Voltaire understands it and does not let you off the hook. It is not enough for him to seize on the many contradictions or even inaccuracies that spot your thinking (you advocate the Republic for both small and poor States, forgetting the Roman and Venetian republics and even the Athens' democracy!), the wise man of Ferney judges your work "childish," and even worse, dangerous. Was he already thinking that this so generous "general interest" might stifle law and liberties and sow Terror if it were wrongly interpreted? "An assembly of the people" suspending all jurisdiction and all executive power "would be a formal invitation to crime," he prophesized.

Considering your recommendations and nothing else, and if one does not read what you are writing and will continue to write on these men that have to be changed—and who are none other than the man you are—Voltaire is not wrong: the Terror, the Gulag, the Holocaust, just to mention these, will, alas, soon prove him right. But those who reduce you to being merely the precursor of these crimes are bound to remain ignorant of the polychrome landscape, the cubist mobile, the musical fluid in osmosis with the genius of the French language, that is, the thinking of the writer Rousseau. Because before the decisive *Of the Social Contract* that political scientists are still reinterpreting, the novelist who never stops writing the novel of his "I alone" had already published *Julie, or the New Heloise* in 1761, sparking much jealousy. The best-selling book of the eighteenth century, this epistolary love story sells like hot cakes in bookshops; out of stock, it is rented weekly or by the hour, and you are inundated with readers' letters asking for news of your totally imagined characters!

The work features a play of ardent and frustrated passions that do manage to work themselves out successfully in a society far more idyllic than the happiness in the society promised in the *Social Contract*. But the folds of their sublimated affects hide a few keys that open the doors of shameful human singularities, burning desires, and painful sexual admissions. Rousseau's own secret garden?

Unassuaged by morality—now called bourgeois—the four protagonists' desires outlive their passion, either by the intermediary of the "triangular constellations" (Saint-Preux-Claire-Julie; Julie-Saint-Preux-Wolmar) that compensated the degenitalization of potential sexual relations or by the intense erotization of the bonds among them and with the world, strongly expressed by music, Jean-Jacque's place of choice and refuge. The modern reader rushes to condemn the sacrifice of women who devote themselves to their duty to the detriment of pleasure and whose virtue should not allow a mother to survive the death of her son. There is also the praiseworthy morality of the males: Saint-Preux discovering new continents, rejecting war; Wolmar as an exemplary spouse. Although tempered, sensuality does not at all disappear. The episode of Milord Edouard and the castrato Regianino introduced a subtle digression on the differences between the sexes. As a counterpoint to Julie claiming her resolute femininity, Rousseau introduced the Italian singer's charms, far from the canon's norms of such a difference! But her seduction is what excites the protagonists' erotic memories that contribute simply to setting up the little ideal cenacle of his guests in a holy effervescence of desires, less, nevertheless, physical love. Might music and sublimation be the guarantors of the conjugal bond? Or maybe even of the *Social Contract*?

Where is Abelard in this new Heloise? Was it perhaps the castrato Regianino's seduction that took over? That means that the bourgeois family, like the State, needs a certain castration if it can be sublimated in the continuous innovation of new seductive languages such as the arts, music, and literature. Tempered voluptuousness provides a fragile but irreplaceable support to moral duty, and sublimation is its republican spirituality. The novelist, Rousseau himself, preceded the lawmaker in his divine task, when souls collapse.

Here, Voltaire, who was suspicious of his philosopher's virtue and well aware of his "sexual anomaly," attacked: "It is rather strange that a man who publicly admits being a corruptor would want then to act as lawmaker: but he teaches men as he directs girls." And elsewhere: "Never has a whore preached more and never has a valet seducer of girls been more philosophic."

Is it Voltaire's or Rousseau's fault? Their coffins had already been placed side by side in the Pantheon when Victor Hugo blessed them from the height of his fame of *Les Miserables*, and not without recognizing in Jean-Jacques both the "solitary" and the one who acted in "solidarity."

Rousseau's probing the depths of denatured humanity is clearly not the most audacious. It was not until the Marquis de Sade that death wishes were unleashed into a boudoir philosophy and shone a sarcastic light on virtues' calamities. Excitable and shy, Rousseau had the brilliant idea to match the rigor of the tormented citizen of Geneva with the hypersensitivity of the women-surrounded orphan, both to dream of a pacified humanity and to admit to his own baseness.

He committed himself to writing about it in a ductile and contagious prose as the only remedy to the criminality dwelling in the social animal. With and beyond his proclaimed solitude, it is the singularity of the excesses and failures of human experience that he offers to those seeking political thought or just simply seeking thought. Not as a replacement of the "general interest" and the risks of its slippery slope toward the automatization of our species. But like a new promised land between the "*state of nature*" and "*sovereign people*," Rousseau erected the cult of the imaginary where the singularity of beings speaking, music-ing, rebeginning, and re–being born is protected and elucidated.

THE SINGULAR SELF

"I am undertaking the same thing as Montaigne," he proclaimed in his "first" *Reveries*. But with one difference: Rousseau's Self was not the royal path toward wisdom that enlightened Montaigne. Nor was it this *amabam amare* that led Augustine to his God, nor the Quietist deduction that annihilated the child for Fenelon. "I intend to present my peers with a man in all the truth of nature. And this man will be me. Myself alone. I feel my heart, and I know mankind. I am not constituted like anyone I have ever encountered. I dare venture that I am not made like anyone else in the world, and though I might be no better, at least I am different" [*The Essential Writings of Rousseau*, trans. Peter Constantine (New York: Modern Library, 2013), 323]. Not everything has been said, but everything begins as of the first lines of the *Confessions* (1770). An impetuous and sovereign singularity, "uneven and natural," a "succession of affections," a "chain of sentiments," a flux of metamorphoses. Like Montaigne, indeed, when the author of *Essays* wrote: "We are all little pieces, and so varied and shapeless that each piece, each moment, does its part."

It is impossible to portray him as La Bruyère might have done because Rousseau had nothing to do with these word statues created by the poetics of Scaliger during the Renaissance, in the "Characters" of classic art. The "I alone" of Rousseau is not statufiable. From the outset he sought himself as both unique and other. From reversal to reversal, unstable and fickle, he seemed to slide the baroque man's mobility into the libertarian projects of the Enlightenment. But passionate about happiness, he reduced the "obstacles" and the "crimes" he attributed to himself in his irresistible urge to say, to signify, to write "quickly and well, twice well," as Baltasar Gracián had said. Listen to these galloping words capturing the thief's drive: "This ribbon alone tempted me, I stole it." That is all. That is me, and me alone.

It is there, in the writing of sensible memory, that Rousseau freed himself from confusion, worry, and passion itself. To give himself over to the jouissance of wandering alone: reverie grasped in this carrier wave of language that Freud called "free association," on which the solitary walker imprinted the mark of a musician's ear, of an often absolute precision.

"Who am I?" Saint-Preux was already obsessed by this question: "Tormented by a criminal passion I can neither bear nor conquer, am I the one I thought I was?" His quest continued in the fugues of the *Confessions*. Their solitary *self*, which seems exalted or even egotistical, and already romantic, does not stop seeking its elusive truth, infinitely rebounding on the wave of his multilayered guilt disappearing as soon as confessed by the verbal magic of his incessant self-analysis. Is Rousseau the missing link between Augustine and Freud with his Dora case and his president Schreber?

He continued this search until the end of his life for which "it is enough for me . . . to enter inside myself," but always open forever, always ready to be completed while walking across lakes, mountains, and meadows, flowers, winds, and stars. Because these *Reveries* are the real walk of his life: "But me . . . who am I myself? This is what I am still seeking," he wrote, ill, two years before his death.

The revelation of this unstable Self, contentious and of a real *processivity* found only in the Taoist sage, is based on a return to childhood, a worship of memory, and a wager on the power of the imaginary.

Traumatic and recomposed childhood, constantly seen in unstable, saturating, frustrating, and incestuous relations. The author's paroxystic sensitivity, always ready to "feel his heart" and careful to improve his fellow man more in theory than in practice, seems to have been constructed less by a parental or institutional authority than from a trauma, an abandon, a "vacuum" that he often complained of.

Jean-Jacques lost his mother when he was nine days old. His father, a bad-tempered watchmaker always spoiling for a fight, left the house when Rousseau was only ten. The eroticized tenderness that mature women afforded him, satisfying the vicissitudes of their displaced mothering through him, nevertheless compensated for these lacks. Mme de Warens, whom he called "Mama," nicknamed him "Little One." Nourished by this mothering, effusive and capricious permissiveness, the orphan covered his abandonment distress by the feeling of a boundless happiness. Was it the prototype for the "natural state"? Or the motor of a fabulous vital enthusiasm? The "I alone" has its roots in this constantly re-created bliss: Herein lies his family, his mother, his country, his Nature, his impetus. His genius made a political project of it for all humans, while childhood, sensations, memory, and imagination became the cornerstones of this universe that the writer never stopped reworking and changing.

"Grasp life by its beginnings": this beautiful Augustinian theme became a therapy for Rousseau: "the great cure for the miseries of life" lay in the ability to put oneself "in the state of a man who is beginning to live." The state of the baby, the "idle life," or the perpetual return to one's beginnings? The goal to reach was not that but the possibility of holding oneself in the opening—of ideas and situations—that coincides with happiness. "Except the Being existing by himself, nothing is beautiful but what is not." Melancholic but not really, Rousseau prefigured the future beyond the vacuum and the nothingness, found pleasure in what was missing, what was desirable more than what was consumed. He prophesized desire projected by the grace of his imaginary construction.

The permanence of the past placed memory at the center of this "broken heart." "It is the history of my soul that I promised, and to write it faithfully I do not need other memories: it is enough for me . . . to enter again into my inner self," he wrote in the *Confessions*, letting a sensorial and vibrant nostalgia shine through the carrier wave of happiness. By the grace of the perceived and the felt, the enigmatic "I alone" settled at the interface between "nature" and these closed and cold "pagodas" that the others are, to feel oneself "alive": "Only on the condition that I tasted an intense sweetness thinking I was not alone, that I was not conversing with an unfeeling and dead being, that my problems were counted . . . and that all the miseries of my life were merely . . . pleasures for a better state" (*1st Dialogue*), and again: "We describe much more what we feel than what is" (*Letter, 1763*); "I feel my heart," "I cannot mistake what I felt?" "I will say each thing as I feel it, as I see it, without self-consciousness, without second thoughts, without worrying about variegation."

This tapped and transmissible memory is found in and by one's imagination, which Rousseau asks not to be confused with the fiction of "those who philosophize in their studies." Colleagues appreciated this. "My imagination, which in my youth was always forward looking and is now regressing, compensates with these sweet memories the hope I have lost forever" (*Confessions*). But if this "imaginary compensation" betrays a renunciation of pleasures lightly called physical, it produces an exquisite experience of language: between things and words, Rousseau's imaginary claims to be consubstantial with the felt, the affects and drives; it is embodied. Thus he is brought to jouissance. For that itself it is worth living as much as or more than the feeling itself: "Why deprive myself of the present charm of jouissance to say to others that I had found pleasure?" Because by saying it the jouissance is fulfilled. "But how to say what was neither said, nor done, nor even thought, but tasted, but felt, but without being able to utter any other object of my happiness but this feeling itself. . . . happiness followed me everywhere; it was not in any determined thing; it was all in myself, it could not leave me for one instant" (*Confessions*).

"I CANNOT LEAD INTO ERROR"

By thus transforming infantile trauma into a joyful reviviscence in memory remade language, "saying" and writing, Rousseau was sure he held the truth: if and only if he managed to contact the things felt with words. In thus making his "soul transparent," he could only be in truthfulness: HIS truth could be claimed as THE truth, facing those who were unable to share the alchemy of this incorporated saying. This remains true even if the person has committed errors, since the folds of his wanderings, which the writer-analyst was and would be able to restore, are so many truths, potentially universal in their very specificity, to be added to the knowledge of the human soul.

In Freudian terms, it is the right to "psychic reality" whose truth the psychoanalyst respects and Rousseau asserted against the partisans of "exterior," "objectal reality" in which "barbarians" imprison the man or woman suspected of committing or not indictable errors. Sovereignty of the imaginary, if it succeeds in translating the sensible melody, without getting blocked, trail-blazing adventurer of the unsayable: "In detailing to him [the reader] simply everything that happened to me, everything

I did, everything I thought, everything I felt, I cannot lead him into error, unless I want to; even in wanting to I would not manage to do so easily in this way" (*Confessions*). Thus understood, "moral truth" is one hundred times more respectable than that of facts.

It is not enough to say everything. "I have often said evil in all its turpitude; I have rarely said good in all its amiability" (*4th Reverie*). It is important to stick to the "atmospheric" fluctuations of the self so that, in the thrall of a "moral reform," the work becomes a "barometer" of the driving pressures that underlie it, even to crimes. "Extravagances," "follies," "deliriums," "annihilations," but also "brief passions": The moments of my life that I became an other must be recalled. . . . Then, my soul in movement did no more than cross the line of rest, and its constantly renewed oscillations never allowed it to stay there" (*Confessions*).

Only the movement of this effort, or rather this joy in the sensible imagination, faithful to the felt, thanks to the contact with nature, and to the "oscillations" of morality itself, can claim to reach the truth of the singular Self, become synonymous of man's "natural state." Style itself "is part of my history," so that "ideas" do not precede me but come "as I like," and "facts" are only "occasional causes" for its moral truths to start moving. The imaginary, thus telling the truth of the one who constructs it, cannot not tell the truth. Whether making a mistake or lying, the writer "is always well painted when he paints himself, even if the portrait does not resemble him" (*Confessions*). Filter of anxieties and desires more than an imitation of external reality, "substance" and "form" are reconciled and intrinsically intertwined—like music!—writing thus understood constructs and circulates singularity. And gives itself a chance to distill the truth in the *Social Contract*.

Is this plea for the power and right of the imagination to make "my soul transparent" an extravagant monument of narcissism? Is it the ultimate megalomaniacal pretention of this "I alone" that Diderot dismissed with a scathing remark: "Only the nasty one is alone" (*The Natural Son*)? It can lead society's accuser to get stuck in the role of the paranoiac panicked by then being accused in the conspiracy of his persecutors. Rousseau was not spared these demons. But through the constantly renewed power of his embodied imagination, he tamed his fantasies and his most outrageous acting out. And he managed to thwart the old couple, inherited from past centuries, "self-love" and "self-esteem." Rousseau's experience concerns a singular yet sharable Self that is neither self-esteem that avoids obstacles but loses itself nor self-love—to which it is closer—that eliminates them without getting sidetracked.

After Voltaire's denunciation and the cold reception of *Confessions*, excessive solitude brought awareness of his overwhelming distress in *Rousseau: Judge of Jean-Jacques: Dialogues*: "The author of the books and that of the crimes seems to you to be the same person; I think I have the right to make two of them." The manic-depressive examined himself and organized his duality: "Let us remember one of these short moments of my life where I became an other" (*Confessions*). Arthur Rimbaud is close by, another ambulating dreamer. And in a furtive rebound, the philosopher, taking refuge in his haven as a music copyist and composer, found in self-analysis this "feeling of existence" that acquiesced to his new happiness. The explored duality here goes beyond the certitude of a sublimated self. But happiness from now on is expressed in negative terms, "without needing to recall the past or to take strides toward the future" (*Reveries*). Out of time, stripped of will and of objects, the solitary walker becomes abstract painter to draw the broken spaces of the natural-maternal repository found in a new state, now ecstatic, "satisfied, perfect, and full."

Another philosophy of creative subjectivity emerges in *Reveries*, his last work: an *ecceitas*, irreducible but nevertheless connected to Providence with its earthly ecosystem, closer to Duns Scotus than to Montaigne or to Vauvenargues.

In the crucible of this new subjective recomposition, the Self cancels itself out: "I can easily say that I only began to live when I looked at myself as a dead person," the *Confessions* predicted. "I never meditate, I never dream more deliciously than when I forget myself" (*Reveries*). Can this spiritual roaming still be called literature? "A language as new as my own project is what is needed" (*Confessions*). In his *Essay on the Origin of Languages* (1781, posthumous), Rousseau dreamed of an idiom able to compact things and words, a fabulous bridge from drives to signs: he alone would have made possible the first encounter of the two sexes and their sources. "From fountains' pure crystal flow the first fires of love." Is this the final reverie on the subject of the primal paradise?

His work as a whole was thus an inner journey toward this felicity of language, toward this antiliterature. The following centuries took it up and developed it: Baudelaire's "correspondences," the metamorphoses of the "hachischins" and the great poets; the search for sensible childhood in Proust's involuntary memory and cursed races; botany for Colette as a spiritual experience, etc.

ON THE ROAD TO VINCENNES

In the *Praise of Folly*, Erasmus (1469–1536) left his mark on Renaissance humanism. Dame Folly, fully part of him and of all humans, finally spoke up in philosophy. Rousseau's imagination prolonged and transmuted it into *Praise of Illumination*.

On the road to Vincennes, the man examined his "state of confusion." But then he drew inspiration from this "delirium-like agitation" that often came upon him in waves and that he shared with Diderot and the Encyclopedists. Their brotherly complicity did not save them from the nasty demolitions that pit the deist, materialist, and atheist clans against Jean-Jacques Rousseau for three decades. He, from Protestantism to Catholicism and vice versa but always in his interior meanderings, confessed: "I often distorted religion to my own fashion but I never was without it."

For the moment, we are in 1749. The neurasthenic and still obscure author went all out for Diderot. With his *Letter About the Blind for Those Who See* (1749)—still mentioned today to promote the "republican work site" for the disabled—the great Diderot who called himself deist became an atheist, which had him imprisoned in Vincennes. This imprisonment put Rousseau in a state of great emotion: palpitations, unending tears, "indescribable distress" that worked itself out in a surge of verbal and creative enthusiasm. Depressed, manic, and unstable, Rousseau composed a hymn to happiness to make his soul transparent and transmuted his amorous fever into an "illumination" that produced the *Discourse on Sciences and Arts*:

[A]rriving in Vincennes, I was in a state of agitation verging on delirium. Diderot noticed it; I told him the cause of it and read him Fabricius' prosopopoeia written in pencil under an oak tree. He exhorted me to develop my ideas and compete for the prize. I did so, and from that moment I was ruined. All the rest of my misfortunes during my life were the inevitable effect of this blunder. My sentiments became elevated with the most inconceivable rapidity to the level of my ideas. All my little passions were stifled by the enthusiasm of truth, liberty, and virtue; and, what is most astonishing, this effervescence continued in my mind upward of five years, to as great a degree perhaps as it has ever done in that of any other man. (*Confessions*)

PERIWINKLES

Might Proust's "little madeleine" be a sign of recognition sent to Rousseau's "periwinkles"? In a few light blue and mauve lines, Jean-Jacques paid tribute to his communion with "Maman," who haunted his pen right up to the last *Reverie* published after his death: "I dwelled seventy-six years on this earth and I lived seven of them," he wrote about the years 1729–1737, close to Mme de Warens, "the best of women," transfigured as a flower.

> The first day that we went to Charmettes, Maman . . . saw something blue in the hedge and said: here are some periwinkles still in flower. I had never seen periwinkles; I bent down to examine one but was too short-sighted to spot plants on the ground from my height. I only glanced at it and almost thirty years have passed without seeing a periwinkle or without paying attention to it. In 1764 . . . I began to collect plants. Climbing up and looking among the bushes I cried out joyfully: Oh! So here's a periwinkle; and there it was. Du Peyrou noticed my excitement, but he did not know what caused it. (*Confessions*)

The "cause," as for little Marcel, is Maman: might it be this periwinkle, spotted by Maman and adored with her, that destined "her little one" to become a herbalist? The real object of happiness had always been "inside myself." The writer analyzing his soul knew this: there is nothing of outside in this sky blue and water paradise. Neither the flower, nor his amorous adolescence and youth, nor even Maman. Nothing but the "feeling of happiness" imprinted in him, induced certainly by maman-periwinkle, by periwinkle-maman, but re-created in style. Explosive "secret affection" that he had to say, he and he alone, to make happiness exist: "But how to say what . . . was felt, without being able to state any other object of my happiness than this very feeling" (*Confessions*).

"Ersatz grief," Proustian excellence in its variations like the periwinkles episode, would always be bittersweet. Only Colette, faithful to her pleasures lived with Sido, succeeds in this innocent, infantile, and solar jouissance called pre-Socratic. But it is Proust, nevertheless, guardian of "involuntary memory," who crowns the imagination as "the only organ . . . for the enjoyment of beauty." Echoing Rousseau: "Saying to myself I have rejoiced, I rejoice again."

CONSPIRACY: IS ROUSSEAU PARANOID?

Where did the evil preying on our enlightened philosophers come from? Their fraternal complicities turned into quarrels, ostracisms, and persecutions. The French have often pushed the truth of these psychodramas of love until death between men, through women if necessary, while living them in full daylight, without necessarily going as far as a homosexual act. Did Rousseau have to be affected with a congenital malformation of the urethra or a metabolic problem called "intermittent acute porphyria," as if the infantile trauma sealed up in incestual effusions was not enough to trigger delirious effervescences?

The political combats in which the men of the Enlightenment were engaged could only exacerbate his private fragilities. Suspicious, anxious, at war against the "barbarians" who were also harming themselves in epistolary battles, the Encyclopedists wounded and even killed with their art of the well-turned phrase. Is that enough to cry conspiracy? Rousseau did so, but modern researchers have shown that he was the one who broke ranks and attacked first. Things really got worse in 1764 when the *Sentiment of the Citizens* denounced an immoral Rousseau, enemy of religion, fraudulent, and above all an unfit father who abandoned "his children at the hospital door." The anonymous pen was Voltaire's who had already written to d'Alembert in 1762: "This monster dares speak of education, he who did not want any of his sons and who put them all in the Foundling Hospital." But the denunciation went public, and even if Rousseau persisted in believing that Voltaire was not the author, he knew that the father of *Candide* harbored a fierce hatred of him.

Rousseau had foreseen the plot even before he could identify it. "It is in the private talks, in the circles, in the little secret counties, in all these little literary courts presided by women that the daggers that covertly stab him are sharpened" (*Dialogues*). As soon as they were drawn, the arrows went right to the heart of the one who, between despondency and exaltation, was persuaded of "being the master of all of nature." That Diderot, Grimm, d'Alembert, Mme du Deffand, Choiseul, and Voltaire denounced him or that they had him investigated by the authorities neither justified nor explained the overwhelming evidence against him: there was a plot against him, and the nameless crowd itself was part of it. He recognized himself in the straw dummy burning at a street fair on rue de la Plâtrière, now rue Rousseau.

The violence of his ex-philosopher friends, resonating with his exaltations of "censor" feeling "censored," the unconscious grip of a fault going beyond what he said soberly about it in the *Confessions*, places the "I alone" in the panic of a persecuted person. More than a "universe of fault," there is in Rousseau a climate of fault, as his weather metaphors suggest, "within" his bipolar-tending Self. Far from being stuck in an inexorable universe, this atmosphere is counterbalanced by his self-analysis of this rupture that *Rousseau: Judge of Jean-Jacques: Dialogues* undertakes. "I had to say with what eye, if I were an other, I would see a man such as I am." "The author of the books and the author of the crimes are not the same man."

With distance and irony, mixing meditation and innocence, without denying the fault but without remorse or repentance either, the writer absorbed the "obstacle," guilt and persecutions concerning his refusal of paternity. He went no further than minimally rectifying what he was criticized for: the children were given to Public Welfare in all legality and not left at the church door, and he justified his refusal of paternity as the best choice for his children considering the family context. That done, and faced with the absurdity of social injustice, Rousseau pleaded for the innocence of the natural man that for him meant remaining faithful to his singular complexity: the interior debates of his divided Self that exposed him to his readers were his only and real defense. And to predict new times where human beings would cease to "mutiny" against their conscience.

The outside enemy did not just disappear, but writing about anxiety did reach the other inside oneself: "Is the essence of my being in their gaze?" "Our true self is not quite in us" (*Rousseau: Judge of Jean-Jacques: Dialogues*), and "I need to commune with myself in order to love" (*Reveries*). This is the beginning of a turning point. As the consciousness of his singularity grew, Rousseau sought another way of being in the world. In examining its many facets, the *Dialogues* pointed to and consolidated a "constant way of being:" less social, more musical—meaning a sharable communing—taken with botany and in an indefatigable wandering across his interior landscapes. And with an extreme surge of sublimation, his newly recovered solitude fit into a now indistinctly spiritual, esthetic, and natural puzzle, absolving him from his psychological, social, and political traumas. So without worldly "worry" or "hope," Rousseau proclaimed a serenity that desired to be freed from freedom itself.

Was he lying to himself? On February 24, 1776, the philosopher-writer tried in vain to leave a manuscript of the *Dialogues* on the altar of Notre Dame de Paris, but its gates were closed. Did he do this to protect himself from some guilt, some original sin? That of having lost his mother, of having innocently killed her, of being born ill? Or the sin of remaining the eternal child, irremediably innocent, incapable of evil, without purpose, alone, abandoned, an orphan? Only good for dreaming of a better world instead of what he did not have, of what he was not. By living the best of social contracts or rather asocial, for the orphans we are, in one way or another, one day or another.

THE ISLE OF SAINT-PIERRE

At the end of his life, Rousseau "fed himself" from his own substance," distilled in the flesh of the world. And like the Taoist sage who dreams only of "feeding life" (*yăng sheng*), his Self had already been forgotten. It was the *ipseity* of the singular walker who took his place, reunited with himself in the processivity of the vital force, abated or almost extinct, always inseparable from his writing. Without time, without success, pure present without duration. "Nothing from outside of oneself, nothing but oneself and one's own existence; as long as this state lasts, one suffices to oneself like God," he said in the fifth Reverie.

The painter of the vital force was now a minimalist. Tucked into the rhythm of the universe, he wrote his ecstasies, like Teresa of Avila returning to her seventh and last mansion. And it was the child Rousseau who emerged, with his abiding taste of spring, of renewal, of rebirth. "Everything is in a constant state of flux on earth: there is no constant and fixed shape." "I was born to life in this instant." "It seemed to me that I was filling all the objects I perceived with my slight existence. . . . I had no distinct notion of my individual."

The memory that returned then was of his refuge in 1765 in the middle of Lake Biel on the Isle of Saint Pierre, after the stoning of Môtiers. The aquatic ecstasy experienced at this beloved place ("of all my homes . . . none made me so truly happy"), abundantly restored and in verbal and physical faithfulness the simple repose of an impersonal existence at one with mother-nature, within and beyond the anguish of thinking, sketched out in the *Confessions*: "O nature, O my mother, here I am in your care alone." From then on, disseminated in the perpetual movement, the "I alone" stops his self-analysis with the gesture of a sometimes impressionistic, sometimes abstract, calligrapher.

In any case, and always defying Pascal's austere restraint, Rousseau "is not waiting to live:" he continued to savor felicity here and now, still "occupied with [his] happiness, able once again to enjoy when [he] wants:"

> The ebb and flow of this water, its noise continuous but louder from time to time, hitting my ear and eyes constantly, compensated for the internal movements that the reverie turned off and sufficed for me to feel my existence with pleasure . . . but soon these slight impressions faded in the uniformity of the continuous movement that rocked me and that, without any active help from my soul, continued to grip me to the point that called by the hour and the appointed signal I could not tear myself from there without effort. (*5th Promenade*)

Inviting us to this concert of words and feelings, Rousseau made good on this wager that seemed to conclude his work: to avoid the judgment that underpinned the Social Contract and replace it with a singular experience. Mixture of meditation and reverie, addition of the particular to the general, this experience took root in sensations, with the most singular being taste, and let itself go like doing an effortless duty. An experience that foresaw Kant's "esthetic judgment," taken up again by Hannah Arendt, to attempt to found a political philosophy able to escape the "banality of evil," in a "Social Contract" that would look like a concert audience. Each citizen would appreciate the work according to his individual taste, and yet a community of singulars would exist when, at the end of the concert, the audience shares the mutual attention that will have been brought to the creation and to the extreme experiences. "We's" without uniformity other than that of continuous movement.

Rousseau certainly did not dream of reworking his *Social Contract* in the aftermath of the *Confessions, Dialogues,* and *Reveries. We* are the ones the dilemma addresses: solitary and sharing, how to be righteous?

If globalization can avoid the automatization of the species under the virtual net of talking points, it has to contemplate the ways of Rousseaian felicity. And to give us the chance of experiencing their risks and serenities.

GLOBALIZED ROUSSEAU

Sofia. Bulgaria. Early 1960s, my native country. The iron curtain is already tearing, but no one has predicted the fall of the Berlin Wall. Students, academics, and intellectuals, we read the author of the *Social Contract* in French, German, and English, a few choice pieces in Russian, or even more rarely, in Bulgarian.

We do not agree. Some of us see him as the inspirer of man's rights—and women's—the inventor of the alienation theory before Marx. To use Kant's idea, he is "the Newton of the moral world," the then much missed founder of social democracy, and even, according to Lévi-Strauss, the "inventor of the social sciences."

"Wrong," counter the others: he is a gentle dreamer who undermines the individual's moral discipline and redeems himself by prophesizing the totalitarian state, by visualizing a "people in bodies," ripe for the Jacobin terror and the Soviet Gulag! How can one give the whole man to the state, this hyperorganism, supposed to make our happiness as citizens through security rules and moral order, under the "supreme direction of the general will"? Your wanderer dreams like a Bolshevik!

Not at all, the former argue: the protective state is just a means of guaranteeing the freedom of the man alone, of the singular, of the incommensurable stranger. Proof? Social convention dissolves if "there remains in the state one citizen who could not be helped," "one prisoner" held wrongly, "one unjust trial." I hear some and approve others.

A journalist friend passing through Sofia brought me the first *Pléiade* volume (*Confessions, Dialogues, Reveries of the Solitary Walker*) from Paris. Just as Rousseau was born again on the road to Versailles, Rousseau was "born again" in my eyes. "Everything is connected," he said, and in my mind, his personal writings do not diminish his political writings. In making his "soul transparent," he produced an antivirus, a counterweight to tyranny—democratic or spectacular. This extravagant shepherd, this "fanatic," as Diderot called him, this person "consumed by the need to love," invites each one to "enter inside oneself" to "feel one's heart." It is more difficult than voting, attested to by literature and psychoanalysis. But "rest and freedom are incompatible; you have to choose," Rousseau wrote to the Polish.

Denounced at the Sorbonne, condemned by the Bishop of Paris, and "taken into custody" in Geneva, stoned in Môtiers, expelled from Basle, exiled to Wotton, Rousseau was oppressed, offended, and exiled. The voice of this humiliated person has spanned the centuries to come to the rescue of victims of social inequalities: "As for wealth, no citizen should be rich enough to be able to buy another, and so poor as to have to sell oneself." "We are approaching the state of crisis and the century of revolutions," was his eloquent-as-a-Mohammed prophesy. "I am seeing all the States of Europe on the road to ruin," a still-fraught threat today.

But happiness still remains a renewable idea, in Europe and elsewhere, for this melancholic person threatened by a conspiracy. Is it this herbalist, consoled by corollas and calyxes, who is leading us, anticipating modern ecology? Is it the "moral religion" of this "champion of God"? A god who was neither Yahvé nor Jesus, and taking inspiration from both, but who moved away from this "apple juice" that Freud considered the god of philosophers? I like to think that Rousseau's form of personal religion is the indefatigable spiral of thought written in his paradoxical and involved way, rejecting the albeit experienced fault, eliminating lack and obstacles in his tireless search for a memory equal to the sensible shock. Derrida and Starobinski subtly pointed out the reversals of the transparences and complements of this vision of modern humanity: "I help you"—the man of need—becomes "I love you"—the man of moral passion, before falling into "I buy you"—the man of technical mediation and generalized corruption. The third millennium adds "I informatize you": you communicate but do you know how to signify? Here again, Rousseau comes to us.

Thinking about the foundations of modern democracy, he understood that it could not survive without finding its own language. *Rousseau the intimate* became an example for Goethe, Chateaubriand, Nerval, Musset, Hölderlin, Flaubert, Balzac, Stendhal, Byron, Tolstoy, Gide, Proust, Colette, and others. And even for the postmoderns who come out with avalanches of confidences in the guise of autofiction. Bergson was right against Benjamin Constant and the French "liberals" of the nineteenth century: no work in any other literature will have had as much influence as that of Rousseau the *visionary*.

Nevertheless, a *political* language that can probe and move the *obstacles* of the current *denaturations* is still lacking. As the ancient rhetoric failed in revolutionary arrogance and its totalitarian or fundamentalist variants, Rousseau's verdict has never been so scathing: "There are tongues (really? more like languages, words: of course!) that promote freedom. Ours are made for the humming of the couch." The metaphor of oriental despotism then referred to the salons, boudoirs, and political and ideological comfort. Today, the humming of screens, the rings of cell phones and the beeps of text messages are noisier than ever. They are even bad for freedom.

Solitary and invisible, Rousseau's imaginary experience remains one of these language revolutions that open paths for freedom, when the social contract is unable to do it and the people seem to abstain from the political cacophony.

16

SPEECH, THAT EXPERIENCE

When the search for God takes place intrinsically in language, does it not immediately open the way to the immanent becoming of transcendence?

Because I speak, my search for God—Love and Word—can only be a loving discourse. I seek myself in Him ("Seek yourself in Me," says the Creator to Teresa of Avila, before she finds him in her "*muy interior*"); "I" seeks itself in speaking the Word, and my God becomes my language.

A crossroads then appears at this point if the seeker dares to forget that his quest leads to Christ. Either I lock language in the absolute triumph of my "subjective arbitrariness" and strangle myself in a sort of *newspeak* or even in its totalitarian politics that George Orwell had already diagnosed and that Benedict XVI had rightly feared in his speech at the College des Bernardins.[1] Or I build my lab in the Word-Flesh in which I probe the acoustic vibrations and organs, I re-create its intelligence and passions, its prosody and narration, its concepts and silences: "I am the journey,"[2] just as much by writing as in psychoanalysis. And yet, as I practice its mysteries, the Word-Flesh dispossesses and alters me: no more lab! I thought my language was my own, but it turns out to be foreign, other than me in me. Am I its author or its product? Unless it transcends me infinitely, insistent infinity in the little point that I am, infinitesimal St. Teresa, acknowledged precursor of Leibniz's infinitesimal calculus.

caught up in fact in the whirlwind of its divine, of its human comedy. Perhaps. But what becomes of the unnamable? What becomes of the separation marking the wish, the breaking of the inscription subtending the stated, the seen, and the heard? Is silence merely speech's way of being, its appeal, and its listening? Or does it reveal another experience of meaning—its reserve, its economy, and its writing? The very *condition* of visibility, before any *Parousia* that the Bible emphasizes?

I go to my bookshelf.

"Our God, *Logos*":[16] such is Freud's legacy to psychoanalysts. But the Logos of the Jewish atheist exists ahead of the audible utterance, in the memory traces of the unconscious "magic writing pad," where drives and desires turn still silent letters into hieroglyphics. The Logos is our God, provided that it can reach "*ça*."

"I am a sound that resonates softly, existing in silence since the beginning":[17] the Gnostic manuscripts already scrutinized speech and silence.

And Sollers: "Inscribing the leap, the breach, forces me to inscribe as if we had gone to the other side,"[18] to bind—on the page of a novel—the evocation of the biblical cut in relation to the Chinese calligrapher's stroke. Resemblance and diversity of writing—this more-than-speech—in two cultures that from now on set the passions of times to come.

Polylogue with amazing potentialities and risky liberties, could the language experience according to the Bible and the Gospels be an antidote to the one single book of "monotono-theism" (Nietzsche),[19] or even "exclude everything that is today known as fundamentalism"?[20] Vigilant of Catholic enculturation, Benedict XVI is convinced of it, if and only if the "culture of the word"[21] finds "its full measure" by taking one road, the one that leads to Christ.

Since when do the roads opened by the Word-Flesh and by the invisible *Bereshit* that preceded it lead nowhere (Heidegger)? Our lost trails open up tracks and ignore Christ less than they say: questioning-challenging-reinventing the Presence, the Cross, Redemption, Resurrection, the beginning, the sense, the non-sense, the flesh and the spirit, the soul and the body. Without necessarily losing oneself in the forest, although that often happens to them, but by tirelessly starting over and over the experience of speech and writing, of music and literature, endless transubstantiations.

Do we lack values? What if the extension of biblical and evangelical word had transmitted an indispensable one: precisely, the singularity of speech to awaken, protect, cultivate, valorize. Advice to humanism, also suffering, to reinvent.

Do we lack an authority? Does not morality at work in the speaking being, which Freud analyzed with his discovery of the death drive doubled with erotic urges, dethrone "His Majesty the Ego" from its "subjective arbitrariness" and up to the "fundamentalist fanaticism"[22] of its explosive furies? And it still has to be informed by the experience of speech whose authority lies neither in the prohibition nor the pardon but in its capacity to tackle the limits, to the limit.

Are we missing a link? Fragile Europe crisscrossed with twenty-five languages is in the process of reinventing one: translation. What if cultural, linguistic, and personal diversity were translatable? Here is a link, a modest weaving of the dream of universal peace! When Europe makes the anamnesis of its crimes against its Jewish and Christian foundations, when it succeeds in its encounter with Islam. . . .

To counterweight the nihilistic crash and its double, the clash of religions, by opposing them with a uniform and absolute universal runs the risk of being as nihilistic as the adversary being fought. We still have one chance: the emergence of cultural and religious diversities, which deserve attention and respect. Let us try to say, listen to, and hear them. And what if that were the ultimate saving metamorphosis of the experience of speech? "The foundation of any genuine culture."[23]

17

DISABILITY REVISITED

The Tragic and Chance

No one has as yet been taught by experience what the body can accomplish.

—BARUCH SPINOZA

What more can I bring, women and men who live with and care for disabilities every day, that you do not know already? Nothing, of course, except a strong emphasis on two aspects of this hardship.

First, the link between disability and mortality. Disability is the modern side of the tragic in that it puts us in front of mortality (individual and social) that we are still today incapable of grasping. Mortality that is not only unthinkable when due to a crime or a war but even more so when it underlies one's entire existence.

Yet the tragic—and that will be the second aspect of my message—*can* become a *chance*. How? By mobilizing an exceptional creativity in each of the protagonists of the hardship, the situation of disability reveals our *irreducible singularity* as speaking beings. That is what I call a chance, and the social link can be rebuilt around this.

"Why are you concerned with disabilities?" I hear your question, I'm often asked it. Generally, I satisfy people's curiosity. Not without noticing that the simple fact of asking the question reveals the particular exclusion that affects those in a situation of disability. Indeed, after two centuries of human rights combats, and regardless of the inadequacy of the gains in this area, we easily accept being against racism, anti-Semitism, or any other form of discrimination related to ethnic origin, social class, race, religion, or sex. But it is not the same for disabilities: here we are not confronted with a "difference" like the others, nor even a "fragility" or a "vulnerability" like the others. Thus the persistent surprise: "Oh, you're interested in that? Whatever for?" Tonight I hope to help you understand what form this particular discrimination takes and what the stakes are.

In reality, my experience with disability transformed me, the rather abstract intellectual on the way to becoming a psychoanalyst, into a novelist, with less conceptual and more sensitive language; besides, as a mother, it committed me to a gigantic task, and every moment I measure its urgency but also its utopia. Because this task really deals—neither more nor less—with refounding humanism.

How does disability change our experience and with that, our idea of the human? Can this upheaval help us build bridges between Christian humanism and the humanism that came out of the Renaissance and the Enlightenment? Such are the stakes implicit—above and beyond the concrete account and the day-to-day living with disability—in my epistolary exchange with Jean Vanier, published under the title of *Leur regard perce nos ombres*.[1]

SECULARISM AND HUMANISM

As you know, an event took place in Europe—and nowhere else in the world—since the Renaissance and the Enlightenment: as "the machine for manufacturing the beyond is no longer working,"[2] so men and women have severed the tie with religious tradition. Rebelling against those dogmas and in order to liberate their bodies and minds and become the sole legislators of their social ties, men and women have rejected the idea of God. From agnosticism to atheism, diverse variations of *secularization* exist. Far from being a nihilism that leads automatically to a Holocaust or a Gulag, as is often too easily said, secularization turns out to be perfectly able to combat obscurantism and religious fundamentalism. "From then on, religion entered the field of social sciences" to the point of "having access" to "what seemed impossible" such as "the word of God," said the grand rabbi of France.[3] This means that secularization reestablishes this "severed tie of tradition" to tame the complexity of the continent of religions and to reevaluate it by elucidating the *limits* as well as the *benefits* of its essential contributions. This vast challenge that the human and social sciences, psychoanalysis and philosophy, have undertaken is one that Jean Vanier and I—modestly and in all sincerity—have tried to maintain all through our correspondence. Today, I can say, without exaggerating but instead by measuring the distance left for us to travel, that our exchange seems to me to be one of the rare concrete examples— maybe the only one—of the missing debate on secularism.

I experienced the recent interreligious meeting that took place in Assisi on October 27, 2011, as a continuation of this process where the Catholic Church invited nonbelievers for the first time. In closing this event, Benedict XVI called on the faithful not to consider themselves as "possessors" of the truth but to take an example of sorts from those who do not believe in an absolute truth and who "are seeking" it as an "approach to existence," a "questioning" and an "interior struggle."[4]

How has the experience with disability led me to this refoundation of humanism based on a new secularization? A secularization for which the era of suspicion no longer suffices because, faced with threats and the deepening of crises, the time has come to wager on the possibility of men and women believing and knowing together. Why is disability not an exclusion or a "fragility" like others, and why, then, does it exhort us to revisit in depth the model of the way we think it—a model passed down to us from Greek philosophy and, in some ways, from Christian humanism?

Before passing on to you some philosophical considerations, I would like to remind you of a few steps in my own personal journey, evoking three examples—John, Claire, and a woman seen on television—three ways of sharing the hardship of disability. If I may, I recommend my book *Hatred and Forgiveness,* [5] because it deals with concrete experience and personalized care of the disabled person that could bring about this change in thinking that I am advocating before you today.

SINGULARITY

So I am using this debate on the "disabled life" to emphasize the right to *irreducible singularity*, because I am convinced that modern and collectivist humanism failed when it tried to turn its back on singularity. This was what totalitarian regimes did. It could happen in different forms with the ongoing trivialization of the human species that some advances in science, technology, and hyperconnectivity are forthcoming.

In this context, the disabled person is this sensible place of the human chain where the "care through integration/collectivization at any price" can lead to an unprecedented automatization, just when it should bring repair and relief. We know today that if the modern meaning of happiness is freedom, freedom is not necessarily "integrative," "collective," and "in the norm" but rather is conjugated in the singular. Duns Scotus (1266–1308) upheld this against Thomas of Aquinas: truth is neither in the universal idea nor in opaque matter, but in "anyone," this man here, that woman there; whence the notion of *haecceitas* or *ecceitas*, of *hoc, haec*, or *ecce*, "this," the demonstrative indexing an unnamable singularity. Besides, this calls up Dun Scotus's finding on reading the words God spoke to Moses: "I Am *Who* I Am." The unpronounceable call of the name is exactly the sign of extreme singularity.

Why bring up this dream today and consider extreme singularity as a pivot of the social pact?

We are witnesses of a new era, and we know it: in this unbridled globalization, we can no longer distinguish Good, thus it is easier to invoke Evil, or more exactly the axis of Evil, against which terrorized humanity must rise up.

Some people are in search of a new foundational myth, or are trying hard to rethink or deconstruct the divine. Never, however, have the "grass roots" of humanity, that is, all these outcasts, diverse though they may be, had either a project or an ambition as tenacious and free—a human ambition, in fact.

There is not really a question here of a possible and new mythology of Love with a capital L. It is instead an appeal launched to nature and the tragic. The men and women who day after day accept and care for disabled people are determined to combat the most unbearable of our fears: one that returns us to the limits of our existence.

I am wary—you know this—of the term "integration" for disabled people: it implies charity toward those who would not have the same rights as others. I prefer to use "interaction," which expresses a kind of politics that has become ethics, by widening the political pact to reach the frontiers of life. And it is not surprising to find a majority of women (maybe it is also the chance to exonerate the feminine side of men?) on this new political front of interaction. Would it be because after years of feminism and recognizing their best ambitions, women are able to renew their immemorial capacity to care for psychic and physical life by making it a political act and in the long term a political philosophy?

MORTALITY

Let us try to get closer to the disability singularity. When it is a question of disabilities (motor, sensorial, mental, and psychic) that show themselves in a specific manner in each concerned person, is it a singularity like others, a solitude like others? On this point, my opinion at first differed from Jean Vanier's. I maintain that disabilities cannot be reduced to the category of "difference." I challenge the "one-size," "catch-all" concepts such as "we are all *different*," all "*others*," all "*vulnerable*," or all "*fragile*." No, we are not "all disabled." And perhaps even less than we are "all gay" or "all German Jews." Why?

I repeat: disabilities differ from other "differences" insofar as they *put us face to face with mortality*. Nonconformity to the norm, which is the situation of disability, is a crossing of *biology* (a biological deficiency) and the *social response* to this deficiency: biological *and* social, nature *and* culture. But more than sexual transgressions, for example, the disparity with biological and social norms that disabilities present is perceived as a deficiency (I'll come back to this) that can in certain cases and within certain limits be repaired will kill me if I am alone, without a prosthesis or without human help.

The anxiety of death, of human finitude, of the limits of the human himself (facing certain onerous multiple disabilities) is, besides, the hidden side of this iceberg—this so insurmountable bloc that the disabled person and his family know so well—that is often the attitude of the able-bodied toward the disabled, this mix of indifference, shame, and, sometimes, arrogance. Of course, all humans know they are mortal, but we prefer not to think about it. And some even count on the eternal. And yet biology has discovered that cellular death (*apopotosis*) is ongoing and parallel to growth from the moment of conception, and this is what sculpts the living.[6] The disabled person lives with mortality at work within, a companion of solitude, as Baudelaire spoke of his pain: "Give me your hand, my Pain, come this way!" Inevitably, the supposed solitude of the disabled person has an absolute companion, a permanent double: the pain of mortality. Even if this person is not ailing, even if he feels no specific pains, his disability constantly reminds him—or at least his entourage if his deficiency deprives him of this consciousness—that he is not like other living people who themselves are able to refuse to know that they are mortal.

Religions and other forms of the spiritual introduce this dimension of mortality into the minds of their followers, although many of those who claim this dimension are in defensive denial in their everyday practice. Secularization, on the contrary, has not constructed an argument on the morality within us. I am not speaking about death: we are experts in celebrations. Nor about dependent old age: the longevity of parents and grandparents makes us happily pay into our retirement funds, for there is a good chance that this disabling "very old age" may one day be our own. I am speaking of "living mortality," from birth or as a result of these "unpredictable biological genetic variables" that can generate disabilities: this mortality called "disabling" is still unthinkable for us. A radical change of thinking is therefore needed so that the hardships of disability make us better assume and accompany the human condition to its limits and in its finitude. The consciousness of our finitude and its accompaniment is an integral part of human singularity.

NORMS

Disability has thus led me to locate the finitude and anxiety of death in the uniqueness of the human person. But another revision of our tenacious prejudices is still needed concerning the disabled: *that of the norm*. Can we approach it without romantic rejection, without servile submission, and with all the seriousness it requires? The norm is not only a discriminating social, economic, and moral constraint; it is inscribed in the social contract starting with language. As soon as I speak, I accept and share norms. To speak is to submit to grammatical norms, and the speaking being must conform to common rules, without which there is no exchange. The compassionate rejection of norms also seems to discount fundamental biological laws that order living organisms (even if current knowledge in this area is insufficient and there is unpredictable biological variability). The idea of a norm, of a typical form, of an appropriate rule is as indispensable in biology as for the social link.

Yet with the development of democracies, and also the achievements of the life sciences, *biopolitics* advances another understanding of the norm. Indeed, thanks to their active adaptation, one that is revolted and creative vis-à-vis norms, new political subjects have come to the fore, such as people living with disabilities who push back the limits of earlier norms and generate new ones. It has thus become normal for the disabled person to lead a social, family, and love life. The norm is no longer an a priori fixed concept but rather a dynamic one. Where is this mutation's motor? How is it that singularities shake up the norms and allow them to evolve?

PRIVATION VS. POSSESSION:
"TO HAVE" OR "TO BE"

Militants for the rights of the disabled reject the very term "disability." The one criticism among the many that I want to point out is that our model for disability results from an Aristotelian conception of human aptitudes that assumes a universal typical form (an archetype) from which "diverse situations" or "cases" deviate *by default*—by deprivation of having (*steresis*). I am blind because I am deprived of the sensation of seeing or the ability to see. In *Physics* and the treatise *On the Soul*, Aristotle analyzed these variants with great subtlety, their "potency" and their "impotence." In Matthew, the Aristotelian *steresis* led to the category of "poverty" (25:35–46): "For I was hungry and you gave me to eat; I was thirsty and you gave me to drink; I was a stranger and you welcomed me;

naked and you clothed me; sick and you visited me; in prison and you came to me. Whatever you do to the least of these, you have done to me." To be clear: of the various "leasts" and "steriles," lacking or poor let us share the impotence with passion; and on this com-passion with the "lack of being," let us found "well-being," the ethics of what Christian humanism will be.

Without being reduced to an ontology of negation, this ontology of privation finds echoes throughout the whole history of philosophy, concerning the "to be" and the "being" in its "finitude," passing by Descartes and Hegel and up to the "ontological difference" of Heidegger.[7] Concerning the specific area that unites us tonight, we can observe that the philosophy of privation includes the poor, the sick, lepers, drifters, and the crippled, without distinction, all those marked by a *lack* or a *flaw*. The magnificent works of charity are inspired by them, the foundation of Christian humanism and of the Church understood as "community of the suffering servant" who will "com-plete," "give" to those who "have not."

This solidarity model based on *poverty/privation/"lack in being"* continues to prove its effectiveness. Not only through charitable works, but also concerning knowledge: it is often through the study of "what is lacking" (pathologies) that the sciences appropriate the complexities of "what is full" (normal functioning). For example, by studying aphasia, the mechanisms of language can be better understood. It is not a question of ignoring the pathological and less still of abolishing it—the inevitability of the norm makes that impossible—but rather of adjoining it to another.

For the paradigm of lack—with its counterpart *compassion* and/or *tenderness*—also has its limits, even flaws, which I did not fail to point out to Jean Vanier in our correspondence. Its theorization comes from a Greco-Christian origin, but the model is now unconsciously universal. As it stands, it risks enclosing the disabled subject in a position of "needy object," of "taken in charge." At best with "tenderness," often neglecting the scientific knowledge that enables the identification and treatment of specific symptoms and that can end up in infantilization. Indeed, the intrinsic logic of this model holds the disabled subject back: it prevents him from opening up to his "potencies," that is, his singular potentialities; does not enable him to use his always irreducible solitude for his *singular creativity*, for his initiative that can be shared according to his own limits. When it does not lead to "integration" at any price, the logic of this model nurtures the fantasy of an ideal jouissance, supposed fusion-confusion of the able-bodied "haves" with the "deprived/have-nots," improbable communion where sects can comfortably do their business.

I support, on the contrary, and counter to the paradigm of "having" and of *steresis*, that the paradigm of the *singularity of the being*—which includes even the deficiency itself, as an indicator of finitude and the frontiers of the living—is not a deprivation, a weakness, or a sin. The contingency of the singular *is* positive, and in it "to be" and "being" merge. The contingency of the singular "disabled" reveals to me my own singularity of "a have," meaning "able-bodied," which I neither exalt nor deny but that I tame for good from the singularity of the so-called have-not. The ongoing mortality touches me in him, I am part of it, mortality falls on me, I accompany it, I love it as it is. By my love for the singular other, I carry it to its specific, singular development—and to mine, equally specific and singular.

Of course, one no longer, or rarely, associates a "disability" with a "fault." But spontaneously, automatically, "normally," one continues to exclude, to "lonelyize," to ostracize. Only later does one pretend to "integrate," but always with the idea in the background of "deprivation," of a "flaw" that essentially "we others," the "haves," would not have in essence. "We possess (aptitudes, strengths), but he/she does not; he lacks them": this model of *lack* remains "the" implicit and indelible assumption of our humanist, Christian, or secular philosophy. Of course, the poet sometimes revolts: "There is none more deaf than the haves," wrote Michaux. But it would be just as false to say that we are all deaf because we are all "haves." As long as we distinguish an *essential being* from an *inessential* and *lacking being*, we will be tempted by the segregation of the living. The essential Being is perhaps no longer Divine, but we have replaced it with Biology, when we understand the disabled person as "deprived" of certain biological aptitudes (Biology—with a capital B—takes the place of the essential Being: might the "divine" return in the postmodern, bioscientific "*being*"?); or when we consider the disabled person as being without cultural and social abilities (Society—still with a capital S—thus assuming the role of an integrative "*being*").

On the contrary, leaving aside this paradigm of "poverty" and "fault," and substituting it with that of the *incommensurate singularity* of each person, including the disabled, we get closer to the Scotist ethic. What is a Scotist ethic?—Here is "the" question to ask at the College des Bernardins, this crossroads of theology and philosophy where specialists like Emmanuel Falque can enlighten us.[8] Is it a more "mystical" ethics (some, like Gilles Deleuze, have said "atheist"), while Thomas Aquinas' would be more "social"? In Scotist-inspired ethics, in any case, singularity could be thought of as the only *positivity,* the only *value,* as one says today. But it was starting from the positivity of *being* that Duns Scotus extended it to the *Being* itself, to God as the *causa singularitatis.* God would be singular, and Christ especially, for Man-God develops the density of his singularity in particular by the trial of his passion in death, and up to his *glorification* as wounded-crucified sur-vivor: since this is neither a *repair* nor a *satisfaction* but precisely the evidence of his singularity.

A militant for the rights of the disabled in the United States, Nancy L. Eiesland, takes up, apparently without knowing it, this Scotist idea in her book *The Disabled God* when she described Jesus as the only "disabled god."[9] Did he not appear to his apostles, even in his glory, with an *unpaired body,* a damaged body? Here, the wound is not a lack, for it is an integral part of the Glory, itself given and perceived as a singularity.

The once-canon Diderot had taken this "positive singularity" up in another way, that of modern humanism," when he undertook to transform the *disabled* person into a *political subject* for the first time in the world. In his *Letter on The Blind for the Use of Those Who See* (1749), he made his point clear: the disabled have rights, are born free and equal in rights. And Declarations of Human Rights would take a lot of time to formulate and implement this principle that transforms, in efficient positivity, the finitude in act in the disabled person. The right to "personalized compensation" in the 2005 law is an outcome of this.

Nonetheless, to accomplish this ambition of modern humanism, political will and laws are not enough. We would have to reinvent this *corpus mysticum* that Kant himself evoked at the end of the *Critique of Pure Reason* (1781), whereby the singularity of the disabled person could transform norms into dynamic, evolutive concepts: reinvent love as *union with singularity* of all others. In other terms: the *love of singulars* must be substituted for *integrating solidarity* with the weak. What love? Love as desire and will so that the singular can elucidate, be recognized, and develop in sharing his own singularity. Far more than solidarity, which itself still has trouble existing, only this love can drive the constitutive singularity (and not "by default") of the-one-who-testifies to mortality to thrive in a society founded on the norm (without which, as I have said, there is no link) but that can make norms evolve.

I am thinking of the *training of caregivers* in place of psychoanalysis in this complex and controversial area when broaching the question of love, understood as a continual and elucidated transference, in caring for the disabled person. We will undoubtedly return to this in the debate. Allow me to conclude—on a more personal note—by calling up the maternal role in this hardship.

MATERNAL RELIANCE REVISITED

"I want you to be," says the mother to the child. *Volo ut sis*, says the Scotist ethic. "I love that you are," I say to David. My empathy, my loving fusion with him, showed me that with his perfect pitch he can make music in spite of his neurological deficiencies. Yet, I really accompany him only by facilitating his means of separating himself from me, of personalizing his languages, his means of expression, and his link with others to the maximum. He will make music, multimedia, an artistic ESAT will be created, he will participate in his singular way, not as *I* want but as *he* wants and can. A new "worksite" will be started: "an "emotional and sexual life," with his pals and care people whose training has to be worked out. He is joining a "personalized" life place: thanks to Jean Vanier, it will be "Simon of Cyrene." He will fall in love, it is difficult, is it possible? I doubt it, I say to him, "David, you're dreaming!"—"But Mama, I dream, therefore I am," he answers me. And the norm itself is beginning to adapt itself to his being. It even becomes "normal" for it to be talked about at UNESCO and the College des Bernardins.

In this central role played by patiently elucidated and problematized empathy and love, which I call a vigilant transference, Jean Vanier's exceptional experience is pioneering. We have recently seen a secular version, which does honor to republican secularity, in the film *The Untouchables* (produced with the support of the Simon of Cyrene association).

The love along with the humor and cheerfulness that results from it, this burst of laughter that pulverizes the pain and this joyful alchemy marvelously epitomize the philosophy of singular sharing that I am probing for you, and it breaks with a certain postmodern and morose humanism, which—when it does not exalt the theomorphism of its integrating all-powerfulness—wallows in depressive and whining despair. You can see an example of this in another equally instructive film, the Iranian saga *A Separation*, the anti-*Untouchables*. Another style of life—the transcendence of the "self-deficient" by the *corpus mysticum* of singularities—is taking the place of the *habitus* of the com-passion of the "haves" with and in the "impotence" of the have-nots. You know this: the extraordinary capacity of sur-vival of these disabled bodies when they are dynamized and express joy in the transferential encounter. They bring to my mind Spinoza's astonishment: "*No one has as yet been taught by experience what the body can accomplish.*"[10]

This secular and bracing *corpus mysticum* that I call before you, that Jean Vanier practices in his fashion, that the film *Untouchables* brings to the public eye, is a horizon and a hope for all parents and caregivers. A true cultural revolution. It is easy to wrap it in ironic skepticism, and I do it sometimes too. But I know that many share this philosophy, its energy and its hopes, and try to put it into practice, in spite of obstacles, delays, and regressions of all kinds in a hostile climate of identarian tension and economic austerity.

18

FROM "CRITICAL MODERNITY" TO "ANALYTICAL MODERNITY"

I am not a specialist on Stéphane Mosès's vast, precise, sober, and ambitious thought whose influence in contemporary culture is just beginning to be recognized. Nor am I any more of an expert in the Bible and the Gospels that continually nourish that culture. I am an atheist, brought up in the spirit of the Enlightenment, a woman who defends European secularization and remains intimately convinced that this radical and healthy change—decried by many today—can only be understood and developed, and consequently avoid its impasses and errors, if one recognizes and analyzes the debt to the tradition it took off from. I will come back to this question that, far from distancing me, brings me closer to Stéphane Mosès, the theorist. But I would like to begin with the man, and with the memory I have of him.

No positive definition of the word "humanity" exists. We are only really familiar with the negative in the expression "crime against humanity." Until I met Stéphane Mosès, rarely, probably never, had a man given me with such acuity the certitude that humanity is a voice, a look, a smile, an ear. Welcoming and clever, this voice immediately grasped your vulnerability, but to better rekindle your ability to live and survive by this original act: thinking.

Stéphane Mosès's gentleness was immediately striking, and it conveyed an unusual happiness: one that penetrated each individual to the core of his distress, and without exaggeration or compassion accompanied this fellow being, this brother, in the development of what his most singular, strange and innovative thought contained. A mixture of classicism and nonconformity, of disconcerting normality and incisive audacity, of tradition and avant-garde (as they said in Paris), which he extended to me from Saint-Germain-des-Prés as well as in Jerusalem by asking for news about my son David, or by writing carefully complicit letters, always on target. This man was eager to reveal himself to himself while at the same time revealing us. Stéphane Mosès or the joy of a thought that is thinking you. A rare quality that he transmitted to his family.

Among Stéphane Mosès's writings that enlightened me on the biblical continent, but that also enabled me to grasp his influence on European literature and taught me a great deal about Rosenzweig, Benjamin, or Scholem, I will focus on three themes. These are apparently secondary but nevertheless essential themes in a work largely devoted to Judaism and its spiritual renewal in the twentieth century: exile, language, and the broken thread of tradition or its refoundation.

EXILE: A STRANGENESS ELEVATED TO THE RANK OF "METAPHYSICAL CATEGORY"

Meditating on the exile experience of Walter Benjamin and Gershom Scholem, Mosès pointed out the differences between, on one hand, the "flight" of Benjamin to Ibiza and Paris as an "extreme form of unhappiness" and, on the other hand, Scholem's "voluntary settling" in a "spiritual homeland" experienced as the "realization of a utopia."[1] Communism vs. cosmopolitism, criticism of official communism vs. political Zionism, life away from home vs. life in a homeland "as problematic as it may be," Jewish intellectual committed to the left vs. Zion as a "symbol," connecting the mythical origin of the Jewish people to its utopian goal. In spite of these divergences, the two men agreed on two points.

Both first regretted the disappearance of transcendence or aura in modernity and then raised, according to Mosès, "exile to the rank of metaphysical category." As of 1933, Scholem sensed a catastrophe of historic dimension, even as God's existence was being felt as less tangible.

Benjamin, referring to Nietzsche, depicted a "bad modernity," a "frozen agony" devoid of symbol, just good for "allegory," which would only express rupture between the sign and its signification. I fully agree with Mosès's reading that recognizes in Benjamin, beyond the expression of his chronic depression, a diagnosis of xenophobia—French and/or republican?—of which many strangers are victim in the country of human rights ("Life among strangers is intolerable, solitary life is no better, a life among the French is impossible"). I raised this observation myself at the end of the 1980s, in *Strangers to Ourselves*.[2]

At this point in his thinking, and without departing from the biblical heights, Mosès's fulguration—not the least of his paradoxes—took him to the dawn of Greek philosophy, to Plato, where he demonstrated that the *bios theoreticos* was inevitably, as Hannah Arendt would remind us, a *bios xenikos*. Describing the "great city desperately fallen," its "starless sky," its "soulless masses," and its "desperately empty destiny of the individual," might Benjamin be the acute consciousness of man alienated by modernity? Or else, does he more radically incarnate the destiny of all men, necessarily alienated in "all societies" (Scholem), and for whom the modern city would only unveil its intrinsic logic? Benjamin, "the very incarnation of the stranger," like Freud and Kafka? And Mosès concluded: "Scholem made us understand that there was no "here," be it the recovered ancient homeland of the Jewish people, other than a utopian "here" "experienced as a place of interior exile."

From this *estrangement*, no longer depressive as for Benjamin but seeking "a hidden dimension only accessible to mystics" and whose sources he recognized from the Kabbalah, Scholem worked his way toward a "dialectic Zionism," where the ability to exile oneself from oneself is the very condition of the act of thinking, of thinking oneself, of infinitely interpreting the tetragram of all identity (national, political, sexual, etc.).

Mosès also introduced raising up foreignness to the "rank of metaphysical category," basing it, as his two masters had done, on the interpretative tradition of Judaism, itself reworked by Greek thought. Yet from the pen of our friend, strangeness as a "metaphysical category" is not crystalized in a philosophical concept but follows another road, both theological and political, in "Trois prières pour l'étranger dans l'Ancien Testament."[3] This is Abraham's prayer for Sodom and Gomorrah—a people outside of Abraham's lineage (Genesis 12:3; 14:1–14, 24; Ruth 4:18–22); of Moses's prayer (Exodus 32) after smashing the Golden Calf—he prays for his people, idolatrous sinners, but accompanied by the "mixed multitudes"; and lastly of Jonah's "nonprayer" concerning the inhabitants of Nineveh (Jonah 4:2). The three prayers that he interpreted in all their diversity inscribed a "principle of ethical universalism into Judaism," which does not depend on "ethnic belonging" but rather on "moral behavior." The biblical character prays for the "salvation of the stranger" in the name of "ethical responsibility toward all men": a salvation that is not "preguaranteed" but depends on the ethical choices of those for whom the prayer is intended.

Stéphane Mosès would have undoubtedly adopted this definition of the Akeda that I found from the head rabbi of England, Jonathan Sacks, for whom "chosenness" goes beyond "narrow particularism" and opens the way to "dignity in difference."[4] With Isaiah (19:24–25), he considered that the "tender care of God" could bless Israel's traditional enemies, such as Egypt and Assyria.

Thus elevated to the rank of "metaphysical category," strangeness as "dignity in difference," found in no other holy text, would be an essential ferment of this "spiritual recognition of Judaism," of this "spiritual and historic surge" in which Scholem and Mosès shared the vision that made the State of Israel a metaphysical necessity for humanity.

LANGUAGE: WHAT SUBJECTIVITY?

In the dialogue between Franz Rosenzweig and Eugen Rosenstock, which Mosès described as "the most overwhelming Judeo-Christian dialogue of the twentieth century," the accent put on the linguistic concept of "dissimilation" at times tends to eclipse the *preeminence of language* over all conceptual speculation in Rosenzweig's work.

Mosès always pointed to this "resurgence of language as a structure of the real," which he dated back to the mystical conception of language in the Kabbalah, and that he defined as an "ontology of Jewish mysticism." It would be interesting in fact to examine its traces in Lévi-Strauss's structuralism, in the poetics of Roman Jakobson, or in the distinction between "semiotics" and "semantics" in Emile Benveniste.[5]

Certain advances in the last courses of the great linguist clarified and completed Mosès's remarks. Mosès was greatly interested in the question of language by disassociating it from the "mystical philosophy of history" specific to Jewish messianism, while spelling out the two areas (mystical ontology vs. mysticism of history), thanks to and through "the belief in a paradigmatic function of language, conceived . . . as measuring the presence or absence of the divine in the world at such and such moment in history." According to Mosès, Rosenzweig placed *subjectivity at the heart of Jewish messianism*. He also considered it at the heart of the speech experience, as opposed to the formal character of language as a system of signs, on one hand, and the impersonal nature of the narrative, on the other. But exactly what subjectivity is it a question of?

This thinking about Rosenzweig led Mosès to a fascinating analysis of the conception of language as an *act of enunciation*, according to Emile Benveniste. This conception has, in my understanding, not sufficiently interested linguists and philosophers.[6] In acknowledging what he generously referred to as my "foundational text" on "the predicative function and the speaking subject,"[7] and in discussing the concepts of semantic/semiotic, language/enunciation, or narrative/discourse, Mosès compared this latter couple—narrative/discourse—to that of narrative (*Erzählung*) and dialogue (*Zwiesprache*) in Rosenzweig's work. Narrative uses the third person and the past tense of the verb; while the personal mode, on the other hand, which is also that of dialogue, is expressed around the pronouns I/you and the predominance of the present in the enunciation. This opposition is at the heart of Rosenzweig's philosophy and governs the whole of his system of thinking. It is enriched by a linguistic approach to texts, shown by two analyses of the first chapter of Genesis as a paradigm of "the narrative" and of the Song of Songs as a paradigm of the "dialogal" mode. But Rosenzweig introduced here a third subjective modality of the enunciation—communitarian and necessarily absent in Benveniste; it favored the singularity and unicity of the I: it is "choral language" (Psalms 115). "Collective evocation of a collective future" founded on a we, the pronoun that Rosenzweig and Benveniste both agree is not the plural of I but that dissolves the singular in an impersonal collective that the author of *The Star of Redemption*[8] had a preference for, and that could not be found in Benveniste.

If I linger somewhat lengthily on this linguistic face-to-face, it is not only to give an additional example of the internal tension of Mosès's thought, here a tension between the specificity of the theological field and that of the rationality of the social sciences, secularized and preserved in their independence and yet tightly intertwined in their reciprocal debt. I underline this point because these echoes of Mosès's customary thinking have made me aware, by contrast, of the philosophical and theological genealogy of this subject of the enunciation, which Benveniste introduced into the general linguistic field and which caused a veritable revolution against Chomsky's "Cartesian linguistics."

Indeed, the "subject of the enunciation" according to Benveniste belongs implicitly to subjective singularity: a complex notion that was forged in Christian and post-Christian philosophy since Saint Augustine, Duns Scotus, Hegel, Husserl, and up to Christian personalism—just to mention the principal stages of its evolution. This genealogy is missing in Mosès's thought; he merely notes the conception of "dialogue" that is a constituent of the meaning of enunciation in Levinas as well as in Benveniste when the latter makes a quick recourse to phenomenology. Yet, according to Benveniste, it is I that "poses" you and "transcends" it, meaning that I is "logically prior" to you—it is I that leads the way, regardless of the linguistic mechanism at work, whereas for Levinas, on the contrary, it is the you that transcends the I: the I does not "pose" the you, it "reveals" it.

There is no question here of "choosing" between these two conceptions of intersubjectivity, Levinas or Benveniste. I observe that in the light of Levinas and Buber, Benveniste's dialogism interpreted by Mosès, far from being immobilized in a minor linguistic formalism—facing the transcendentalism of the Revelation affirmed in Levinas—brings a specific modernity to our interpretation. I thus see emerging, in the unspoken of Mosès's text and even in his argumentative economy, the dividing line where secularization, along with phenomenology and the language sciences, constructs not a "bad" but what I will call a "good" modernity. This modernity is possible only thanks to the emergence of a new subjectivity, which is not that of a "speaker" isolated in the unity of his psychological "ego" but refers to the "emergence in the Being of a fundamental property of language." The only Being is the Being of language, Benveniste seemed to be saying, echoing Heidegger. Therefore whoever says "Ego" is "Ego," as the linguist wrote. An ego never says "ego" on her own, as Descartes would have it (*Cogito ergo sum*), but from the outset transforms the "semiotic" linguistic system into the "semantic" dynamics of an always and already "dialogic" saying. Ego acts intersubjectively: it only ever discloses its constitution in the act of speaking in and for "being other."

We thus have to avoid the Cartesian Ego, as well as the psychological "ego" (*moi*): we must think of the ego as outside itself and as correlated with "being other" and so constitute the ego as a speaking subject and/or a fundamental property of language—not as the subject of the statement but as the subject of the enunciation or of the procedural signifyingness reviving the memory of the modi significandi of the medieval logicians. Here is where the Word of Christianity takes back its rights.

Thus framed, more than a new light was shone on the question of the other/*You* (with a capital Y); it would also lead to a radical displacement in Christian theology and its relationship to language. Who is this other with whom *I* dialogue so that my enunciation will carry not "lies" but "truth," if not "the truth"? Saint Augustine (De Magistro) had already responded by taking up the subjectivity of incarnation, in his revisited and corrected Platonism: *I* only becomes the "speaking subject" by transferring itself, in a vertical dialogue, to the ecstatic subjectivity of a third, a God-man, Son and Father, Same and Other, of the Master of which *I* was "before Abraham was." Such will be the Christic invention of subjectivity as subjectivity loving the laws of the Father in love unto death. In the celebrated *De Magistro*[9] dialogue, does not Saint Augustine posit that *I* says the truth only if it identifies indefinitely with this absolute Subject, with this loving/loved *you* who is the Son-Father? *I* must transfer itself in place of this magisterial *I* to control the verbal flux and direct it toward true speech.

A long history of subject-and-language followed: with Duns Scotus who understood truth only in the singularity of the *haecceitas*, and for whom the Being itself is singular; with the mystical research of a Saint Teresa of Avila and the vision she had of the Other by inviting him: "Seek yourself in me"; with the negativity of the subject in the Hegelian dialectic; and to the dialogism of Christian "personalism," in the wake of the phenomenology that John-Paul II took up.[10] The Christian tradition of creative subjectivity—altered in its loving link with the Other—transformed this horizontal alterity that is the *you* of the interlocutor, into a vertical instance, principal of alterity, "Grand Other" as Lacan called it: at once external to the *I*, and immediately interiorized (me/*I*), constant motor of its active unicity which is none other than its singular creativity.

Obviously, no element of this complex tradition was evoked by Benveniste, who went no further than to refer to "phenomenology" in general and to Husserl in private. It was only when he became aphasic and shortly before his death that I saw him trace, on my own chest, the word THEO, which even today I still do not know if it was a question. Nevertheless, Benveniste was the first, and perhaps the only, linguist to have studied the role of language in the Freudian exploration of the unconscious.[11]

It is thus through the intermediary of psychoanalysis, having a firm grip on the radical impact of intersubjectivity rebuilding the subject in this loving link known as "transference," that the linguist attentive to phenomenology sought the necessary support for his initial conviction. It is indeed through the link of *I* to *you*—by this affirmation of *I* if and only if *I* takes the other into consideration—that this fundamental property of language that phenomenologists and psychologists call a "subjectivity" is constructed. But it is up to psychoanalysis to explore the anthropological secret of the Revelation of *I* to *you* and vice versa, that of Love.

For Benveniste, the practice and the theory of psychoanalysis, and, by extension, the vast field of the language sciences and/or social sciences, thus occupied the role of Revelation. In the analytic experience of speaking, *I* is able to "believe" in *you*, to "invest" in you: loving belief, credence, and identifications proceed from the same seme;[12] but they also allow questioning I and you, going as far as putting the fundamental properties of language and Being itself into question. This is the way the I has access to the Unconscious that reveals itself to the Subject, in spite of its Ego (*moi*), and thanks to you: in an infinitely reconstructable dialogue, in this endless "transference" that takes place for the other as well as for oneself.

Evoking Benveniste-Augustine-Freud, I do not distance myself from Levinas-Mosès. On the contrary. Mosès is a careful reader of Freud, of his dream analyses as of his studies of "Freudian slips" or "negation."[13] His discovery of Benveniste in the light of Levinas made it possible for me to better identify the function Benveniste attributed to the "speaking subject" as an indispensable hyphen between phenomenology and psychoanalysis, between Husserl/Heidegger and Freud.

Further still, Mosès demonstrated that where Levinas referred to the Bible to structure the essential dialogism of language, Benveniste drew from the history of religions and psychoanalysis. And that the speaking subject from this point of view showed itself to be the subject of desire, while for Levinas, *I* was a subject of the Alliance. In this interpretation and according to me, the speaking subject is one of these precious creations of modernity that reestablish and link the Jewish and Christian traditions, with and in spite of the thread broken by secularization.

I would like to thank Stéphane Mosès for his interpretive daring that put linguistic thought and Messianic philosophy into perspective and thus opened new inroads for reading Benveniste's work and the linguistics of subjectivity that resulted from it. A daring that helps us as well to grasp that this inherited subjectivity of the Jewish-Greek-Christian tradition is at the heart of secularized European culture, its plinth and the jewel. I am sorry to say that we are not proud enough of it to be the true guardians and transmitters of that tradition.

THE BROKEN THREAD OF TRADITION OR ITS REFOUNDATION

Mosès was attached to the theme of a double Jewish modernity: a *normative* modernity (which began with Hermann Cohen and Franz Rosenzweig, developing in the 1950s with the renewal of Jewish thought in France, notably with Levinas); and a *critical* modernity (Franz Kafka, Walter Benjamin, Hannah Arendt).

Normative modernity contrasts with historic positivism, as it deciphers modern significations in traditional texts. Hermeneutic, it integrates the subjectivity of the interpretant and, in the same surge of Heidegger proclaiming that the "hermeneutic circle" belongs "to the very structure of meaning," it updates the meaning of the ancient text. The modern author lends an "aura" ("transcendence") to the sources of Jewish tradition—an aura linked to their anteriority—but equally an argumentative force compatible with a philosophical theorization.

For enthusiasts of *critical modernity*, on the other hand, the Jewish tradition is reduced to a series of fragments of texts, scattered remains in a world without God, defined thus by Arendt, taking up Tocqueville's expression: "the thread of tradition is broken, and we cannot repair it . . . what is left to us . . . is a shattered past, no longer able to inspire value judgments."[14]

Thus Benjamin declared, referring to Kafka, that only "the rumor of real things" would survive, "a sort of theological gossip, where there are outdated and obsolete things." And Mosès rereading Benjamin showing that even this shattered universe, made up of disparate myths, decomposed and recomposed, initiated a "recycling" of ancient meaning.

In Kafka's "The Silence of the Sirens," these mythological creatures no longer sing; it is their silence that bewitches the hero, contrary to any original likelihood. Yet, far from sinking into meaninglessness, the "broken thread" of tradition expresses the ingenuity of this Kafkaesque Ulysses, an ambivalent ingenuity to be sure, ludicrous, or very simply uncertain and turned toward the unknown.[15]

Likewise, Kafka's *Letter to His Father* rejected the empty legitimacy of his de-Jewished father. But by encouraging the reinvention of another legitimacy based on the past, abject and yet enviable, Kafka proposed a permanent and infinite ambiguity to modern thinkers.

Mosès concluded from this that like some rabbinic exegeses that do not hesitate to radically subvert the apparent meaning of the texts, "hope is perhaps found" in "the dazzling discovery of the unhoped for" "at the bottom of the junk heap of a shattered tradition, enabling us thus to find sparks of hope in the past that are still buried there."[16] Mosès's optimism led him to this final paradox that is the balance between "conservatives" and "revolutionaries," between the "nothingness of the Revelation" (where Revelation maintains its validity but signifies nothing, according to Scholem) and the "rumor of real things" or "theological gossip" (according to Benjamin).

Based on my analytical and linguistic experience, I propose another bridge between modernity and tradition. The groundwork exists already in the obscurity that still surrounds psychoanalysis and those who take inspiration from it, on the edge of a globalized spectacle, dazzled and blind, and to which that bridge remains imperceptible. It concerns interpreting Jewish and Christian tradition without being limited to the melancholic contemplation of the "heap of ruins" and "scattered debris" (Benjamin) alone. The time has come for the prodigal sons and daughters not to return to their father's house (it does not exist in itself) but to acknowledge their debt to him by patiently and indefinitely refounding it. And this would be accomplished thanks to the meticulous scholarship of archeologists and historians as well as the visionary interpretation of those able to inscribe their analysis in today's context.

Mosès seemed to say that this had always been an ongoing process. His work helps us not only to recognize it but also to accelerate its perpetual refoundation. Arendt's critical modernity is right: the thread was broken here, in the Greek and biblical traditions, only by the double caesura, first of Christianity, then of the Enlightenment, both prepared by the Baroque flowering. However, a nostalgic reading cannot exhaust the meaning of this double rupture, which a continuously refreshed creative subjectivity relaunches and radicalizes.

It is up to us at this beginning of the third millennium to continue the *reassessment* undertaken by normative and critical modernity. And, from there, to apply it to the whole of Jewish-Greco-Christian tradition as well as to its Muslim contribution, bearing in mind the Freudian discovery of the unconscious and the dynamic subjectivity that it led to, following in the steps of the pioneers who came before us, but also *in other ways than* those who advanced before and after the Second World War, by going beyond their normative transcendentalist modernity or their sad critical modernity.

This revival of the "hidden dimension," born of the Christian break that accentuated the infinite creativity of the speaking subject, was activated by the Renaissance, then stoked and sealed by the Protestant Reformation. It then became accessible to the mystics, and notably to those of the Baroque revolution, too easily called the Counter-Reformation. The extraordinary vitality of the Baroque age was in fact far more than that dubious and unstable gap between sign and signification, bound up by allegories and ready to topple into the void as Benjamin diagnosed. While relevant for the nineteenth century, this melancholic verdict had no hold on Teresa of Avila's jouissance, the whirlwinds of voices in Vivaldi, or the undulations of the marble in Bernini.

The Baroque age introduced transcendence in the immanent jouissance of the bodies of both sexes, and a prodigious loving subjectivity invaded Europe—destructible and constantly being reborn. Borne by European humanism, stopped or energized by the conflictual cohabitation of Jews and Christians—exterminating cruelty and sublime duo, more often apocalyptic than fertile—this jubilatory subjectivity would take democratic or elitist, mystical or social forms. It then declined into ravages and persecutions—expulsion of the Jews from Spain, Russian pogroms—and ended with the horror of the Holocaust. But it resisted and survived. The complex dynamic of this historical and spiritual momentum distanced itself from tradition only to better reinterpret and renew it: not as "eternal return" but in the form of a reworking in which the "broken" foundation would continue to function, underground or unconscious.

After the Renaissance and the Baroque age, this permanent *rupture and/or refoundation* would become radicalized. Beyond the "bad" modernity, which "wiped the slate clean" and made way for the Terror, then postromanticism and positivism at the end of the nineteenth century, another modernity saw the light of day, reborn, baroque, and heir to the Enlightenment. Often occult, even initiatory, it has since then not stopped working to search for past time, to transmute, rediscover, and re-create.

Let us not fear these modernities: they are our own. The Enlightenment uncovered obscurantist abuses of the need to believe, and we have obtained this incommensurable liberty that other traditions envy, copy hypocritically, and often flout. But we know today that the boldness of this rift turned bad, soiled by its crimes, in particular with revolutionary terror and totalitarianisms to the point of *denying* anthropological, prereligious universality, of this same need to believe that invests *I* in *you* and *you* in *I*. In this negation itself is a *radical evil* that can henceforth be denounced: it begins with the individual and collective repression of this "emergence of fundamental properties of language in the Being" that the speaking subject constitutes, according to Benveniste, its singular liberty, and it culminates in declaring the superfluity of some humans. Might this be the major symptom, a terrible impasse that condemns the "broken thread"?

Facing these symbolic ravages that were preludes to the programmed extermination of men and women, psychoanalysis has the means to help elucidate the horror. How? The Freudian discovery of the unconscious provides one of the major keys for accessing the singular memory and thus for the survival of Tradition in history. By establishing that God has become unconscious and in restoring the unconscious subject of desire, psychoanalysis calls for a transmutation of values that overcomes individual resistance that undermines desires and thoughts as well as the loss of collective meanings. A new modernity is emerging in the historic perspective that I have just reformulated: a *more-than-critical* modernity, call it *analytical.*

Am I too optimistic in wagering that it is possible not to establish the "eternal return" of tradition but to refound it? Only an *analytical modernity*, concerned with clarifying its antecedents, would be able to take on this challenge. Is this analytical modernity, elitist and in the minority, withering in Europe today? Perhaps it is only waiting to bounce back—transferring the historical and spiritual momentum of Judeo-Christianity to other geographical areas. It will discover and is already discovering in ancient texts anthropological constants that secularization had too quickly repressed and that came back in psychisms and societies throughout history. We have no other choice, faced with the resurgence of conservatisms, obscurantisms, and fundamentalisms of all kinds, but to join *normative* and *critical* modernities to this *analytical* modernity that takes up and questions a mutating anthropological permanence.

Benjamin found in Proust traces of infinite sensorial empathy with lost esthetic and spiritual experiences.[17] When I hear them uttered on the couch, the need to believe and the joy of knowing seem to be like prepolitical and prereligious needs that have to be satisfied or else the child would acquire neither speech nor thought. But did the psalmist, repeated by Saint Paul, not already say: "I believed and I spoke"? The ecstasy of Saint Teresa of Avila explored the psychic life that is the essence of loving. And "seek yourself in Me" is possible only if I am in love with the other. Only the passionate, sensual, and sublime risk transmutes the fundamentally sadomasochistic burn of desire in this purity that brings the transcendence of self to realization outside of self, an open-ended work, an active existence: for the life of the saints themselves is social and infinitely transmittable.

Stéphane Mosès's thought encourages us to situate the breaks effected by Christianity and the Enlightenment in the complex history of the ruptures and reweaving of Judaism and Christianity. Thus only the stranger like the modern (be he hermeneutic, critical, or analytical) is part of this "hidden figure" par excellence through which the Revelation renews itself in and from its own scansions.

Thank you, Stéphane Mosès, for having accompanied me throughout the years in these reflections, and for having legitimatized them, enabling me to reformulate them here, and so I dedicate this to his memory. The exigency and the subtlety of this man—Jew and European—help us think when the ground gives way.

19

IN JERUSALEM

Monotheisms and Secularization and the Need to Believe

Barely two years ago, when I came back to Israel for the publication of my book *Tales of Love* (1985) in Hebrew, I shared a dream with you of creating a permanent center for thinking about religions, right here in Jerusalem, drawing inspiration from the history of this world-unique city and from Freud's legacy still insufficiently reflected on. I envisioned a forum with its basis in psychoanalysis and in other human and life sciences, perhaps even including one day the participation of theologians from different religious traditions to attempt to analyze—without preconceived ideas and fratricidal rivalry—these enigmatic constructions currently reactivated in their very crises that are systems of belief whose "clashes" seem to threaten today's globalized planet. At the time, as I shared my ideas for the project with you, I did not think it would develop beyond the utopian stage, and I certainly did not expect it to take shape so quickly. I clearly underestimated the enterprising spirit lying dormant among psychoanalysts as well as our accomplices' energy! Here we are today, about to lay the first stone of the edifice, hoping that this same passion and efficiency will see us through the immense work we have ahead of us. For this task reaches beyond the destiny of each of us. By addressing the memory of religions, psychoanalysis takes full responsibility for its epochal vocation and justifies its experience, not beyond the treatment that absorbs us daily in the experience of transference but to better hear the logics of this very transference in the memory of history and for the future horizon.

Thank you also and especially for entrusting me with this inaugural conference that the organizers have opened up beyond psychoanalysts and experts in religion to a larger and historically concerned audience—Jerusalem warrants it—this major problematic. You will understand then, I am sure, that the honor you have shown me comes with a worry I would like to share with you straight off. I would like to convince you that—in spite of the seriousness of our session—what I have to say should be heard with neither more nor less than a "great question mark" at "the most serious place," as Nietzsche wrote. Such is my challenge: to raise questions, and to question the very answers I sketch out, all the answers. Might this be an exorbitant wager in the guise of humility? An impossible challenge? It is, in any case, my own right now, and for me it is "cruel and long term," to quote Sartre on the subject of atheism.

BRIEF HISTORICAL OVERVIEW

My thoughts are currently directed to Sigmund Freud, to his genius which, from *Totem and Taboo* (1912) and *Moses and Monotheism* (1930), to cite only these two, opened up a new way of thinking religion. By thinking it, I mean living it. It seems to me that one of the missions of this forum will be to plan a future session devoted to rereading his *Moses* and from there to exploring the paternal function and its modulations today. Freud analyzed this line of monotheism while attentively listening to neuroses and psychoses, going through Sophocles's tragic dramatization and focusing on the anthropology of the late nineteenth and early twentieth centuries. He followed this line of thought to the discovery of the Oedipus complex and the incest taboo; to their role in the emergence of the capacity for psychic representation, access to language, and the development of thought as well as to their fantastical investment in diverse religious constructions. Without delving further into Freud's work here, but to which I will return several times, I will emphasize only the necessity never to forget this specifically Freudian positioning, constantly at the interface—in transference—history, biology, and what we call today "sciences of the mind," but also a bit of theology (with Pastor Pfister, for example)—an "interdisciplinarity" that his successors are often tempted to reduce to only one of its components, if not purely and simply to ignore it.

In beginning our work we cannot forget the considerable contributions for the interpretation of religious values and behaviors, from Ernest Jones to Wilhelm Reich, from Melanie Klein to Heinz Kohut, D. W. Winnicott, or W. R. Brion, and many other disciples of Freud. I could never mention them all. You will hear about them in our discussions.

An essential step in the post-Freudian approach to religion was taken by the structuralist-inspired work of Claude Lévi-Strauss and Jacques Lacan. Observing the universality of the incest taboo,[1] Lacan advanced his conception of the "symbolic" as the realm of Law that regulates desire in the oedipal complex. This complex is then understood as deriving from a primary or symbolic prohibition against incest, without anything biological necessitating such a taboo. "Transcending" in a way human lineage, might the "symbolic" coincide, in fact, with the *incest taboo*[2] and be the substratum or at least a condition, the condition of the "divine"? Moreover, the "symbolic" has come to be defined as encoded by linguistic structures and as if framing kinship relations themselves.[3]

Would God be "unconscious,"[4] "structured as a language"?[5] If and only if "the symbolic position" of the Father maintains itself as a paradigmatic and unconscious anthropological constant, whatever the historical variants of social paternal roles throughout history may be.

Would the "symbolic" as posed be a "theological" drive that seeps into psychoanalysis, the "symbolic position" being understood as an idealization of the norm or the Law as an unsurpassable authority, even as a transcendental function of the speaking being—because of the very fact that he speaks and regulates his kinship? Would saying the symbolic "is not in man but elsewhere" be a way of "showing God out one door" (which Freud does by chasing "the future of an illusion")[6] "to let him back in through another"[7]—as Lévi-Strauss feared? Lacan responded that there "is no Other of the Other"; we understand this as meaning that no exterior mandate can guarantee the foundations of the symbolic order. This is only the chain of linguistic, parental, interpretive, and cultural signs in which the speaking being is caught: "We are so far inside it that we cannot get out of it."[8]

A third poststructuralist and feminist-inspired movement examines the role of the "second sex" in the attempt to deconstruct the monotheist and paternal onto-theology. It behooves our forum to highlight and discuss the work of our divinity schools and gender study colleagues, notably from American universities. And because the maternal vocation is a key figure of the sacred, on the border of biology and meaning, and because secularization is the only civilization that lacks a discourse on motherhood, it is up to us here to further current research on the early mother-child bonds, so as to better contribute to the survival of our species. A major part of my own work concerns this problematic that I propose to deal with another time.

To further simplify this perfunctory overview of several essential points of the interface between psychoanalysis and religion, I add that listening to the Freudian unconscious allows us to think *transcendence* (Husserl's transcendental ego with its phenomenological consequences comes to mind) as immanent to the speaking being. It is like an irreducible *alterity* that inhabits us and that is modulated in the power struggles of the *bonds of desire* in the oedipal triangle, between the speaking being and its maternal and paternal imagos. There is an irreducible alterity that is universal and dual (father/mother, man/woman) and no less plural because it conjugates in the singular for each of us: an ardent pole of singular desires, this alterity makes me speak, think, love/hate. Religions celebrate it as a limit or figure of the sacred: the Other, which manifests itself in the plurality of polytheist gods while monotheism emphasizes the unicity and singularity of this universal and irreducible alterity coextensive to the unicity of the speaking being. Do you call this God? Let's talk about it.

What exactly is the Copernican discovery of psychoanalysis? Psychoanalysis did not discover that "all men are mortal" (the Greeks realized it and founded philosophy); nor that "all men desire death in their malady of love" (the Marquis de Sade had already pointed that out); it did not discover that "all men are babies" (which women knew, but since they did not have the right to speak, no one much talked about it). Psychoanalysis insists on the fact that *there is something of the other*: the other that makes me speak—that I invest and from whom I separate myself—by love-and-hate. The traces of these immemorial experiences that are inscribed in me and that I do not control, traces of "love-hate," install a strangeness in me, which alters and transcends me, and which will be called the unconscious. Recognizing it in me makes me consider each person as a subject in her/his irreducible alterity: *every I is an Other.*

This immanentist conception of transcendence (which inscribes the Other in Me) is already ongoing in Christian theology and in Christian-inspired philosophy. Saint Augustine comes to mind: "God, thanks to whom we learn that what we thought was our own is sometimes alien and what we thought alien is sometimes our own."[9] Or Leibniz: "God, land of possible realities."[10] Our interpretation of the Freudian unconscious is enriched and refined if we dare decode in it also a kind of reappropriation of the transcendental Ego (which was Christian before being phenomenological), of the singularity (*haecceitas*) of Duns Scotus, or even the well-known words of Rimbaud: "I is an other."

More radically than the other monotheisms, Judaism became the witness of the speaking being's founding alterity. A neurologist friend recently reminded me of a story my grandmother used to recount, of a gentile who asks a rabbi to teach him the Talmud. The rabbi begins with the story of two Jews who, walking on a rooftop, fall down the chimney. One comes out all black, the other all white. Who will go wash? The dirty man, answers the gentile. Wrong, objects the rabbi, because each one judges himself by looking at the other's face; the clean man seeing that the other is dirty takes himself for him and goes to get washed. Confused, the gentile recognizes his mistake and asks for another test. The rabbi tells the same story. The gentile, believing he has understood, responds that it is the clean man who goes to clean up. Wrong again, replies the rabbi, for learning from the previous episode, the man with the dirty face sees that the clean man goes to wash his face and deduces that it is his face that is dirty, and therefore he goes to wash up.

In regard to world history, and with a rare obstinacy, the Jewish people testify that there is something of the other: by dedicating themselves to the worship of Yahweh who chose them from among the others, and simply by existing politically as the "chosen people," thus other, and without proselytism. There were and would be violent offshoots from asserting this alterity, this chosenness. The history of religions is made up of them, and the threats weighing on this region of the world today are proof enough. Constant vigilance is imperative. And yet, that the assertion of this existence of the Other can take the shape of a state—the State of Israel—seems to me more than a metaphysical necessity today. It becomes an anthropological necessity if it makes all others try to think from the point of view of the other. Is it possible? We all know that the question is open. And difficult for each of us.

After this sweeping overview of the psychoanalysis/religions interface and before the immense continent in front of us, I suggest four themes which we will surely elaborate on in our forthcoming forum:

1. The need to believe and the desire to know[11]
2. The Bible: the prohibitions against sacrifice in order to construct the subject in man
3. The beaten son/father of Christianity: from loving unto death to sublimation
4. Islam or how to understand the problem of murder
5. Secularization and cultural diversity: ruptures and questionings

THE NEED TO BELIEVE AND THE DESIRE TO KNOW

Take the Psalm 116:10: "*He'emanti ki adaber 'ani aniti me'od*"; "I had faith even when I said: 'I am greatly afflicted' [I who spoke in my trouble]: "All men are liars!" Saint Paul wrote in his Second Letter to the Corinthians 4:13, echoing Psalm 116 in the Greek translation: "*Epistevsa dio elalissa*" (Greek);[12] in Latin: "*Credidi, propter locutus sum*"; in French: "*J'ai cru et j'ai parlé*"; in German: "*Ich glaube, darum rede ich*"; in English: "I believed and therefore I spoke."

Since the psalmist evokes the merciful listening of God, loving Other, a few lines before this utterance, and in assembling the various interpretations of the Hebrew term *ki*: "and," "because," "in spite of," I understand the verse this way: "Since You speak to me and listen to me, I believe and I speak in spite of the unnamable."

The context of the psalm is thus very explicit: it associates faith (*emuna*, in which we hear the root *amen*, faith or belief) that commands the act of speaking with specific, indifferent, and, here, deceptive, utterances. ("I am afflicted," "people lie to me," etc.) Faith, that is, "there is something of the other that I listen to and that listens to me," holds the key—the condition and the deep meaning—to the act of speech itself, even if it is one of complaint. Because I believe, I speak; I would not speak if I did not believe; believing in what I say and persisting in speaking grow out of the capacity of believing in the Other and not at all from the inevitably disappointing existential experience (unhappiness and lies). But what is "believing"?

The Latin credo comes from the Sanskrit *kredh-dh/srad-dhā*, which denotes an act of "confidence" in a god, involving restitution in the form of a divine favor accorded to the faithful; the secularized financial term "credit" stems from this root; I deposit a good and await a compensation (Emile Benveniste meticulously argued this development).[13] Belief is a credit: not surprising that the two are in the same state of crisis today.

What is the connection with Freud?

The psychoanalytical experience of the child and the adult, which reestablishes the metamorphoses of our personal as well as phylogenetic evolution, attests to this crucial moment of development where the *infans* (the one who does not speak) projects himself in a third party with whom he identifies: the loving father. Primary identification with the "father of individual prehistory,"[14] dawn of the symbolic thirdness that replaces the fascination and horror of the dual mother-and-child interdependence: this trusting recognition given to me by the father loving the mother and loved by her and that I, in turn, devote to him changes my stammering into linguistic signs whose value he determines.

Signs of objects, but mostly signs of my jubilations and my fears, of my early experience as a speaking living being, they transform my angst into "expectant faith": *gläubige Erwartung*, wrote Freud.[15] The loving paternal listening gives meaning to what would otherwise be an inexpressible trauma, a nameless excess of pleasures and pains. But it is not I who construct this primary identification, nor is it the loving father who imposes it on me. The *Einfühlung* with him—this zero degree of becoming One with the third—is "direct and immediate," like lightning or a hallucination. It is through the sensitivity and discourse of the mother loving the father—a mother to whom I still belong and from whom I am still inseparable—that this "unification" of me-in-the-other-who-is-a-third imprints itself in me and founds me. I cannot speak without this shoring up that is my "expectant faith," addressed to the loving father of individual prehistory: this other of the mother, loving the mother no less than the mother/the woman in me, and who possesses the "attributes of both parents." This father who was already there, who had to be there before Laius was, before the henceforth famous father called "oedipian" came to formulate his prohibitions and laws. Knots of differences between the sexes and generations; and emergence of identities, of the freedom to make sense.

A myth, you think? Rather a romanticized reconstruction that I tell myself with Freud, embroidering more or less unconsciously on the 116th Psalm and the Second Letter of St. Paul to the Corinthians, 4:13? Not only.

It is readily said, too readily, that everyone speaks his/her "mother tongue." Winnicott studied the conditions that enable the mutual excitation between mother and baby to be transformed into language: a "transitional space" is necessary, he concluded.[16] For example, the mother's reverie, or a third object between her and the baby, but which one? It had been forgotten that Freud himself had sketched out, without dwelling on it, this "believing" destiny of the father of primary identification.

An imaginary father thus arises who, in recognizing me and loving me through my mother, signifies to me that I am not she but other, who makes me believe that I can "believe," that I can identify with him—Freud even uses the word *cathexis* (*Besetzung* in German). To believe and/or to invest, not in him as "object" of need or desire (this will come later; for the moment my "object" of need and desire is rather mommy); but to believe and/or to invest in the representation he has of me and in his words—in the representation that I make of him and in my words. "I believed and I spoke."

On this one foundation, my *need to believe* thus satisfied and offering me optimal conditions for developing language can be accompanied by another capacity that is both corrosive and liberating: the *desire to know*. Carried by this faith that lets me hear and speak to a loving/loved third, I burst into questions. You see that I have not forgotten our "big question mark," my sign for this talk and, if you will, our forum.

Who has not witnessed the jubilatory trance of a child asking questions? Still straddling the border between the flesh of the world and the kingdom of language, the child knows with a hallucinatory knowledge that all identity—object, person, himself, as well as the adult's response—is a constructible-deconstructible chimera. And he continuously brings us back to this flimsiness of names and beings, of the Being who no longer frightens him but makes him laugh because he believes it is possible to name and to have things named. Before this young, vibrant Ego gets trapped in the certainties of the superego, this "pure culture of the death drive." And before "I believed and I spoke" is transformed into clichés, into "PR," into depression.

Lacan thought that the motto for psychoanalysis should be "*Scilicet*": "You can know."[17] Indeed, you can know where children come from, where that you speak comes from, what you say, etc. He forgot to mention that "you can know" if and only if you *believe* you know, to be able to understand why you believe, what you mean by believing, what you believe. . . . Lacan, originally Catholic, must have believed that it was obvious and not worth emphasizing. Now, it would really seem that the time has come to return to this "value-added" of the word and to what subtends it, its "jouissance-added," he said. By going even further, up to *believing*. . . . From knowing to believing and vice versa, the eternal turnstile of speaking-being. Carrying the possibility of knowing to the point of the need to believe, and still questioning the historical contents of beliefs and their truths: absolute or constructive? Protective or passing? Illusionary, beneficial, or deadly? Ad infinitum.

According to Freudian theory, the Ego separates and connects the Id and the Superego. This is at the very heart of the treatment, composed of verbal traces and sensations/perceptions, which are no more than the conversion of mnemic traces of traumatic excitation, with the prior condition being oedipal transference. The psychoanalytic interpretation thus obtains, like a singular poetics, by detecting the particularity of each analysand viewed through an oedipal lens but not limited to it.

For Freud there was no doubt that speech in psychoanalysis can only reach the drives and passions by first passing through pre- or translinguistic sensations. Until the last words of his apophtegm in 1938, he is emphatic about the mystic: "Mysticism: the obscure self-perception of the reign of the Id, beyond the Ego."[18] This legacy relates to his formula from the *New Introductory Lectures* (1932): "Perception can seize (*Erfassen*) relations in the deep Ego and in the Id."[19] This must be understood: the psychoanalytic treatment dissociates itself from the "gap" of mystical experience insofar as, in rapture, the ecstatic Ego gives way to the self-perceiving Id. The "vision" creates a breach in verbalization, and the fantasy acts in silence, a lightning-flash of insight accompanying the underlying drive. Language only reappears with Eros, which the mystics have to transmit and retransmit. By contrast, analysis is a procedural event, temporal and interactive, that continually constructs and deconstructs the oedipal link. This distinction needs to be emphasized: what specifically psychoanalytical underlying structure differentiates speech in psychoanalysis from the esthetic or mystical raptus?

In the death drive as defined by Freud, and against which narcissism is powerless, only the *object relation* seems capable of acting on the *unbinding* that contradicts Eros and feeds the deadly powers. But while the object of desire holds all of our attention, we neglect the deep and so fundamental explorations of the Oedipus complex that Freud addressed in *Totem and Taboo* (1912) and studied until *Moses and Monotheism* (1939): explorations of the symbolic capacity ("I believed and I spoke") facing the evolutions of paternity as a regulator of the destructiveness of the speaking animal.

Freudian psychoanalysis bequeathed to us precisely that capacity to signify, that *signifying process* as promised by and resulting from the paternal function. The evolution of family structures and reproduction, the onto- and phylogenetic *signifying process* uncovered through transference-countertransference fused the most intimate with historical upheavals, introducing history onto the couch experience.

When certain people, lost to the point of asphyxia, no longer know from where they are speaking, nor even what they think they are saying, they begin a psychoanalysis. Speaking in analysis thus takes up the form of questioning, no longer consciential but vertical to the system of language, to the point of canceling out the work of language as a system of signs, and with it, the tyranny of identification with family triangle substitutes in the structure called oedipal. Borderline states are thus "semi-oticized," if not "signified" in the *signifying* process of transference, before reproducing, for a time only, the fragility of the paternal function and the inexhaustible resistance of the maternal vocation.

Analysis makes new links possible: that is at least what most analysands hope for. In fact, the only link that the patient succeeds in establishing within the framework of treatment is that of the investment of the process of symbolization itself. Whatever it is, optimal or not, the "object" (sexual, friend, or professional partner, symbolic ideal, etc.) endures only on the condition that the speaking-analyzing subject be capable of tirelessly constructing-deconstructing meaning: from the need to believe to the desire to know, and vice versa.

Outside ethics and religion, but also the new "sciences of the mind," speaking in psychoanalysis opens new perspectives in the process of signification and in the relations that the human being keeps up with it. To explain my thinking: it is this shift of saying in relation to himself, this infinitesimal revolution, constitutive of our practice, that disturbs the world. Psychoanalysts are unfortunately not skilled enough in highlighting this exceptional singularity of "speaking in psychoanalysis": *I believe that I can know.* Yet this experience seems to be not only one that can save us from a culture that psychoanalysis has revealed to be dominated by the death drive, but one that can create a diversion from it, deter it, and divert it in full consciousness. Endlessly, and through the test of language alone that subtilizes language by making it sensible to the indescribable and by questioning the very conditions of speech, including the need to believe.

THE BIBLE: PROHIBITIONS AGAINST SACRIFICE; OR, HOW TO CONSTRUCT THE SUBJECT IN MAN

Whereas the biblical chosenness constructs the subject in man, a psychoanalytical reading of the Bible will find therein a "strategy of identity." In *Powers of Horror*, I studied how the emergence of the subject occurs when prohibitions, notably dietary, replace sacrifice.[20]

The distinction clean/unclean, *tôhar/tâmê*, was established in the biblical episode of the burnt offerings that Noah offers to Yahweh after the deluge: "Noah built an altar to Yahweh and, choosing from all the pure animals and all the pure birds, he presented burnt offerings on the altar" (Genesis 8:20). By endorsing this distinction, Yahweh had no choice but to defer his judgment: which led to clemency, on one hand, and offered time, on the other.

Neither the fault of Cain nor Adam's wandering (*nâd*—which refers back to female uncleanliness, *niddah*) soiled them. *Tôhar/tâmê* was a kind of arrangement based on a particular bond established with God. The opposition was certainly not absolute, but it testifies to this essential characteristic of the biblical text that always distinguishes identities without ever confusing them. It thus becomes a question of separating man and God in the constitution of the theological corpus.

But in the complex journey of the Yahwehist and the Eloist, one can follow how this fundamental difference subsumes, in fact, the others: life and death, vegetal and animal, flesh and blood, healthy and sick, alterity and incest. If one holds to the semantic value of these oppositions, they can be grouped into three main categories of abomination: (1) dietary taboos; (2) bodily deterioration and its apogee, death; (3) the female body and incest. Topologically, these variants correspond to the admission to or the ban from the holy place of the Temple. This is logically a matter of conforming to a law, the Law of cleanliness or the Law of holiness, as specifically summarized in Leviticus (11–26).

Commentators note that while biblical impurity was first linked to religious worship since the unclean was excluded from the Temple, it concerned things (food, menstrual blood, leprosy, gonorrhea, etc.) not immediately related to the sacred place. It was therefore secondarily, and by metaphor, that uncleanliness concerned the relation to the Temple, just as, consequently, that which was excluded from it, in particular, idolatry. In fact, it was only during the Second Temple, upon return from exile, after Ezekiel, and particularly in Isaiah (56–66), that the clean/unclean distinction became fundamental for Israel's religious life. Nevertheless, without undergoing great changes, it became still more allegoric or metaphoric, for the accent was henceforth placed less on the religious aspect of cleanliness than on uncleanliness, which became a metaphor for idolatry, sexuality, and immorality.

When the Temple was destroyed, its function persisted for the Jews, organizing certain oppositions in a "metaphoric" way. There was no opposition between material abomination and topological (holy place of the Temple) or logical reference (Holy Law). The place and the law of the One did not exist without a series of oral, bodily, and, even more generally, material separations, and which were ultimately relative to the fusion with the mother. The clean/unclean configuration bears witness to the harsh battle against *paganism* and its *maternal cults* that Judaism had to fight in order to constitute itself. This configuration accompanied the sharp edge of the fight that each subject in his own life must wage throughout his/her personal history to separate him/herself and only then become a speaking subject and/or a subject of the law. In this sense, the "material" semes of the clean/unclean opposition that punctuate the Bible are not metaphoric rituals of divine prohibition based on archaic material customs but rather provide the answer, concerning the subjective economy and the genesis of the speaking identity, of the universal symbolic Law that constitutes language and/or even the possibility of making sense.

The introduction of the clean/unclean opposition coinciding, as we have seen, with the burnt offerings thus immediately posed the question of the relationship between *taboo* and *sacrifice*. It would seem that God used the flood to sanction a violation of the taboo-regulated order. Noah's burnt offering must then repair the order disrupted by breaking the taboo. It was a question of two complementary movements.

The taboo implied by the clean/unclean distinction prescribes differences; an articulation that could be called metonymic becomes possible in which, to maintain himself in it, man is part of the order of meaning experienced as a sacred order. The sacrifice itself constitutes the Alliance (Akeda) with the One when the ensuing *metonymic order* is disturbed. Sacrifice thus works between two heterogeneous, incompatible, and forever irreconcilable elements. It necessarily connects them with violence, because it violates the semantic isotope of each of them (man and his God) at the same time that it poses it. Sacrifice is thus a *metaphor*. The question is which came first, the metonymic taboo or the metaphoric sacrifice. In the end, as sacrifice extends the logic of the taboo only when that logic is disturbed, it is clear that taboo came before sacrifice. It seems safer to say that the focus some religious bodies put on the taboo protects them from all sacrificial intervention, or at least subordinates it to the taboo. *The biblical abomination would thus be an attempt to stop murder.* By the sustained abomination, Judaism distinguishes itself from sacrificial religions. And insofar as religion and sacrifice overlap, biblical abominations constitute perhaps the logical explanation of the religious experience (without actually killing which had become unnecessary with the revelation and observance of taboo strictures). With biblical abomination, might religion be wending its way toward obsolescence?

The list of often specious prohibitions, which makes up Leviticus (11:1–4), becomes clear if it is understood that it is a question of strict compliance with the logic of the divine word. However, this logic is based on the initial biblical postulate of the man/God difference, co-extensive to the prohibition against killing. As in Deuteronomy (14), it means constituting a logical field to keep man from being carnivorous. One must shield oneself from murder, not ingest meat or carnivorous birds, and there is one criterion only for that: eat ruminant herbivores. Some ruminant herbivores depart from the general rule of ruminants by having a cloven hoof, so they would be ruled out. The clean would be those who conform to an established taxonomy; the unclean, those who disrupt it, introduce mixing and disorder.

Patiently, meticulously, the obsessive defenses against the desire to kill transform themselves into an ideal self, and the taboo into ethics. Ritual distinctions (vegetal/animal, flesh/blood) that initially appeared to us as an expression of a foundational opposition between man and God and signify the initial contract ("Thou shall not kill") become an entire system of logical oppositions. Different from the burnt offerings, this system of abomination presupposes it and guarantees its efficiency. Semantically dominated, at least initially, by the life/death dichotomy, it eventually becomes a code of differences and similarities in relation to the burnt offerings. A system of taboos is constituted as a true formal system—a taxonomy. Mary Douglas brilliantly highlighted the logical compliance with the Leviticus abominations, which would be incomprehensible without this aim of "separation" and "individual integrity."[21]

Fighting against mixing and promiscuity, uncleanliness finally recedes from the material register and expresses itself as a profanation of the divine name. The defiled will now be what upsets the symbolic unicity, such as simulacrums, substitutes, doubles, and idols. Moreover, it is in the name of this thus unified "I" to whom, through Moses, an entire people conforms, that moral prohibitions subscribing to the same logic of separation follow: justice, honesty, and truth (Leviticus 6–9).

Deuteronomy takes up and varies the Leviticus abominations (14, 22, 32), which in fact underlie the whole biblical text. But the recurrence of a specific figure incarnating this affirmed logic of separation attracts our attention, because it indicates that the unconscious founding of this persistence of separations, for the purpose of unity and/or the One, is ultimately the *incest taboo*: "Thou shall not boil a young goat in the milk of its mother" (Exodus 23:19; 34:26; Deuteronomy 13:21).

The abomination is not to feed but rather to cook the young goat in the milk of its mother: in other words, it means using the milk, not in function of the needs for survival but for a cultural construction, a culinary myth establishing an abnormal bond ("incestual") between a mother and her child.

We therefore see that the dietary prohibition, just as the more abstract expression of the Leviticus abominations in their logic of the differences dictated by the divine One, was about the incest prohibition. Far from being one of the semantic values of the Bible's vast project of separation, the mother taboo seems to be its originary mytheme.

Yet it is the prophetic current that steers this "mytheme" to its full eclosion. In particular through Ezekiel, heir to the Law of cleanliness and the Leviticus Laws of holiness, that moves toward a *theological distinction* between cleanliness and uncleanliness. And as Isaiah announced, this distinction would rule Israel's life from stem to stern upon return from exile. Neither banished nor cut off, uncleanliness is pushed away and folded under, always there, operating, constitutive: "Your hands are soiled with blood/and your fingers with guilt" (Isaiah 59:3); "All of us have become like one who is unclean, and all our righteous acts are like filthy rags" (Isaiah 64:6). "A people who continually provoke me to my very face: / offering sacrifices in gardens/and burning incense on altars of brick; / who sit among the graves / and spend their nights keeping secret vigil; who eat the flesh of pigs / and whose pots hold broth of impure meat" (Isaiah 65:3–4).

Abjection—dietary, sanguine, and moral—renewed within the chosen people, not because they might be worse than others but because, in the eyes of the contract that they alone sealed, they are able to identify abjection and only then to rid themselves of it without end. It is thus the very position of the logic of separation, as well as its severity, on which the existence and degree of abjection depend that the man of God can and must combat. Such is at least the conclusion that can be drawn from the prophets' emphasis on abjection.

Still more, and contrary to certain structuralist psychoanalytic currents that absolutize the cleansing efficacy of the symbolic Law, the permanent prophetic resumption of abomination in "chosenness" itself points out that the strategy of identity is never acquired once and for all. The paternal symbolic order in which the identity of the speaking being constitutes itself is of course absolute and universal; it is nevertheless singularly contingent: to be constantly conquered and particularly by the one who is chosen to it with the highest standards.

There is still a tendency to reduce Freud to *The Future of an Illusion* (1927), and it is not exactly wrong to do so, for it is always a question of combating the excesses of deadly religious obscurantism the identarian conflicts lead to. One should not forget that not only is illusion indispensable to psychic life (as attested to by the role of fantasy in psychoanalytical listening), it even very simply constitutes it (think of the "transitional" role according to Winnicott). One should not forget how imaginary constructions (myths, fables, narratives, religious stories, rites, and all the arts) constituted "precursors" for Freud in his quest for logics intrinsic to the life of the "psychic apparatus."

With this in mind, think about Kant's effort to find the foundation (*die Grundiegenung*) of metaphysics in "the most intimate part of man." This "subjective deduction" would lead to moving backward in relation to the stated metaphysical ambition, to the point of obscuring it, maintained Heidegger. Does it mean, then, freeing oneself of the subject by the Being? Or rather, as Freud did, to "move backward," but better and differently than Kant, "toward the beginning of the subject" to elucidate it (the *analysis*): to look into the foundations of metaphysics at the same time as of the subject itself?

The logics of biblical abominations and their psychoanalytical interpretations seem to me to provide a radical means of probing the emergence of the subject in man, insofar as they present in acts and in metaphor-metonymy the series of separations that articulate singular identity and/or his symbolic chosenness, as it functions by the posed/supposed instance of the Other as Creator.

THE BEATEN SON/FATHER OF CHRISTIANITY: FROM LOVE UNTO DEATH TO SUBLIMATION

Although paternal connotations of the Divine Creator abound in the Bible, it is Christianity that actively and perseveringly exploits the paternal axis of the symbolic order, and it does so specifically through the complex relationship between Jesus-the Man-God-Son-of-God *and* God the Father Himself. Without claiming to offer an exhaustive analysis of this complex topology, I would like to propose a possible interpretation alongside a rereading with you of *Totem and Taboo* (1912) and "A Child Is Being Beaten" (1919) by Freud, yet also informed by my clinical understanding of the "desire for the father," of sadomasochism and of its sublimation.

Remember that for Freud killing the father is a foundational act, a historical reality in human civilization. Likewise, for Christians, Christ is a historical character and the killing that believers commemorate is a real one. As a psychoanalyst, I am only interested in the *psychic reality* that generates fantasies in the subjects who believe in such events, whether or not they actually occurred. In addition, from the perspective of the Trinity, it seems difficult to dissociate the suffering to death of the Son from that of the Father who is consubstantial. A new construction, different from Freud's, thus claims our attention: what if Jesus were not only a child or a beaten brother, but a beaten father—beaten to death?

By combining the son (the beaten boy) and the father (authority by law), this scenario has the advantage of both appeasing the incestual guilt that weighs on the desire for the Sovereign Father, the Other, and of encouraging virile identification (including in the case of girls and women) with this tortured man: but only under the cover of a masochism promoted, even recommended, by this double movement. "This beaten father and/or brother is my double, my fellow, my *alter ego*, myself provided with a male organ."[22]

However, there is another moment, essential to the "a father is being beaten to death" fantasy that not only strictly speaking liberates the death drive as sadomasochistic aggressiveness but, even more, confronts this drive in its deep and radical Freudian sense, as unbinding[23] of the drive-based links and of the living itself. It is precisely what slips in to the gospel story when God the Father Himself reaches nothingness. Is not the *kenosis* or Christic "annihilation" in the descent into hell the death of God Himself? Reconciliation through resurrection very quickly follows. And the invitation to the believer is to retrace this process, to live it, and to sublimate it. Wonders of Christian art!

In other words, Christianity has at the same time admitted and denied the killing of the father. Such is precisely the particular solution it has succeeded in imposing on the authority of the universal dead father whose religious commemoration characterizes our human condition. From then on, Christianity, and in particular Catholicism after the Counter Reformation, took over the Greco-Roman body: it absorbed the ancient body discovered by the humanists by pushing it to its limits in man's Passion. Painting, music, and literature would develop the passions of men and women, heralded by mysticism before Baroque art, and radically overturn the subject of monotheism.

ISLAM; OR, HOW TO REFLECT UPON THE PROBLEM OF MURDER

Is Islam involved in this monotheistic movement? Might there be more similarities between Allah and the Aristotelian God than with the Creator Father?

Benedict XVI's speech in Ratisbonne on September 12, 2006, relaunched the debate on "reason" according to Islam and the place "holy war" occupies therein. The subject is so sensitive that it too often inflames passions: the specialists can deal with this at another meeting. Remember only the commentaries that emphasize the similarities between Allah and the Aristotelian God—the latter supposedly being the Prime Mover on the periphery of the universe (*Physics* 8:10), much more than a world cause removed from the world. These same specialists carry the hypothesis to affirming that it would be the inspiration for mechanical obedience and terror, thus having a link with radical Islam. Others, fortunately, recognized that Islam rejected as much as it was inspired by Hellenism (and in particular, Aristotelianism); that in the eighth century a "rationalist" school tried to understand faith through reason; but also that the "discovery" and diffusion of Aristotle, notably in the Christian culture, would be above all the work of great masters like Avicenna and Averroes.

I hold that one of the essential questions Islam poses is the role of the *divine* and its link with the *paternal function*. In sparing Isaac, Abraham became the pivotal figure of this juridical and loving paternity: his obedience to the divine word moved God so that he then suspended, by the sacrificial judgment of the son, passion among men, the "oedipal" desire

(Freud would say) for death. This event thus laid the foundations for the Messianism of the *pistis:* Jesus, accomplishing "faith working through love" of the biblical God (Galatians 5–6), temporarily dies on the cross to be resurrected by and for the love of the Father, thus embracing the Abrahamic destiny. This foundational event presents itself differently in Islam that, according to Freud, recuperates (*Wiedergewinnung*) the unique and great originary-Father (*Urvater*) but omits "the development that in the Jewish case produced the murder perpetrated against the founder of the religion,"[24] and that Christianity was ready to recognize. I agree with this point of view, as I pointed out in my ideas about the place the "father being beaten to death" holds in Christianity.[25]

Islam also does not say who should be sacrificed and/or spared: Hagar's illegitimate son Ishmael or the legitimate Isaac, son of Sarah? Furthermore, how do we interpret the fact that in the Koran Abraham *dreams* of the sacrifice (rather than receiving the injunction from God Himself): is this an unconscious desire to possess the son, in all senses of the term, to take pleasure from him and to abolish him? Or is it a means to renounce immolation and murder?

With these "details," the subject is constructed differently in each of the three monotheist religions, not only in its relationship to the Law and in the bonds between men, but also in the sadomasochistic jouissance experienced in the murder of the other, whether by the killing of the child in oneself or in facing one's own death.

I would like to return to Freud's idea that Islam remains outside of this movement of deepening "love-hate" of and for the father present in Christianity: the explanation lies not in a supposed loyalty to Aristotle but rather in the exclusion of any idea of paternity in the divine—as opposed to Jewish and Christian monotheisms—but also in the exclusion of many fundamental points of the biblical-Gospel canon that join the Creator to his creatures in a loving bond. Thus there is an absence of original sin in Islam (guilty for having believed Satan; Adam and Eve are expelled from paradise, but their posterity does not bear the burden of their fault). Likewise, the sacralization of the Koran was revealed to Mohammed alone so that the Jews and Christians are supposed to have only partially received the revelation and have therefore deformed it.

Return to these different elements that seem crucial to me in an attempt to understand today's political crises: why is a dialogue with Islam so difficult, even impossible, today? The "Aristotelianism" cited above does not constitute a satisfactory explanation. By invoking it, to my mind, we are not dealing with the real question that Islam raises concerning the believer's link to divine authority. I would formulate it this way: limiting the authority of Allah to a juridical pact only, does not Islam depart from a paternal Creator whose function is to *choose* (in Judaism, even though the spirit is legalistic, it does not suspend the creationist component which underlies the effort of reflection and questioning), or to *love* (in Christianity, even at the price of abandonment and passion)? Of course Sufism—and notably Ibn Arabi (1165–1240)—proposed subtle variants to the "big sacrifice," such as sacrifice of self, the "*nafs*" or *psyche,* in the face of nothingness. These particularities of Islam, which I have pointed out very schematically, could create an obstacle to an Islamic theology and dialogue, not only between its Sunni and Shiite branches but with the two other monotheisms as well. They also limit the potential opening of Islam to the ethical and political problems of men and women confronting the libertarian challenges of the third millennium.

These reflections should enable us to turn toward the most liberal currents and go back to the work that anthropologists, sociologists, and psychoanalysts devote to Islam, thus opening and pursuing dialogue and not giving in to terrorizing and terrorist movements that Islamic observance is prey to.

If today Islam is not up to undertaking an interpretive return on its history and its connection with the landscape of monotheist religions, and whether for political or for economic reasons, the structural difficulties that underpin them must not be neglected either. For this reason, it behooves anthropologists, sociologists, and psychoanalysts, with or without specialists of religion, to make a concerted effort to elaborate tools that create bridges in spite of the differences defined and analyzed as to their anthropological consequences. Is this utopian? Or is it the only answer possible when faced with today's "clash of religions"?

The manner in which Islam has become stuck in the fundamentalist mire raises the question of *Homo religiosus* in its very structure. *Homo religiosus* could not transcend the "love-hate" that constitutes him without sidestepping. He must shore up his theology, accept himself as a thinking object, and accept the current interpretations of the multiple and infinite needs to believe. Is this not what Freud said when he advised

speaking one's love of the other, infinitely? Of analyzing oneself by analyzing it, constantly? Might psychoanalysis be a descendant of theology?
Its ultimate variation, *hic* and *nunc*?

SECULARIZATION AND CULTURAL DIVERSITY:
RUPTURES AND QUESTIONINGS

Last, I will not dodge the question that is inevitably put before us, actors
of secularization and more or less formed by it, united here today. Even if
Europe has now become the only democracy able to realize Kant's dream
of "universal peace," its "repentance" clearly does not protect it from racism and anti-Semitism; and its offspring, what is commonly called the
"West," is always ready to lead new crusades in the name of Good against
Evil. Religious fundamentalism does not spare Christianity, of course,
and this tendency is quite significant with neoconservative Protestantism
in the United States. One can wonder if Catholicism itself, since John Paul
II and in spite of its humanitarian and humanist developments, is not
flirting with a defensive identarian hardening: as if the survival of the
Catholic faith "depended" on the Jihad, to the point of seeking its authenticity by withdrawing into its own conservatisms, or even in a paradoxical "identification with the aggressor"!

But let us get back to secularization and the Holocaust. In *The Origins
of Totalitarianism* and elsewhere, Hannah Arendt strongly emphasized
this new phase of anti-Semitism that was driven in Europe by many
causes, and also by the "assimilation" of the Jews in the wake of the
Enlightenment. The philosopher-political theorist drew back in horror
before the Nazi and Stalinist extermination camps and concluded in substance that "its horror *can* never be fully embraced by the *imagination*."

Questioning the responsibility of secularization in these "somber
times," Arendt condemned the reduction of human differences to the
generality of *zoon politikon*, which became the generic "Man" in a reduc-
tive understanding of "human rights." Nonetheless, when Waldemar
Gurian and Eric Voegelin from the important political science department at the University of Notre Dame in Indiana wanted Arendt to
adhere to their thesis that totalitarianism was more the product of

modern atheism than a sociohistorical process, or the "spiritual sickness of agnosticism," Arendt did not disagree that a certain atheism may have contributed to the end of ethics. But she maintained that the totalitarian phenomenon was unique, and that there were no prior cases, either in the Middle Ages or in the eighteenth century, that could qualify as "totalitarian."[26] She also took great care to differentiate her philosophical questioning from any religious position and connected the political use of the "divine" to the pernicious nihilism she combatted: "Those who conclude that because of the terrible events of our time we should turn back to religion for political reasons seem to me to show as little faith in God as their opponents."[27]

The last but not least enigma that the third millennium and its galloping globalization confronts us with concerns the *mutations of the singular subject* that constituted itself in the wake of the Greco-Judeo-Christian tradition. The disruption of oedipal structures in the recomposed family—due to the weakening of paternal authority, the assertion of the psychic bisexuality of the two sexes, and assisted reproduction—does not really abolish the universality of the anthropological constants that were discovered and then set down by the monotheist religions, and that the psychoanalytical experience has been trying to elucidate since Freud.

Transgressive contingencies have always inhabited the order of free legitimacy (what Hegel called *Sittlichkeit*) in the guise of "aberrations," and as criminal as they might often seem—as in the story of "soiled" Antigone against Creon the ruler—they are in reality internal and inherent to the ethic of free identity, its internal double. There is something new though: modern secularization and new technologies accept these transgressions not as *perversions* (of Oedipus, the Law, symbolic order) but as invitations to modernity to invent new kinships, new families, and *new legalities*.

They first coexist at the edge of the symbolic order as a *père-version* to begin with, accepted or not as part of the democratic debate and with the input of all available knowledge, in particular that of psychoanalysis, before—perhaps?—modulating, covertly and over time, the regulating institutions of kinship and of family themselves.

Alternatively, people whose psychic life has been formed by different religious contexts—Buddhism, Confucianism, Taoism, Shintoism, animism, etc.—do not seem to share the same logics of *libertarian singularity*.

While seduced by globalization, through some of its standards that psychoanalysis uncovered and continues to probe, these people often put extreme pressure on us to rethink them (hence oedipal triadic trials, psychic bisexuality, among others).

In this context where religions harden more than deal with these challenges, it is up to psychoanalysis to interpret cultural diversities and to assure their respect as well as their defense and illustration of this model of individuation and human freedom revealing, thanks to our therapeutic experience, the fecund complexity for individual and collective fulfillment. This heritage was bequeathed to us by a tradition symbolized by Jerusalem and of which psychoanalysis is the rebellious child who recognizes its debts.

To conclude, let us stop bemoaning the sensational pseudodiscovery that "all civilizations are mortal"; or rejoicing that the twenty-first century will be religious (Malraux); being "sanctimonious" about religion and knowledge out of "fear of being nothing" (Voltaire). The Greco-Judeo-Christian civilization is the only one that has lasted from rupture to rupture, while breaking "the thread of tradition" (according to Tocqueville and Hannah Arendt). Today we know that this "broken thread" triggers extravagant freedoms, the most precious of which is thinking, which presents a major risk if we do no more than point to the abuses of obscurantism and forget to probe the benefits of this "thread."

God is not necessary, indeed, but the need to believe—both a carrier net as much as a strangling knot—is, in my listening, both a prereligious and prepolitical anthropological necessity. I have discovered that the illusion of eternal Life can attenuate the anxiety of death and turn a Carmelite called Saint Teresa of Avila into an ecstatic writer who self-analyzed: "Look for yourself in me," the eternal Other was to have said to her—before she became a "business woman" who shook up the politics of the Church. I hear that the Marian myth bandages wounds of the sexual jungle so the brutality of rape ends up in immaculate rebirth; and I observe, still on the couch, that the immaculate conception fable counters the fantasies of the primal scene but, while turning the unbearable into a pure enigma, prepares it for sublimation or even to become analyzable. Present and past history teaches me that the promise of absolute love, lavished by an Ideal God the Father, soothes the sadomasochistic rivalries of brothers . . . when it does not sharpen them to death. And I ask myself.

Because secularization alone was able to "cut the thread of tradition," we can now think all traditions. Without ecumenism, and by putting them in perspective and in tune with each other. This is our advantage, and an exorbitant ambition.

The heirs of Judaism have paved the way by opening a philosophical dialogue with biblical tradition. That led to the normative modernity of Hermann Cohen, Franz Rosenzweig, Gershom Scholem, and Emmanuel Levinas; but also to the critical modernity of Kafka, Benjamin, and Arendt, who reappropriated Nietzsche and Heidegger. A third modernity is now being sought: the modernity of analytical atheism, which, inspired by Freudism, can open all the globalized world's religious traditions to the experience of thought. "There where it was, I can venture." You say: "spiritualities"? I answer: "I am a journeywoman."[28]

We are going to journey down a long road that goes back to prehistory, traverses the thoughtless, and heads toward the unknown: a new stage opens before us by our common ambition to explore the memory of religions using the analytical experience and with the contributions of all who would like to come along with us.

20

DARE HUMANISM

WHAT IS A COURTYARD (PARVIS) OF GENTILES?

Herod expanded the site of the First Temple of Solomon to establish a place of sacrifice for Jewish pilgrims, pagans, Greeks, and other "infidels," "unclean" people, "outside of the Alliance" with Yahweh; but this courtyard was also a place where the sick begged and merchants traded, activities that were prohibited inside the temple. Christianity afterward transformed this separating space. "[T]he court, which is without the temple, cast out, and measure it not: because it is given unto the Gentiles, and the holy city they shall tread under foot two and forty months"[1] (the number forty-two signifies as long as imperfection in the world lasts, until the Messiah comes). The revolution of Paul of Tarsus began with his address to these Gentiles that he brought from the court into the temple. "He has even brought Greeks into the temple, and defiled this holy place" (a foundational act leading to his being dragged from this place.[2] Did not the same Paul perceive an "unknown God" (*Ignoto Deo*) announced on the peristyle of a Greek temple, like a divine need, or even a premonition of Christianity among these not so "unclean" "Gentiles" for him after all: enough to justify this true abolition of the court that Paul achieved by introducing them into the "Holy of Holies"?

In the nineteenth century the German philosopher Schelling developed this Paulist intuition by interpreting Greek polytheism as an integral part of what he called a "theogonic process": this is coextensive to and resulting in self-awareness after having gone through the "mythological representations" that inhabit it when it does not yet have a hold on itself.[3]

So does not the mythology of these "Gentiles" ultimately become Freud's "unconscious": with Oedipus, Medea, and others such as Diane of Ephesus, without forgetting *Totem and Taboo*?

I mention some of these elements of this long history to point out that, far from remaining in the courtyard as we are encouraged today, Gentiles have long since integrated a conception of the human with the debatable (more later) name humanism. But back to the courtyard.

In the Middle Ages the courtyard was the place of mysteries. But in earlier times the Church space itself was open to extravagant and carnival-like shows, a multiform combination where the sacred mixed with burlesque, misogyny, and triviality. The Church hierarchy condemned these fantasies for offending God, and they were firmly exiled to the courtyard around the fourteenth century. A courtyard, as you can see, is not a safe place.

The term *Gentiles* is nonetheless confusing. Thomas Aquinas, in his famous *Summa Contra Gentiles* (the title was not in his own hand but that of a copyist), understood "Gentiles" in the sense of Paul who was the "Apostle of the Gentiles." It referred to people of the non-Jewish nations of antiquity who were "Gentile," although the theologian used this term primarily for the Greek philosophers, introduced to him by this "Gentile" Aristotle whose logic he readily borrowed. But in order to consolidate the "true religion," he also discussed what he called the "errors" professed and practiced by Jews, Muslims, and heretical Christians against the Catholic faith and reason. Would they all be Gentiles, in fact, if they were not Catholic?

The ever ambiguous and polemical polysemy of the terms *court* and *Gentiles* makes the project of this dialogue hard to grasp, as relevant as it might be. The metaphor, especially as applied to the present, disregards the incredible break that took place within Christianity, and then outside it, that saw the birth of the humanism of the Renaissance, the philosophy of the Enlightenment, the freedoms and impasses of secularization, and finally of the dangers and promises of technology. The novelty of these events has been anything but "gentle" in the meaning of the word that interests us, not only because Jews were involved in this secularization but above all because it was not premonotheistic paganism. By "cutting the thread" with Greek, Jewish, and Christian tradition, but also "very close to it," secularized humanism offered an unprecedented conception of human universality, whether consisting of a diversity of religious practices or professing no faith at all.

Can the opening of a dialogue between believers and this secular humanism find accommodation in the metaphor of a space so laden with identarian separations? Could it share the ambition of a Henri de Lubac, who in 1968 in *Athéisme et sens de l'homme*, when commenting on *Gaudium et Spes*, described a dialogue between "secular humanism" and "Christian anthropology" by the term "*confrontation*," to be carried out "by the force of a spiritual penetration of the two protagonists"?[4] A confrontation that would be an "art of spiritual communication," "which does not end with a smile," but remains a "combat" around conceptions of man (that of Catholics being a "cult of man," he wrote).[5]

Is this confrontation, this combat, this mutual aggression through the art of spiritual communication, possible if one of the parties is placed in the courtyard and the other holds the place of the holy of holies? This is doubtful, and it is to be feared that the salutary confrontation desired by Henri de Lubac would end in parallel discourses and in spatial separation. But the intention is for an opening, beyond the weight of the words that are not. And those who today are engaged in it will surely do their best to meet the challenge. Thank you then for this project, for this invitation, for this challenge.

WHY DARE: SARTRE AND HEIDEGGER

I entitled my remarks "Dare Humanism." Why? When humanism is rigidified into *systems*—Auguste Comte's or Marx's, or Sartre's "radical secularism," which he assured conserved religion's moral values but abandoned their divine guarantee and are consequently as many theologies that ignore each other—it becomes a metaphysical relic. It moves divine worship of the Absolute in society or human nature to wind up in a "sociolotry" or a "humanolatry" that contemporary philosophy has not failed to deride.

The two seminal texts on humanism since the Holocaust, Sartre's *Existentialism Is a Humanism* (a 1945 conference) and *Letter on Humanism* from Heidegger to Jean Beaufret in 1946, barely allude to the biblical and evangelical genealogy of this concept. Heidegger especially emphasizes its Roman origin, while Sartre emphasizes *freedom in existence*, which in humans precedes *essence*; Heidegger developed the *ecstatic proximity* of the Being of which man would be the "shepherd": he takes refuge in *language* but remains "concealed," inaccessible to philosophy. Incompatible and incomparable (an *ad hoc conference*, for Sartre; a *meticulously written text* for Heidegger), these two major reflections, however, have in common that they offer visions of man that bypass atheism even to the point of not commenting on the idea of God (*man chosen* by Yaweh in the Bible; a *God of Love made man*, according to the Gospels).

With feigned naivety, Sartre declared that it was "very vexing that God does not exist because all possibility of finding values in an intelligible heaven disappeared with Him."[6] Thereafter "man, without support, was constantly condemned to invent man"; this freedom was as rich in promise as in risks, for "value is nothing more than the meaning we give to it."[7] More prudent and "poiesis," Heidegger "did not decide for or against the existence of God," but nor did he accept "indifferentism" (agnosticism), since, "where we are in our global destiny," "thought does not surpass metaphysics by surmounting it . . . but by descending to the nearest proximity. . . . [This] descent leads to the *poverty of ek-sistence* of *homo humanus*."[8] This *poverty* where the philosopher seeks the human resides in the "clarification" that comes from language: by the unusual simplicity of speech, where ethical laws have "come (back) down," before yielding to the "slow steps" of the "peasant across the countryside," to close this "love of wisdom" that is humanism, according to the *Letter to Beaufret*.

Whatever the many faces of HUMANISMS outlined here in broad strokes that are accepted as atheist (Sartre) or are not dealt with (Heidegger), questions on humanism leave "the empty party empty" and "fill it with the strongest, the most august, and most opaque name that can be found." These questions attempt to construct a representation of man, by "transvaluing" (Nietzsche) some previous representations coming from the Greek-biblical-Gospel tradition: "Humanism does not place the *humanitas* of man high enough," Heidegger wrote,[9] not so hostile to humanism after all . . . endless rethinking. But as long as he seeks this "high" in the "descent" toward the deepest poverty of language.

In this spirit, if not in this school, I will talk about three periods in which the idea of the secular man crystallized, debating with the traditions of antiquity, Judaism, and Christianity, and facing historical, technical, and scientific mutations: Erasmus, the eighteenth century, and Freud. And to show that this particular history of humanism does not offer a denial of God but a questioning of the "being of man." This proves coextensive to both the *need to believe*, specific to anthropological religiosity (as opposed to institutionalized religion), and the desire to know that drives the freedom to think: two *human universals* that led so-called secular humanism to renounce establishing an absolute Object of desire for all, men and women, without necessarily renouncing the need to believe or the desire to know, let alone renouncing the means to explain and accompany them.

AMONG THE BUILDERS: ERASMUS, THE ENLIGHTENMENT, FREUD

ERASMUS OR HOW TO TAME FOLLY

Contrary to popular belief, Erasmus (1469–1536) did not bring back *Homo romanus* when he wrote his *Praise of Folly* (1509, published in 1511). Humanism, at the time of its crystallization for Erasmus, was neither a philosophical system nor a political program but a language experience that tamed folly and dreamt of peace. Was it a message of moderation? More precisely, Erasmanian humanism, by describing man's wildly errant ways, strove to prove the absurdity of wars, beginning with those set off by religious conflicts. Erasmus the "eel," an elusive dissident, slithered out of Luther's hands as well as the Vatican's control. His intimate knowledge of Greco-Roman culture that he had studiously learned enabled him to retranslate the Vulgate written by Saint Jerome whom he nevertheless praised. But this Dutchman was emerging as the major figure of reviving humanism by his art in taming our worrisome strangeness, most disturbing because it is also "the nearest": folly (in *Praise*) and childhood immaturity that continues to live within us (in *On Civility in Children*, 1530, intended for Prince Henry of Burgundy).

And so the theologian Erasmus, lover of Greco-Roman rhetoric, broke with theology and founded reborn humanism when he spoke through the words of Lady Folly: "Without me (she/he says) the world cannot live a single instant." Neither sacred essence nor rational animal, does the human being lead a mad existence? Would this constitute a tragic or comic aberration, or more certainly both? Lady Folly is my alter ego, yours and the saints' too. All split, dissociated, "cleaved," as the shrinks today say, and each one differently. What should one do?

Erasmus did not propose absolution but offered us language: a *declamation*. He set up Lady Folly as if at a country fair: might his *Praise* be a satire? Yet it is not he who speaks; *I* is already an *other* (*man* or *woman*): a raving woman. I/she reviews the turpitudes, the devastation, wars, and bloodshed, results of passions in heat that spare no one: the apostles themselves, mystics, and lovers could not escape Lady Folly. This is a satire. Not quite, I quipped. Theatrical, carnivalesque, polyphonic, the humanism of *Praise* does not transcend us, it gets to us at our most shameful. In counterpoint to a certain "Christian humanism" that cultivates the surpassing of self, a form of heroism, Erasmus recognized how to tame human beings' vulnerability, and he took the risk of a common life, even when passions often won over morality.

Simple "ironic esthetic stage" in the guise of propaedeutics? When Erasmus had become a teacher twenty years later, he continued to reject theomorphism in his teaching and asked teachers to "relive childhood" through play; if it is backed up by an ethical code, it turns into a life project. Paul of Tarsus had said: "Brothers, do not be children in your thinking. Be infants in evil, but in your thinking be mature" (1 Corinthians 14, 20). Erasmus knew that, and he changed the Paulist message into an interior experience and transmission.

DIDEROT AND SADE: INFIRMITY, PASSION, AND THE IMPUDENCE OF UTTERING

Let us try to understand how this reactivated humanism separated itself from what is a posteriori called "Christian humanism," summed up as

"transcendence" according to Pascal: "Learn that man infinitely transcends man. . . . Listen to God."[10] Since Nietzsche, who formulated it in
the late nineteenth century, the diagnosis is found everywhere and is
worsening today: by assigning humans the responsibility of elevating and
of transcending themselves, Christian humanism and certain subsequent
currents called humanist have imposed a double and dangerous image of
man. Presented as a sinful creature, fallen, miserable, or "bionegative,"
man is nonetheless capable of heroism that culminates in the daily "existentialism of obstinacy" (Sloterdijk), if not in Olympian worship.

In perpetual quest of God and struck by an originary flaw ("original
sin" for theologians; "prematuration," in a biopsychological approach),
humanity would be a kind of cripple while the resulting humanism would
be condemned to withdraw into the only universality left to it, that of the
suffering and the infirm.

These vestiges of expiatory Christianity coexist with their symmetrical and concordant other side, the heroization of universal vulnerability:
for example, in the Olympic Games ceremonies or in this politically correct form of disability that is tolerable in the journalistic/telegenic meaning of the word only if the disabled athlete wins a medal in these same
games. One main current of so-called modern humanism—normative,
normalizing, infatuated with performance and entrepreneurial competitiveness in the "work more to earn more" race—shares this philosophy.
There is another, under the pretext of deconstructing it, that flatters the
denial of disability, this most insidious of exclusions, as it frightens people because it puts us in front of psychic and physical mortality and exacerbates the growing indifference of the social body and political powers
on this subject.

I feel the diminution of humanism in these two extremes
(miserabilism/"fragilitism" and reparative or heroizing obstinacy) as a
real abuse of the specific and complex experience of the disabled. But I
also see it as an oversight of an essential component of humanism: that of
the French Enlightenment, principally through Diderot and Sade, who
rip away the curtain of miserabilism as well that of the "existentialism of
obstinacy" and, more courageously than anywhere else, open the scene
of singular passions and of "how to live together with them."

Remember that former canon Diderot knew well the misery of the
human body. He sought it specifically in the disabled body of a blind man

from Cambridge, a genius surveyor who had his "soul at his fingertips" and calculated volumes he had never seen like no one. Diderot devoted his *Letter on the Blind for the Use of Those Who Can See* (1749) to him, and he rose up against predestination theology using disability; from deist he became an atheist, which cost him being sent to the Bastille: *political humanism* was born.

In addition, Diderot would soon develop this horizontal dimension of the new *political humanism*. His *Letter on the Deaf and Dumb* (1751) gradually was addressed *to all those who no longer know how to listen or hear*. At the same time as he challenged obscurantism and called for freedom of thought under the monarchy, he appealed to everyone's *interior space*, the subjective experience of what is meant by "listening" and "hearing." Was he thinking of the Apocalypse of John? "Blessed is he who reads and those who hear" (1:3). In times of social or cosmic catastrophe, it is through reinvention of our abilities to think that life can begin again, not a purely physiological life, which would be *zoology*, but *biography*: an irreducible subjectivity that is sharable.

With the Enlightenment and until Freud, humanism was mostly an *eroticism*, in the etymological meaning of the word, the desire and pleasure of creating links, of living together, without forgetting the ability to be alone; this eroticism is given as the solar side of our vulnerability, not "from a lack" or something tragic but creative and innovative. From the outset, however, there is an accompanying aporia: how would it be possible to live this eroticism without the mix of repression and illusion that religions have woven around it?

Diderot valiantly tackled the dilemma and strove to find an answer in the *Conversation with a Christian Lady*; "Christian Lady," echoing the Pascalian wager, asks this master in disbelief, "What do you gain in not believing?" One is not moral for nothing, implies the interlocutor, and if the philosopher Thomas Crudeli sought neither compensation in heaven nor jouissance on earth, "that's sad," she concludes. The only alternative that the atheist offered the Christian lady against religion that represses bad passions was "the natural penchant for benevolence" reinforced by education and age. The good Catholic was not convinced, and it was necessary to wait for the philosopher's clincher argument to put an end to the dialogue: religions are not a substitute for passions but rather fuel them. They are source of dissension and are founded on an incomprehensible being on which men fail to agree.

The scoffing writer's accusation against the abusive confinement in *The Nun* fell short: his friends found him in tears, unable to finish the manuscript of "this tale of mine that I tell myself." For leaving the convent—where she was forced to mortify her body or on the contrary yield to the abuse of a nymphomaniac superior—his nun did not find meaning in life. No more than Diderot himself, who could not turn it into a novel. It was only a few years later in *Rameau's Nephew*, in the dialogue between Him, the libertine and spastic musician, and Me, the philosopher, that the humanism of psychosexual complexity emerged through an unprecedented liberation of speech—liberation that Hegel, meditating on *Rameau's Nephew*, would call an "impudence of utterance": the distinctive mark of culture and in particular of French culture.

At the same time, while Rousseau (in *The New Heloise* and *Emile*) invented the modern biface couple, shelter for the procreation of the species and a nursery of citizens for the bourgeois State, the Marquis de Sade's impudence of uttering revealed the cruelty of men's and women's all-powerful drives when they dare to compete with infinity no longer in the beyond but in the thick of human passions. From the *Dialogue Between a Priest and a Dying Man* to Silling Castle in *The 120 Days of Sodom*, the free rein given to the most singular desires comes up against both the denial of pleasure because of religious prohibitions and the massification of this pleasure by religious and political dogmas. Freed from the divine cause and the moral constraints it decrees, the infinite transcendence of our desires can only be replaced by infinite pleasures unto death: cruelty and what will be called "sadism" follow, when one pretends not to see that the phantasmagoric imaginary of Sade, necessarily asocial, is made of words.

In the refined precision of language and in both secret and phantasmatic micro societies such as a discreet reminder of very strict and observant monasteries, this cruel truth of desire infinitely unfolds in its most extravagant singularity. Unbearable transgression of moral law, fundamentally divine moral law, singularized jouissance unto death is formulated necessarily as a blasphemy jealous of the power of the Supreme Being Himself, be he religious or republican, *ultimately* unmasked as a

"Supreme Being in wickedness." As the realization of this monstrously particular *jouir* could only be depraved, by renouncing the world, Sade's writing comes (*jouit*) to light up the infinite excesses of passions by an unbridled imagination.

For Sade, his predecessors' humanist caution is jettisoned for the dark energy of this new *Praise of Folly*, like a satanic underside of theism and a sarcastic catastrophe of humanism, and his own paradoxes point out to the fascinated or tortured reader this void that modernity is far from having filled: how to think "world"; can one share the infinite thrust of desire and its collapse in the reality of human bonds without the protective code enacted by Divine Cause and its consubstantial moral conscience?

FREUD: BETWEEN THE NEED TO BELIEVE AND THE DESIRE TO KNOW

At this point came the discovery of the unconscious and the outlines of a new version of humanism: again and again passed over in silence. As of 1911, in his "Formulations Regarding the Two Principles in Mental Functioning," Freud posited a "mental revolution of matter" that constituted hominization and specified the human being: the establishment of the "reality principle" succeeded the omnipotence of the "pleasure principle" that dominated the living and the human at their beginnings. When a part of drive-based energy is invested as psychic representation, the assumption of its singularity is represented to the speaking being as a symbolic unit transcending the organism as well as objective exterior reality.[11]

By this I mean that while animal drive follows the general route of the species, the psychic representation (*psychization*) waives immediate drive satisfaction, and it is a *psychic reality* distinct from *exterior reality* that the human takes as the aim of his pleasures of a new type. It can be said that he "invests" it (*Besetzung* [in German], *cathexis* (remember these words). Psychic reality, distinct from the reality of the body and its milieu, thus becomes in turn a source of pleasure in the infinite pursuit of an object of desire that constantly steals away.

There is a major indispensable condition in this psychization. Whereas Romain Rolland led Freud to recognize an "oceanic feeling" in the maternal contact as the prototype of the ecstasy in which religious experience thrives, it was the primary identification, *Einfühlung*, with the figure of the Father of "individual prehistory"[12] that guides, according to Freud, the drive aim, detaching it from sensorial satisfaction alone and supporting its ability to invest psychic representations. Note that this experience is situated before Oedipus's revolt against Laius. So very early on, the future speaking being invested the function of the father who recognized him and whom he recognized. This father of "individual prehistory" was not an "object" of satisfaction but a "pole of identification," reciprocal gifts, and expectations of recognition.

The psychic act shown here, the "investment," is in Sanskrit **kredh*, **sraddha*, and in Latin *credo*. Carried by maternal desire for the father (hers and/or the child's), this *Einfühlung*—"unification," "becoming ONE with the father"—constitutes a prereligious occurrence of "believing" as a universal anthropological need. Therefore this *Einfühlung* in the need to believe appears as a precondition of language crossing the dyadic oceanic mother/*infans* and addressing a third party where "the assumption of the subject" is accomplished. "I believed and I spoke," said the psalmist (Psalm 116), repeated by Paul in the Second Epistle to the Corinthians (4–13).[13]

Monotheism celebrates this anthropological truth that is the father's desirance through the intermediary of the need to believe opening the way to speech. This is how Lacan explained it: "It takes nothing for saying to make God."[14] Freud himself became convinced that religions institutionalized some steps of this dynamic and sometimes consolidated the pleasure of imagining and thinking, but more often they hampered the desire to innovate in thinking. On the contrary, a certain drive-based renunciation and the need to believe taken up by the desire to know in the complex experience of subjectivity seemed to him necessary for culture, whatever it may be: they cannot be dissolved, they can only "be sublimated."[15]

To be vertical in its ascensional surpassing toward the Law or the Ideal (going through the individual prehistoric father and then Oedipus), this dimension of the *Homo religiosus* is not exclusively ascetic; it has its hell as well as its paradise. The interior experience of the mystic has, in particular, constructed the psychosexual complexity of the Western man and woman: "*Ego affectus est*" and "*Credo expert*," said Saint Bernard, warrior crusader but great lover, contemporary of the troubadours, precursor of the Renaissance. "I ask God to leave me free of God," countered Meister Eckhart on his end, bequeathing his mystical vocabulary to German philosophy. "Play chess, my sisters, yes, to checkmate the Lord," then suggested Teresa of Avila with a smile.

However, along with these advances in the need to believe, where again according to Freud, mysticism and psychoanalysis seek a "similar point of attack," psychoanalysis—with the humanities—raises a more general question concerning the very structure of *Homo religiosus*. He could clarify the "love-hate" that carries him only by stepping aside and taking himself as object of thought. Is it by developing his theology, opening it to the multiple interpretations of the multiple variations of the needs to believe? Does psychoanalytical research bet on the fact that it is possible to say the love of another, infinitely, to analyze oneself by analyzing it infinitely? Would psychoanalysis be one of the variants of theology? Its ultimate variant, perhaps, *hic* and *nunc*?[16]

HUMANISM'S NEW PLAYERS: WOMEN, MOTHERS, ADOLESCENTS

With passions thus liberated, psychoanalytical listening enables us to address the new players of humanism—women, mothers, teenagers (among others)—whose entrance into culture and politics disrupts traditional ideologies, be they revealed religious dogmas or declining humanism.

It can never be repeated enough: from Theroigne Mericourt to Louise Michel and Simone de Beauvoir, *humanism is a feminism.* Yet the access—uncompleted—to women's freedom to love, to procreate, to think, to undertake, indeed to govern, cannot hide the fact that while a great deal of the research in contemporary psychoanalysis is centered today around the early mother / child relation, the civilization born of secularization is the only one that has no discourse on motherhood.

What is a mother? She is the actress in what I call *reliance.*[17] Before the need to believe that the primary identification with the Father of individual prehistory crystallized, maternal reliance intervened at the dawn of the development of the psychism, thus preceding the need to believe that religions institutionalized. With every newcomer, the mother constructs a sensible code, prelanguage, to bring him/her to language. How can a woman subject, a lover to boot and constantly more in demand professionally, say "I" in this intersection of maternal passion/vocation? There will not be a new humanism as long as mothers as actresses of this reliance are not able to speak out.

But if humanism is a feminism, it is also an *adolescence*. Why do these teenagers—anorexic, suicidal, drug addicted, arsonists, or dreamers, innovators, liberators, romantics—fascinate and scare? Because they are lovers in need of an ideal who believe with all their might that there is an Object of absolute love. When they do not find it, these Adams and Eves, these Romeos and Juliets, become nihilistic thugs, kamikazes, and so on. The civilization born from secularization is also the only one without initiation rites for its adolescents. Will shrinks, educators, sociologists, and parents know how to read these "ideality diseases," this need to believe that the erotic excesses and deadly acting out (thanatic),[18] for example, that they indulge in, reveal?

In conclusion, I will speak about the challenges of technology and interculturality that humanism, which is so disparaged, is called on to renew, for I am bold enough to think that it can rebuild itself in a continuous way.

INTERIOR EXPERIENCE AND HYPERCONNECTIVITY

On the threshold of the third millennium, in the hyperconnected–smart technologies corporate culture that intrudes into our strictest intimacy and is now being colonized by biotechnology, are we witnessing the disappearance of the *interior space* that Teresa took pleasure in with her seven "mansions" and that Diderot, already attentive to the deaf and dumb, was attempting to redeem?

At the end of his *Critique of Pure Reason*, Kant foresaw the possibility of the relationship of the "idea of a moral world . . . to a *corpus mysticum* of rational beings in it."[19] The new links created by the internet's social networks, the brotherhood and solidarity that they seem at first to promote, have nothing in common with this metaphor of the union with oneself and the wholly other. Similarly, it was vain to hope that the universalization of the principles that founded human rights—globalization at its most promising—might put an end to barbarism, whose persistence in the world is all the more cruelly displayed through media transparency.

This pact with the wholly other to whom the mystical subject is in thrall cannot be reduced to moral laws alone that it converts into absolute love. And if today many of us try to discover or revisit the *corpus mysticum* to reinvent ourselves, it is the absence of a modern loving discourse and experience that sustains our quest.

Others of our contemporaries argue that a third-millennium version of humanism, abolishing the subjective and supposedly narcissistic and "human worshipper" space, should necessarily emerge from the all-powerful finance, communications, and smart technologies, that should be given a free rein. The biotech century Big Brother promises a "win-win" virtual self and has no interest in the incommensurable intimacy that the Freudian breakthrough bequeathed us. I search, I discover, I hear, I share the singular language of this man, of that woman: the refoundation of humanism listens to the singular.

Whatever forms they take, they are *mutations of the singular subject,* formed in the wake of Greco-Judeo-Christian traditions that constitute the last enigma modern times confronts us with. The recomposed family and the upheaval of the resulting oedipal structures, but also the emergence of cultures that seem not to share our principles of individual liberty, however significant they may be, do not deeply abolish the universality of anthropological constants as they were uncovered and then set by monotheisms, and as the analytic experience since Freud endeavored to elucidate them. These mutations force us nonetheless to consider, tolerantly, of course, but also firmly, both ethical codes without which autonomy of thought and the free subject that were crystallized in the wake of this tradition and through its ruptures could not survive, as well as their transgressive, protesting, "*queer*" or "unclean" contingencies.

I believe that a third modernity is finding itself, one that was inaugurated by the Renaissance and the Enlightenment, followed by the *normative modernity* of modern Judaism (Hermann Cohen, Franz Rosenzweig, Gershom Scholem, and Emmanuel Levinas) and *critical modernity*

(Nietzsche and Heidegger revisited or reinvented by Kafka, Benjamin, Arendt), that of *analytical humanism*. Freudian-inspired, it can open all the religious traditions of the globalized world to the experience of thought.

CHINESE AND EUROPEANS: UNIVERSAL OR MULTIVERSE?

The meeting of cultures is certainly the other key challenge that today's globalization confronts us with. A most significant example is that of the meeting of Chinese tradition with Jewish and Christian monotheism.

Leibniz, a contemporary of the Jesuit mission in China, considered along with his forefathers that not only did the Chinese not know "our God," but they understood the subject itself as endowed with a kind of intelligence, of Law, *li*. And thus the mathematician became a visionary of a Chinese-type "humanism" whose enigma still escapes us, and that we are quick to stigmatize as "arrogance." Would it be because he seems more comfortable in adapting to the logic of business and connectivity where the Self is reduced to a point of impact of the infinite cosmic and social recesses (clearly national today, and that manage to cancel it)? Facing it, would the permanent deconstruction/construction be a handicap that risks hindering our entrepreneurial competitiveness?

I maintain, on the contrary, that by pretending to ignore the rationales of inner experience, there is the risk of seeing the anxiety of finitude and the explosion of violence constantly thwart connectivity, cooperation, and repair by *homeotechnique* of this ideal world that the New Alliance promises us in complexity. Globalized humanity is seeking a coming together between, on one hand, the Chinese adaptability to cosmic and social intelligence and, on the other hand, the political interaction among psychosomatic complexities of which Proust summarized post-Christian humanism: "Those who are sick feel closer to their soul."[20]

I have suggested only some varieties of this humanity that seems no longer like a universe but what I call a "multiverse," a metaphor that, at a time when astrophysics is reshaping our understanding of the human, I gladly borrow from the so-called superstring theory (quantum physics that proliferates possible universes, and inflation that pushes them to exist). A metalaw governs it all: there is a universal humanity of which the concept and practice come from universalist monotheism and the rupture with it, but the singularity of each of its components is of such delicacy that the general law takes on specific modalities. It is possible that, confronted with emerging diversities, we are witnessing the advent of a *multiversal humanism*. If so, this will be possible only from and with OUR tradition of the universal.

21

TEN PRINCIPLES FOR TWENTY-FIRST-CENTURY HUMANISM

What is humanism? A big question mark on the most serious of issues? This event with its unending promise, disappointment, and reconstitutions took place within the Greek-Jewish-Christian, and European, tradition.

When Jesus described himself (John 8:24) in the same terms as Elohim speaking to Moses (Exodus 3:14) saying, "I am," he defined man—and anticipated humanism—as an "indestructible singularity" (in the words of Benedict XVI).[1] Indestructible singularity that not only links him to the divine beyond the genealogy of Abraham (as the people of Israel already did) but also innovates. For if the "I am" of Jesus spans the past, the present, and the future, and the universe, the Burning Bush and the Cross become universal.

When the Renaissance with Erasmus, and the Enlightenment with Diderot, Voltaire, Rousseau, but also the Marquis de Sade and up to the atheist Jew, Sigmund Freud, proclaimed the freedom of men and women to revolt against dogmas and oppressions, to free their bodies and souls, to question all certitudes, commandments, or values, did they open the way to an apocalyptic nihilism? In attacking obscurantism, secularization forgot to look into the *need to believe* that implies the *desire to know*, as well as the limits to put on the desire unto death—in order to live together.

Yet it is not humanism but rather the sectarian, technicist, and nega-
tionist deviations that have sunk into the "banality of evil" and that promote the current automatization of the human species. "Be not afraid!"
(Isaiah 44:8; Matthew 17:7). These words of John Paul II are not directed
solely to believers that they may take heart in their resistance to totalitarianism. The appeal of that pope, an apostle of human rights, also
encourages us not to fear European culture but, on the contrary, to dare
humanism: by constructing bridges between Christian humanism and
that emerging from the Renaissance and the Enlightenment that aspires
to puzzle out the risky ways of freedom. Thank you today, Pope Benedict
XVI, for having invited humanists among you for the first time in this
place.

Thus my thoughts with you here in Assisi are addressed to Saint Francis, who "seeks not to be understood as to understand," nor "to be loved
as to love";[2] who awakened women's spirituality with the work of Saint
Claire; who placed the infant at the heart of European culture by creating the Christmas holiday; and who, before he died as a humanist before
his time, sent his letter "to everyone in the whole world."[3] I also think of
Giotto, who unfolded the sacred texts in living images of the everyday life
of men and women of his time and challenged the modern world to shake
up the toxic ritual of today's omnipresent entertainment.

Can we still speak about humanism; better still, can we still speak
humanism?

Danté Alighieri comes to me right now, celebrating Saint Francis in
Paradise in his *Divine Comedy*. Danté founded a Catholic theology of
humanism by showing that humanism exists only if we transcend ourselves in language by inventing new languages, as he himself had done in
writing ordinary Italian in a new style and inventing neologisms. "Going
beyond the human in the human" (*transhumanar*) (Paradise 1:69), he says,
would be the road to truth. It is a question of "intertwining" in the sense of
"coupling" (*s'indova*, putting oneself there, in the "where") (Paradise 33:138),
as the circle and the image intertwine in a rose window, the divine and the
human in Christ, the physical and the psychic in the human.

From this Christian humanism, understood as "a going beyond" of the
human in the coupling of desires and meaning through language, and if
it is a language of love, secularized humanism is the often unconscious
heir. And it separates itself from it by refining its own rationales, which I

outline here in *Ten Principles*. They are not ten commandments but ten invitations to think of bridges among us.

1. Twenty-first century humanism is not a theomorphism. The capital letter man does not exist. Neither superior "value" nor finality," nor arrival of the divine in the highest acts of those called geniuses since the Renaissance. After the Holocaust and the Gulag, humanism has a duty to remind men and women that if we consider ourselves the only law-makers, it is uniquely through the continuing questioning of our personal, historical, and social situation that we can decide on society and history. Today, far from deglobalization, it is necessary to invent new international rules to regulate and control global finance and the economy and, in the end, to create an ethical universal and collective world governance.

2. Humanism is a process of permanent refoundation that develops only through ruptures that are innovations (the biblical term *Hiddouch* signifies inauguration-innovation-renovation; *enkainosis* and *anakainosis*; *novatio* and *renovatio*). Understanding the Greco-Judeo-Christian heritage in depth, thoroughly examining it, transvaluing (Nietzche) tradition: there is no other way to fight ignorance and censorship, and to thus facilitate the cohabitation of cultural memories constructed over the course of history.

3. Child of European culture, humanism is the meeting of cultural differences that globalization and digitalization promote. Humanism respects, translates, and reevaluates the various needs to believe and desires to know that are universal to all civilizations.

4. Humanists, "we are not angels, we have bodies," said Saint Teresa of Avila (*Life* 22:10) in the sixteenth century, inaugurating beyond the Counter-Reformation a true baroque revolution that initiated the century of the Enlightenment. Nonetheless, free desire is desire unto death, and it took psychoanalysis to include, in the sole and ultimate regulation of language, this liberty of desires that humanism neither censors nor flatters but proposes to clarify, accompany, and sublimate.

5. Humanism is a feminism. The liberation of desires could only lead to the emancipation of women. Once the Enlightenment philosophers opened the way, women of the French Revolution demanded it with Theroigne de Mericourt, Olympe de Gouge, and up to Flora Tristan,

Louise Michel, and Simone de Beauvoir, and I am not forgetting the struggles of the English suffragettes, nor those of Chinese women from the beginning of the bourgeois revolution of May 4, 1919. Combats for economic, legal, and political parity require new thinking on the choice and responsibility of motherhood. Secularization is still the only civilization that fails to have a discourse on motherhood. The passionate bond between mother and child, this first other, the dawn of love and hominization, this link where biological continuity becomes sense, alterity, and speech, is a *reliance*.[4] Distinct from religiosity as from the paternal function, maternal reliance completes them and is fully part of humanist ethics.

6.   Humanists, it is through the sharable singularity of the interior experience that we can combat this new banality of evil of the ongoing automatization of the human species. Because we are speaking, writing, sketching, painting, music making, playing, calculating, imagining, and thinking human beings, we are not condemned to become "talking points" in speeded up hyperconnection. The infinity of capacities of representation is our habitat; depth and deliverance are our freedom.

7.   But the Babel of languages also generates chaos and disorders that humanism will never regulate by just the attentive listening to the languages of others. The time has come to go back to the immemorial moral codes: without weakening them so as to problematize by renewing them in the light of new singularities. Far from being pure archaisms, prohibitions and limits are the safeguards that cannot be ignored without suppressing the memory that constitutes the pact humans have with each other and with the planet and planets. History is not of the past: the Bible, the Gospels, the Koran, the Rigveda, and the Tao live within us in the present. It is utopic to create new collective myths, and it is also insufficient to interpret the old ones. It is up to us to rewrite, rethink and relive them, in the languages of modernity.

8.   There is no longer a universe; scientific research discovers and ceaselessly probes the "multiverse." Multiplicity of cultures, religions, tastes, and creations. Multiplicity of cosmic spaces, of matters and energies coexisting with the void, composing with the void. Have no fear of being mortal. Able to think the multiverse, humanism is confronted with an epoch-making task: inscribing mortality in the multiverse of the living and the cosmos.

9.   Who will be able to do it? Humanism, because it cares. The loving care (*cura*) of the other, the ecological care of the Earth, the education of the young, attending to the sick, the disabled, the elderly, and those who are dependent, do not interrupt either science's advances or the explosion of virtual money. Humanism will not be a docile regulator of economic liberalism that it should try to transform without apocalyptic jolts or sunny tomorrows. By taking its time, by creating a new proximity and basic solidarities, humanism will elucidate and reorient the anthropological revolution already announced by the biological emancipation of women, by the uncontrolled processes of technology and finance, as well as by the inability of the powerless democratic pyramid model to channel innovations.

10.   Man does not make history, but history is ourselves. For the first time, *homo sapiens* is capable of destroying Earth and himself in the name of his religions, beliefs, or ideologies. Similarly, for the first time men and women are able to reassess in total transparency the constituent religiosity of the human being. The diversity present here in our meeting in Assisi attests to the fact that the hypothesis of destruction is not the only possible one. No one knows which human beings will follow us, we who are engaged in this unprecedented anthropological and cosmic transvaluation. The refounding of humanism is not a providential dogma nor a mind game; it is a wager.

The age of suspicion is no longer enough. Faced with increasingly grave crises and threats, the time has come to wager. Let us dare to bet on the continuous renewal of men's and women's ability to believe and know together. So that in the multiverse surrounded by a void, humanity might long continue its creative destiny.

22

ON THE SANCTITY OF HUMAN LIFE

Octor 10, 2012: Tenth World Day for the abolition of the death penalty. Mobilization, ignorance, hostility, misunderstanding, solemnity, and gravity suspend time in the global crisis, in the hyperconnected acceleration and in the various threats of destruction. And they call for contemplation and invite meditation and questioning: what is the meaning of a call for the universal abolition of the death penalty?

I

I am neither a lawyer nor a specialist of abolitionism. I have never witnessed an execution, and no one in my circle has been a victim of murder, sexual abuse, torture, or degrading violence. I will not read you medical reports chronicling the tortures of the guillotine that Camus copied to impress on us his nausea. Nor have I felt this romantic empathy that enthralled Hugo comparing his pain at being exiled to that of an outcast. I consider that pain is incommensurable, even incommunicable, and that the death wish that is within us threatens us all, in the singular.

I hear my analysands confide in me the sufferings they endured at the hands of torturers in Latin American prisons or their inconsolable grief after the extermination of their parents in concentration camps. I come apart with them, and I will not attempt to say that evil is without reason, like the mystic who states that the rose has no reason. Because I search for and with them: why? So that meaning returns, because meaning gives life back.

Abolish the death penalty: what wish and what project are we conveying here? And what does it mean?

Abolishing the death penalty signifies that we are positing "the inviolability of human life" as the foundation of the humanism of the twenty-first century, as Victor Hugo called it, more than 150 years ago (in 1854).

Since the beginning of time, humans have been afraid of death; yet they give it to better preserve life and try to save the *good* by inflicting the supreme *evil*. For the first time in history, however, we realize that it is not enough to replace old values by new ones because these new ones also get stuck in dogmas and impasses that are potentially totalitarian. And life is not a "value" like others, nor even THE value. Even more, for the last two centuries, and particularly today, life is not only a question: What is a life? Does it have a meaning? If so, what is it? But life is now a requirement: it has to be preserved and its destruction prevented—because destruction of life is a radical evil. While everything seems to be collapsing, and wars, the threat of ecological disaster, the frenzy of virtual finance and the consumer society constantly remind us of our fragility and vanity, the *inviolability of human life* calls on us to think of the meaning of our existence: this is the cornerstone of humanism.

What LIFE are we talking about? The abolitionist answers: ALL LIFE, whatever it is, including "accepting the life of those who horrify," the demented, the criminals, as Robert Badinter proclaimed when he introduced a bill in the French parliament in 1981 to abolish the death penalty. Can today's humanity feel deeply enough and stand by its beliefs to the point of "accepting the life of those who horrify"? We abolitionists say yes. Even if 141 countries out of 192 members of the United Nations have already abolished the death penalty, 60 percent of the human population lives in a country where it is still applied (since it is in effect in four of the most heavily populated countries of the planet: China, India, the United States, Indonesia).

Bolstered by its plural heritage—Greek, Jewish, and Christian—Europe chose secularization, thus effecting an emancipating mutation unique in the world; but its history was also marked by its too long litany of horrors—wars, exterminations, colonialisms, totalitarianisms. This philosophy and history impose on us a political and moral conviction that no state, no power, and no person can dispose of another person and has the right to take his life from him. Regardless of the man or woman we condemn, justice must not be one that kills.

Pleading for the abolition of the death penalty in the name of the *inviolability of human life* cannot be classified as either naïve or smugly and irresponsibly idealistic, nor is there any question of forgetting the victims and the pain of their families. NO. I do not believe either in human perfection or even in absolute perfectibility through compassionate grace or education. I am betting only on our ability to better understand human passions and to accompany them to their limits because experience teaches us that it is impossible (unthinkable) to respond to crime by crime.

I repeat: the human being's greatest fear is that of seeing his life taken away, and this fear is the basis for the social pact. The oldest jurisprudence treaties in our possession testify to this. Take the Babylonian code of Hammurabi (1792–1750 BC) or the Greek philosophers Plato and Aristotle, but also the Romans, or the Jewish and Christian holy books: all societies plead for and implement the death penalty for criminals in order to defend, protect, and dissuade.

Voices were, however, raised against this killing: today's abolitionists have found and listened to them to support their combat. Already In Ezekiel: "I take no pleasure in the death of the wicked but that the wicked turns away from his life and lives" (33:11); but especially Saint Paul: "Death, where is your victory? Where is it, O death, your poisonous stinger? Death has been buried in the victory (of the Resurrection)!" (1 Corinthians 15:55). And in their wake, Maimonides: "It is more satisfying to acquit thousands of the guilty than to put to death one living person."

It is rare, but some religions or politicians have come out against the death penalty: Tibetan Buddhism banned it in the seventh century; and in 747 a first abolition was proclaimed in China that Montesquieu pointed out, praising its Chinese authors who said: "The more the torture, the closer the revolution; torture increased as morals decreased." Shouldn't Chinese authorities be reminded of that? China eliminated the death penalty in 2011 for thirteen nonviolent crimes, but executions for corruption continue and are increasing. As for Islam, there is little question of challenging the death penalty.

In France, the abolitionist movement began after the torture of Damiens, who attempted to assassinate Louis XV. While Diderot advocated the death penalty for its dissuasive effect, Voltaire was one of the rare people to support the work of Cesare Beccaria, who, as of 1764, was thinking: "What right do men have to allow themselves to kill their fellow men?" In the spirit of the Enlightenment and of libertarian humanism, abolitionism developed throughout the nineteenth century. Think of Clemenceau, Gambetta, and those lucid words of Jean Jaurès, proclaiming that the death penalty "is contrary to both the spirit of Christianity and that of the Republic." Closer to us, I am thinking of Camus, who saw that "capital punishment is written about only in whispers" because "the new murder, far from repairing the offense done to the social body, adds a new strain on the first. . . . The capital judgment breaks the only indispensable human solidarity, solidarity against death."

II

The abolitionists put forward three main arguments against the death penalty: the ineffectiveness of vengeance and dissuasion; the fallibility of justice; the pain this elimination locks in.

In the first place, nothing proves the effectiveness of the death penalty against human destructiveness: there is no correlation between the maintenance of the death penalty in a legal system and the crime rate. Furthermore and on the contrary, the possibility of death, far from annihilating criminal passion, exalts it. He who sows terror and transcends it by his own death is not seeking expiation. The stigmatization of his acts and his very sacrifice in reality have no other end than to enflame martyrs ready to die in their turn. Far from being dissuasive, fear becomes temptation and then feeds the desire to inflict death by inflicting death on oneself. The death penalty as the "eye for an eye, tooth for a tooth" law turns out to be ineffective as vengeance as well as dissuasion.

The second argument refers to what Victor Hugo called the "derisory brevity of human justice": the judiciary lottery and its fallibility. In what name does an institution, a man, or a woman grant themselves the right to pronounce and carry out a death sentence?

The third argument is only whispered because it addresses the pain of the victims and their families. Some people think that even if putting the criminal to death does not avenge his crime nor dissuade those who come after him, it does at least get rid of the perpetrator. The death penalty as elimination of its agent would thus alleviate the unbearable and soothe.

But does the image of the criminal in his tomb really relieve the pain of those who have lost someone close to them, victim of the worst atrocities? This pain that has to be soothed is as inexpressible and unable to be shared as it is legitimate and respectable: who would dare deny this? No one and especially not those who, indignant at the death of innocent victims, desire also to defend and protect life in the name of its inviolability. Because they know that death as the ultimate and unique recourse is an illusion.

When will we stop making the tomb our savior? Let us separate ourselves from the jouissance that the vengeful act provokes. Victor Hugo pointedly drew our attention to this religion of death as savior: "Do not dig a tomb with your own hands around us," he wrote from Guernsey. "Men who know so little and who can do nothing, you are always face to face with infinity and the unknown. Infinity and the unknown are the tomb." What I hear is do not hope to find "the unknown or infinity" in the sacrifice of the condemned, even an assassin. And I add: the only unknown or infinity are human passions whose experience we do not stop probing and whose knowledge we do not stop acquiring.

By abolishing the death penalty we are not shouting victory over death as Paul of Tarsus wanted and who called for believing in the Resurrection. We encourage knowing and accompanying passions better, and the most terrible of them, the death drive.

III

Psychoanalysis discovered that *Homo sapiens*, who is both *Homo religiosus* and *Homo economicus*, is a Homo eroticus inhabited not only by a life force but also by a death drive: the one that Freud, as if he sensed the

Holocaust, explored at the end of his life and that contemporary research continues to elucidate today.

The human being is fundamentally binary: digesting the good and expelling the bad, oscillating between the inside and the outside, pleasure and reality, prohibition and transgression, one's self and the other, body and mind. Language itself is binary (made of consonants and vowels, and other dual forms that were a boon for structuralism). Thus children gain access to the difference between good and evil at the very moment they begin learning the mother tongue: the universe of meaning leads one to distinguish between good and evil, before refining their nuances, perceiving their polyphonies, their excesses, their transgressions, or creating works of art.

Our desires prove to be more or less compatible with those of others. They draw us toward the other, and to love, but to a love that in itself contains aggression: I love you, me neither, hatred and guilt; such is the alchemy of the word. These are precisely the convergent and divergent libidinal interests, founded on our conceptions of good and evil, that our loftier values are constructed on and that become competitive or conflictual. Desires and values lay down religions, philosophies, and ideologies that live off them, kill each other because of them, or attempt to explain and understand each other.

These so-called values often capture destructivity, taking the form of a fascination for evil that is sought in the other, and which then leads to searching for the scapegoat to get rid of him mercilessly, in favor of the Sovereign Good, my very own Good, my religion. This is the *rationale for fundamentalism*, which carries out a relentless war in the name of an absolute ideal erected against the one facing you. Whether individual or collective, this fundamentalism is fed by a total and blind faith that suffers absolutely no questioning. As I stated before, the condemnation to death of the fundamentalist does not eliminate fundamentalism itself; on the contrary, it makes its agent a martyr and exalts the rationale, one that has economic and social roots but also a psychosexual nerve, by the very structure of its passion, and it remains unassailable if it is not defused from within.

There are, however, only the superficial layers of radical evil here. There is also a *pure death wish*, dissociated from any desire (or *désintriquée* from desire). This death wish does away with the distinction between good and evil, between me and other; it *abolishes the meaning* and dignity of the other and of self. The destructivity I have just highlighted here yields to *unbinding*. These extreme states of almost total unbinding of the death wish touch the limits of *Homo sapiens* as a speaking being and capable of values (beginning with *good* and *evil*). The person in thrall to this unbinding expresses himself in a language that is now only mechanical, an instrument of destruction without either code or communication: without reason, without remorse, nor expiation nor redemption.

Such borderline states do not take refuge only in hospitals or on couches; they do not strike serial killers alone or explode brutally only in the chaos of an adolescence doomed to indifference and insensibility to the stranger to get rid of. Borderline states of the death wish also break out in sociopolitical crises and catastrophes. These abject states can lead to the cold and planned extermination of human beings, as was the case for the Holocaust and other genocides.

IV

I hear your question and share your indignation: so the abolitionists want to save the life of these criminals?

If I have carried this thinking to the idea of dehumanization, it is to demonstrate more clearly that the humanism the abolitionists of capital punishment advocate is a wager against horror. Knowledge of human passions enables us to look at these borderline states and deal with them clinically, even if such knowledge makes us neither all powerful nor able to cancel out this pathology when a whole society is suffering from it. But after Ezekiel, Paul of Tarsus, and Maimonides, after Beccaria, Voltaire, Hugo, Jaurès, Camus, Badinter, and so many others, greater knowledge of the range of human passions would seem to be the only way to spot and deal with the many faces of this radical evil. When compassion and forgiveness abdicate because they have no hold on this evil, it still becomes possible to probe it down to its depths. How?

- By relaying the horrified emotion by a more precise diagnosis of the complex aspects of radical evil. Vigilance, objective analysis, care, and education do not do away with any of the criminals' guilt, but they do mobilize us as of their early symptoms:

- by replacing the death penalty by strict sentences that prevent recidivism;
- by organizing the indispensable care of these people, convicted criminals or political criminals, to lead them as far as possible in their restructuration. And to thus better analyze the springs of destructivity and of unbinding that generate crime.

Hannah Arendt, philosopher and political journalist, denounced the Nazi horror as an unprecedented radical evil but argued that it is not the *evil* but the *good* that is radical. Because *good* is not a symmetric reversal of *evil*; it is found in the infinite capacities of human thought to find the causes and the ways of fighting the *malaise* and the *malignity of evil*.

V

Allow me to conclude on a more personal note.

As a child in Bulgaria, my native country, I heard my parents discuss the death penalty the communist regime inflicted on the previous parliament but also the Stalinist purges and trials. I was studying French when my father, a man of faith, explained that while the revolutionary terror had been inevitable, the language, like French culture, also carried light within it. I was already in France when he was hospitalized for a benign operation and assassinated in a Bulgarian hospital in 1989, a few months before the fall of the Berlin Wall—they were then carrying out experiments on old people. The death penalty was abolished in Bulgaria in 1998, even though today 52 percent of the people polled in this country say they are in favor of it.

It is not a question of saving society, which can perpetuate itself only by steeling itself against the infinite complexity of passions. It is a question of using our knowledge of the passions to help the human being, to better protect us against ourselves. The new humanism should be able to defend the principle of the inviolability of human life and to apply it to all, without exception, as well as to other extreme situations of living experience: eugenics, euthanasia, etc. Far be it from me the idea of idealizing the human being or of denying the evil he is capable of. We can, though, care for him, and by abolishing capital punishment—which, remember, is a crime—we fight against death and against crime. This means that the abolition of the death penalty is a lucid revolt, the only worthy one against the death wish and ultimately, against death. It is the secularized version of resurrection.

You no doubt know that the Italians light up the coliseum, the bloody memory of many Christian gladiators and martyrs put to death, each time a country abolishes the death penalty or decrees a moratorium on executions.

I suggest that every night a country gives up the death penalty its name be seen on a specially installed giant screen on Place de la Concorde (former Place of Revolution) and the Hotel de Ville (former Place de Grève), in memory of Mme Roland, Mme du Barry, Charlotte Corday, the knitting women, the guillotine, Fouquier-Tinville, André Chénier, etc. Would this extra expense risk exacerbating the state of our finances? Optimists predict that virtually the whole world will have abolished the death penalty by 2050. It is up to us to see that the majority of the people are in favor of this abolition.

V

FRANCE, EUROPE, CHINA

23

MOSES, FREUD, AND CHINA

I must confess: my four-year degree in Chinese has not made me a
Sinologist (so I'm not a China "specialist"), and as a psychoanalyst, I
have treated only two Chinese analysands: a perfectly Westernized
man and woman born in France of Chinese parents, only occasionally
speaking Mandarin, sharing only partially in Chinese cultural traditions,
and thus more representative of these polyphonic personalities that
globalization produces than of "modern China."

I am nonetheless responding to your invitation in spite of these most
modest contacts with the Chinese continent, because, as a semiotician,
philosopher, psychoanalyst, and woman, on one hand, I cannot ignore
the immense challenge the face-to-face between the European culture
and the Chinese one presents—with and beyond the economic, financial,
military, and political competition; and on the other hand, because I
believe that psychoanalysis holds a specific and perhaps unique place, in
any case a decisive one, as to the possibility of having a real dialogue
between these two cultures.

WHICH ONE IS THE MORE BELIEVABLE?

In the seventeenth century, Blaise Pascal had already called attention to
the inevitable meeting of our two worlds when he wrote in his *Pensées:*

FIGURE 23.1 François Wahl, Marcelin Pleynet, Philippe Sollers, Roland Barthes, and Julia Kristeva, 1974, in front of Longmen Grottoes, China.

"Which is the more believable of the two, Moses or China? There is no question of taking this lightly; I tell you there is something in it to blind and something to enlighten. We must put papers on the table."[1] There is no question of the broad view. I tell you there is enough here to blind and to enlighten.

Was Pascal thinking of Elohim's word speaking to Moses (Exodus 3:14) and taken up by Jesus (John 8:24): "I am (the one) who is/will be"? In the wake of the Enlightenment and after Kant, Freudian psychoanalysis went back to and turned this affirmation into "Who am I?" That is the question the analysand brings to the analyst's couch, searching for a creative singularity.

But it must first be stressed that no more than the singularity of the "I," the verb "to be" does not found Chinese thought, which is concerned with neither *foundations* nor *origins*. In its triple Taoist, Confucian, and Buddhist configuration, this Chinese thought appears to us as a "fluid of

FIGURE 23.2 Julia Kristeva, 1974, in front of Longmen Grottoes.

unitary processivity" that has no other meaning than to "maintain and enrich life (*yang sheng*)."[2]

Is the encounter between psychoanalysis and China doomed because of this considerable "gap" (nor am I forgetting the economic and ideological obstacles linked to the political regime)? I do not think so, for two reasons. Not only are Chinese men and women part of the globalized world and integrate its logic and practices for better or for worse since the bourgeois revolution of 1919 going through communism and finally by its adaptation to globalization today.[3] But mainly because psychoanalysis, while being the heir to Greek-Jewish-Christian onto-theology (that of "Moses," according to Pascal), is no less the result of its deconstruction in and by modern philosophy and the social sciences. In addition, it carried out—more than other disciplines—a reworking of this heritage, of its categories and its aims, even of their languages, because of the status of free association and interpretation. So many specific traits, according to me, of assets that make psychoanalysis able not only to shed light on human experiences heterodoxal to its classical heritage but to modulate itself and to continually reinvent itself in this search.

Freudian psychoanalysis is this revolution in European thought that we have not yet fully measured and that does not cancel out the specific contribution of the Greco-Judeo-Christian "I am"; but it does not absolutize it either. For it inscribes its discovery, based on the unity of the singular and on a controlled and controlling subjectivity, in the very heart of the Oedipus complex and the paternal function. And it weaves, with them and around them, a real panoply of psychic structures, their catastrophes, and creativities which through their ambiguities, ambivalences, and recompositions cross and reconfigure the dichotomies transmitted by onto-theology: body/soul, nature/culture, even feminine/masculine. So this Jewish atheist Freud, without really becoming Chinese with a Taoist body, gave us the means to bring up and question the numerous gaps vis-à-vis the "I am" that specified the varieties of human experiences.

Yes, it is urgent, as Pascal already had it, to "put papers on the table": to open the immense Chinese archive, probe its specificities in relation to European ways of thinking that are "universal" only when they are able to be modified and attuned to the exotic experience of emerging cultures.

But above all, we cannot forget the truly revolutionary contribution of psychoanalysis in Western culture. A contribution that neither Sinologists (from Marcel Granet[4] and Henri Maspero[5] to Kristofer Schipper)[6] nor philosophers (François Jullien)[7] take into consideration when they deal with the coming together of Europe and China, from the angle either of universalism or of relativism. Some have the tendency to assimilate, reduce, and integrate the Chinese difference into our ways of thinking; the others run the risk of granting a superiority to the Chinese world vis-à-vis the West that is supposedly stuck in its metaphysical categories, tired and obsolete.

Universalism caricaturized as if it were only a greedy colonialism ready to swallow up the other was succeeded by a new hierarchy in which the exotopic Chinese are called to the rescue to revitalize Western thinking, blocked and paralyzed without this amphetamine. Caught in the game of the repressor (the West) and the repressed (China), relativism's claim forgets that the very ones who practice it develop their reasoning in the stream of contemporary thought, at the crossroads of philosophy and its dismantlings and deconstructions, as well as the social sciences that came after them. It is indeed with the tools of those same ideas that the relativists locate and examine the differences in Chinese thought; while, on the contrary, Taoism, Confucianism, and Buddhism have neither the intention nor the means to interpret Greco-Judeo-Christian cultural heritage and less to suggest bridges among the cultural diversities of a new universalism.

I will first maintain that a true heterogeneity between our ways of living and thinking exists that is important to bring out in order to elucidate the irreducible singularity with which the Chinese woman and man approach experiences as fundamental to psychoanalysis as the "body" and the "soul," the "mother" and the "father," the "woman" and the "man," but also "language," "writing," or also "meaning" and "signification."

Then I will call to mind the fact that the transvaluation through psychoanalysis of these experiences and categories already gives us the possibility to address *Chinese differences* not as enigmatic oddities but as facets of psychosexuality certainly centered on the Oedipus complex, but also opening onto other configurations when speech is lived as an experience.

And my conclusion, however, is that a better understanding of male and female Chinese analysands enables us to better understand these "gaps" and to take them into account so as to avoid the temptation of normativism and reductionism that might also tempt psychoanalysis, and to expand that listening to human singularities that characterizes the ethics of psychoanalysis.

BODY, SOUL, PERSON: WHAT CHINESE "SELF"?

The Iliad had already distinguished the soul of warriors, *psuché*, connected to their head ("Like a phantom in a dream," "vaporous," "it flies far away") from their *thumos*, the body as seat of energy and courage. But it was Socrates in *The Phaedo* who separated the soul "isolated in itself" (64c–d) from the body, before Aristotle declared it as "cause" and "principle" of the body, and that its immortality was debated. And although the "psychic" no longer corresponds to that soul, Western thought from the "innermost being" with the Christian prayer of the soul traveling

FIGURE 23.3 Julia Kristeva 1974, in front of the imperial concubine Yang Guifei's pool in Xi'an, China.

toward God, and up to the "psychic apparatus" of psychoanalysis, conveys that archeology of the psyche-soma separation inherited from Greek ontology. The Freudian revision of this dichotomy by "Freudian dualism" that maintains "psychic representations" to better articulate their diversity with "drives," which are already psychosomatic from the beginning, cannot be stressed enough.[8] I have myself concentrated on the "heterogeneity," always already *psychic-and-physic*, of the Freudian constituents of the "psychic apparatus" that numerous authors (from Klein to Bion or André Green, and, in another way, Lacan) developed and enriched.

On the contrary, in China, shamanism deals with "vagabond souls" without unifying the notion. For the Taoist Zhuangzi, the soul was the interior of the physical form, always with a vital potential in mind: a principle of *animation* (rather than a "soul" entity) progressively separating itself from the physical being; the "refined," the "subtle" (*jing*) (think of an effect similar to that of "sublimation" in psychoanalysis?); the "quintessence that renews itself," integral part of a purification process and of progressive disengagement. "Nourishing quintessence" thus means sharpening one's capacities and keeping oneself alive.

It is thus clear that China never elaborated an apology of *Amour-Agapê* as a monologue or dialogue of the soul but conceived of love as an emotion or sexual cosmic regulation. Likewise, it follows that the transference toward the Other, the worship of Alterity, does not exist as an objective aim of a distinct plan. Transcendence would be only an opening of another dimension in the tangible and concrete. Thus Confucius distinguished the "physical *state*" from "what this physical state used," in other words, its "capacity" (*Dé*), and says that a dead body "has not lost its soul" but its "capacity." It follows that Chinese thought, which is "soul-less," does not function from the notion of subjectivity transferring itself to an alterity but rather from a notion of invisible "communicative efficiency" flowing from the human belonging to Tao. Heavenly capacity, internal to natural processivity.

Moreover, this "communicative capacity" does not only dissolve our soul, it dilutes the body as well (*wo xíng*, my body, for Zhuangzi, or more precisely "my actualized form"). This means that the notion of body is gradual and appears as a continuous modification.

Without "essence," and without individuation, there is no concept of "matter" either but of "materialization" by continuous concretion,

FIGURE 23.4 Julia Kristeva, 2009, in the Forbidden City, Beijing, China.

integrating death itself. It is clear that in this processive dimension of existence, tragic mourning has no place since death itself nourishes the life of the processual body.[9]

While one can appreciate the flexibility and adaptability of this mechanism, one can perceive its limits as well. Do not the restrictive morals of Confucian rituals and codes, their rigid, even tyrannical, prohibitions (such as the submission of the subject to the sovereign, son to father, wife to husband), remain a nominalist symbolism, exterior and intrinsically dictatorial, for the very reason of the absence of subjectivation, of the introjection of the One (the psychoanalyst would say) by an individuality? In other words, "dead skin," both despotic and without a real grasp on the life process?

A historical example serves as example of the entanglements in which Western thought found itself facing these procedural bodies and souls, but also the innovations they led some bold thinkers to. In the seventeenth century, when the Jesuit Longobardi[10] (*Treaty*, 1701) considered that the Chinese did not know "our God" because their celestial emperor was only one attribute of the matter that government or causality is endowed with, he did not overlook the fact that this kind of thinking could lead to atheism. Furthermore, he asked, can this kind of "causal matter" reveal the *truth*?

Leibnitz detected in this immanent causality, if not a Chinese-style humanism, a kind of "self" inseparable from its cosmic and political affiliations that would not be an "individual" but a point of impact of an actualized infinite combinatory of forces and logic systems.[11]

Might this experience or this Chinese thought be intrinsically hostile to the concept of an individuality open to freedom and truth, one that thrives in the complex history of Greek/Jewish/Christian crisscrossings and their Muslim transplant? There is no lack of similar fears and worries in Chinese history. Yet is it not this same "ontology of self inseparable from the logic of the living and the social," specifying the individual according to the Chinese experience, that is equally likely to harbor the "human rights" of an *other species*, in greater harmony with the laws of the cosmos and social conflicts? Provided there is the unfolding of the complexity of signifying desires and acts that constitute the innermost being of such a Chinese "self," its specificity compared to a European one, still already open to the signifying desires and acts of its natural and social environment. And by beginning to interpret the specific role of the woman and the mother, as well as the inseparable belonging of the meaning of language to both music and gesture.

MATRILINEAL FAMILY, *YIN* AND *YANG*, BISEXUALITY

During my first trip to China, in May 1974, with Philippe Sollers and Roland Barthes (we were the first delegation of intellectuals invited after China was admitted to the United Nations), our hosts proudly showed us "archeological proof" of "matriarchy" in ancient China. In the Xi'an region, excavations had uncovered the existence of necropolises with the Mother installed in the center. Around her, skeletons of other members of the family were exposed, undoubtedly a twofold funeral rite: first, separate graves for the two sexes (mothers buried with their children on one side, men on the other), and then laying out the family around the Great Mother.

In Chinese mythology, the goddess Nüwa created the first humans out of clay and gave them procreation powers. Goddess of marriage and fertility, she was the sister and wife of Fuxi, and they were two of the three legendary Augusts. Nüwa invented the *se*, a kind of zither, and she also repaired the leak in the heaven caused by the war between the gods of water and fire.

The Chinese ideogram *xing* (姓), which means "name" or "family name," is composed of a pictogram *nü* (女, "woman") to the left of the phonic complex *sheng* (生, "to grow," "to be born," "life." Unlike the patrilineal filiation and in the *father's name*, the term "name" in Chinese designates an origin of the *woman-mother*, literally "born of the woman." The Chinese family name was originally the name of the clan in the matriarchal epoch, a female name. And so the eight great names of Chinese high antiquity were all composed with the pictogram *nü*, woman.

Recent anthropological research has drawn attention to an ethnic minority—the Na—still present in modern China on the frontier of Yunnan and Sichuan Provinces, where people generally do not marry and where, because there is no marriage, there are no fathers, except societal. Relationships themselves are thus reduced to "individual" relationships between "individuals" (but we already know that the word is inappropriate;

maybe "the actives"?) linked together by women. The Na have no term in their language for "father" or "husband," as their society is composed of matrilines descending from a common ancestor and divided into groups of sisters and brothers living under the same roof and bringing up in common the children of the sisters as well as those of the previous generations (grandmothers, great uncles, great aunts, mothers, aunts, etc.). The men come to "visit" the women, one, two, or several sisters, and still today in Na villages a special room is reserved for the woman who will be visited by the "rain" or the "wind" of a visitor. Men occupy the place of "exchange object" among women and the maternal uncle brings up the children. Sexual exchanges are "substance" exchanges and not exchanges between "persons," so they do not create alliances.[12] Incest is nonetheless prohibited between consanguine members of the same house.

Now this maternal ascendancy as well as the vital role assigned to the sexual and notably male substance seems to underlie a rich variety of erotic techniques that order Taoist sexuality. Thus in *The Book of the Yellow Court* innumerable prohibitions were imposed on the man to withhold his semen, make possible his jouissance, and protect him from the Mother with vampirical desires. Henri Maspero reckoned that the "unfavorable days" and/or sexual prohibitions were so numerous that only a few were left for making love![13] To escape the lustful Mother, Taoism became macho and recommended to the man to have multiple partners a night, preferably very young so they would be ignorant of erotic secrets. Other texts describe orgiastic rites like the *union of breaths* practiced by the couple under a master's guidance, in a refined choreography of breathing and visualizations of the body's inner organs that mime the cosmic energies, with the man and woman alternatively assuming the active and passive roles. Remains of these hierogamic practices can be found in *Inner Alchemy*: coupling where the partners seek total abandon, the absence of thought and feeling (neither sight nor hearing), and to rebecome an embryo, to find the Mother's belonging to her embryo and vice versa—this "alchemy" being described as an immersion in original Taoism when the *yin* is naturally born in the *yang*, and the *yang* naturally in the *yin*. Echoing Laozi, the body of an "old infant" without a father is thus sought, but reverting to his own mother with this regressive jouissance being lived as a way to immortality.

Without a veritable incest prohibition, appealing to the fragmented body and bisexuality, denying death by the fantasy of a return to intrauterine life, these practices revive the unconscious trace of the matrilineal memory as well as the extreme fragility, even the censorship, of the paternal function and of individuating castration. Like the other side of biblical circumcision of the male sex, the woman's "bound foot" punishes the imperious jouissance of the *yin* and thereby implicitly recognizes feminine sexual power.

In contrast, Confucian ancestor worship with its rigid rituals had a mission to impose a varnish of feudal patriarchal morality to contain the eroticism of this cosmic Taoist body. It strove to rein in a jouissance that one would be mistaken in seeing it as "leaving our *jouissance* cold";[14] or moreover qualifying it as perverse, since it is so close to the innocent ecstasy of a polymorphic narcissism, specific to borderline cases, which clinical experience is beginning to show us and to discover in the Western mystical tradition, among others.

I mention these legendary excesses of Taoist eroticism because in a secret, preconscious, and unconscious way their logic structures the psychosexuality seen in the modern Chinese novel and cinema. The result is the certitude of having a psychosexual duality split dependence in relation to both the mother and the father and guilt-free bisexuality that is not strictly "psychic" since body and soul interlace in the "life-nourishing" procedure, more strongly than in other cultures, notably in the Christian West dominated by the patrilineal model. This internal cohabitation—the most significant trait of all, even though the *yin* and the *yang* combine in each of the two sexes on both sides of the sexual difference—does not erase the external biophysiological and social difference between man and woman. It is favorable, on the contrary, to the procreating couple, while granting female jouissance a central place and an inexhaustible "*yin* essence." And so this question for future research in psychoanalysis: what to think, then, of the Chinese mother, of Chinese maternal eroticism coming close to the woman lover's?

LANGUAGE, MUSIC, WRITING

The particularities of the Chinese language cannot escape the analyst's attentive listening. Without morphology, declination, or conjugation, without morphologically separating the noun from the adjective, without the verb "to be," thinking in polar terms (the word "thing" is said in terms of complementary oppositions: *dong xi*, literally east-west), the Chinese utterance gets its definitive meaning in the addressee's reception of the whole message, in its context, and in adding the memory of the dialogical link. In this sense, it is a veritable "transfer" that nevertheless is precise, so the fans of clear messages assure us. Wittgenstein said it: "Essence is expressed in grammar."[15] Like a swimmer in the processivity of verbal flux, the Chinese interlocutor is shaped from the start by this spatial grammar, like a hypervigilant and polymorphic interpreter.

I would like to underline another aspect of the Chinese idiom that enriches its fluidity even further: its *musicality*, which like other languages (Vietnamese, for example), conserves and develops the imprint of the *infans*'s prelinguistic capacities left by the trace of the early mother-child link. Contemporary semiology is aware of this temporality of the newborn who is not yet a speaking subject but who makes *sense* with his intonations-vocalizations-echolalia, with the "semiotic'" but who is not yet able to construct a *signification* with phonemes, morphemes, and a syntax, who has thus no "symbolic" performance, in my terminology.[16] All children, whatever the language, develop a semiotics; but only a tonal language conserves and deploys this *semiotic* capacity in integrating it in the *symbolic*, by making it signifying in linguistic communication. If I say "table" in French with an ascending or descending intonation, it still means "table"; but if I say "*ma*" in Chinese with a high, rising, falling, or light intonation, the word changes meaning: "mother," "horse," "to scold"—there are no fewer than seventeen different meanings, in addition to the pictorial writing. The tonal language alone bears these traces of early mother-child interdependence, engrammed on the verbal flux frequencies, and integrates, transfers, or "socializes" them in adult usage.

Writing itself, pictorial in origin, then more and more stylized, abstract, and ideogrammatic, preserves its evocative visual and gestural character. In addition to the memory of meaning, a memory of movement is required to write Chinese. That is added to phonetics to give different meanings to the same syllable with the same tone. As the graphic elements come from psychic layers even more archaic than that of the syntactic-logical meaning, Chinese writing could be considered as an unconscious sensorial depository from which the thinking subject in

Chinese will never be definitively cut off, a laboratory par excellence of its evolutions, innovations, and resurrections.

CHINESE AMONG US

What then do these specificities of Chinese culture teach us about its possible—or its impossible—encounter with psychoanalysis?

It is imperative to train Chinese analysts, for that they must take on the study of the various psychoanalytical currents but also of their own cultural tradition, neglected or deformed by totalitarianism, but that many intellectuals are today beginning to reappropriate and reevaluate.

If we take Chinese women and men into analysis speaking French, English, etc., on our couches, the analyst must familiarize him/herself with the specificity of Chinese thought—a fascinating and difficult task, and a real civilizational challenge, particularly for psychoanalysis. The development of modern research in social sciences and psychoanalysis itself should not be underestimated. I mentioned my analysis of tonal languages in referring my semioticians' observations to the psychosexuality of the early mother-child link. I could also mention recent work on maternal eroticism.[17]

Before the separation of *subject* and *object* of desire, the analyst identifies the maternal body status as "Thing" (*Das Ding*, according to Lacan, adapting Heidegger) or, in other words, not yet "object of desire" but a gripping pole and/or a real possession that reappears in the melancholic's or depressive's "Thing" for which he is specifically incapable of the mourning that precedes the putting into place of an "object" separated from the "subject." Another analysis is this other economy of psychosexuality prior to the crystallization of the dual subject/object, but where attraction combined with rejection reduces the mother and the child to "abjects," in an inseparable *abjection*.[18] And another in which there is vital and vitalizing cathexis, beyond the possible ascendancy over or even the mother's destructivity of the newborn who becomes the first other, what I called a *reliance*:[19] this is to be distinguished from religion that connects to the paternal function as an ideal and/or symbolic pole of cathexis. These are so many links that precede and exceed the very appearance of the

Oedipus complex and its corollary, castration. This enables us to think the differences in Chinese subjectivity as it appears in modern Sinology.

In conclusion, to those relativists, fascinated by the exotopia of Chinese men and women, who doubt our Western capacity to listen to and get to know them, I will give three examples that argue for the possibility of such an encounter.

The first case is that of a Chinese man of letters who was my professor and who extolled the advantages of this Chinese universe, made of adaptive vitality and permanent processivity, defying our static binary categories. At the same time he admitted: "When depression strikes us, I have no recourse. I need an object to invest, someone I can believe in." The only path he could take was either salvation through religion or psychoanalysis to learn transference: this cathexis of the other, paternal and maternal at first, thanks to which separation but also loss become tolerable.

The next example I was confronted with came after giving a lecture at Beijing University on "female genius," where I acknowledged the emancipation of Chinese women (unique in emerging nations and based on this tradition that I just broadly outlined here today). While it is true that there are no "human rights" in China today, it is nevertheless relatively possible to claim "women's rights," and we awarded the Prix Simone de Beauvoir in 2010 to a jurist and a video maker, both Chinese. At the end of the lecture a very anxious male student asked me this question: "Madame, who will save us from women? We men are being scorned; we only have the choice between conjugal violence and homosexuality to protect us." I was told that bisexuality does not automatically bring about singular jouissance, and that the Taoist "interior alchemy" with its polymorphic pleasures could not replace the working-through of violence and the access to alterity that the analytic experience works toward.

And finally, there is no lack of "Chinese" differences in European culture, especially in literature. I am thinking of Colette, who, in *The Pure and the Impure*, glorifies a primary female homosexuality, which became a paradisiacal life style (with her "ladies of Llangollen"), but mother-daughter incest as well in *Green Wheat*, always with infantile innocence as opposed to the guilt-ridden homosexual in Proust and to his "race of the damned." Would Colette be like the Taoist sage who "nourished himself only from his mother"? Perhaps Marguerite Yourcenar thought so, when she said she was "as complicated as an old China."[20] I recommend reading Philippe Sollers's novels, a mix of the infantile and incestual, and Jean-Michel Lou's *Corps d'enfance, corps chinois. Sollers et la Chine.*[21]

So if the Chinese have a lot to teach us about polymorphic narcissism and borderline cases inasmuch as they are endogenous, and about sublimation as well, psychoanalysis in turn, provided it is able to hear them, could bring much to those who call on it. This is in order to have access to the Other being, which is not really salvation but opens the way to freedom and its risks. In other words, to another jouissance.

So, Freud or China? Let us wager that there will be no domination of one over the other but a "multiverse" of crossovers. But first of all, there is "putting papers on the table"—and especially a lot of listening, risking transferences, and analyzing.

24

DIVERSITY IS MY MOTTO

S o wrote Jean de la Fontaine in "Eel Pâté."[1] Is there a more French genius than that of a fabulist? And yet with all due respect to the advocates of the famous "French cultural diversity," there are many people who suspect our country of cherishing only its own diversity—cultivating the palette of its wines, cheeses, perfumes, and other decadent refinements—but barely opening its heart and republican institutions to the world's diversity.

As a European citizen of Bulgarian origin with French nationality and American by adoption, I am not unaware of this scathing criticism. Nevertheless, after some decades spent in the Hexagon, I would like to emphasize three aspects of my experience that seem to me to illustrate the French contribution to European specificity.

First, Europe is now a political entity that speaks as many languages as, if not more than, it has countries. This multilingualism is the basis of the cultural diversity to be preserved and respected—in order to preserve and respect national characters—but it is also important to exchange, mix, and cross. In the twelfth century Saint Bernard[2] made love the subject of European man by mixing the Song of Songs, his experience as a crusader, and his self-analyzed knowledge of the body inseparable from a tormented mind that was nevertheless able to find peace in beatitude. The Renaissance reconciled us with the Greek miracle and Roman pomp. In the seventeenth century Descartes introduced an *ego cogito* to budding science and growing economic development. The eighteenth century, along with its charms of libertinism and the misery of the destitute, brought this concern for singularities that would crystallize in "the rights of man." After the horror of the Holocaust, the bourgeois born in the nineteenth century and the rebel of the twentieth century have had to contend with another era. Today European linguistic diversity is creating kaleidoscopic individuals able to defy both *globish* English bilingualism brought about by globalization as well as the good old French-speaking world that has trouble waking up from its Versailles dream world to become the carrier wave of tradition and innovation in the melting pot. A new species is surfacing: the polyphonic subject, a polyglot citizen of a plurinational Europe.

I would like to begin by expressing some necessarily subjective comments on this ongoing modulation that singularizes, to the limit, the intrinsically plural psychic universe of future Europeans. This is the polyphony that young Europeans are progressively trying their hands at and that I was lucky enough to glimpse almost fifty years ago when General de Gaulle granted me a scholarship to study in Paris: this skeptical European yet confirmed visionary was already speaking to a Europe from the "Atlantic to the Urals." Then I will broach diversity informed by the chimera of the "French social model"—to maintain and perfect—and argue that it belongs to a European model of liberty, so necessary today faced with the automatization of the species in the grip of technology. Last, surprised that we put so little effort into trying to explain what French secularization means outside our borders, I want to express my worry that this other "French exception" is taken seriously throughout the world by all those who are more and more aware that flirting with identity politics is not far from the "clash of religions."

THE OTHER LANGUAGE OR THE CONDITION OF BEING ALIVE

What separates the stranger from one who is not one is that he/she speaks another language. The European who goes from one country to another speaks the language of his/her country with the language or even languages of the other countries and thus cannot, from then on, escape this condition of stranger that adds to his originary identity while becoming a more or less permanent double of his existence.

An extraordinary destiny—the stranger hovering between tragedy and chosenness. I recognize in my own parlance the inextricable mixture of the logical clarity of French and the orthodox accent of my Bulgarian heritage. If suffering there is in the junction of these two languages, it is linked to the *symbolic* matricide implicit in the abandonment of one's native language, an always renewed suffering that my imagination, nourished by the return of my maternal memory, gives rise to in French.

This dialogue with Bulgaria, inscribed in the "other language" experience, makes France resonate with suffering for me. The chosen language, language of reason, can only parallel one's native language, language of passions. Considered by the Americans as an intellectual and a French writer, I do not always recognize myself in this French discourse that turns its back on evil and treasures the tradition of indifference, when it is not just nationalism. This happens especially when I return from a trip.

Yet I feel protected in the French landscape; I like its logical wholeness. I even sometimes think I belong to it. In spite of their cultural successes and international exploits, French musketeers, Crusaders, explorers, and colonizers returned home opting for a serene pleasure. And while leaving behind them their conquering intentions, they continue to believe they are a great power.

Does our pride in disseminating Francophony that runs up against the expansion of English and *globish*, among others, take these delights and pains into account? To transmit the taste for the French language, its literary tradition, and its ongoing mutations, it is perhaps necessary to begin by elucidating and making French life sharable: its debates, ideas, and arts. And by expressing them in the languages of the others—Europe and the world also invite us on this trip where French people, by birth and by adoption, have everything to gain—we could convince and seduce before spicing up the taste for Francophony and sharing (let's dream a bit) its attractions and glories.

THE PRIDE OF THE UNFORTUNATE AND
THE RIGHT TO PLEASURE (*JOUIR*)

Without belaboring this cohabitation with the "other language," I would like to address the cultural and political context where it occurs. The social and political situation attests to the fact that freedom in our country understood as revolt has a considerable scope, perhaps unique in the world.

French national unity, a historical realization, is nevertheless worshipped like a cult or a myth. This national unity anchored in the language is perhaps a weightier heritage than elsewhere and harks back to the monarchy and republican institutions and condenses the art of living and French taste—fruit of a harmonious sharing of customs.

Unlike the Anglo-Saxon world based on the family, the French world proudly promotes what Montesquieu called in *The Spirit of Laws* a "nation's way of thinking."[3] Recent history has clearly shown how this "nation's way of thinking" can degenerate into rawboned nationalism and xenophobia. Yet to neglect it would be, to say the least, irresponsible.

Moreover, our national cohesion is not without fragmentation: networks, subsets, and clans that are by nature insidious and always in rivalry lead to an amusing diversity as well as a dangerous dissonance. But this balance is just as unstable in France as elsewhere. While the French like to exhibit their malaise, they are also able to laugh at its theatricalization.

When national pride morphs into Poujadist arrogance, it paralyzes all initiative and takes refuge in the past looking for a feeling of superiority, that of belonging to a prestigious civilization that one refuses to swap for the attractions of globalization. On the other hand, when impossible work schedules, unemployment, and absence of social protection bring about human beings' automatization, our sense of dignity—removing the stigma of poverty and valorizing the quality of life—becomes an incomparable comfort for those who feel oppressed. But right away the supposedly desired dialogue between "the humiliated and the offended" and the "officials" gets transformed into resistance. And the "communist hypothesis" that France might be able to reconcile the rhythm of globalization with people's demands, thus promoting a competitive but also free European model, endures. What would happen if the demands to better share national and world wealth were taken seriously? The "French exception" wavers between an indebted utopia and justice for all.

Countries are like people: they suffer from the same illnesses of our times, and even depression. If recent statistics are to be believed, France has one of the highest rates of suicide in the world: fourth in Europe behind Finland, Denmark, and Austria. As for individual depression, narcissistic wounds, deficiencies in maternal relations, and absences of paternal ideals add to neuronal fragilities that cause the subject to under-estimate the connections of language and life. To these very complex causes are added the expression of greater and greater social distress, namely, the loss of work, unemployment of varying durations, professional humiliations, poverty, and the paucity of ideals and of possibilities.

No longer able to identify with the glorious and Gaullist great power image, weak and almost inaudible in European negotiations or in com-petition with North America, having lost its belief in the ideals and facile perspectives of demagogic ideologies, and feeling more or less threatened by migratory influxes, France is reacting like a depressed patient. The depressed withdraws, closes himself off, becomes silent, incapable of articulating his unhappiness. For many French people, the fear of the other and the fear of Europe take the place of political and community mobilization. National arrogance goes along with self-depreciation, and that leads to the undervaluing of self and of others. In fact, it is the intran-sigent superego, despotic ideals, and implacable perfectionism that drive the person—or the State—to depression.[4]

Just as the depressed patient has first to recover confidence in herself to then delve into a real analysis of her ill-being, the depressed nation also has to recover a more satisfying image of itself and then to undertake a European integration and to better welcome immigrants. The nation's cultural heritage is not sufficiently valorized, especially by intellectuals who prefer to promote doubt and push Cartesianism to self-hatred. It is possible that an excess of universalism, when it is not self-hatred, made us be "imperceptibly bad-mannered,"[5] exacerbating our national depression. The time has come to treat it; once suicide is no longer an option, the depressed has only a manic reaction: in place of depreciation or inaction, it is better to designate some enemy, usually imaginary, to declare wars obviously holy ones (see the National Front and fundamentalisms).

The French embody both the dissatisfaction of the unfortunate (those of Robespierre and of Hugo) and the presumptuousness of a nation that seeks pleasure (from Rabelais to Colette). Is it a handicap? It could be good fortune, within European space, so as not to die while celebrating the end of history by being bombarded with marketing. New forms of revolt nevertheless demand more than ever the involvement of the elites and so-called specialized groups that become the new political players (professions, age-groups, etc.).[6] Would it be impossible to reconcile the "people," the "elite," and "public opinion groups"? Difficult, yes, but impossible? To speak of just the "elite," it is not the people who underestimate them but the "elite" themselves who close themselves off in their technical expertise and tear each other up in internecine battles. But the elites exist, and there is no dearth of ambitious French achievements in laboratories, universities, and artistic creation.

So are we regressing compared to the 1960s as is often claimed in the Hexagon and on the other side of the Atlantic? What is apparently happening is less spectacular—the spectacle is saturated with shows; serious work comes across badly or is rarely seen on television. But it is chugging along, perhaps even more seriously than before or elsewhere.

Europe is waiting for France: it is perhaps up to a foreigner, a French woman by adoption, to emphasize this because I am persuaded that France is one of the privileged countries that can uphold a model of freedom in its European birthplace and one that the world needs.

WHAT FREEDOM: ADAPTATION OR CHALLENGE?

The difference between the European and North American cultures has become clearer since the fall of the Berlin Wall in 1989. These two cultural models are based on *two conceptions of liberty*, worked out by Western democracies, as a whole and without exceptions, two conceptions of freedom based on fundamentally complementary Greek, Jewish, and Christian traditions that often find themselves in opposition. Upon examination we will be better able to understand what separates Europe and North America; it cannot be reduced to current economic and political interests.

In *Critique of Pure Reason*, 1781, and *Critique of Practical Reason*, 1788, Kant came out with a previously unknown definition of freedom: freedom is not negatively an "absence of constraint" but is positively the possibility of a self-beginning, *Selbstanfang*. Identifying freedom with self-beginning, Kant advocates an enterprising subjectivity, a self-initiative, if I translate his "cosmological" thinking onto a personal level. This freedom of Reason, be it pure or practical, is, however, subordinate to a Cause, be it divine or moral.[7]

But in a world in which technology has become the supreme power, this freedom becomes identified with the ability to submit oneself to a "cause," always exterior to self, from now on less and less a moral cause and more and more an economic one, or the two together in the best of cases. In his analysis of the connections between capitalism and Protestantism, Max Weber shows freedom as the possibility of adapting to the logic of causes and effects,[8] what Hannah Arendt called the "calculation of consequences," the logic of production, science, and economy. To be free would be to be free to adapt to the production and profit market.

This logic of instrumentalization, one of globalization and the market economy, imposes a schema of freedom beholden to the supreme cause (God) and the technical cause (the dollar). This is a form of freedom adapted to the cause-effect chain and also in agreement with scientific thinking, that is, thinking-calculation. This decisive moment in humanity's development brought about access to technologies, the free market, and automation. American culture seems to be the best suited to this form of freedom.

The other model of freedom is to be found in Greek philosophy, from pre-Socratic thought to the Platonic dialogues. This fundamental liberty, as Heidegger made clear in his discussion of Kantian philosophy,[9] is in the Being of Language that reveals itself to itself and to the other and in this sense liberates itself and is a prerequisite to the concatenation of Aristotelian "categories"—which are already in themselves premises of scientific reason—and not subject to a cause. Before freedom is submitted to the cause-effect chain, it manifests itself in the Being of Language, through the Presence of Self to Other. This freedom, inscribed in the essence of philosophy in its infinite questioning, is situated as a counterpoint (and counterweight) of the laissez-faire free market.

This freedom at work in *poetry* animates the experience of the *liber-tine* who confronts his transgressive desire with the social chain of causes and effects; the *analytic experience*, founded on transference and coun-tertransference; the *revolutionary act* that places singularity at the sum-mit of the hierarchy of conventions by recognizing human and citizens' rights and abiding by the French Revolution's motto, Liberty, Equality, Fraternity, which radicalizes the English habeas corpus declarations. Revisiting these eighteenth-century experiences and discourses enables us not to confuse the heritage of the Enlightenment with an abstract universalism.

When the European Union tries to construct itself by conforming to the "American model," France painfully tries to counter it with a "model of society" that would not be or would not only be that of the "free mar-ket." This constant reminder of our cultural difference not only is the result of being rooted in an older or more experienced tradition but has to do with another conception of freedom that puts the emphasis on the singular being against economic and scientific necessity. This is the model of freedom put forward by the French government, be it the left or the social Gaullist right, when it emphasizes "solidarity" challenged by the "free market" and virtual finance.

Not forgetting the constraints of the cause-and-effect chain and thus ignoring economic reality, one has to recognize the advantages of this other model of freedom that constitutes more an aspiration than a fixed project. The European model is animated by the concern for human life in its most fragile specificity (the poor, the disabled, the old) as well as in respect for sexual and ethnic differences in their intimacy.

Is it pure utopia to envisage this conception of singular freedom for all of humanity? Thought-calculation and consumption are abetted today by the revival of sectarian religious offshoots where the sacred, rather than being a "permanent challenge" in line with human dignity and religious vows (in Saint Augustine, for example), is subjected to the same logic of causes and effects that is carried to the extreme when disguised as power in the service of a sect or fundamentalist group.

In this context, there is no abstract and utopic European homogene-ity. It has been said that there is a chasm between the "old" and the "new" countries of Europe. "Old Europe," and France in particular, has to take seriously the economic problems of "New Europe" that make these countries dependent on the United States or the International Monetary Fund. But it is also essential to recognize and respect the cultural and particularly religious differences that separate the various countries so as to avoid the "clash of civilizations" in *Pax europeana* itself.

Although this second model of freedom is of Greco-French origin, it can be spotted in both the Protestant as well as the Catholic worlds. Moreover, it goes along with the Judaic notion of chosenness, enabling people from this tradition to implement the crossover between these two versions of freedom, "free-market" and "solidarity," "technical" and "poetic," "causal" and "revelatory."

Can globalization adapt to the multiple conceptions of the human being brought by other civilizations? For this humanity that can only be defined in terms of *hospitality*, the only guarantee is the respect of diversity; technical and robotic uniformization is the easiest betrayal of it. But hospitality is neither the juxtaposition nor the hierarchization of differences. I am speaking of hospitality in diversity, which requires that other conceptions of freedom must be taken into consideration in order to complexify each way of being. So this humanity whose meaning escapes us makes sense to us only when we speak of "crime against humanity," this humanity that I am trying to define, would in fact be a *process of complexification*.

In this way, Europe could form one of the determinant stages leading to the experience of our multiple freedom. It would be in the interest of North America, which seems to be leading the globalized world game, even while understanding the disastrous consequences of this uniformization.

HAS SECULARIZATION PERISHED IN THE RIOTS OF THE POOR SUBURBS?

Among the many causes that enflamed the poor suburbs, the denial by French society and the international community of what I call a *sickness of ideality*, specific to the adolescent,[10] must be included.

It is well known that the child, in his perverse polymorphism, constructs himself as a "theorist" who "wants to know" where children come from. On the other hand, the adolescent could be described as a "believer" inasmuch as he is pushed toward an insatiable search for ideal models (partner, job, etc.) allowing him to separate himself from his parents and to become an ideal being himself.

While the dream of an ideal couple or life belongs to every age-group, it does nevertheless remain an adolescent invention. From courtly love to Dostoyevsky and Gombrowiz, the novel as genre has constructed itself on adolescent figures: passionate for the absolute and easily devastated, depressed or perverse, naturally sarcastic, always believing and thus indefatigable rebels, and potentially nihilistic. As a prereligious and prepolitical form of believing, the *need to believe* erected as *a shared ideal* contributes to psychic life construction. An absolute necessity remains that as such can easily be inverted; idealism becomes nihilism in differing forms: disappointment, boredom, depression, destructive rage, vandalism, etc.

If the initiation rites of so-called primitive civilizations were examined, one would note that they had a dual role: they consolidated symbolic authority (divine or political), and at the same time they authorized taking action, today considered as perverse. In mortification rituals and excessive fasting in medieval Christianity, adolescents' anorexic behavior and sadomasochistic tendencies were considered both banal and heroic.

As for modern society, along with the dissolution of the family and the weakening of authority, it has nothing to offer but its inability to understand the structuring necessity of the need to believe, of the quest of ideality. The result is an endemic impotence in dealing with the adolescent crisis that, in addition, concerns immigrant adolescents who are victims of social and ethnic discrimination. While severe sanctions for barbaric behavior are obviously indispensable and urgent, its significance depends on our ability to help these torn psychisms to rebuild themselves, beginning by really understanding that behind the vandalism is the too-long-neglected need to believe.

In this context, I argue that France is more "advanced" than "behind" other countries in the crisis of adolescents from an immigrant background. Why?

Perceived as more serious for the person and the social group, the malaise is analyzed here at a more radical level: at the intersection of social distress *and* psychosexual lack of being (*désêtre*). It becomes clear, then, that the adolescent violence destroying our poor suburbs is not *beneath* but *beyond* the "clash of religions." What is exploding is not a religious conflict, in spite of pyromaniacs' religious manipulations and arsonists' sectarianism; nor is it an a posteriori demand against the "wearing of religious signs," because neither spiritual authorities nor parents approve of violent acts. It is also not interethnic and interreligious rivalries, as has occurred in other countries. In fact, these acts confirm the failure of the integration these young people aspire to; they burn what objectifies their desires: cars, supermarkets, warehouses, buses (the "success" and "wealth" highlighted by their friends and parents); schools, crèches, police stations, all the way up to their "foreign" fellow creatures from "intruders" to the "evil eye," or who seem to be "making it" (symbols of social authority and of a fantastical power they would like to share in).

No speech, no program, no real claim can explain these acts of violence. Nothing but an unnamable suffering, strictly speaking, *senseless*, without sense, that clumps together this need for ideals, recognition, and respect: the suffering of parental abandon and social impotence that underlie discrimination.

These explosions of destructivity, pure death wish, do not seek a protection or a religious justification that would provide a way out for the need for ideality. Is the fault due to French secularity that is supposed to have abolished these ramparts, these religious norms? I do not share these insinuations. The criminality of "underprivileged teens" reveals a more extreme version of nihilism: having to do with the prereligious[11] need to believe constitutive of the psychic life with and for others. The resulting sickness of ideality provokes or exacerbates identarian catastrophes and pathologies of what is called *unbinding*[12] that abolish the distinction between *good* and *evil*, *self* and *other*, and touch the limits of the speaking being able to have "values." Faced with these borderline cases where politicians must exercise pragmatism and generosity, the parent, teacher, and intellectual have to come up with supports and ideals suitable to modern times and the plurality of cultures.

All forms of adolescent nihilism immediately show the present inefficacy of religious treatment and its inability to respond to the paradisiac aspirations of the paradoxical and necessarily nihilistic believer—the young person who is discriminated against in his inexorable globalized migration.

When religious armor no longer can retain this *crisis of belief*, a historical challenge is addressed to republican humanism: is it capable of mobilizing all the police, economic, educational, and psychological means to deal with this troubling malady of ideality?[13]

The French crisis of diversity, interpreted here in its most painful symptoms, reveals the deep existential distress that concerns the whole of European and worldwide diversity. But it is first in France that this secular philosophy of tormented passions and ideals demands to be better known, explained, and understood. Our experience can then complete the diversity of the means modern democracies can muster to mobilize for the fight against new barbarisms, always secretly based on what we have forgotten or lost or on the challenges to our identity.

25

THE FRENCH CULTURAL MESSAGE

IS THERE A FRENCH CULTURAL MESSAGE?

The question arises by default when we realize that culture, far from being absent from Brussels politics (subsidies for the cinema or translation, heritage labeling, "European cultural capitals," Europeana Digital Library, etc.), does not provide much inspiration for the European project. The Treaty of Rome does not even mention the word "culture," and the awareness of a European cultural unity is being defined only gradually as the cultural policies of the Union are developing. Too heavy-handed in its aspiration to universality, guilt-ridden under the weight of inquisitions, persecutions, colonialism, the Holocaust, and the Gulag? We lack the intellectual and political audacity that would affirm the specificity of European culture, of its limits and its crimes, but also of its progress and its future. This is where the sense of a "French cultural message" takes on an added depth and urgency: can the voice of France help promote a new European cultural consciousness while preserving its own national singularity?

The UNESCO Convention on Diversity of Cultural Expressions (2005) sketches a vision of multicultural civilization by proposing to preserve and promote the cultural singularities of all the peoples in the world as an antidote to this new banality of evil, which is the automatization of minds bent by the *globish* of globalization. But who is aware of this initiative that works not in favor of the diversity of skin color and of communities but rather with and through them, for the diversity of cultural expressions? Certainly not French public opinion. France itself, which energetically promoted it with Canada, has trouble applying it. And yet it is a French cultural message that serves as the basis for this vision perceived and adopted by the signatories of the convention.

Could we contribute to the renewal of international culture that the constructive criticism of globalization is asking for? The French conception, rooted in the Enlightenment and driven by republican goals, respects diversities while affirming that they are translatable, interpretable, and sharable; it runs counter to the universalism that trivializes cultural traditions and modern expressions, counter to identarian communities that juxtapose social and cultural entities. This third way that France is actively championing on the international scene remains poorly understood by its very promoters—the French—as well by their annoyed partners. It deserves to be spelled out. Leaving aside all nationalistic patriotism, the time has come to liberate national identity and assert the specific contributions of our country in various areas of social life: cultural development, its role in the history of the French, and its international value that other peoples can adopt and adapt for themselves.

DESIRE FOR FRANCE AND FOR FRENCH

While our investigation has brought out the deep malaise that touches all the sectors of foreign cultural life, the cultural message of France and the intercultural vocation of Francophony remain respected, desired, and expected realities. You think that the French language is declining in the world, and you are not entirely wrong. But do you know that, unlike English, which is regressing in certain regions of the United States in favor of Spanish, French has never been so widely spoken, and the number of its speakers is increasing for demographic reasons both in France and in Africa? Some 115 million people use French every day, or 7.7 percent more than in 1990, and 61 million use it "partially." According to some demographic projections, the population speaking the language of Voltaire could increase fourfold in fifty years, thus attaining more than 8 percent of the world population.

You are persuaded that the International Organization of Francophony (OIF) is a colonial legacy, and Francophony is a circle of local, not really respectable, potentates. Do you know that the OIF has fifty-six state and government members and fourteen observers divided into three categories: those whose inhabitants use French as their native language; those for whom French is the official or second language (mainly sub-Saharan Africa and the Maghreb); and countries that have "chosen Francophony" for whom French is a foreign language but who identify with the respect of diversity embodied in France's cultural and/or political message (since 1995, Eastern European countries but also countries in Asia and the Pacific)?

Did you know that Radio France Internationale (RFI), which you hear only in the Parisian area and which is going through an alarming crisis, records its highest audience ratings in . . . China? That with French aid the Polytechnic Tongji University in Shanghai has created an "Academy of European and Chinese Cultures and Religions" so that graduate engineers of this prestigious institution "do not become suicide bombers when they encounter a staff or social conflict," explains the director of Tongji? That the Alliance Française in New York welcomes new demographics, delighted to discover programs where the charms of Vaux-le-Vicomte neighbor the surprises of our neighborhoods' urban cultures? And that in Florida the only place Americans can see Spanish, Italian, Mexican, and German films is the French Cultural Center? Because the "cultural exception" à la française tries to balance old and new, and that is applied to cultural expressions of all nations whose diversity it respects. In the best of cases.

I can hear the objections already: can one speak of "message" without bordering on arrogance that the misunderstanding about the "French exception" did not fail to worsen (when it was precisely about "excluding" cultural expressions from consumer products)? Contaminated by the ongoing homogenization and trivialization, a harmful "declinology" is at work, pushing "politically correct" thinking to challenge the creativity of nations within multiculturalism. Let us not give in to this defeatism: let us take on the innovative potentials of heritage, notably linguistic, in and by which cultural, regional, and national diversities are constituted, as well as the republic's respect and promotion of individual and collective liberties.

IDENTITY AT STAKE . . .

Of the multiple facets of the French cultural message, I will take up two traits that underlie and could consolidate the consciousness of a European cultural unity: the challenge of identity and multilingualism; and two courses of action that enrich but also handicap France's cultural politics: the role of the State and the importance of networks.

Running counter to current politics where identarian certitudes always and still pave the way for new and maybe nuclear wars, Europe—and France within it—is the space of an identity (national, ethnic, racial, religious, sexual) that a growing number of people experience less and less as an *absolute* and more and more as an *anxiety* or a *question*, which does not preclude them from being proud of it and claiming it as their own. Because the "I'm French, a woman, a teacher, Jewish, Catholic, Muslim, mother, ecologist, etc." is a refuge that comforts me. I prefer "to be part of it" when I do not know how "to be" simply, when I do not know who I am and even if I am: belonging is a transient antidepressant but no longer an absolute value. Subject to question, national identity is lived more and more here in France and in Europe as a living organism, evolving, constructible-deconstructible, an indefinitely surpassable identity, one that resists identarian and community tensions and ethnic and religious clashes in this beginning of the third millennium. A distinctive trait of the cultural message of France in Europe and of Europe in the world: it is a defused area of peace, fragile, never safe from fundamentalisms of all kinds but the only livable and enviable one, because its culture questions identity certitudes by trying, for better or for worse, to share them.

Where does this come from?

I hear the Jewish God's words: *Eyeh hasher eyeh* (Exodus 3:14), "I am who I am" (or "I am what I is," or "I am who I will be," taken up by Jesus according to John 8:24: "You will die in your sins; for unless you believe that I Am who I claim to be, you will die in your sins"). It means that "I" does not define me, "I" am an unrepresentable and eternal return on my very being.

I also find it in the journey as defined by Saint Augustine, for whom there is only one country, one precisely of journey—*In via, in patria*:[1] a journey indistinctly spiritual, psychic, geographic, historical, and political.

It guides Montaigne's pen in his *Essays* devoted to the identarian polyphony of the Self: "We are all patchwork, and so shapeless and diverse in composition that each bit, each moment plays its own game."[2]

The mixture of the Greek miracle with the three monotheisms—Christianity with its Jewish substratum and its Muslim graft—has now led to secularization, this phenomenon unique in the world: nowhere else has the "thread of tradition" been severed as in France and, thanks to France, in Europe. This has opened the way to an extraordinary liberty, unknown anywhere else. But one laden with risks and, just as unheard of, that gave birth to Nazi and Stalinist totalitarianisms.

Yet France and Europe are neither a beautiful Harlequin's cloak nor a hideous grinder of victimized strangers. No, a coherence has crystallized out of its diversities which, for once in the world, asserts an identity while opening it to its own critical examination and to the infinite potentialities of others. After having fallen prey to identarian dogmas to the point of crimes, and perhaps also because it fell prey and then analyzed it better than many others, a French-and-European "we" is in the process of emerging today, one that brings to light a conception and practice of identity as a questioning anxiety. And it is not because voters lacking purchasing power and threatened with unemployment shun the European elections, sabotaged by the political class itself, that this mutation of civilization is not making progress: slowly, with difficulty, but definitively.

. . . AND MULTILINGUALISM

Alongside this identity questioning that asserts itself against the tide of always threatening identarian clashes, Europe is a political entity that speaks as many languages as, if not more than, the countries that make it up. This multilingualism is the core of the cultural diversity to be respected—with national characters—and to exchange, intermix, and cross. The least one can say is that France is late in joining the movement. Why?

European linguistic diversity could generate in the long run a plural psychic space, because it is trilingual, quadrilingual, multilingual, and able to challenge the *global English* bilingualism imposed by globalization.

On the other hand, the French show notorious difficulty in acquiring fluency in foreign languages. This stems less from an alleged and imaginary "inaptitude," often advanced to explain this failure, than from a persistent deficiency in teaching in this area, as well as an absence of a proactive policy able to break the still tenacious debilitating remainder of a "delusion of grandeur." Plurilingualism is no longer a utopia: would it not be a concrete and nuanced remedy for the latest versions of trivialization and totalitarianism? Indeed, the stranger is different from one who is not one insofar as she speaks another language: this is now the case for any European passing from one country to another, speaking his or her country's language along with that/those of others. We can no longer escape the condition of stranger that adds to our original identity and becomes the double of our existence. The French worship their mother tongue, more passionately than other peoples worship theirs, and it keeps them from adopting a foreign idiom with which they can create a place of life and thought equal to French. Yes, this attachment to native speech has many connections to the current strong tendencies for diversity that are shaking up the uniformism of globalization, for better or for worse.

REINVENTING FRANCOPHONY

Indeed, a hallmark of French culture lies in the close links that the country's history has forged between various cultural expressions and the French language itself. The *French Academy Dictionary* and the enthusiasm for literary prizes are striking examples of this attachment that makes our literary culture a privileged place of thought, fields in general having to do with philosophy or theology. From the Renaissance and the Enlightenment until today, the conversation on language and the profusion of literary experimentation have become the laboratory of this "French exception" called secularism. This alloy, which makes language and literature almost sacred in France, and at the same time calls for the universal respect of others, is unique in the world. The desire for the French language persists through globalization perceived as a way of being in the world (subjective experience, taste, social and political model, etc.).

And yet the very term *Francophony* has become a trap. Younger generations with immigrant backgrounds as well as those of French origin mistrust it; writers challenge the discriminatory risks (what difference is there between "French" literature and "Francophone" literature?); political personalities want figures. Concepts and institutions of Francophony must be reinvented for it to become an important factor of social cohesion within the country and an intercultural message vehicle for the world. The first step would be to associate the defense and promotion of French culture as a whole in a spirit of diversity, cooperation, and solidarity.

A UNIQUE AND PRESTIGIOUS NETWORK

France's foreign cultural policy has a tremendous cultural network, unique in the world in its diversity, scope, and functioning. In addition to its Service for Cooperation and Cultural Action (SCAC), headed up by a cultural adviser reporting to the ambassador, this network includes 151 institutes and cultural centers reporting directly to embassies; 449 accredited French schools and lycées hosting more than 253,000 students, of whom only 95,000 are French; the Alliance Française, which today number 1,071 associations now grouped in a foundation and established in 131 countries. Each year they train over 450,000 students and accommodate 6 million participants for French-language events. Their attendance increases by about 4 percent a year; 85 percent of the alliances are independent nonprofits, run by volunteers at their own expense in their respective countries.

Thus constituted, the French cultural network—in its conception, in the management of its organization and players, and in its activities—suffers from an often very traditional approach concerning the world's sociocultural reality. There are also problems linked to the many places and participants involved as well as to the fact that one cannot be sure how long an action can go on and what its means are, while the British Council and the Goethe Institute offer a single and clear image. Last, and above all, it has to deal with new partners (private, public, and individual) growing exponentially to adapt to a decentralized globalization. Despite its considerable efforts to modernize, the players in foreign cultural policy, its users and recipients, do not clearly perceive its specificity. Given the complexity of cultural options and their promoters on the international scene, the multiple French departments are struggling to be in the center of diplomatic action and to find their specific place that will be attractive.

This network must continually adapt to changes in the world and budgetary constraints. Nineteen centers were closed in Western Europe from 2000 to 2006. But others opened in other regions of the world: in Tashkent and Tbilisi in 2002, Baku in 2003, and Beijing in 2004. The closings are the object of much criticism, especially as all the centers suffer from credit cuts for the overall management of the network (71.9 million euros in 2008, 65.8 million euros in 2009). All the contributors and concerned parties denounce a "disaster-stricken budget" that provides no vision in terms of restructuring.

AN AFFAIR OF STATE

Last—and one of its main features from the monarchy on, including the Enlightenment and the evolutions of the republic—France's foreign cultural policy was and still is a state affair: it is the foundation of its diplomacy, and the promotion of the French language is at the heart of this arrangement. Concerned about safeguarding cultural autonomy and freedom, other countries have chosen not to include it in diplomatic parameters with the risk of seeing political action reduced to economic and strategic management. It is clear that even before the present financial and social crisis, many countries turned to the French model of foreign cultural management in order to make cultural inroads more effective than the French and better adapted to ongoing changes, while the centralizing French statism borrows rather a more managerial approach relying on agents' greater responsiveness. At a time of these crisscrossing influences, the French experience of promoting the inclusion of culture in state political action must be even more vigilant than others in preventing political manipulation of cultural creations. For this purpose, France's cultural message guarantees freedom of expression and pluralism; defends the absolute right of choice and access to knowledge and expertise; encourages the assistance of independent agents capable of multilateral effectiveness; assures the open exchange of ideas; supports the diversity of languages and practices and their translatability in terms of languages but also mutual interaction and acculturation among the various areas of social life. And it contributes—through culture too—to refounding the meaning and practice of democracy.

ENDEMIC FRAGMENTATION AND LACK OF DIRECTION

The advantages of these specific features of the French cultural message only reveal more cruelly the shortcomings that handicap it today. They can be summarized in a phrase: the French cultural policy abroad suffers from endemic fragmentation and lack of direction. This is the consequence of a "cultural Yalta," already criticized by André Malraux, and by most observers ("to the Culture Ministry goes French culture; to the Foreign Affairs Ministry goes the monopoly of culture abroad"), and this dangerously harms the efficiency of our foreign cultural policy. Only a real interministerial interaction will enable the state agencies and their different agents to properly carry out the various missions under their responsibility. The separation between missions in the traditional Quai d'Orsay and those of the former Cooperation Ministry is still very much alive, in spite of the integration of its activities with the Foreign Affairs Ministry in 1996 and the new general management of globalization, development, and partnerships. Two cultures and management styles coexist: the world remains divided between industrialized and developing countries. The Francophony galaxy is dispersed between the OIF and its agents (in particular the University Agency of Francophony [AUF] and TV5) and the various ministries and their departments. As for the French language, the basis of Francophony, it comes under the General Delegation of the French Language and Languages of France (DGLFLF) under the Ministry of Culture and Communications, in charge of French usage in France and interministerial coordination. Last, the Ministries of National Education and Higher Education and Research play an essential role in teaching French and foreign languages as well as in welcoming foreign students.

Faced with the blurring of boundaries between "home" and "foreign," culture and economy, and cooperation and development, the administrative fragmentation brings out the inadequacy of our foreign cultural action and calls for political will as well as structural changes. The assessment is that in spite of the undisputed assets and the expectations it raises around the world, foreign cultural action reveals a lack of real direction and a crisis of cultural diplomacy that translate into a strong gap between political discourse and reality; poor interministerial action; insufficient priorities in terms of influence and funding given by the Ministry of Foreign and European Affairs (MAEE); scattered and uncoordinated actions; flowchart reforms in the place of substantive reforms; and steady reduction in budgets.

Foreign cultural policy is more than ever confronted with a recurrent dilemma: Will it be a defensive patch-up job to manage the inexorable decline of an old country? Or will it become, on the contrary, a catalyst for political innovation inside and outside the country? A strategy of "beautiful leftovers" to make us forget the insults of history? Or a search for a "politics of civilization"? Foreign cultural action seems reduced to a relic, to the superfluous, when it is not condemned to a chronicle of death foretold. Indeed, the vigor of the official commitment cannot hide the fuzziness of its project as well as the devaluation of its institutions and its professionals. Without a vision, this assessment spares neither politicians nor public opinion. It is blatant in the obscure pile of administrative "reforms," "rationalizations," and "restructuring" of a privileged but fragile sector, burdened by its budgetary cuts that seem to fall on it naturally.

There is a resounding urgency to build a strategic project and to undertake decentralized measures to clarify France's cultural message and adapt it to the different regions of the world.

BUILDING A STRATEGIC PROJECT

To effectively respond to this situation, it is necessary to reiterate this message and develop an international cultural offensive in priority areas with selected measures that would accompany an active strategy in international media.

Such an international cultural offensive requires first a *proactive stewardship at the highest level of the state* in order to build a strategic plan and carry out a decentralized action.

It would be helpful to create a *Council of Foreign Action for Development and Culture* attached to the president of the republic, as there already is for national defense and strategy. And to form an *Agency for International Cultural Action*.

Some priorities for foreign cultural action could be singled out and implemented: to develop an uninhibited French language and Francophony policy in France and abroad; to provide more content and visibility for the policy of plurilingualism: to effectively organize the teaching of two languages in French secondary school and higher education; to rely more heavily on translation, interpretation, and subtitles; to implement a more dynamic strategy to spread France's message; to reinforce the place of foreign broadcasting: TV5 Monde, France 24, RFI, and also ARTE and RFO, as well as the legal provision of online content together with books, movies, and artistic exchanges. Last, welcoming foreign students is a major part of France's cultural message, and its shortcomings continue to worsen the paltry international image of our higher education. We shall not be able to remedy the debacle of the university without an energetic modernization of exchange policies and follow-up of foreign elites, moving from a passive attitude to a dynamic recruitment supported by international action from autonomous universities. And it is urgent to implement a French-language editorial policy for advanced scientific research to compete with publications in English.

The European Union and UNESCO have put culture at the heart of their policy. France has the necessary means to be more active and imaginative in the implementation of the Convention on the Diversity of Cultural Expressions.

Intellectuals, prompt to get involved in the Middle East or African conflicts, are in no rush to construct the new European culture by transvaluing the old. Could that be because intellectual discourse is confined to a discourse of confrontation, contradiction, and polemics once it leaves archives and high technology? While, on the contrary, the specificity of European projects and the UNESCO Convention is the wager that the coexistence of diversities is possible. And far from being resigned, weak, or lazy, this coexistence demands the most difficult courage: that of putting one's self into question and questioning others instead of affronting them and the most subtle of languages: translation. This wager demands time, thrives on peace, and enjoys diplomatic influence more than bellicose pathos.

To contribute to the affirmation of an awareness of European cultural unity, France could take the initiative to create in Paris a permanent European Forum on the theme "What European Culture Today?" with the participation of intellectuals, eminent writers, and artists of the twenty-seven countries representing the European linguistic, cultural, and religious kaleidoscope. Its purpose would be to think of the Union, this plural and problematic body, in terms of history and current events to bring out the originality, the vulnerabilities, and the advantages. It would be interesting to continue the identification of symbolic sites of European heritage and to expand this idea to literary and artistic works, giving an annual title of "European exposition, work, or spectacle" to three achievements of this type in the member states and in third countries. The creation of a European Bookshop containing books translated or in their original languages of all of Europe would go in the same direction.

France should participate right now in UNESCO's actions and propositions sharing this aim, such as the "Global Alliance for Cultural Diversity" that tries to foster cultural diversity by developing cultural industries, trade, and best practices; the "Observatory on the Artist's Status" that optimizes training and assures social protection for multicultural exchange participants; and World Anti-Piracy Observatory, likely to help countries who have not signed the convention to join in certain actions in favor of diversity.

France should conceive of measures to sustain this convention in the North/South partnership with the creation of a Global Translation

Observatory for translation as the "language of diversity" that opens new potential for human thought; or the organization in Paris of an international college for cultural diversity and plurilingual development, with chairs awarded in turn for intellectuals, writers, and artists from various countries whose work and world renown contribute to informing and promoting these objectives (it could take over from the Universal Academy of Cultures presided by Elie Wiesel).

FRENCH PEOPLE, KEEP TRYING!

In the eighteenth century the Marquis de Sade addressed the French in these terms to appeal to them to rise up against obscurantism and to be republicans. Today the time has come to free up the French by mobilizing them to bring their rethought and renovated cultural experience to the world, like an invitation to found multipolar governance on the respect and sharing of cultural diversities around the world. For culture is neither a remedy against declining purchasing power nor an outlet for social malaise but rather the privileged space where new languages come together, where thought and the meaning of living and taking action are renewed.

Yes, in France's foreign action for culture and in Francophony, there is room for a message. When emergent movements tempted by totalitarianism and fundamentalism threaten democracies shaken by neoconservative inflations, there is no other recourse to outdated political and administrative models than to mobilize cultural energies, our era having the advantage over the others to look for them not in a civilization but in the sharing of diversities everywhere and among everyone.

Thus understood, France's cultural message can be used also as an incentive to protect and promote other cultures in the same spirit of appreciation, dignity, creativity, and mutual sharing. French "exceptionality" is not the issue but rather the universal philosophy of cultural experience to forge from our ambitions and our impasses and to encourage other countries to assume and to grow their own specificities.

At a time when the base of the economic and social models that yesterday were still arrogant and supposedly infallible is collapsing and ruining all certitudes, the role of culture in this fragile international context becomes a priority. It is urgent to appeal to governments and public opinion to valorize France's cultural activities. Since culture has no meaning other than to make incommensurable differences sharable; since it is the exchange among differences that creates this universal complexity called humanity and its world—Frenchmen, Frenchwomen, onward and upward, so as to exist in the world!

VI

POSITIONS

26

THE UNIVERSAL IN THE SINGULAR

Europe and the United States are signing on to President Karzai's project of "integrating" those Taliban qualified as "lower-rank insurgents," now that the Western democracies' commitment is bogging down in Afghanistan. Even though the Taliban themselves immediately rejected this offer, the plan will obviously be implemented: is it not worth trying everything, including the impossible, in the hope of placating, however relative it might be, Iran's neighbor? The question lies in the limits of this impossible, if the price to pay means *giving up on the rights of men and women* and thus opening the way to new forms of totalitarianism—contrary to the initial strategic calculation. It is as of now essential, therefore, for the Karzai government to ensure through legislation and whatever its future composition the rights of girls and women to education and job training as well as their protection against forced marriages, domestic violence, and discrimination (in the workplace, in inheritance, divorce, etc.). This is the proposal I and others made to the EESC Delegation for the Rights of Women, which was accepted and submitted for examination by the London Conference. I was personally involved in the international support of Afghan women in 2006 when I had the honor of receiving the international Hannah Arendt Prize for Political Thought: I dedicated it to those women who sacrifice themselves by fire, unable to otherwise express their revolt against social and religious obscurantism. The NGO Humani Terra of the Marseille

Hospital that runs the Herat Hospital in Afghanistan is in charge of providing them medical and psychological care. Before the Taliban, Afghan women were beginning to experience some emancipation, and still today global media keeps them informed of the progress of women's rights worldwide. Thus many of them do not blindly submit to fundamentalist repression, and we are trying to help them find ways out other than despair. But what is the link with Hannah Arendt? At a time when Nazism was considered to be pitted against Stalinism, Arendt understood that they were both part of the same totalitarian horror, because they declared the human life they were destroying by the Holocaust and the Gulag superfluous. Today it is revolting to tolerate these new forms of barbarism that consider some human beings as superfluous, especially women. In Afghanistan and beyond, globalized society is at stake.

Will the third millennium be religious, sinking into an apocalyptic "clash of religions"? Or will it be one of cultural diversity? I am betting on the second hypothesis, which happens to be that of UNESCO in its Convention on the Protection and Promotion of the Diversity of Cultural Expression of 2005.[1] However, things are not so simple. It is first necessary to agree on what is meant by "diversity."

In the name of "diversity," some people want to impose mind-sets and archaic rituals that violate individual and social freedoms, acquired at the price of painful historical combat. It is no coincidence that women are often the first victims of such regressions: Freud wrote that since prehistoric times in religions and still today, more or less unconsciously, "the whole woman is taboo."[2] People claim to "respect diversity" by allowing genital mutilation of African women, and chadors and burkas of Muslim women. Why not a return to Chinese women's "bound feet"?

Better than "cultural diversity" would be the promotion of interculturality. It would take into account cultural traditions, including religious beliefs. Not to mention the crucial component of the human experience called *history*. Having led humans to think that the universal and freedom are accessible to all humanity, history also gives us the audacity to turn them into realities. What universal? What freedom? The "universal" finds its full libertarian value only if it is a *universal in the singular*. Let me explain.

Going back to the Jewish and Christian origins of these philosophical and political notions, we tend to oppose a "Jewish universal" (biblical and

Talmudic), which would be diversifying because of its concern for singular chosenness to a "Catholic universal" (Paulist Roman heritage) that would be generalizable, assessable, and measurable. Ignoring the complexities of these two traditions, this opposition is clearly simplistic: the singular Alliance of Judaism with the divine, while having the exceptional metaphysical advantage of creating the subject in man, does not exclude approaching the world in terms of absolute truth, nonproblematizable and without exteriority; while Catholic spirituality, albeit expansive, colonizing, and inquisitorial, does not ignore either singularity (with Duns Scotus) or the uncontrollable desire for the infinite (with the baroque revolution). Moreover, instead of opposing the two universalisms, it would be politically more reasonable and fruitful to go beyond the duel between Jews and Christians to rethink the tensions of the Jewish-and-Christian duo and their reevaluation in and by secularization and human rights, a rupture not found in other religions and that led to French secularism. The universal, attentive to the singular rights of each woman and each man, is its precious heritage, which, in the name of human rights, today seems to be the only one able to reach out to emerging countries.

European culture is the crucible of all this, for better or for worse. The horror of the Holocaust will not cease to inspire the greatest suspicion, if not hostility, to Europe. It has to be recognized that the critical return of racist, anti-Semitic, and xenophobic crimes committed by Europeans makes the European political debate an exceptional forum, one that becomes an example in a world pulled apart by nationalist or religious identity clashes.

Thus, while the cult of identity (national or sexual) engenders new militancies, the European space runs against this trend, since in Europe "national identity" is no longer a cult but is now a constantly evolving reality to question. Yes, there is a European identity open to the plurality of national and regional identities and to their languages and which, by questioning memory and becoming, is trying to find the best interaction with the migratory flows of globalization. We are neither aware enough nor proud enough of this identarian innovation emerging in Europe slowly, painfully, but more resolutely than anywhere else.

Is this European interculturalism an impossible dream? Certainly. But this is the utopia that gives the European project all its energy, above and beyond economic and political uncertainties. Because it is based on sharable diversities provided each person's rights to his/her optimal development are guaranteed, this intercultural utopia is the exact opposite of that fantasy of a new "communism" being proposed as a "courage option" to "get out of the crisis." Did not the Communist universal fail precisely because it refused to recognize that freedom is conjugated in the singular? No solidarity or fraternity with the "diverse," the "different," or the "undocumented" can be built without leading to the full materialization of human rights, namely, the right of this man or of that woman: in the *singular*, with and through their "community."

Procedural, legal, and social humanism is often criticized for lacking the sacred. I contend that when the universal merges with the concern for each person's incommensurability, the boundaries of the social pact widen to an indefensible vulnerability and the unpredictable creativity of the nondescripts, and *humanism in the singular introduces the sacred* into the world.

Going back to women, let us remember the warnings of the author of *The Second Sex:* individuals' possibilities are not defined "in terms of happiness, but in terms of freedom"; and that if "freedom is the only way to establish the value of all life," "freedom is never given, but always has to be won."[3] And, I add, to be questioned, to be renewed. In creating the Simone de Beauvoir Award for Women's Freedom, the International Jury awarded it first to women under a fatwa (Taslima Nasreen and Ayaan Hirsi Ali) or fighting for their rights (the Iranian women's NGO One Million Signatures). Women's rights, like men's rights, cannot be exported. At the crossroads of cultures benefiting from interculturalism that should be optimized, these rights emerge slowly, specific to each country, culture, and religion.

Two Chinese women, the lawyer Guo Jianmei and literary and video artist Ai Xiaoming, received this award in 2010. They are part of a complex tradition of women's emancipation, which accompanies Chinese history alongside—and against—oppression: from Taoism to the bourgeois liberation movement passing through the women imperial court writers, the suffragettes who invaded the parliament in 1912 and then claimed the right to vote via the 1920 movement called feminists' "Five proposals" (equal inheritance rights, the right to vote and to be elected, the right to education and work, self-determination in marriage, and open marriage), and up to Mao's writing on women's suicide or the international commitments of the current communist government. Attached to these cultural traits, albeit rare but concerned with law and women, the action of these award winners, which they define as a "building a strategy of building and not of opposition," was not perceived as foreign interference and was well received by public opinion. In the spirit of this singular universal that calls on each person's creativity, the prize wished to distinguish Ms. Ai's and Ms. Guo's specific genius, their initiatives, and their pathbreaking acts of liberty. I gave a provocative title to my trilogy on women that is against massificating feminism, *The Female Genius*.

At the diametrical opposite of this spirit, the "veiled [woman] candidate of the *banlieue*"[4] attaches more importance to the sign of religious affiliation than to the person of this woman and thereby encourages fundamentalism's influence: the far left prefers the teaching of imams to women's emancipation. Since violence against women was a national cause in 2010, it would have been more revolutionary to choose a woman candidate from the *banlieue*, subjected to a forced marriage, domestic violence, denial of access to knowledge, as well as discrimination in the workplace and other infringements and deficiencies of republican law itself. There is much left to do to open politics to "women of the *banlieue*," without locking them complacently in their religious affiliation. Could this be the famous "affirmative secularism" practiced by the Ligue Communiste Revolutionnaire (LCR) rather than the demagogic PR that perpetuates exclusion?

I am not an expert on Islam, and it is difficult to move forward on this touchy field without offending sensibilities, even among secular intellectuals of Muslim origin, without awakening colonial memories and postcolonial resentment. Whatever the variants of Islam and its rationalist, mystical, or poetic developments, it seems that the role of the father figure and of symbolic authority (what Freud called *Urvater*) is so powerful, even unsurpassable, that it imposes obedience and hinders the man's freedom and, even more, the woman's. I take note, as do some French-speaking writers and philosophers of Muslim origin, that the rupture of secularization has not taken place in Islam. Or would it be so invisible and inaudible that it is received as a foreign transplant? No Enlightenment, no Haskalah.[5]

Under these conditions, can Muslim "identity" become a question and evolve from there? Political and economic changes are undoubtedly needed, which would enable Muslims to get out of the position of the "vengeful persecuted." More deeply and at the same time, a transvaluation of Islamic and Islamist values is required (Koranic rules, sacrificial rituals, tyrannical grip on gender relations, obedience, holy war, walled women, etc.), which could take place through integration of the history of religions in school and university programs. All religions, including Islam, could thus become objects of interpretation in the light of contemporary social and human sciences and philosophy. This revaluation would join together women and men from the Koranic tradition, as NPNS[6] is trying to do in its own way. "Cruel and protracted" work, in Sartre's words on atheism,[7] but essential, if we recognize that a refoundation of humanism is necessary, one that will not neglect religious facts but will interpret their needs as well as the dangers in a universal that guarantees the liberating values of the person.

27

CAN ONE BE A MUSLIM WOMAN
AND A SHRINK?

There could not be a better new life breathed into the homage to Lacan than to broaden this meeting—springing up amid the hottest of current events—around psychoanalysis, politics, and women. This is a period that has to be called historic for psychoanalysis, for politics, and for women that will surely mean new struggles, thinking, colloquia, seminars, movements, and pages to come. Allow me to sketch out a few leads before broaching the essential: the fragile female genius of the Syrian psychoanalyst Rafah Nached.

There is no such thing as a politics of psychoanalysis. Psychoanalysis is the intimate experience par excellence, as Freud and Lacan, each in his unique way, constantly reiterated. On the other hand, the Copernican revolution of values and norms that opens new possibilities of links to others forming the very essence of politics comes from listening to the speaking being. Since listening to the unconscious reveals the singularity of the speaking being, it is inevitable for psychoanalysis to come face to face with the third millennium's central preoccupation, which I define this way: what meaning can be given to the singularity that has become synonymous with happiness through freedom? Psychoanalysis is called on to answer this question. Why? Because Freud's discovery of the unconoscious transferred the religious and philosophical ambitions of a Western world concerned with human rights to the very heart of scientific rationality. And this approach, our psychoanalytic approach of the human being, counters the pseudo-humanism that is ready to harden the patient under the armor of a worker to assess as well as the terror that the political and religious fundamentalisms sow, and various relentless scientistic attacks. Nached is the witness of this resistance when she tries to give words to the fear of the Syrian regime.

Is it a woman's resistance? A feminist's? But what is feminism? What is a woman? Far be it from me to have you enter this complex continent, especially—to repeat—as it is Rafah Nached's singularity that I want to highlight, her singularity as a woman psychoanalyst in a specific culture. After the suffragettes and before the feminist movement's interest in psychoanalysis in the May 1968 period, Simone de Beauvoir was the first one to bridge the movement for woman's emancipation and the unconscious. This cannot be repeated enough: not only toward the end of her life did she write that Freud was "one of the men of this century for whom [she] had the most respect and affection,"[1] but in spite of her criticism (based on misunderstandings) of psychoanalysis, as of *The Second Sex*,[2] Beauvoir delved into psychoanalysis for the founding idea of her book that had the effect of a slap in the face of the *establishment*, a book that still disturbs. "Sex," she said, referring to the "psychoanalytic point of view," is "the body experienced by the subject." "It is not nature that defines the woman: it is the woman who defines herself by taking nature into account in her affectivity."[3] Beauvoir thus endorses the Freudian refoundation of the metaphysical dualism body/soul, flesh/spirit, nature/culture, and considering "sex" as a "psychosexuality," the existentialist proved herself to be more complicit with Freud than so many phenomenologists who accused the Viennese doctor of "biologizing man's essence." It was Lacan who radicalized this refoundation of metaphysics while Beauvoir's ambivalence would feed into the rush of a certain feminism, especially in the United States, against psychoanalysis. Yet, and conversely, these misunderstandings gave rise to movements that tried to keep abreast of psychoanalytic developments and led to the birth of Psychanalyse et Politique in France.[4] Above all, contemporary analytic theory and practice are developing an unprecedented analysis of female sexuality and more recently of passion, or what I call maternal "reliance."

The Rafah Nached phenomenon is inscribed in this history and has its place in the new context of globalization. I will first deal with the social aspect of her research and action, which has provoked the scandal that we are vigorously protesting today. I will end with the more secret dimension of her practice and thought published in the journals *Topique* and *Psychanalyse*.⁵

"HAVE NO FEAR"

Since there has been no formal charge, one can assume that Rafah Nached is accused of a breach of security because of the discussion group she leads every Sunday with the Jesuits of Damascus. Open to citizens of all tendencies, these meetings attempt to help Syrians overcome fear.

After studying clinical psychology under Sophie de Mijolla-Mellor at Paris-Diderot, Nached said in her articles published in French that she worked in Alep in an "old persons' hospice," "an environment of an unbelievable mixture of people suffering from psychoses, epilepsy, hysteria, mental retardation, and physical handicaps covering all age-groups, from two to old age." She continued this difficult job in Damas in centers for the mentally disabled, where she tried to create "a talking space to help [these people] accept the disabilities they were confronted with and to consider the children as sensible beings, wounded by their disabilities." Little by little, her personal practice became a "talking and listening place for people suffering from those prohibitions" characteristic of the social climate of her country in her opinion. "Outside," she says, "free speech is forbidden, so that a thousand detours are necessary to *express anything the least bit personal*." It is also very difficult to "*say or express a 'no' and that goes for all areas, which is a cultural* aspect." Her psychoanalytic office thus became a "place for the ego to exist whereas outside it is blocked. A place where one can take some distance from one's family, job, or society where fusion reigns.⁶

Thus, faced with the backwardness of Syrian psychiatry, with the problems Rafah Nached had in introducing psychoanalysis in an environment dominated by behaviorism, with the fear of saying "I" and "no" in a country where tradition discourages singular speech, even more so under a regime of excessive violence and repression, she managed to undertake group therapy work based on psychodrama, with a colleague, Jesuit and psychoanalyst. There were a French Jesuit, a Dutch Jesuit, and some others, one of whom a young Syrian Jesuit who had the courage to criticize the Church hierarchy, complicit with the Damas regime (in an article in a Syrian newspaper in August 2011) and specifically in the Jesuit places of worship in Damas.

What does this act, at the outset strictly clinical, say? It says: "Have no fear!"

You heard me right: I am suggesting a comparison between Rafah Nached's analytical work and John Paul II's remarks that triggered Solidarity—before leading, in the midst of and following a series of economic, political and social causes, to the fall of the communist bloc itself.

My juxtaposition might be shocking to some, but I maintain it. Comparisons are misleading. Without setting up equivalences between Rafah's psychodramas to treat fear and a pope's appeal in Poland, yet while suggesting a resemblance, the rhetorical figure maintains the irreducible differences between the two fields: Syria and Poland, Rafah and John Paul II. This paradox produces a shock that lets you transform the emptiness of thought not into aggressiveness but into this desire for signifyingness, into psychic curiosity. That is what Rafah tries to generate in those who are afraid. Have no fear, you can know and say it: "*Scilicet*," she says, but in Arabic. It is with this fragile spark, psychic curiosity, that Rafah rose in opposition to Syrian power. And that is what I am trying to maintain in us today so that we might give a future to this modest and scandalous act, Rafah's treatment, that worries every dictatorial regime.

Let us be serious. No one knows what will happen after today's dictatorship. There are many of us who fear that the libertarian revolt will bring to power a fundamentalism that is at first insidious and then virulent. Another aspect of Rafah Nached's work deals with this very fear: her research goes back to a long process of translation of psychoanalytical vocabulary (of Freud and Lacan) into Arabic that she is trying to resuscitate, and then her attempt to interpret the religious experience of Islam in the light of psychoanalysis.

Here is the heart of the fundamentalist threat that politics cannot solve with laws only, with economic measures or even war campaigns that are more or less supported by the United Nations. Friedrich Nietzsche's ambition must be recalled: addressing the "hooligans in public spaces" and taking seriously the "death of God," he posed "a great question mark at the most serious place,"[7] that is, the place of God. In other terms, it is a question of constantly continuing the "transvaluation of values," necessarily and traditionally religious. Psychoanalysis, more than all the other human sciences, is at the heart of our specific singularities where this great question mark concerns every person's intimacy.

Rafah Nached's work in this area is still embryonic, timid, and hesitant. "Barely simmering," Jacques-Alain Miller said when I spoke to him about it. But this work is ongoing, and this is for me the most impressive, the most promising part of the Rafah phenomenon.

After recalling the works of Moustafa Safouan, Moustafa Hijazi, and Sami Ali translating Freud and Lacan in Arabic, the group around Rafah Nached who is carrying on this effort is "tormented trying to find the unfindable appropriate word that carries meaning in Arabic"; "we have to generate psychoanalysis in Arabic"; "we experienced psychoanalysis as a metaphor of translation and translation as a metaphor of psychoanalysis": "we have discovered that psychoanalysis is a work of civilization, that is, of life," "of everything that relates to the Arabic language"; this "society has not yet entered postmodernism."[8]

And here is this discovery that perhaps only a woman could emphasize with such force—listen: unlike the German language of Freud (and the French of Lacan), where sexual metaphors are so rich and have immediate access to the unconscious, "in Arabic metaphors [concerning sexuality] are situated in the area of death."[9] Furthermore, seeking to diagnose what the analyst finds specific to Damascus, and in particular "why this fear of the psychoanalytic word," Rafah Nached wrote: "Psychoanalysis is situated perhaps between the rejection of sexuality in the general meaning of the term and the esoteric language of divinity."[10]

You get it: the fears that this woman analyst tries to hear go much further than the fear of a political regime; they are locked up in the religious attitude.

Yet Rafah Nached does not attack them head-on. She does not target headscarves or burkas, the confinement of women, or the calls for jihad. Concerning Islam's religious practices, Rafah and her group are interested in Sufism because that is where a psychic deepening of the amorous link between Me and You develops: "Betrayal or love?" This is the title under which Rafah Nached devotes a succinct study in *Psychanalyse*[11] about the amorous link between the mystic and his God in the work of

Hallaj (famous tenth-century rebel mystic), and his "interior experience" that resonates as well with Georges Bataille's text as with the Freudian "psychic apparatus" or Lacan's "topologies."

While very dependent on the works of Henry Corbin and Louis Massignon, the psychoanalyst prudently suggests an interpretation of the ambiguity of this mystical love that links the Ego to his Great Other. Both illusory union (with Allah) and diabolical rebellion (close to Iblis), the Sufist faith is like the *height of fanaticism* where the subject identifies with the all-powerful Other and turns it around so as to dominate it in the *père-version* that culminates in the omnipotence of Self.

But this ambivalent liaison continues on as well in surpassing the symptom itself, by the acceptance of *désêtre* and frustration, and even of the jouissance of disengagement and self-annihilation, as of any power. Furthermore, the sacrificial position, the feminization of the Islamic soul in its uniquely masculine subordination to the divinity, the question of the "other" jouissance (neither man nor woman but "pure subjectivity" without necessarily being either ecstatic or exterminating à la Al-Queda), are set out in the article "Dire l'indicible."[12] In conclusion, it is "in passing by the mystical and its relationship with *jouissance* that its language [Lacan's language? Psychoanalytic language?] can be understood and accepted by us," Rafah Nached concludes in *Topique*.[13]

I see this work as the beginning of a path our Syrian colleagues are trying to navigate, not to stigmatize the religious experience but to question it, to analyze it, to deconstruct it infinitely. Is that another reason to put this woman in prison? Of course. But I bet that her jailers do not know it. And that this progress can only get stronger in spite of and against the persecution crashing down on Rafah.

Last, her group points out that it continues to monitor the "new maladies of the soul" the current situation produces. For example, it works with Iraqi refugees on the pain, shocks, and violence they have undergone or have committed; it attempts to "dig out something that comes from our language and our culture," said the colleagues Rafah quoted: "We do not want to make psychoanalysis an empire of which Paris is the capital."

I hear the pride and ambition of this project and this criticism. This is what I suggest:

The Simone de Beauvoir Prize for Women's Freedom that I created in 2008 has awarded six exceptional women from India, Somalia, Holland,

Iran, China, and Russia. It will be meeting next week to choose the 2012 winner of the prize that will be given on January 9 in Paris. It will probably be a woman from the Maghreb or the Mashriq. I would like the board to reflect on the nomination of Rafah Nached even though we [have received] the candidacies of several remarkable women whose body of work is quantitatively greater and qualitatively more accessible.

Alongside the Rafah Nached phenomenon, I want to suggest that our Women's Forum carry forward with a permanent forum that could be called the "Rafah Nached Forum: Psychoanalysis and Cultural Diversity." It would gather French and other psychoanalysts from various cultural traditions that today are dying out or fighting on this planet, on a regular basis. Its aim would be to stimulate the transvaluation of the traditions that haunt the unconscious, this transvaluation that I consider as the only radical opposition to fear and trivialization. With a bit of luck, a Rafah Nached prize given by this forum could reward the excellence of a clinical or theoretical work that contributes to developing psychoanalysis in the critical climate of globalization.

With the liberation of Rafah that we demand, it would be our answer to fear and to those attempting to silence this woman who is trying to say the unsayable.

28

ONE IS BORN WOMAN, BUT
I BECOME ONE

Q: Do you remember when you discovered Simone de Beauvoir? A: I was still in Bulgaria, Beauvoir was not yet really a star, and I had the feeling that women were free. Something was not right, but I did not know what it was. A French friend brought me *The Second Sex*, I think around 1958. It was the post-Stalinist thaw, and we were beginning to openly talk about freedom. The Hegelian dialectic analyzed it in terms of ideas, but this French existentialist broached it from the sexed body and in the polyphony of literature. Neither proletarian revolt nor a spiral of the mind freedom took shape for me with Simone de Beauvoir: freedom had to encompass women, and it could be written.

Q: *Did she turn you into a feminist?*

A: No one was talking yet about feminism. She revealed to me that the enigma of female sexuality, secret and scandal, was becoming a political reality that went along with the possibility of "transcending one's self." "One is not born, but rather becomes, woman." Today, between biological determinations and psychosocial reconstructions, we would say: "one" is born woman, but "I" become woman. If I cannot find either who I am or my place in society, it depends on me and on us to change things. On *us*, in the social battle: "We are free to transcend all transcendence," but this "elsewhere" is "within our human condition" (*Pyrrhus and Cineas*).[1] And on me, through thought and writing: "I would create myself anew and justify my existence" (*Memoirs of a Dutiful Daughter*).[2]

It seemed to me that this vision of women as the actresses of their freedom could arise only with the emergence of the modern consciousness of Europe and even more from France's history, with the legacy of Mlle de Gournay, Théroigne de Méricourt, Stendhal, and Colette. My admiration for French culture was reinforced, and I admit that it still holds up in spite of the reality checks inflicted on it. I am even convinced that women in China or in Iran who today are trying to acquire their rights must imbue themselves with this European humanism, with the secularization that came out of the Enlightenment and the freedom to surpass one's self according to Beauvoir.

Q: *In* The Second Sex, *Beauvoir criticizes psychoanalysis, then in* All Said and Done *she says that she "adores" Freud. What is your opinion as a psychoanalyst?*

A: In *The Second Sex*, Beauvoir nonetheless pointed out that her understanding of sex stemmed from the "psychoanalytical point of view": sex is the "the body lived by the subject. . . . Nature does not define woman: it is she who defines herself by reclaiming nature for herself in her affectivity." Neither pure biology nor pornographic, and even less, spiritualist excitation, sex according to her was inseparable from the work of the psyche: it is an *experience* (*Lived Experience* is the subtitle of the second volume). I read this in the scientific and psychic sense of the word. I do not identify Beauvoir in the feminist cliché reduced to a political and legal militant. For me, she is a laboratory researcher who permanently takes risks in her private life and thought, and who urges every woman to reconstruct her personality and to develop her creativity. That is why I dedicated the conclusion of my trilogy, *Female Genius*, to her.[3]

Q: *At a conference on "Beauvoir and psychoanalysis," you concluded your remarks saying, "Not only does Beauvoir not let herself be challenged by psychoanalysis, but she challenges the psychoanalytical microcosm and invites it to take its place in history."*

A: This subject that "accomplishes its freedom only by its perpetual surpassing toward other freedoms" and that she called for to get women out of their "facticity" and their role of the object of the Other, was founded for her on all of Western philosophical history (including the Hegelian dialectic, phenomenology, and, of course, existentialism). But perhaps more than for her contemporaries, psychoanalysis nourished this woman's thought. She scandalized the *establishment* by teaching it in the lycée, and Anne, a psychoanalyst, is the heroine of the *Mandarins*, which did not prevent her from remaining very ambivalent about Freud. Her often simplistic criticism (reducing the Oedipus complex to a match between sexual organs, accusing Freud of an "absence of originary intentionality of existence" or of "a systematic rejection of the idea of choice," etc.) was picked up and exacerbated by the onrush of feminists, mostly American, hostile to psychoanalysis. But it also gave rise to reverse movements that tried to better understand what was happening in psychoanalysis, leading to the emergence of the MLF[4] and Psychanalyse et Politique. On the other hand, by constantly remaining at the intersection of the intimate and the social, Beauvoir demonstrated the limits of psychoanalytic intimism when it neglected the social and historic mutations that every person we hear on the couch undergoes or tries to assume.

Q: *In* All Said and Done, *she recounts her dreams. What does that mean to you?*

A: Why tell her dreams in public? A cruel Beauvoir who exposed herself to get the upper hand, for which she was often denounced? An attempt to seduce, a desire for control over the intimate lives of her readers, an ultimate desire for power? I think that she was a woman of great intellectual honesty: thinking was jouissance for her; she thus put herself unremittingly in question. To the point of interpreting her own dreams, by unabashedly unveiling her often painful specific traits: her inability to let go, her tendency to "play a psychodrama rather than to simply live," to "rationalize" her anxiety where every emotion triggered an avalanche of trips, trains, stations, planes, Sartre himself as a helicopter, everything "unchecked," and that "cold water" that separated her from her mother but also from her favorite lover Nelson Algren, or else plunging a knife into the paternal throat, without forgetting the fear of breaking raw eggs after a demonstration against abortion. The shadow of the "broken woman" stands alongside the emancipated lover, the traveler, and the hiker in her dreams. In showing her fragility here as in her novels, she kept her readers from cementing her in the role of boss; she made a Simone de Beauvoir cult impossible. In turn, some men delighted in making her the cry-baby, the infantilized woman in love, the inexorable correspondent shackled to her "dear little you-other," either to mock or to reduce the "truth" of Beauvoir and of women to a kind of tormented and talkative sensitivity that reassured them after all.

Q: *What do you think of her compulsion to write interminable letters?*

A: She seemed possessed by a verbal drive that nothing could stop, the way nothing could stop the walker devouring space. Did she ever realize that her sharp intelligence, her total commitment, life itself, and, after all, writing are the work of language? Her very precise assessments of great women writers barely take into account what is called "form." But taking hold of the overflowing drive in language has always acted as an antidepressant in the culture of the word. In writing about Teresa of Avila's mystical experience, I realized that in the sixteenth and especially the seventeenth centuries, men of the Church asked nuns and lay women penitents to write their "spiritual life," resulting in a rich feminine literature. The escape into the French language of Beauvoir, this fallen-away Catholic, is indeed an original way to appropriate and "transvalue" Catholic tradition: I am thinking of Mme Guyon's *Torrents* and the magnificent letter-writers like Mme de Sévigné. Dismissing her insatiable attention to detail and her semiautomatic volubility is to overlook the fact that she put them to use for the anthropological revolution she brought about: showing women that the mothers of the species are also free subjects.

Q: *How do you judge her passion for walking to exhaustion, wanting to see every site in a place?*

A: Arousal, for women as for men, abates with long hikes. This permanent race is also a "language" that reveals the immense dynamism of the *subject* Beauvoir. And she succeeded in infusing her immense energy into history.

Q: *Do you agree with her definition of universalism?*

A: I do not see it in the same way as the universalists who think they are expressing her ideas today. Her declared equality of the sexes, this "brotherhood" (note the masculine) between men and women, belongs philosophically to the universal system whose genealogy dates back to the Platonic Ideal, to the republican ideals of Universal Man and his rights cherished by the French Enlightenment. Thanks to psychoanalysis, it is clear that these values are supported by the denial of the feminine body and share the phallic veneration of the Great Man, not without ambivalence, aggressiveness, and dependence. Beauvoir was right to encourage women to measure themselves against this requirement, to transcend themselves in the universal, which necessarily entails a development of psychic bisexuality that Freud said was more pronounced in women than in men.

But because what interested her were "the chances for the individual" and his/her "happiness" defined "in terms of freedom," a constant tension shaped her thinking: the universal is incarnated (already in *The Second Sex* and in her novels) in the experience of each man and each woman. One can never say it enough: Beauvoir's universal is conjugated in the singular. She was not a militant who confined all women in a Promethean totality, as did the libertarian movements after the demise of the religious continent promising universal freedom for "all men," necessarily starting with choice communities (all the bourgeoisie, all the workers, all the third world, etc.). Before realizing that this denial of singularity opened the way to banalization and totalitarianisms.

Q: *Without citing anyone, you criticize "rationalist repression with which some present-day universalists reinforce their virile ambitions and sneer at childbearing and, worse still, at breast-feeding, as if that brought about the degradation of the feminine condition."*

A: Beauvoir's universalism is constantly being rethought and recomposed. There is no universal formula for what *the* woman or *the* mother should be. Coming from a totalitarian country, I was particularly sensitive to this. I particularly saw this concern for singularity in her constant thinking in novelistic terms. While Sartre, after "The Words," associated the imaginary with neurosis, Beauvoir continued to write—biography or autofiction (who knows?)—it speaks of her mother, her lovers, of death using "I." To say in short that it is only by including the most singular experience possible in the endless march toward the universal that "I will set hearts on fire" and that we all, men and women, will be able to "justify our existence."[5] If that is forgotten, feminism will become a certainly necessary militant project, but one that would quickly turn dogmatic and sectarian.

Q: *But you also speak about difference, which would take shape in her experience. Are you not drawing her toward differentialist ideas that are rather your own?*

A: It is possible. In reading a work as sensational and disturbing as this one, every one of us tries to see what it corresponds to in everyday life and in ourselves. But I do not think I am betraying her. She was often trapped by her "fraternal" universalism and reverted to stereotypes to describe some women's lived experiences imposed by specific historical conditions, as if they were essential. Thus women have "maladies of the womb," "the species eats away at them," an infant is a "polyp," the female body is a "swamp that insects and children sink into," as opposed to the male sex, "clean and simple as a finger," etc. From there she tried to move toward that universal liberator, the male philosopher, the great man philosopher. This great man who could be a woman. This is what many feminists have retained, especially a certain American feminism before it became more differentialist. On the other hand, in the variants of the life of the couple with Sartre, Algren, and others, it was the loving woman who came to life, capable of caring and complicity. And the couple emerges as a space for exchange, without crushing each other and without being a place of worship. Where in spite of differences of opinions and issues, it is possible to remain united and respect the body and thought of the other. An example not to repeat but one that is an encouragement to innovate. How to live with a man without fixed hierarchies, while being different? By working out free thoughts that remain a conversation, together and each in her/his singularity?

Q: *Their couple was not set up as a model and yet some people made a model of it and afterward said they were disappointed.*

A: Could they have escaped a kind of early version of media hype? It was Saint-Germain-des-Prés; they lent themselves to this mythification, which is always a misunderstanding in which one becomes complicit. But reading *The Mandarins* or later *Adieux: A Farewell to Sartre*,[6] I picked up no obsequious religiosity of the woman in regard to the man. On the other hand, they gave the impression of a couple who used "contingent love affairs." They have been criticized for turning these "contingent partners" into victims. Was this cruelty not paid back by a lot of cruelty to one's self? Held in the clutch of jealousy, the Castor painfully passed through the ghost of the "disillusioned woman" to transcend herself in her writing, and by relying on her cult as master thinker who would not let herself be shaken even by the discovery that Sartre's "vocation" for "contingent love affairs" hides the "Bringing Up Baby" type of indefensible erotic dependence.

Did the couple's sadomasochistic logic escape Simone de Beauvoir? In any case, that is what she described in man/woman relations, in the war between the sexes. I do not think she analyzed it, and even less, dispassionately.

Yet she pursued the formula Hegel highlighted in *She Came to Stay*: "Each consciousness seeks the death of the other" even to the sexual scenarios of Sade's death wish.[7] Fascinated by the daring of the Divine Marquis, she devoted an astonishing text to him, *Must We Burn Sade?*, before *The Mandarins*.[8] Inescapable cruelty, she implied, against the terrifying optimism of a feel-good conscience: "In a criminal world, it is necessary to be criminal." But is this really what Sade said? His terrible sadomasochistic jouissance unfurls in the imaginary, and even the unlimited freedom of the grand lord bad man is not equal to his murderous phantasms. One is not obliged to act out, any more than erect guillotines, which he disapproved of. Always attentive to dominant/dominated logic that structures desire and sexual relations, Beauvoir detected their sociohistorical inflections and put forward the idea that all universal laws rest on homicides, that passions are deadly, and that ethics are only an ethics of ambiguity. She tried to unravel the ambiguities in Stalinist communism, for example, getting trapped, in passing, by her indulgence for the passions of revolt. To stick just with couples, strangely it was Colette who succeeded in dedramatizing feminine love affairs by ironizing this "great big love" and "these men that other men call great." As for Beauvoir, something of the grand woman in love always remained in her, till the end.

Q: *When you speak of her "tender cruelty toward Sartre," are you alluding to* Adieux: Farewell to Sartre, *which was seen more as revenge than the last act of their contract of truthfulness?*

A: Some people saw it as vengeance, others as the ultimate veneration of Sartre. I think that there was cruelty but not really vengeance, if one considers that the love relation is intrinsically sadomasochistic. Obviously, we are far from the bourgeois couple hallowed by Rousseau to assure the procreation and upbringing of the subject-citizen, but who hides skeletons revealed by Sade in his closets. *Exit* also the Surrealist crazy love and Georges Bataille's mystical love. Sartre and Beauvoir understood that religion today took refuge in the idyll of Love and the Couple, with capital letters. Can one live without that consecration? Maybe, not really, with the unsaid, censure, and victims. "Do you know Casanova, darling?" she wrote to Algren. She could have added Sade. Beauvoir and Sartre went far into atheism lived as deconstruction of the love idyll, and in exposing its endurance as well as its cracks. Atheism, this "cruel and long-lasting experience," wrote Sartre. They maintained this cruelty in their tête-à-tête, trying to soften it when possible. Do you know any others who have stood in full light like this?

Q: *Do you think there is, on one side, motherhood disparaged by Beauvoir, and on the other, motherhood reduced to an instinct of the species? Is there a third way for women?*

A: The path is narrow. It should be neither one nor the other. But what is a mother? Would it be that dream about her mother, rue de Rennes: "I'm uneasy about her; and in fact we can't reach each other: or I can't manage to get to the house where she's absent." "I dreaded falling back under her power." To transcend herself in these conditions would mean tearing herself from this cold and domineering motherhood. And, of course, freeing herself from the historical situation of the women of that period and before that, of these serial pregnancies, mothers dying in childbirth, back-alley abortions, and the battles of breathtaking courage for the contraceptive pill and the right to abortion. . . . It must be recalled because many young people forget. Beauvoir rejected this victimizing motherhood for mothers and a vehicle of victimization for children. That kept her from seeing the situation today, that is, when motherhood becomes a choice, it can be lived differently. With its difficulties, of course, for economic and psychic means are needed to assume this burden and transform it into creativity.

We have not yet found the discourse for these new forms of motherhood. Secularization is the only civilization that does not know what a good mother is. Winnicott cautiously advanced that she was the one who could dream next to her child, enabling him to play, speak, and think. Question: how can this woman-mother construct her sexuality as a lover, her professional autonomy, and her maternal availability for this first other, her child? A whole plural universe, a "pluriverse," as astrophysicists say, is emerging for the first time in human history. Beauvoir in fact developed a true *adoption motherhood* that accompanies all motherhood: by legally adopting Sylvie, and through her political solidarity with her feminist "girls" in the combats where she recognized a transmission of her ideas beyond the differences. This is the emancipated woman's complex world that Beauvoir urged us to rethink. She gave us keys, but not all of them. There are still many things for us to say after her, but without incriminating her failures as some differentialists do.

Q: *In* The Second Sex *she said, "The free woman is just being born."* *Since then, has she been born?*

A: She is now in the process of being born. When we see what some women of our generation have accomplished, it cannot be compared to the previous generation of women, but also in relation to what is happening in developing countries where this message has not yet reached. The free woman has been born through those who were sensible to Simone de Beauvoir's breakthrough and what came afterward. There were three waves of feminism in the twentieth century: suffragettes, Simone de Beauvoir, and after May 1968, new emancipations and new obstacles. This is the progressive birth that must be understood by women in advanced democracies who fall under the heavy lid of conservatism and other crises. But also by those in other countries with their different historical traditions, exposed to other pressures and persecutions. It is often too quickly said that the Castor was a rebel who wanted to impose her will on the world rather than be subjected to the world. I think she did better. Her existentialist notion of freedom meant not only not giving in but also living by surpassing one's self in a world that is neither to be endured nor managed but to be compatible with my initiative of surpassing and only then to be transformed.

Q: *When she began to write* The Second Sex, *she was madly in love with Nelson Algren. Did that play a role in her book project?*

A: That was not the only impetus for the book. First, she discovered Michel Leiris's *The Age of Man* and wanted to do the same. But the intellectual stimulation came from Sartre, who asked her to think about what it meant not to have been brought up like a boy. And then her meeting with Algren was a radical experience. She was attracted to this man from a lower social milieu, an antifather, the polar opposite not only of her "dear little philosopher" with whom she was living through her first serious crisis but also her noble father who "every morning went to "the courts," who seemed to her "a type rarer than the rest of men," and who, in addition, "was a dramatic actor." Impossible to kill, impossible to marry! A passion was thus born for this Jewish writer, for his authenticity of a man coming from the poor, the male who would awaken her body. A new experience of freedom. But in which she would end up assuming a man's role in the classic meaning of the term. For, while being convinced that her "true and warm place" was "next to the loving heart" of this American

lover, she used him as a sexual object. And told him that she was returning to Paris to be with Sartre because what interested her was to write
and be able to think. Algren obviously was not about to accept this compromise, and she was extremely hurt when he broke off the relationship.
But it was she who would renounce the happiness of their sensual couple
and the role of genitor.

Another and a new freedom followed in the aftermath of *The Second
Sex*, but also with the discovery of America. Beauvoir constructed a polyphonic vision of the world that she scoured and analyzed tirelessly with
this principle: "Faced with complex situations, one must think" (*America Day by Day*).[9] Whether it was her critical solidarity with Israel ("The
idea that Israel might not survive as a state . . . is unbearable to me")[10] or
her indulgent wager on China (which was carrying out "its growth and
expansion step by step").[11]

Q: The Second Sex *is sixty-two years old. Some women think it is
outdated.*

A: They are wrong. They have not read it. They have to read it first. And
then each one can question her own experience.

Q: Why was the Simone de Beauvoir Award created?

A: At her centennial (2008), the feminists were not all in agreement,
so I was asked to take over the international conference in Paris. I wanted
to do something that would leave a mark after the celebration, so that this
true anthropological revolution that she accelerated would continue to
nourish minds, notably in other cultures that seemed to be unaware of
the subject in man and even more so in woman.

Q: When you wrote *The Samurai,* was it a nod at Simone de Beauvoir's
Mandarins?

A: Yes, an IOU for her, because her message got through. But times
have changed, and I assume my difference; I even assert my foreignness
that sees France from the outside. Olga in *The Samurai,* an immigrant
who stands in for me, comes from afar and could never be compared to a
French Normalian aristocrat.[12] I stress this nomadism that is gaining
ground and that prefigures a reunited Europe or globalization. By the
same token, while the Chinese mandarins were power figures and
the Saint-Germain-des-Prés ones had assumed a similar role as master
thinkers, the term *samurai* no longer emphasizes power but rather the
war between the sexes and the mortal risk that the fight for freedom

entails. In my generation, and mainly in the structuralist and poststructuralist Tel Quel movement, it was and still is a question of going to the limits of self. Thwarting identities and complicating certitudes. An endless analysis, to bring to the world. "I am a journeywoman"[13] in my essays and my "more-than-novels" that are only questions in the bud.

NOTES

1. MY ALPHABET; OR, HOW I AM A LETTER

1. Cf. Marcel Proust, *Finding Time Again*, in *In Search of Lost Time*, trans. Ian Patterson (New York: Penguin Classics, 2003).
2. Cf. "Diversity Is My Motto," chap. 24 in this volume.
3. Cf. Thomas Mann, "Germany, My Suffering," in *Order of the Day: Political Essays and Speeches of Two Decades* (Manchester, N.H.: Ayer, 1969).
4. Marcel Proust, *Contre Sainte-Beuve*, in *Marcel Proust on Art and Literature: 1896–1919*, trans. Sylvia Townsend Warner (New York: Carroll and Graf, 1997).
5. Proust, *Finding Time Again*.
6. Cf. Stéphane Mallarmé, "Verse Crisis," in *Mallarmé: The Poet and His Circle*, trans. Rosemary Lloyd (Ithaca, N.Y.: Cornell University Press, 2005).

2. RELIANCE

1. Stéphane Mallarmé, "Mystery in Literature," in *Mallarmé in Prose*, trans. Mary Ann Caws (New York: New Directions, 2001).
2. Dante Alighieri, *Paradise*, canto 33, trans. Dorothy Sayers (New York: Penguin Classics, 1962).
3. Religious theme appearing in fifteenth-century Italian painting.
4. Cf. Julia Kristeva, "Motherhood According to Giovanni Bellini," in *The Portable Kristeva*, trans. Thomas Gora, Alice Jardine, and Leon S. Roudiez (New York: Columbia University Press, 2002), 303.

3. HOW TO SPEAK TO LITERATURE WITH ROLAND BARTHES

1. Philip Roth, *Exit Ghost* (New York: Houghton Mifflin Harcourt, 2007).

2. Julia Kristeva, "How Does One Speak to Literature?" in *Desire in Language: A Semiotic Approach to Literature and Art*, trans. Tom Gora and Alice Jardine (New York: Columbia University Press, 1980), 93.

3. Cf. Georges Bataille, *Inner Experience*, trans. Leslie Anne Boldt (Albany: State University of New York Press, 1988); and Philippe Sollers, *Writing and the Experience of Limits*, trans. Philip Barnard and David Hayman (New York: Columbia University Press, 1983).

4. Roland Barthes, *Criticism and Truth*, trans. Katrine Pilcher Keuneman (Minneapolis: University of Minnesota Press, 1987).

5. Cf. Julia Kristeva, *Hannah Arendt*, trans. Ross Guberman (New York: Columbia University Press, 2003).

6. Barthes, *Criticism and Truth*.

7. Barthes, *Criticism and Truth*.

8. Barthes, *Criticism and Truth*.

9. Maurice Merleau-Ponty, *The Visible and the Invisible*, trans. Alphonso Lingis (Evanston, Ill.: Northwestern University Press, 1968).

10. Cf. Julia Kristeva, *Proust and the Sense of Time*, trans. Stephen Bann (London: Faber and Faber, 1993).

11. Kristeva, *Proust and the Sense of Time*.

12. Julia Kristeva, *The Revolution in Poetic Language*, trans. Margaret Waller (New York: Columbia University Press, 1984).

13. Cf. Julia Kristeva, *Powers of Horror: An Essay on Abjection*, trans. Leon Roudiez (New York: Columbia University Press, 1982).

14. Maurice Blanchot, *The Space of Literature*, trans. Ann Smock (Lincoln: University of Nebraska Press, 1982).

15. Jean-Paul Sartre, *Critique of Dialectical Reason*, trans. Alan Sheridan-Smith (London: Verso, 2004).

16. Cf. Julia Kristeva, "The Novel as Polylogue," in *Desire in Language*, trans. Thomas Gora (New York: Columbia University Press, 1980).

17. Barthes, *Criticism and Truth*.

18. Barthes, *Criticism and Truth*.

19. Barthes, *Criticism and Truth*.

20. Cf. Julia Kristeva, "Roland Barthes and Writing as Demystification," in *The Sense and Non-Sense of Revolt*, trans. Jeanine Herman (New York: Columbia University Press, 2001), 187–216.

21. Barthes, *Criticism and Truth*.

22. Barthes, *Criticism and Truth*; and Barthes, *Writing Degree Zero*, trans. Annette Lavers and Colin Smith (London: Jonathan Cape, 1967).

23.   Marcel Proust, "Time Regained," in *In Search of Lost Time*, trans. Ian Patterson (New York: Penguin Classics, 2003).

24.   Proust, "Time Regained."

25.   Barthes, *Criticism and Truth*.

4. EMILE BENVENISTE

1.   His mother, Maria Benveniste (born in Vilna, today Lithuania), taught Hebrew, French, and Russian at the Alliance Israelite Universelle school in Samokov (Bulgaria); his father, Mathatias Benveniste (born in Smyrna), spoke Ladino; his childhood environment was made up of Turkish, Arabic, modern Greek, and likely Slav. Many of the great linguists of the twentieth century, of Jewish origin, tended to study languages because of the multilingualism in their family milieu (the Darmesteter brothers, James and Arsène, Michel Bréal, Sylvain Lévi).

2.   A "Talmud Torah" would give students a Jewish cultural baggage, preparing them for the baccalaureate and enabling them to prepare for rabbinical studies. There the students learned Latin, Greek, Hebrew, German, and, with most particular care, French.

3.   Cf. Françoise Bader, "Sylvain Lévi," in *Trois linguists (trop) oubliés, Anamnèse*, no. 5 (2009) (Paris: L'Harmattan, 2010), 141–70.

4.   The signers implore the UFJ (UGIF) "to maintain as tight a union as possible between our French brothers and ourselves . . . encouraging nothing . . . that would morally isolate us from the national community to which we remain faithful, even punished by the law." Our translation. Cf. Marc Bloch, *The Strange Defeat* (New York: Norton, 1968).

5.   His *Vocabulaire des institutions indo-européenes*, 2 vols. (Paris: Minuit, 1969), is the most concrete example.

6.   Echoing Rilke, this condensed and allusive confession expresses the young linguist's nostalgia for a mother whom he left at the age of eleven, and who died when he was seventeen without his seeing her. Sensitive to the "latent virile violence" that attracted him in the "superficially feminine" appearance of a vigorous and "strong-as-a-man" maternality, Benveniste composed his self-portrait featuring poets (bachelors?) from Homer (the "Old Man of the Sea") to Lautréamont ("Old Ocean, Oh great celibate"). Cf. *Philosophies*, no. 1 (March 15, 1924), year of the publication of the first Manifeste du surrealism.

7.   The Rabbinic School on rue Vauquelin trained rabbis in Europe for the Eastern and African communities, "just as teachers were trained for schools." In a letter dated October 1918, the student's mother wrote that "the school situation" of her son Ezra has "become unbearable": he is drawn to languages and will study literature. Cf. Françoise Bader, "E. Benveniste, A Literary Anamnesis," *Incontri Linguistici*, no. 22 (1999): 20 (Rome).

8.   Cf. Emile Benveniste, *Problems in General Linguistics*, vol. 2, trans. Mary-Elizabeth Meek (Miami: University of Miami Press, 1971) (hereafter *PGL*).

9. Emile Benveniste, *Dernières leçons, College de France (1968–1969)*, coll. "Hautes Etudes," EHESS (Paris: Gallimard, Le Seuil, 2012) (hereafter cited as *DL*).

10. *DL*, 60.

11. Antoine Culioli created this project with his "theory of enunciatives," in studying the activity of language through the diversity of national languages.

12. Manuscripts in the BNF, PAP. OR. DON 0429, approx. 6–22; Chloé Laplantine presents an annotated transcription in *Emile Benveniste, Baudelaire* (Limoges: Lambert-Lucas, 2011).

13. But Benveniste borrowed the term *interpretant* from the American philosopher while specifying that he only used this "isolated denomination" and in particular in a "different" meaning (lesson 5), presumed to be phenomenological. Peirce's "thirdness" could nonetheless have supported the structure of the subject of the enunciation (Freud's oedipal structure) in Benveniste's semantics.

14. With Roland Barthes, *Zero Degree of Writing* (1953), *Elements of Semiology* (1956), Jacques Derrida, *Of Grammatology* (1967), *Voice and Phenomenon* (1967), and in the literary domain, after the "nouveau roman," with Philippe Sollers, *Drama* (1965), *Logic* (1968), *Numbers* (1968), *Writing and the Experience of Limits* (1971).

15. Edmund Husserl, *Ideas Pertaining to a Pure Phenomenology—First Book*, trans. F. Kersten (Leiden: Njhoff, 1982).

16. Cf. BNF, PAP. OR. DON 0429, env. 22, f. 260, cited by Laplantine in *Emile Benveniste, Baudelaire*.

17. Cf. Julia Kristeva, "Engendering the Formula," in *Desire in Language: A Semiotic Approach to Literature and Art*, trans. Thomas Gora (New York: Columbia University Press, 1980).

18. BNF, PAP. OR. DON 0429, env. 20, f. 204.

19. BNF, PAP. OR. DON 0429, env. 12, f. 56.

20. BNF, PAP. OR. DON 0429, env. 23, f. 358.

21. The quote in the heading is from a letter from Emile Benveniste, October 17, 1954: "Linguistics is universality, but the poor linguist is torn apart in the universe," in Georges Redard, "Biobibliographie d'Emile Benveniste," *DL*.

22. Cf. *DL*, 8.

23. I was finishing my doctoral thesis, which I defended in June 1968, as a foreign student exception, and I was beginning my research on the poetic language of Mallarmé and Lautréamont for my state thesis.

24. Madeleine Biardeau (1922–2010), *Théorie de la connaissance et philosophe de la parole dans le brahmanisme* (Berlin: Mouton, 1964).

25. Cf. Charles H. Kahn: "The Greek Verb 'To Be' and the Concept of Being," *Foundations of Language* 2, no. 3 (August 1966): 245–65.

26. Five letters of Antonin Artaud written in 1945 to Henri Parisot. Cf. Antonin Artaud, *Letters from Rodez* (Paris: GLM, 1946).

27. "We consider the bloody Revolution as the inevitable vengeance of the humiliated spirit. We . . . conceive it only in its social form. . . . The idea of Revolution is the best

and most effective safeguard for the individual." Cf. "Revolution, First and Always!" in *The Surrealist Revolution*, no. 5 (October 15, 1925): 31–32.

28.   Stéphane Mallarmé, "Mystery in Literature," in *Mallarmé in Prose*, ed. Mary Ann Caws (New York: New Directions, 2001).

29.   Cf. *DL*, 152.

5. FREUD, THE HEART OF THE MATTER

1.   Sigmund Freud, *The Interpretation of Dreams*, trans. A. Brill (New York: Macmillan, 1913).

2.   Sigmund Freud *The Complete Letters of Sigmund Freud to Wilhelm Fliess, 1887–1904*, trans. Jeffrey Moussaieff Masson (Cambridge, Mass.: Belknap, 1986); Max Schur, *Freud: Living and Dying* (New York: International Universities Press, 1972).

3.   Sigmund Freud, *Sexuality and the Psychology of Love*, trans. Shaun Whiteside (New York: Penguin, 2006).

4.   Freud, *Sexuality and the Psychology of Love*.

5.   Freud, *Sexuality and the Psychology of Love*.

6.   Debate on January 19, 2004, organized by the Bavarian Catholic Academy, Munich. See Jürgen Habermas and Joseph Ratzinger, "Les Fondements prépolitiques de l'Etat démocratique," trans. J. L. Schlegel, *Esprit*, no. 306 (July 2004): 5–28; republished in *Raison et religion. La Dialectique de la sécularisation* (Paris: Salvator, 2010). Cf. Julia Kristeva, "Penser la liberté en temps de détresse," in *La haine et le pardon* (Paris: Fayard, 2005), 15–27.

7.   Habermas and Ratzinger, "Les Fondements prépolitiques," 11; *Raison et religion*, 43.

8.   Habermas and Ratzinger, "Les Fondements prépolitiques," 8; *Raison et religion*, 36.

9.   Habermas and Ratzinger, "Les Fondements prépolitiques," 6; *Raison et religion*, 33.

10.   Habermas and Ratzinger, "Les Fondements prépolitiques," 16; *Raison et religion*, 55.

11.   Habermas and Ratzinger, "Les Fondements prépolitiques," 28; *Raison et religion*, 83.

12.   Sigmund Freud, *The Future of an Illusion*, 1927, in *The Standard Edition of the Complete Psychological Works of Sigmund Freud*, vol. 21, trans. James Strachey (London: Hogarth, 1968).

13.   Freud, *The Future of an Illusion*.

14.   Sigmund Freud, *Civilization and Its Discontents*, trans. James Strachey (New York: Norton, 1961); and "The Sigmund Freud-Romain Rolland Letters (1923–1936)."

15.   Cf. Julia Kristeva, *Tales of Love*, trans. Leon Roudiez (New York: Columbia University Press, 1987).

16.   Cf. Julia Kristeva, *The Incredible Need to Believe*, trans. Beverley Bie Brahic (New York: Columbia University Press, 2009).

17.   Jean-Paul Sartre, *The Words*, trans. Bernard Frechtman (New York: Vintage, 1981).

18.   Cf. Hannah Arendt: "The thread of tradition is broken and we shall not be able to renew it." In *The Life of the Mind* (New York: Harcourt, 1978); and Arendt, "The Crisis in Culture," in *Political Theory* (1988).

19. Marcel Proust, "To My Friend Willie Heath," in *Pleasures and Days*, trans. Andrew Brown (London: Alma Classics, 2013).

20. Marcel Proust, *Swann's Way*, trans. C. K. Scott Moncrieff (London: Chatto and Windus, 1921).

21. Cf. Julia Kristeva, *New Maladies of the Soul*, trans. Ross Guberman (New York: Columbia University Press, 1995).

22. Julia Kristeva, *The Black Sun: Depression and Melancholia*, trans. Leon Roudiez (New York: Columbia University Press, 1989).

23. Simone de Beauvoir, *All Said and Done* (New York: Knopf, 1972).

24. Simone de Beauvoir, *The Second Sex*, trans. Constance Borde and Sheila Malovany-Chevallier (New York: Knopf, 2010), 57.

25. Cf. "Reliance: What Is Loving for a Mother?" chap. 2 in this volume.

26 Cf. Julia Kristeva, "Adolelscence, un syndrome d'idéalité," in *La haine et le pardon* (Paris: Fayard, 2005), 447–60.

27. Zones of educational priority [translators' note].

6. THE CONTEMPORARY CONTRIBUTION OF PSYCHOANALYSIS

1. Julia Kristeva, *Hatred and Forgiveness*, trans. Jeanine Herman (New York: Columbia University Press, 2010).

2. Sigmund Freud, "Was Moses an Egyptian?" in *Moses and Monotheism*, trans. Katherine Jones (New York: Vintage/Random House, 1955).

3. Better known under the name Akhenaton.

4. Jacques Lacan, *The Subversion of the Subject and the Dialectic of Desire*, trans. Alan Sheridan (New York: Tavistock/Routledge, 1977).

5. Cf. Julia Kristeva, *Powers of Horror: An Essay on Abjection*, trans. Leon Roudiez (New York: Columbia University Press, 1982).

6. Cf. Julia Kristeva, *Tales of Love*, trans. Leon Roudiez (New York: Columbia University Press, 1987).

7. *Revolution in Poetic Language*, trans. Margaret Waller (New York: Columbia University Press, 1984).

8. Daniel N. Stern, "'The Pre-Narrative Envelope': An Alternative View of 'Unconscious Fantasy' in Infancy," *Bul. Anna Freud Centre* 15 (1992): 291–318; and Kristeva, *Hatred and Forgiveness*.

9. Cf. Julia Kristeva, "Oedipus Again; or Phallic Monism," in *The Sense and Non-Sense of Revolt*, trans. Jeanine Herman, 65–90 (New York: Columbia University Press, 2001).

10. Cf. Yirmiyahu Yovel, *Spinoza and Other Heretics* (Princeton, N.J.: Princeton University Press, 1989).

11. Cf. Julia Kristeva, *The Portable Kristeva*, *The Female Genius*, vol. 1: *Hannah Arendt*; vol. 2, *Melanie Klein*; vol. 3 *Colette*, trans. Ross Guberman (New York: Columbia University Press, 2000).

12. Colette, *The Break of Day*, trans. Enid McLeod (New York: Farrar, Straus and Giroux, 1961).

13. Cf. "The Dead Father," a two-day international symposium, Low Library, Columbia University, New York, April 29–30, 2006.

14. Julia Kristeva, "Open Letter to the President of the Republic on Citizens with Disabilities, for the Use of Those Who Are Disabled and Those Who Are Not," in *Hatred and Forgiveness*.

15. Cf. "Disability Revisited: The Tragic and Chance," chap. 17 in this volume.

7. A FATHER IS BEING BEATEN TO DEATH

1. Julia Kristeva, *The Old Man and the Wolves*, trans. Barbara Bray (New York: Columbia University Press, 1993).

2. Sigmund Freud, *Totem and Taboo*, trans. James Strachey (Abingdon: Routledge and Kegan Paul, 1950).

3. *National Geographic* 80 (May 2006) (French ed.): 5–19.

4. Sigmund Freud, "A Child Is Being Beaten, in "A Contribution to the Study of the Origin of Sexual Perversions," trans. A. and J. Strachey, *CP* 2 (1924), 172–201.

5. Julia Kristeva, "On the Extraneous of the Phallus; or, the Feminine Between Illusion and Disillusion," in *The Sense and Non-Sense of Revolt*, trans. Jeanine Herman (New York: Columbia University Press, 2000).

6. Julia Kristeva, *Tales of Love*, trans. Leon Roudiez (New York: Columbia University Press, 1987).

7. Julia Kristeva, *Revolution in Poetic Language*, trans. Margaret Waller (New York: Columbia University Press, 1984).

8. Julia Kristeva, *This Incredible Need to Believe*, trans. Beverley Bie Brahic (New York: Columbia University Press, 2011).

9. Kristeva, *The Sense and Non-Sense of Revolt*.

10. Cf. André Green, *La Déliaison, psychanalyse, anthropologie et littérature* (Paris: Les Belles Lettres, 1982; and Pluriel, 1998).

11. Julia Kristeva, "Suffer," in *This Incredible Need to Believe*.

12. Gilles Deleuze, *Présentation de Sacher Masoch* (Paris: Minuit, 1967), 100.

13. Georg Wilhelm Friedrich Hegel, *Lectures on the Philosophy of Religion*, trans. Robert F. Brown, Peter C. Hodgson, J. Michael Stewart, and H. S. Harris (Berkeley: University of California Press, 1988).

14. Friedrich Nietzsche, *The Anti-Christ*, trans. H. L. Menken (New York: Cosimo Classics, 2005).

15. Meister Eckhart, *The Essential Sermons, Commentaries, Treatises and Defense*, trans. Bernard McGinn and Edmund Colledge (New York: Paulist Press, 1981).

16. John of the Cross, *The Spiritual Canticle*, trans. David Lewis, Catholic First (online text).

17. Julia Kristeva, *Black Sun: Depression and Melancholia*, trans. Leon Roudiez (New York: Columbia University Press, 1989).

18. Kristeva, *Tales of Love.*

19. About sublimation in psychoanalysis, Kristeva, *Sense and Non-Sense of Revolt*, and Kristeva, "L'impudence d'énoncer: la langue maternelle," in *La haine et le pardon* (Paris: Fayard, 2005), 393–410.

20. Colette, *Break of Day*, trans. Enid McLeod (New York: Farrar, Straus and Giroux, 2002).

21. Kristeva, *New Maladies of the Soul.*

8. MATERNAL EROTICISM

1. Sigmund Freud, *Formulations on the Two Principles of Mental Functioning*, 1911, Papers on Metapsychology; *Papers on Applied Psycho-Analysis* (London: Hogarth and Institute of Psycho Analysis, 1924–1950).

2. Jean-Michel Hirt, *Vestiges du Dieu: athéisme et religiosité* (Paris: Grasset, 1998).

3. Lou Andreas-Salomé, *Anal and Sexual* (Sesto S. Giovanni: Mimesis, 2012); also her letters and the *Journal*, from her meeting with Freud in 1895 to the last Open Letter to Freud, 1931. Freud did not go along with her/take up this position of hers as he was in a dangerous position in 1911 (this was also the date of the Weimar Congress to which he invited Lou) due to Ferenczi's dissidence, but especially to that of Jung, who distanced himself from sexuality tied to the oedipal myth and incest.

4. Sigmund Freud, "The Ego and the Id and Other Works (1917–1919)," in *The Standard Edition of the Complete Psychological Works of Sigmund Freud*, trans. James Strachey with Anna Freud (London: Hogarth and the Institute of Psycho-Analysis, 1953–1974).

5. Lou Andreas-Salomé, *Lou Andreas-Salomé: The Freud Journal (1958/1964)*, trans. Stanley A. Leavy (New York: Basic Books, 1964).

6. Sigmund Freud and Lou Andreas-Salomé, *Sigmund Freud and Lou Andreas Salomé Letters*, trans. William and Elaine Bobson-Scott (New York: Norton, 1972).

7. Lou Andreas-Salomé, Letter to Rilke, March 1, 1914, in *Rainer Maria Rilke and Lou Andreas-Salomé*, trans. Edward Snow and Michael Winkler (New York: Norton, 2006).

8. Maurice Merleau-Ponty, *Phenomenology of Perception* (London: Routledge, 2012), 106.

9. Maurice Merleau-Ponty, *The Visible and the Invisible*, trans. A. Lingis (Evanston, Ill.: Northwestern University Press, 1968).

10. Cf. "Reliance: What Is Loving for a Mother?" chap. 2 in this volume.

11. The woman is a "hole," *nakèva* in Hebrew; and Marie, Queen of the Church, is no less of a "hole" in the Son-the Father-the Holy Ghost Christian trinity. Cf. Philippe Sollers, "Le Trou de la Vierge," in *Eloge de l'Infini* (Paris: Gallimard, 2001), 921–33.

12. Julia Kristeva, *The Revolution in Poetic Language*, trans. Margaret Waller (New York: Columbia University Press, 1984).

13. Colette, *Break of Day*, trans. Enid McLeod (New York: Farrar, Straus and Giroux, 2002).

14. Bernard Brusset, *Psychanalyse du lien* (Paris: Presses Universitaires de France, 2005).

15. Martin Heidegger, *What Is a Thing?* trans. W. B. Barton and Vera Deutsch (London: Gateway, 1968); Jacques Lacan, *The Ethics of Psychoanlysis*, trans. Dennis Porter (New York: Norton, 1992).

16. Sigmund Freud, *Repression*, in *The Standard Edition of the Complete Psychological Works of Sigmund Freud*, vol. 13, trans. James Strachey (London: Hogarth, 1974). Cf. J. Laplanche and S. Leclaire, "L'inconscient, une étude psychanalytique," in *Problématiques*, vol. 4 (Paris: Presses Universitaires de France, 1981), 303 sq.

17. Donald Woods Winicott, "Mind and Its Relation to the Psyché-soma," paper presented to Medical Section of the British Psychological Society, December 14, 1949, rev. October 1953.

18. Cf. "Antigone, Limit, and Horizon," chap. 12 in this volume.

19. Cf. Jacques Lacan, *The Seminar*, book 7: *The Ethics of Psychoanalysis, 1959–1960*, trans. Dennis Porter (New York: Norton, 1992).

20. Ilse Barande, "Antinomies du concept de perversion et épigenèse de l'appétit d'excitation. (Notre duplicité d'être inachevé ou la mère-version)," 42nd Congress of Psychoanalysis for French-Speaking Analysts, *Revue française de psychanalyse* 47, no. 1 (1983): 143–282.

21. Julia Kristeva, *Powers of Horror: An Essay on Abjection*, trans. Leon Roudiez (New York: Columbia University Press, 1982).

22. Baudelaire associates the "rotting carcass" with "sensual pleasure," an association of which Jean-Michel Hirt offers an exquisite analysis; Céline is torn between the graceful dancer and his "female companions who squander you ad infinitum"; and there are de Kooning's hideous matrons (among so many others) who testify to the same.

23. André Green, *On Private Madness* (London: Hogarth Press, 1986).

24. Cf. Julia Kristeva, *Tales of Love*, trans. Leon Roudiez (New York: Columbia University Press, 1987).

25. Julia Kristeva, "On the Extraneousness of the Phallus, or, the Feminine Between Illusion and Disillusion," in *The Sense and Non-Sense of Revolt*, trans. Jeanine Herman (New York: Columbia University Press, 2000).

26. Julia Kristeva, "La passion maternelle et son destin aujourd'hui," in *Seule une femme* (Paris: Editions de l'Aube, 2007), 170–82.

27. Cf. Roland Barthes, *Mourning Diary*, trans. Richard Howard (New York: Hill and Wang, 2010).

28. Cf. Judith Thurman, *From Secrets of the Flesh: A Life of Colette* (London: Bloomsbury, 1999).

29. Georges Bataille, *My Mother, Mme Edwarda and the Dead Man*, trans. Austryn Wainhouse (London: Boyars, 1989).

30. Sigmund Freud, "On the Most General of Debasements in Love Life," in *The Sexual Life of Man*.

31. Man holds to it religiously (Barthes, *Mourning Diary*: how "not to pray, to bless" in mourning the mother) because the anxiety of narcissistic collapse—opening to an abyss beneath castration anxiety—exercises a literally sovereign hold on him.

32. Cf. Kristeva, *Powers of Horror*.

33. Cf. chap. 2 in this volume.

34. Cf. Jean-Michel Hirt, *Les Infidèles, s'aimer soi-même, comme un étranger* (Paris: Grasset, 2003). This work is the third part of a trilogy he wrote with *Vertiges de Dieu* (1998), and *Le Miroir du Prophète* (1993).

35. Kristeva, "Stabat Mater," in *Tales of Love*.

36. Simone de Beauvoir, *The Second Sex*, trans. Constance Borde and Malovany-Chevallier (New York: Knopf, 2010), 775.

9. SPEAKING IN PSYCHOANALYSIS

1. "La cure de parole," presented at the 67th Congress of Psychoanalysis for French-Speaking Analysts, Paris, May 17–20, 2007.

2. Dominique Clerc-Maugendre, "L'écoute de la parole," *Revue française de Psychanalyse* 71, no. 5 (December 2007): 1285–1340; and Laurent Danon-Boileau, "La forge du langage," *Revue française de Psychanalyse* 71, no. 5 (December 2007): 1341–1409.

3. Maurice Merleau-Ponty, *The Visible and the Invisible*, trans. Alphonso Lingis (Evanston, Ill.: Northwestern University Press, 1968).

4. Crossing of terms in which elements of parallel groups are reversed, following the AB/BA structure—for example, the flesh of the world/the world of the flesh.

5. Maurice Merleau-Ponty, *Phenomenology of Perception* (London: Routledge, 2012). This modern use of the term *flesh* refers back to its Greek tradition. In the first place, *Chair*, sarx, is linked to sensations: *Sextus Empiricus* (Against the Professors, 7:290) posits that the "carnal mass" is the seat of sensations; Plato attributes desire to the body, *soma* (Phedon, 82), more "figurable," as the Latin corpus demonstrates; but Epicurus goes back to the idea of "pleasure of the flesh:" the flesh aspires to an infinite pleasure, that only reason (*dianoïa*) can restrain. Judaism resembles this Epicurean association, while exploring it in its own fashion. In the Bible, flesh, *basar* or *scherr*, represents the deadly nature of man capable of sin, without developing the struggle between flesh and spirit. With the New Testament comes the ambiguous notion of the flesh, sick body, weakness of knowledge, defilement even, which, according to Paul, nonetheless is the corporal condition indispensable to really participate in Christ's message—to truly believe. I use the term *flesh* in what follows according to Merleau-Ponty, in giving it a psychoanalytic interpretation.

6. I will not discuss here the distinction between sensation (conscious reflection of exterior reality through the sense organs) and perception (conscious representation of it).

7. Emile Benveniste, "Remarks on the Function of Language in Freudian Theory," in *Problems in General Linguistics*, trans. Mary Elizabeth Meek (Miami, Fla.: University of Miami Press, 1971).

8. He is at the top of the scale when he says that a well is deep, and at the bottom when he names its height.

9. Brought back by Saussure at first in a restricted way, as signified-signifier unconcerned by the referent, and then in a way more attentive to the unconscious, through the Kabbalistic web of anagrams.

10. Cf. Julia Kristeva, "The Metamorphoses of Language in Freudian Theory," in *The Sense and Non-Sense of Revolt*, trans. Jeanine Herman (New York: Columbia University Press, 2000); and Kristeva, "The Impudence of Uttering: The Mother Tongue," trans. Anne Marsel, http://www.kristeva.fr/impudence.html.

11. On this point I agree with Daniel Widlöcher, "Psychoanalysis of the Instant," *L'Inactuel*, no. 2 (1994): 75–88.

12. Daniel N. Stern " 'The Pre-Narrative Envelope': An Alternative View of 'Unconscious Fantasy' in Infancy," *Bul. Anna Freud Centre* 15 (1992): 291–318.

13. This is close to Laurent Danon-Boileau's "nostalgia" (cf. "La forge du langage").

14. "As low as it gets"; "sleep staves off hunger"; "have eyes bigger than your belly" [translators' note].

15. Alphone Daudet and Paul Arène, "Mr. Seguin's Goat," in *Letters from My Windmill*, trans. Frederick Davies (New York: Penguin, 1978).

16. Brevity has the merit of revelation; Heracles knew this already when he wrote: "Oracles do not speak nor do they hide, they make signs." Cf. Emile Benveniste, "A Linguist Who Neither Says nor Hides, but Signifies," chap. 4 in this volume.

17. Reciprocal permutations and substitutes of the five senses with each other.

18. "The Poem of Hashish," trans. Aleister Crowly, 1895, https://www.erowid.org/culture/characters/baudelaire_charles/baudelaire_charles_poem1.shtml.

19. Widlöcher, "Psychoanalysis of the Instant."

20. Cf. Julia Kristeva, *Proust and the Sense of Time*, trans. Stephen Bann (London: Faber and Faber, 1993)

21. According to Frances Tustin's "latent and endogenous autism" in *The Black Hole of the Psyche*, trans. Fr. P. Chemla (Paris: Seuil, 1989).

22. Marcel Proust, *Finding Time Again*, in *In Search of Lost Time*, trans. Ian Patterson (New York: Penguin Classics, 2003).

23. Cf. letter to Lucien Daudet, November 27, 1913, in *Correspondance*, vol. 12 (Paris: Plon, 1984), 342–43.

24. Cf. Julia Kristeva, "In Search of the Madeleine," in *Proust and the Sense of Time*).

25. Colette, "Fleurs," "La Treille muscatel," in *Prisons et Paradis* (Paris: Livre de Poche, 2004).

26. Colette, *Break of Day*, trans. Enid McLeod (New York: Farrar, Straus and Giroux, 1961).

27. Cf. Julia Kristeva, "The Tender Shoot," in *Female Genius*, vol. 3: *Colette*, trans. Jane Mary Todd (New York: Columbia University Press, 2004).

28. "Note for a letter to the Balinais," quoted in Julia Kristeva, *The Revolution in Poetic Language*, trans. Margaret Waller (New York: Columbia University Press, 1984).

29. Jacques Derrida, *Writing and Difference* (Chicago: University of Chicago Press, 1978). Derrida talks about the trace as an archi-writing, "first possibility of speech," and also the first possibility of graphism. Cf. also Derrida, *Mal d'archive: Une Impression freudienne* (Paris: Galilée, col "Incises," 1995).

30. André Green, *Le Discours vivant* (Paris: Presses Universitaires de France, 1973), 227–50. Green juxtaposes the language of linguists, a formal system uniting homogenous elements, with the language of psychoanalysts, consisting of a heterogeneity of the signifier, supported by the Freudian theory of the drive and its representatives (affect/representation).

31. Cf. Green, *Le Discours vivant*, 17–100; and "Narration in Psychoanalysis," in Julia Kristeva, *Hatred and Forgiveness*, trans. Janine Herman (New York: Columbia University Press, 2010).

32. Cf. conference organized by Julia Kristeva, Daniel Widlöcher, and Pierre Fedida in 1994, "Actualité des modèles freudiens: language, image, pensée," in *Revue internationale de psychopathologie*, no. 2 (Paris: Presses Universitaires de Paris, 1995).

33. I have built my conception of heterogeneity relative to "speech in psychoanalysis" on George Bataille's research on "heterology," in *Oeuvres completes*, vol. 2: *Oeuvres posthumes (1922–1940)* (Paris: Gallimard, 1987), 171. Cf. also Green's notion, *Le Discours vivant*, 139.

34. Sigmund Freud, *The Ego and the Id*, trans. Joan Riviere (New York: Norton, 1960).

35. Freud, *The Ego and the Id*.

36. "Mystik die dunkle Selsbtwahrnehmung des Reiches ausserhalb des Ichs, des Es"; Sigmund Freud, note from August 22, 1938, in "Schriften aus dem Nachlass," *Gesammelte Werke*, vol. 17(London: Imago, 1946); cf. also *Résultats, idées, problèmes* [1921–1938], vol. 2, trans. J. Altounian, A. Bourguignon, P. Cotet, and A. Rauzy (Paris: Presses Universitaires de France, 1985), 288.

37. Sigmund Freud, *New Introductory Lectures on Psycho-analysis*, trans. James Strachey (New York: Norton, 1990).

38. Cf. Julia Kristeva, "Symbolic Castration: A Question," in *New Maladies of the Soul*, trans. Ross Guberman (New York: Columbia University Press, 1995).

39. André Green, "The Unbinding Process," in *On Private Madness* (London: H. Karnac, 2005).

40. Cf. Daniel Widlöcher, "L'inconscient psychanalytique, une question toujours ouverte," *Cahiers philosophiques*, no. 107 (2006): 32.

41. Freud, *The Ego and the Id*, 57.

42. Cf. Sigmund Freud, "Traitement psychique," in *Résultats, idées, problèmes*, vol. 1 (Paris: Presses Universitaires de France, 1984), 8.

43. Sigmund Freud, "Sigmund Freud, "Die Verneinung, la dénégation," 1925, *Le Coq héron*, no. 8 (1982).

44. Cf. Kristeva, "Symbolic Castration."

45. Freud, *The Ego and the Id*.

46. Cf. "Maternal Eroticism," chap. 8 in this volume.

10. AFFECT, THAT "INTENSE DEPTH OF WORDS"

1. Baltasar Gracián, *The Art of Worldly Wisdom*, trans. Christopher Maurer (Radford, Va.: Wilder, 2007).

2. Teresa of Avila, *The Interior Castle*, *The Collected Works of St. Teresa of Avila*, trans. E. Allison Peers (Radford, Va.: Wilder, 2008).

3. Teresa of Avila, *The Interior Castle*.

4. Jacques Lacan, *The Seminar of Jacques Lacan*, trans. John Forrester (New York: Norton, 1991).

5. Sigmund Freud, "Freud's Comparative Study of Hysterical and Organic Paralyses," *Archives of Neurology* 60, no. 11 (2003): 1646–50, doi:10.1001/archneur.60.11.1646.

6. Cf. André Green, *Fabric of Affect in the Psychoanalytic Discourse*, trans. Alan Sheridan (New York: Routledge, 1999).

7. Sigmund Freud, *Studies on Hysteria*, trans. A. A. Brill, Nervous and Mental Disease Monograph Series no. 61 (New York: Nervous and Mental Disease Publishing, 1937).

8. Cf. Lacan, *The Seminar of Jacques Lacan.*

9. Sigmund Freud, *An Outline of Psychoanalysis*, Standard Edition of the Complete Works of Sigmund Freud, ed. James Strachey, vol. 23 (1938), 141–207.

10. Sigmund Freud, *New Introductory Lectures on Psycho-Analysis*, Standard Edition of the Complete Works of Sigmund Freud, ed. James Strachey (1933); and Green, *Fabric of Affect.*

11. Cf. Julia Kristeva, *The Revolution in Poetic Language*, trans. Margaret Waller (New York: Columbia University Press, 1984).

12. Julia Kristeva, *Teresa, My Love. An Imagined Life of the Saint of Avila*, trans. Lorna Scott Fox (New York: Columbia University Press, 2014).

13. Kristeva, *The Revolution in Poetic Language.*

14. Cf. Stéphane Mallarmé, *Variations sur un sujet. Crise de vers*, in *Oeuvres complètes* (Paris: Gallimard, coll. "Bibliothèque de la Pléiade," 1945).

15. Donald Woods Winnicott, "Mind and Its Relation to the Psyche-Soma," *British Journal of Medical Psychology* 27, no. 4 (September 1954).

16. Cf. "Speaking in Psychoanalysis: From Symbols to Flesh and Back Again" and "In Jerusalem: Monotheisms and Secularization and the Need to Believe," chaps. 9 and 19 in this volume.

17. Sigmund Freud, note of August 22, 1938. Cf. "Speaking in Psychoanalysis," n. 1.

18. Ignatius of Loyola, "Rules for Perceiving the Movements Caused in the Soul," in *The Spiritual Exercises of St. Ignatius*, trans. Elder Mullan (Santa Cruz, Calif.: Evinity, 2009); and Julia Kristeva, "La Loquella," in *Intimate Revolt and the Future of Revolt*, trans. Jeanine Herman (New York: Columbia University Press, 2002).

19. Cf. Julia Kristeva, "Ego affectus est," in *Tales of Love*, trans. Leon Roudiez (New York: Columbia University Press, 1987).

20. Saint Bernard, *Bernard of Clairvaux, Selected Works*, trans. G. R. Evans (Mahwah, N.J.: Paulist Press, 1987).

21. Cf. Kristeva, *Teresa, My Love.*

22. French: *connaissance, co-naissance* [translators' note].

12. ANTIGONE, LIMIT AND HORIZON

1. Sophocles, "Antigone," http://records.viu.ca/~johnstoi/sophocles/antigone.htm, trans. Ian Johnston (2005).

2. G.W.F. Hegel, *Phenomenology of Spirit*, trans. A. V. Miller (Oxford: Clarendon, 1977).

3. Nicole Loraux, "La Main d'Antigone," 1985, postface, in Sophocles, *Antigone*, trans. P. Mazon (Paris: Les Belles Lettres, 1997), 105–43.

4. Loraux, "La Main d'Antigone," 110.

5. Jacques Lacan, *The Seminar of Jacques Lacan*, trans. John Forrester (New York: Norton, 1991).

6. V. 509, "And Justice living with the gods below sent no such laws for men." Not *laws*, but *horizons*?

7. Lacan, *The Seminar of Jacques Lacan*.

8. Emile Benveniste, *Indo-European Language and Society*, trans. Elisabeth Palmer (London: Faber and Faber, 1969).

9. Cf. "The Bible: Prohibition Against Sacrifice," in "In Jerusalem: Monotheisms and Secularization and the Need to Believe," chap. 19 in this volume.

10. Cf. "A Father Is Being Beaten to Death," chap. 7 in this volume.

11. Cf. "The Passion According to Teresa of Avila," chap. 13 in this volume.

12. Cf. Judith Butler, *Antigone's Claim* (New York: Columbia University Press, 2002).

13. Cf. Julia Kristeva, "The Extraneousness of the Phallus or the Feminine Between Illusion and Disillusion," in *The Sense and Non-Sense of Revolt*, trans. Jeanine Herman (New York: Columbia University Press, 2001); and Kristeva, "The Two-Sided Oedipal," in *Hatred and Forgiveness*, trans. Jeanine Herman (New York: Columbia University Press, 2010).

13. THE PASSION ACCORDING TO TERESA OF AVILA

1. Cf. Julia Kristeva, *Teresa, My Love*, trans. Lorna Scott Fox (New York: Columbia University Press, 2014).

2. Cf. Sigmund Freud, "Drives and Their Fates," in *The Unconscious*, trans. Graham Frankland (London: Penguin, 2005).

3. F. M. Dostoevsky, *The Insulted and Humiliated*, trans. Ignat Avsey (Richmond: Alma, 2012).

4. Cf. "A Father Is Being Beaten to Death" and "In Jerusalem: Monotheisms and Secularization and the Need to Believe," chaps. 7 and 19 in this volume, respectively.

5. Cf. Julia Kristeva, "God Is Love," in *Tales of Love*, trans. Leon S. Roudiez (New York: Columbia University Press, 1989).

6. Teresa of Avila, *Thoughts on the Love of God*, in *The Complete Works of Saint Teresa of Jesus*, trans. E. Allison Peers (London: Continuum, 2002).

7. Cf. Kristeva, *Teresa, My Love*.

8. Cf. Rudolph M. Bell, *Holy Anorexia* (Chicago: University of Chicago Press, 1987).

9 *The Life of Saint Teresa of Avila by Herself*, trans. J. M. Cohen (Harmondsworth: Penguin, 1957) [translators' note].

10. Jacques Lacan, *Encore: The Seminar of Jacques Lacan*, book 20, trans. Bruce Fink (New York: Norton, 1999).

11. Kristeva, *Teresa, My Love*.

12. Cf. "Affect, That Intense Depth of Words," chap. 10, this volume.

13. Kristeva, *Teresa, My Love*.

14. Kristeva, *Teresa, My Love.*

15. Kristeva, *Teresa, My Love.*

16. Edmund Husserl, *Ideas Pertaining to a Pure Phenomenology—First Book*, trans. F. Kersten (Leiden: Njhoff, 1982).

17. Kristeva, *Teresa, My Love.*

18. Kristeva, *Teresa, My Love.*

19. Kristeva, *Teresa, My Love.*

20. Gottfried Leibniz, letter to André Morell, Dec. 10, 1696, trans. Lloyd Strickland, http: //www.leibniz-translations.com/morellmay1697.htm.

21. Cf. Kristeva, "In Jerusalem."

14. BEAUVOIR DREAMS

1. Simone de Beauvoir, *All Said and Done* (New York: Knopf, 1972) [our translation].

2. Simone de Beauvoir, *The Second Sex*, trans. Constance Borde and Sheila Malovany-Chevallier (New York: Knopf, 2010), 49.

3. Beauvoir, *The Second Sex*, 49.

4. Beauvoir, *All Said and Done.*

5. *Totem and Taboo* is dismissed as one of the "strange novels"; there is again a serious lack of understanding of "progress," which for Freud is represented by paternal religion and Judaism's intellectual spirituality, according to Moses and Monotheism, in Beauvoir, *The Second Sex*, 53.

6. Beauvoir, *The Second Sex*, 55.

7. Beauvoir, *All Said and Done.* All quotations in the remainder of this chapter are from this work.

8. Emphasis by Simone de Beauvoir.

9. Julia Kristeva, *Hatred and Forgiveness*, trans. Janine Herman (New York: Columbia University Press, 2010).

16. SPEECH, THAT EXPERIENCE

1. Benedict XVI, *To Seek God, Meeting with Representatives from the World of Culture*, Paris, September 12, 2008, College des Bernardins, Libreria Editrice Vaticana.

2. Julia Kristeva, *Murder in Byzantium*, trans. C. Jon Delogu (New York: Columbia University Press, 2006).

3. Sigmund Freud and Carl Gustav Jung, *Correspondence (1906–1914)*, trans. R. F. C. Hull and Ralph Manheim (Princeton: Princeton University Press, 1994).

4. Cf. "Affect, That 'Intense Depth of Words,'" chap. 10 in this volume.

5. Benedict XVI: "*It perceives in the words the Word, the Logos itself, which spreads its mystery through this multiplicity and the reality of a human history.*" Cf. *To Seek God.*

6. Benedict XVI, *To Seek God.*

7. Benedict XVI, *To Seek God.*
8. Stéphane Mallarmé, "Mystery in Literature, Music and Letters," in *Mallarmé in Prose,* trans. Mary Ann Caws and Jill Anderson (New York: New Direction Books, 2001).
9. Benedict XVI, *To Seek God.*
10. Antonin Artaud, *L'Enclume des forces,* in *Oeuvres complètes* (Paris: Galllimard, 1976).
11. Benedict XVI, *To Seek God.*
12. Marcel Proust, Letter to Lucien Daudet, November 27, 1913.
13. Benedict XVI, *To Seek God.*
14. Benedict XVI, *To Seek God.*
15. Benedict XVI, *To Seek God.*
16. Sigmund Freud, *The Future of an Illusion,* trans. James Strachey (New York: Norton, 1989).
17. Cf. Philippe Sollers, *Les Voyageurs du temps* (Paris: Gallimard 2009), 143–51, coll. "Folio," n. 5182, 151–60.
18. Philippe Sollers, *Nombres,* (Paris: Gallimard, 2000), coll. "L'Imaginaire," n. 425, 105.
19. Friedrich Nietzsche, *The Antichrist,* trans. H. L. Mencken (New York: Cosimo, 2005).
20. Benedict XVI, *To Seek God.*
21. Benedict XVI, *To Seek God.*
22. Benedict XVI, *To Seek God.*
23. Benedict XVI, *To Seek God.*

17. DISABILITY REVISITED

1. Julia Kristeva and Jean Vanier, *Leur regard perce nos ombres* (Paris: Fayard, 2011).
2. Philippe Sollers, in *Picasso le héros,* Le Cercle d'art, 28, reprinted in *Eloge de l'infini* (Paris: Gallimard, 2001), 142.
3. Cf. Gilles Bernheim, *N'oublions pas de penser la France* (Paris: Stock, 2012), 119.
4. Cf. Speech by Pope Benedict XVI at St-Mary of the Angels Basilica, Assisi, October 27, 2011, http://www.vatican.va/holy_father/benedict_xvi/speeches/2011/october/documents/hf_ben-xvi_pre_20111027_assisi_fr.html.
5. Julia Kristeva, *Hatred and Forgiveness,* trans. Jeanine Herman (New York: Columbia University Press, 2010).
6. Jean-Claude Ameisen, *La Sculpture du vivant* (Paris: Seuil, 1999).
7. Especially in his description of its own-most possibilities as an analytic of finitude: i.e., the "proximity" of the being with the "privative" character of the disjointure of being, which is prior to all singularity. Martin Heidegger, *Basic Concepts,* trans. Gary Aylesworth (Bloomington: Indiana University Press, 1941).
8. Cf. Emmanuel Falque, *God, the Flesh and the Other from Irenaeus to Duns Scotus,* trans. William Christian Hackettis (Evanston, Ill.: Northwestern University Press, 2014).
9. Nancy L. Eiesland, *The Disabled God: Toward a Liberatory Theology of Disability* (Nashville, Tenn.: Abington, 1994).
10. Baruch Spinoza, *Ethics,* 3, proposition 2, trans. Samuel Shirley (Indiana: Hackett, 1992).

18. FROM "CRITICAL MODERNITY" TO "ANALYTICAL MODERNITY"

1. Cf. Stéphane Mosès, *The Angel of History: Rosenzweig, Benjamin, Scholem,* trans. Barbara Harshav (Stanford, Calif.: Stanford University Press, 2006).

2. Julia Kristeva, *Strangers to Ourselves,* trans. Leon Roudiez (New York: Columbia University Press, 1991).

3. "Trois prières pour l'étranger dans l'Ancien Testament," 1997, in Stéphane Mosès, *L'Eros et la loi. Lectures bibliques* (Paris: Seuil, 2010 [1999]).

4. Jonathan Sacks, *The Dignity of Difference* (London: Bloomsbury Academic, 2003).

5. Cf. "The double signifyingness," in "Emile Benveniste, a Linguist Who Neither Says nor Hides, but Signifies," chap. 4 in this volume.

6. Cf. chap. 4 in this volume.

7. Cf. Julia Kristeva, "La fonction prédicative et le sujet parlant," in *Polylogue* (Paris: Editions du Seuil, 1977), 323–56; and Stéphane Mosès, "Emile Benveniste et la linguistique du dialogue," *Revue de métaphysique et de morale* 4, no. 32 (2001): 9n.

8. Franz Rosenzweig, *The Star of Redemption,* trans. Barbara Galli (Madison: University of Wisconsin Press, 2005).

9. Augustine of Hippo, *The Master (De magistro),* ed. Günther Weigel, Corpus Scriptorum, Ecclesiastorum Latinorum (Vienna: Tempsky, 1969).

10. Cf. John Paul II, "Faith and Reason," Encyclical Letter (London: Catholic Truth Society, 1998).

11. Cf. chap. 4 of this volume.

12. Emile Benveniste, *Dictionary of Indo-European Concepts and Society,* trans. Elizabeth Palmer (Chicago: University of Chicago Press, 2016).

13. Cf. Julia Kristeva, "Sur les pas du passeur" (preface), in Stéphane Mosès, *Rêves de Freud* (Paris: Gallimard, 2001), 9–34.

14. Cf. Julia Kristeva, *Hannah Arendt,* trans. Ross Guberman (New York: Columbia University Press, 2003).

15. Cf. Stéphane Mosès, "Ulysse chez Kafka," in *Exégèse d'une legende. Lectures de Kafka* (Paris: Editions de l'Eclat, 2006), 15–46.

16. Cf. Stéphane Mosès, "Brecht and Benjamin interprètent Kafka," in *Exégèse d'une legende,* 71–101.

17. Walter Benjamin, "Image of Proust," trans. Carol Jacob, *Comparative Literature* 86, no. 6 (December 1971): 910–32.

19. IN JERUSALEM

1. Cf. "A Father Is Being Beaten to Death," chap. 7 in this volume.

2. Chap. 7 in this volume.

3. Jacques Lacan, "Symbol and Language as Structure and Limit of the Psychoanalytical Field" and "The Symbolic Debt," in *Ecrits,* trans. Bruce Fink (New York: Norton, 2006).

4. Jacques Lacan, "The Four Fundamental Concepts of Psychoanalysis," in *The Seminar of Jacques Lacan*, book 11, trans. Bruce Fink (New York: Norton, 1998).

5. Jacques Lacan, "The Psychoses: 1955–1956," in *The Seminar of Jacques Lacan*, book 3, trans. Russell Grigg (New York: Norton, 1993).

6. Sigmund Freud, *The Future of an Illusion*, 1927, in *The Standard Edition of the Complete Psychological Works of Sigmund Freud*, vol. 21, trans. James Strachey (London: Hogarth, 1968).

7. Jacques Lacan, *The Seminar of Jacques Lacan*, book 2: *The Ego in Freud's Theory and in the Technique of Psychoanalysis 1954–1955*, trans. Sylvana Tomaselli (New York: Norton, 1988).

8. Lacan, *The Seminar of Jacques Lacan*, book 2.

9. Saint Augustine, "The Soliloquies of Augustine," in *The Call and the Response*, trans. Gerard Watson (Warminster: Aris and Phillips, 1990).

10. G. W. Leibniz, "Remarks on M. Arnauld's letter touching on the proposition: Because the individual notion of each person contains once and for all everything that will ever happen to him," http://www.earlymoderntexts.com/pdfs/leibniz1686a_1.pdf.

11. Cf. Julia Kristeva, *The Incredible Need to Believe*, trans. Beverley Bie Brahic (New York: Columbia University Press, 2009), preface.

12. Although he knew Aramaic and Hebrew, Paul of Tarsus cites the Hebrew Bible in the Greek translation called the Septuagint.

13. Emile Benveniste, *Vocabulaire des institutions indo-européenes*, vol. 1 (Paris: Minuit, 1969).

14. *The Ego and the Id*, in *Introductory Lectures on Psychoanalysis* (New York: Penguin, 1991); cf. also Julia Kristeva, *Tales of Love*, trans. Leon Roudiez (New York: Columbia University Press, 1987).

15. Sigmund Freud, "On Psychotherapy," in *The Standard Edition of the Complete Psychological Works of Sigmund Freud*, vol. 7, trans. James Strachey (London: Hogarth, 1953).

16. D. W. Winnicott, "Transitional Objects and Transitional Phenomena," *International Journal of Psychoanalysis* (1953).

17. Jacques Lacan founded a journal entitled *Scilicet*; seven issues were published between 1968 and 1976 with Editions du Seuil. In the first issue (pp. 3–13) he made this declaration of principles concerning psychoanalysis.

18. Sigmund Freud, *Results, Ideas, Problems* [1921–1938], vol. 2.

19. Freud, *New Introductory Lectures to Psychoanalysis*. Cf. note 2, this chapter.

20. Julia Kristeva, *Powers of Horror: An Essay on Abjection*, trans. Leon Roudiez (New York: Columbia University Press, 1982). Cf. also, among others, Jacob Neusner, *The Idea of Purity in Ancient Judaism* (Leiden: Brill, 1973), 12.

21. Cf. Mary Douglas, *Purity and Danger*, ARK ed. (London: Routledge, 1966).

22. Cf. chap. 7, this volume.

23. André Green, *La Déliaison. Psychanalyse, anthropologie et literature* (Paris: Les Belles Lettres, 1982; and Pluriel, 1998).

24. Sigmund Freud, *Moses and Monotheism*, trans. Katherine Jones (New York: Vintage/ Random House, 1955).

25. Cf. chap. 7 in this volume.

26. Cf. Julia Kristeva, *Hannah Arendt*, trans. Ross Guberman (New York: Columbia University Press, 2003).

27. Hannah Arendt, response to Eric Voegelin, in *Review of Politics* 15 (1953): 81.

28. *Murder in Byzantium*, trans. C. John Delogu (New York: Columbia University Press, 2008), translators' note.

20. DARE HUMANISM

1. Apocalypse of St John 11:2.

2. "And here again that he brought the Greeks into the temple and profanes this holy place," Acts of the Apostles 21:28, King James Bible.

3. "Consciousness has God in it, and not as object in front of it," he wrote in his lessons on *Monotheism*, before suggesting that the Universal is no more than a "reversal" of the one God of monotheism, "the extra-verted One" and "returned" on the All, the One-All projected on tangibles in actuality and in potentiality. Cf. F.W.J. von Schelling (1775–1854), *Le Monotheism* [1828], trans. Fr. A. Pernet (Paris: J. Vrin, 1992).

4. Henri de Lubac, *Athéisme et sens de l'homme* (Paris: Cerf, 1968), 17.

5. Lubac, *Athéisme*, 17, 19.

6. Jean-Paul Sartre, *Existentialism Is a Humanism*, trans. Philip Mairet (New York: World, 1956).

7. Sartre, *Existentialism*.

8. Martin Heidegger, *Letter on Humanism*, trans. David Farrell Krell (London: Routledge, 1977).

9. Maurice Blanchot, *The Infinite Conversation*, trans. Susan Hanson (Minneapolis: University of Minnesota Press, 1993).

10. Heidegger, *Letter on Humanism*.

11. Blaise Pascal, *Pensées*, trans. W. F. Trotter (Boston: Dutton, 1958).

12. "[A]nd our libido is once more free . . . to replace the lost objects by fresh ones equally or still more precious." Matthew von Unwerth, "On Transience," in *Freud's Requiem*, trans. James Strachey (New York: Riverhead, 2005).

13. Cf. "In Jerusalem: Monotheisms and Secularization of the Need to Believe," chap. 19, this volume.

14. Jacques Lacan, *Encore, The Seminar of Jacques Lacan*, book 20, trans. Bruce Fink (Pittsburgh: Duquesne University, 1999).

15. Cf. Sigmund Freud, Letter to Jung, February 13, 1910.

16. Cf. Julia Kristeva, *Teresa, My Love*, trans. Lorna Scott Fox (New York: Columbia University Press, 2014).

17. Cf. "Reliance: What Is Loving for a Mother?" chap. 2, this volume.

18. Cf. Julia Kristeva, "Adolescence, a Syndrome of Ideality" in *Hatred and Forgiveness*, trans. Jeanine Hermann (New York: Columbia University Press, 2012), 447–78.

19. Emmanuel Kant, in *Philosophical Writings*, trans. Ernst Behler (London: Continuum, 1986); and Julia Kristeva, *Pulsions du temps* (Paris: Fayard, 2013), 467, n. 3.

20. Marcel Proust, *Pleasures and Days*, trans. Andrew Brown (London: Hesperus, 2004).

21. TEN PRINCIPLES FOR TWENTY-FIRST-CENTURY HUMANISM

1. Benoit SVI, *Jesus of Nazareth*, vol. 1, *From Baptism in the Jordan to the Tranfiguration* (San Francisco: Ignatius, 2007).

2. Traditional prayer attributed to Saint Francis, perhaps inspired by *The Little Flowers of St. Francis of Assisi*, trans. Madeleine l'Engle and W. Heywood (New York: Vintage, 1998).

3. Francis of Assisi, "Letter to the Faithful" (Santa Cruz: Evinity, 2009).

4. Cf. "Reliance: What Is Loving for a Mother?" and "Maternal Eroticism," chaps. 2 and 8, respectively, this volume.

23. MOSES, FREUD, AND CHINA

1. Blaise Pascal, *Pensées*, trans. W. Trotter (Boston: Dutton, 1958).

2. François Jullien, *Vital Nourishment. Departing from Happiness*, trans. Arthur Goldhammer (Cambridge: Zone, 2007).

3. Julia Kristeva, *About Chinese Women* (London: Marion Boyers, 1977).

4. Marcel Granet, *Chinese Civilization*, trans. Innes and Brailsford (London: Kegan Paul, Trench, Trubner, 1930).

5. Henri Maspero, *Taoism and Chinese Religion*, trans. Frank A. Kierman, Jr. (Amherst: University of Massachusetts Press, 1981).

6. Kristofer Schipper, *The Taoist Body*, trans. Karen C. Duval (Berkeley: University of California Press, 1993); Schipper, *La Religion de la Chine. La Tradition vivante* (Paris: Fayard, 2008).

7. Jullien, *Vital Nourishment*.

8. Cf. "Affect, That 'Intense Depth of Words,'" chap. 10, this volume.

9. Jullien, *Vital Nourishment*.

10. Jesuit Father Nicoló Longobardi, or Nicolas Lombard (1559–1654), is one of the founders of Sinology and in particular the author of *Traité sur quelques points de la religion des Chinois* (Paris: Guérin, 1701).

11. Cf. Julia Kristeva, "Une Européenne en Chine," in *Pulsions du temps* (Paris: Fayard, 2013).

12. Maurice Godelier, *The Metamorphosis of Kinship*, trans. Nora Scott (London: Verso, 2012).

13. Maspero, *Taoism and Chinese Religions*.

14. Cf. Jacques Lacan, *Television*, trans. Denis Hollier, Rosalind Krauss, and Annette Michelson (New York: Norton, 1990).

15. Cf. Ludwig Wittgenstein, *Philosophical Investigations*, trans. G. E. M. Anscombe (Oxford: Basil Blackwell, 1963).

16. Cf. Julia Kristeva, *The Revolution in Poetic Language*, trans. Margaret Waller (New York: Columbia University Press, 1974).

17. Cf. "Maternal Eroticism," chap. 8 in this volume.

18. Cf. Julia Kristeva, *Powers of Horror*, trans. John Lechte, *Oxford Literary Review* (1982).

19. Cf. "Reliance: What Is Loving for a Mother?" chap. 2 in this volume.

20. Cf. Julia Kristeva, *Female Genius*, vol. 3: *Colette*, trans. Jane Marie Todd (New York: Columbia University Press, 2001).

21. Jean-Michel Lou, *Corps d'enfance, corps chinois. Sollers et la Chine* (Paris: Gallimard, 2012).

24. DIVERSITY IS MY MOTTO

1. Jean de la Fontaine, *The Complete Fables of Jean de La Fontaine*, trans. Norman R. Shapiro (Champaign: University of Illinois Press, 2007).

2. Cf. "'Affect, That 'Intense Depth of Words,'" chap. 10 in this volume.

3. Cf. Montesquieu, *The Spirit of Laws*, trans. Thomas Nugent, rev. V. Prichard, based on public domain ed. (London: G. Bell, 1914).

4. Cf. *Open Letter to Harlem Désir, Nations Without Nationalism* (New York: Columbia University Press, 1993).

5. Jean Giraudoux, *The Trojan War Will Not Take Place*, trans. Christopher Fry (Oxford: Oxford University Press, 1955), act 22, scene 13.

6. Cf. Julia Kristeva, *Intimate Revolt: The Powers and Limits of Psychoanalysis*, trans. Jeanine Herman (New York: Columbia University Press, 2002); and Kristeva, "Thinking About Liberty in Dark Times," in *Hatred and Forgiveness*, trans. Jeanine Herman (New York: Columbia University Press, 2010).

7. Cf. Emmanuel Kant, *Philosophical Writings*, trans. Ernst Behler (New York: Continuum, 1986).

8. Cf. Max Weber, *The Protestant Ethic and the Spirit of Capitalism*, trans. Talcott Parsons (New York: Routledge, 2001).

9. Cf. Martin Heidegger, *The Essence of Human Freedom*, trans. Ted Sadler (London: Continuum Impacts, 2002).

10. Julia Kristeva, "L'Adolescence, un syndrome d'idéalité," in *La Haine et le pardon* (Paris: Fayard, 2005), 447–60.

11. Julia Kristeva, *This Incredible Need to Believe*, trans. Beverly Bie Brahic (New York: Columbia University Press, 2009).

12. André Green, *On Private Madness*, trans. Katherine Aubertin (London: Karnac, 1996).

13. Cf. Kristeva, *This Incredible Need to Believe*.

25. THE FRENCH CULTURAL MESSAGE

1. Saint Augustine, *Confessions*, book 7, chap. 21:27.
2. Michel de Montaigne, *Essays*, book 2, chap. 1, "Of the Inconsistence of Our Actions," trans. Donald Frame (Stanford, Calif.: Stanford University Press, 1965).

26. THE UNIVERSAL IN THE SINGULAR

1. Cf. "The French Cultural Message," chap. 25 in this volume.
2. Cf. Sigmund Freud, *Sexuality and the Psychology of Love*, trans. Philip Rieff (New York: Simon and Schuster, 1963), 65. "Not merely is woman taboo in special situations connected with her sexual life, such as during menstruation, pregnancy, child-birth and lying-in; but quite apart from these occasions intercourse with a woman is subject to such heavy restrictions that we have every reason to question the apparent sexual liberty of savages."
3. "The free woman is just being born." Simone de Beauvoir, *The Second Sex*, trans. Constance Borde and Sheila Malovany-Chevallier (New York: Vintage, 2011).
4. Poor suburbs—Trans.
5. Cf. "Jerusalem: Monotheisms and Secularization and the Need to Believe," chap. 19, this volume.
6. Ni Putes Ni Soumises, feminist movement founded in 2003 by Fadela Amara that focuses primarily on the feminine condition in the *banlieue*.
7. Jean-Paul Sartre, *The Words*, trans. Bernard Frechtman (New York: Vintage, 1964).

27. CAN ONE BE A MUSLIM WOMAN AND A SHRINK?

1. Cf. Simone de Beauvoir, *All Said and Done* (New York: Knopf, 1972).
2. Simone de Beauvoir, *The Second Sex*, trans. Constance Borde and Sheila Malovany-Chevallier (New York: Knopf, 2010).
3. Beauvoir, *All Said and Done*.
4. Psychanalyse et Politique was one of the discussion groups linked to the women's liberation movement as of 1970.
5. Cf. Rafah Nached, "Histoire de la psychanalyse en Syrie," *Topique*, no. 110 (2010): 117–27; and Nached, "Dire l'indicible," *Psychanalyse*, no. 21 (May 2011): 33–36.
6. Nached, "Histoire de la psychanalyse en Syrie," 118, 119 (Kristeva's emphasis).
7. Friedrich Nietzsche, "Pourquoi j'écris de si bons livres," in *Ecce Homo* (Paris: Flammarion, 1992 [1888]), 12.4.
8. Nached, "Histoire de la psychanalyse en Syrie," 123, 12.
9. Nached, "Histoire de la psychanalyse en Syrie," 124.
10. Nached, "Dire l'indicible," 33.

11. Rafah Nached, "Tâsîn de la préexistence et de l'ambiguïté," *Psychanalyse*, no. 21 (May 2011): 53–59.
12. Nached, "Dire l'indicible," 33–36.
13. Nached, "Histoire de la psychanalyse en Syrie," 126.

28. ONE IS BORN WOMAN, BUT I BECOME ONE

1. Simone de Beauvoir, *Pyrrus et Cineas*, trans. Marybeth Timmerman, in *Philosophical Writings*, ed. Margaret A. Simons, Marybeth Timmerman, and Mary Beth Mader (Champaign: University of Illinois Press, 2004), 89–149.
2. Simone de Beauvoir, *Memoirs of a Dutiful Daughter*, trans. James Kirkup (New York: Penguin, 2001).
3. Cf. "Beauvoir Dreams," chap. 14 in this volume; and Julia Kristeva, *Female Genius*, vol. 3: *Colette*, trans. Jane Marie Todd (New York: Columbia University Press, 2004).
4. MLF is the Mouvement de la liberation de la femme—women's lib—TRANS.
5. Beauvoir, *Memoirs of a Dutiful Daughter*.
6. Simone de Beauvoir, *The Mandarins*, trans. Leonard M. Friedman (New York: Norton, 1956); Beauvoir, *Adieux: A Farewell to Sartre*, trans. Patrick O'Brian (New York: Pantheon, 1985).
7. Simone de Beauvoir, *She Came to Stay*, trans. Yvonne Moyse and Roger Senhouse (New York: World, 1954).
8. Simone de Beauvoir, *Must We Burn Sade?* trans. Annette Michelson (London: New English Library, 1952).
9. Simone de Beauvoir, *America Day by Day*, trans. Carol Cosman (Berkeley: University of California Press, 2000).
10. Simone de Beauvoir, "Solidarity with Israel: A Critical Support," in *Political Writings*, trans. and ed. Margaret Simons, Marybeth Timmerman, and Mary Beth Mader (Champaign: University of Illinois Press, 2012).
11. Simone de Beauvoir, *The Long March: An Account of Modern China*, trans. Austryn Wainhouse (China: Phoenix, 2002). Cf. Denis Charbit, "Voyage en Utopie: La Chine de Simone de Beauvoir," *Perspectives* 11 (2004): 209–37; and Julia Kristeva, "Beauvoir in China," http://www.kristeva.fr/beauvoir-in-china.html.
12. Julia Kristeva, *The Samurai*, trans. Barbara Bray (New York: Columbia University Press, 1992).
13. Julia Kristeva, *Murder in Byzantium*, trans. C. Jon Delogu (New York: Columbia University Press, 2008).

INDEX

EUROPEAN PERSPECTIVES

A SERIES IN SOCIAL THOUGHT AND CULTURAL CRITICISM

Lawrence D. Kritzman, Editor

Gilles Deleuze, *Nietzsche and Philosophy*

David Carroll, *The States of "Theory"*

Gilles Deleuze, *The Logic of Sense*

Julia Kristeva, *Strangers to Ourselves*

Alain Finkielkraut, *Remembering in Vain: The Klaus Barbie Trial and Crimes Against Humanity*

Pierre Vidal-Naquet, *Assassins of Memory: Essays on the Denial of the Holocaust*

Julia Kristeva, *Nations Without Nationalism*

Theodor W. Adorno, *Notes to Literature*, vols. 1 and 2

Richard Wolin, ed., *The Heidegger Controversy*

Hugo Ball, *Critique of the German Intelligentsia*

Pierre Bourdieu, *The Field of Cultural Production*

Karl Heinz Bohrer, *Suddenness: On the Moment of Aesthetic Appearance*

Gilles Deleuze, *Difference and Repetition*

Gilles Deleuze and Félix Guattari, *What Is Philosophy?*

Alain Finkielkraut, *The Defeat of the Mind*

Jacques LeGoff, *History and Memory*

Antonio Gramsci, *Prison Notebooks*, vols. 1, 2, and 3

Ross Mitchell Guberman, *Julia Kristeva Interviews*

Julia Kristeva, *Time and Sense: Proust and the Experience of Literature*

Elisabeth Badinter, *XY: On Masculine Identity*

Gilles Deleuze, *Negotiations, 1972–1990*

Julia Kristeva, *New Maladies of the Soul*

Norbert Elias, *The Germans*

Elisabeth Roudinesco, *Jacques Lacan: His Life and Work*

Paul Ricoeur, *Critique and Conviction: Conversations with François Azouvi and Marc de Launay*

Pierre Vidal-Naquet, *The Jews: History, Memory, and the Present*

Karl Löwith, *Martin Heidegger and European Nihilism*

Pierre Nora, *Realms of Memory: The Construction of the French Past*

Vol. 1: *Conflicts and Divisions*

Vol. 2: *Traditions*

Vol. 3: *Symbols*

Alain Corbin, *Village Bells: Sound and Meaning in the Nineteenth-Century French Countryside*

Louis Althusser, *Writings on Psychoanalysis: Freud and Lacan*

Claudine Fabre-Vassas, *The Singular Beast: Jews, Christians, and the Pig*

Tahar Ben Jelloun, *French Hospitality: Racism and North African Immigrants*

Alain Finkielkraut, *In the Name of Humanity: Reflections on the Twentieth Century*

Emmanuel Levinas, *Entre Nous: Essays on Thinking-of-the-Other*

Zygmunt Bauman, *Globalization: The Human Consequences*

Emmanuel Levinas, *Alterity and Transcendence*

Alain Corbin, *The Life of an Unknown: The Rediscovered World of a Clog Maker in Nineteenth-Century France*

Carlo Ginzburg, *Wooden Eyes: Nine Reflections on Distance*

Sylviane Agacinski, *Parity of the Sexes*

Michel Pastoureau, *The Devil's Cloth: A History of Stripes and Striped Fabric*

Alain Cabantous, *Blasphemy: Impious Speech in the West from the Seventeenth to the Nineteenth Century*

Julia Kristeva, *The Sense and Non-Sense of Revolt: The Powers and Limits of Psychoanalysis*

Kelly Oliver, *The Portable Kristeva*

Gilles Deleuze, *Dialogues II*

Catherine Clément and Julia Kristeva, *The Feminine and the Sacred*

Sylviane Agacinski, *Time Passing: Modernity and Nostalgia*

Luce Irigaray, *Between East and West: From Singularity to Community*

Julia Kristeva, *Hannah Arendt*

Julia Kristeva, *Intimate Revolt: The Powers and Limits of Psychoanalysis*, vol. 2

Elisabeth Roudinesco, *Why Psychoanalysis?*

Régis Debray, *Transmitting Culture*

Steve Redhead, ed., *The Paul Virilio Reader*

Claudia Benthien, *Skin: On the Cultural Border Between Self and the World*

Julia Kristeva, *Melanie Klein*

Roland Barthes, *The Neutral: Lecture Course at the Collège de France (1977–1978)*

Hélène Cixous, *Portrait of Jacques Derrida as a Young Jewish Saint*

Theodor W. Adorno, *Critical Models: Interventions and Catchwords*

Julia Kristeva, *Colette*

Gianni Vattimo, *Dialogue with Nietzsche*

Emmanuel Todd, *After the Empire: The Breakdown of the American Order*

Gianni Vattimo, *Nihilism and Emancipation: Ethics, Politics, and Law*

Hélène Cixous, *Dream I Tell You*

Steve Redhead, *The Jean Baudrillard Reader*

Jean Starobinski, *Enchantment: The Seductress in Opera*

Jacques Derrida, *Geneses, Genealogies, Genres, and Genius: The Secrets of the Archive*

Hélène Cixous, *White Ink: Interviews on Sex, Text, and Politics*

Marta Segarra, ed., *The Portable Cixous*

François Dosse, *Gilles Deleuze and Félix Guattari: Intersecting Lives*

Julia Kristeva, *This Incredible Need to Believe*

François Noudelmann, *The Philosopher's Touch: Sartre, Nietzsche, and Barthes at the Piano*

Antoine de Baecque, *Camera Historica: The Century in Cinema*

Julia Kristeva, *Hatred and Forgiveness*

Roland Barthes, *How to Live Together: Novelistic Simulations of Some Everyday Spaces*

Jean-Louis Flandrin and Massimo Montanari, *Food: A Culinary History*

Georges Vigarello, *The Metamorphoses of Fat: A History of Obesity*

Julia Kristeva, *The Severed Head: Capital Visions*

Eelco Runia, *Moved by the Past: Discontinuity and Historical Mutation*

François Hartog, *Regimes of Historicity: Presentism and Experiences of Time*

Jacques Le Goff, *Must We Divide History Into Periods?*

Claude Lévi-Strauss, *We Are All Cannibals: And Other Essays*

Marc Augé, *Everyone Dies Young: Time Without Age*

Roland Barthes: *Album: Unpublished Correspondence and Texts*

Étienne Balibar, *Secularism and Cosmopolitanism: Critical Hypotheses on Religion and Politics*

Dominique Kalifa, *Vice, Crime, and Poverty: How the Western Imagination Invented the Underworld*